Enjoy!

Helen, and John too of course x

THE BOMBER AND THE WEATHERVANE

TONY ASTON

Best Wishes

Tony Aston

First edition published in paperback July 2024

ISBN 978-1-3999-8381-5

A catalogue reference for this book is available from the British Library.

Printed and bound in the UK by Kindle Direct Publishing

Also by Tony Aston

Non-fiction

REDDITCH – From the Chip Shop to the Batchley

Helen Theron, JB453 crews' family descendants, and the author have agreed that all royalties earned from the sale of this book will be donated to the Royal Air Force Benevolent Fund. Registered Charity No: 1081009

"People who have served in the RAF are trained to be self-reliant. They don't want to make a fuss and they don't want to be a burden. So, all too often, when life gets tough they suffer in silence.

We don't believe anyone who has served their country should have to struggle through life.

We're the RAF Benevolent Fund, and we're here to support people who are serving – or have served – and their families, when they need it most.

From counselling and financial support to adapting homes or replacing boilers, from the big challenges to the small changes, we can help people live with the dignity and independence they deserve.

For over 100 years, we've been the RAF's most devoted friend, supporting the whole of the RAF Family – from the oldest veteran to the youngest child. Together, we'll continue to be here for as long as they need us."

IN MEMORY OF THE CREW OF

83 (PATHFINDER) SQUADRON

LANCASTER JB453 OL-F

AND ALL BOMBER COMMAND CREWS

WHO MADE THE ULTIMATE SACRIFICE

"They shall grow not old, as we that are left grow old:
Age shall not weary them, nor the years condemn.
At the going down of the sun and in the morning
We will remember them"

AND DEDICATED TO THE MEMORY OF THE WONDERFUL JOHN THERON WHO SADLY PASSED IN APRIL 2024

ACKNOWLEDGMENTS

There have been so many people who have helped and supported me in authoring this book. In particular I would like to thank:

Kay Aston, Peter Aston, Helen Theron, John Theron, Julie Mustafa, Di Ablewhite, Brenda Kelly, Nicky van der Drift, Mike Osborne, Alex Osborne BBC, Olive Lacey, RAF Benevolent Fund, Dick Raymond, Sarah Raymond, Wim van Djik, Marcel Kasper, Hahn Friedhelm, Jacquelin Magnay, Janine Jansen BBC, Lothar Wiegmann, Steve Wigley, Julie Wigley, Elizabeth McLachlan, Mike McKendry, Terry McKendry, Ryan Traynor, Katie Ashby, Mark Leyden, BAE Systems PLC, UK Ministry of Defence, Commonwealth War Graves Commission, Stockport Heritage Trust, Luq Toefy BBC, The Mayor's office at Blankenburg, Ollie Fletcher RAF Benevolent Fund, Nancy Quinlan and all family descendants of the JB453 crew.

Permission to use the lyrics of *"No Moon Tonight"* at the beginning of Chapters 1, 2, 3, 4, 5, 6, 7, 8, 9, 10 and 11 kindly granted by Julie Wigley.

Permission granted by the RAF Benevolent Fund for the use of its logo.

TABLE OF CONTENTS PAGE

"The gratitude of every home in our Island, in our Empire, and indeed throughout the world, except in the abodes of the guilty, goes out to the British airmen who, undaunted by odds, unwearied in their constant challenge and mortal danger, are turning the tide of world war by their prowess and by their devotion. Never in the field of human conflict has so much been owed by so many to so few. All our hearts go out to the fighter pilots whose brilliant actions we see with our own eyes day after day, but we must never forget that all the time, night after night, month after month, our bomber squadrons travel far into Germany, find their targets, often under the heaviest fire, often with serious loss, with deliberate, careful discrimination, and inflict shattering blows upon the whole of the technical and war-making structure of the Nazi power. On no part of the Royal Air Force does the weight of the war fall more heavily than on the bombers, who will play an invaluable part in the case of invasion and whose unflinching zeal it has been necessary in the meantime on numerous occasions to restrain."

Winston Spencer Churchill, Prime Minister 1940-1945

CHAPTER 1

WHERE THE STORY BEGINS

No moon tonight
Above the cloud, stars bright.
Orion in the east, Polaris high,
A thousand airmen's eyes fixed on those points of light.

© Julie Wigley, *No Moon Tonight*

A number of friends and family, together with the occasional total stranger, have asked the question of me, "what inspired you to write a book about an old, slightly beaten-up, metal weathervane?" That is not a question I can answer in one simple sentence. Events that occurred during World War II, particularly those that took place in Europe, have always intrigued and enticed me. My father served as a Petty Officer in the Fleet Air Arm during those years of conflict. Perhaps the stories that he told me and my brothers as we grew up were a significant factor.

Maybe it was the sheer, overwhelming enthusiasm and passion shown by my good friends, Helen and John Theron, when they first spoke to me about the information they had discovered about the old weathervane they had bought, in 2009, from a salvage yard in leafy Surrey.

Or perhaps it was the opportunity for me to put pen once again to paper – or fingers to keyboard – that stimulated and encouraged me.

In truth, it was probably a combination of all of these, that led to a prodigious and overpowering urge to write Helen's story. Once I had finished listening, in late 2021, to the story she couldn't wait to share about the links between the weathervane she had bought, a Lancaster bomber serial number JB453 OL-F lost to enemy fire in January 1944 over Berlin, the tragic loss of all crew members, the amazing amount of research she, and others, carried out in locating the crews' families, and the dedication of the weathervane as an official war memorial, supported by the International Bomber Command Centre, the flames of passion, excitement and emotion deep inside me had been well and truly ignited. The first thing I said to Helen was, *"This needs to be written down. Your story deserves to be told."* And so it was, over tea and cake in my Devon lounge – very British - that the embryo of a plan was hatched for me to do just that. For somewhere approaching two years after this meeting, I poured over official documents, photographs, emails, and letters that had been sent, received, and kept for almost 80 years, all of which Helen had collated and sent to me.

It also led to me, as a direct result of the work Helen carried out, to having contact with members of the crews' descendants in the UK, Canada, South Africa and Ireland, with various RAF and linked civilian organisations across the globe and, incredibly, to a man of 98 years in north Devon who had actually served in the same Pathfinder Squadron as the fated JB453 crew at RAF Wyton in Cambridgeshire between 1943 and 1945, as a flight engineer on Lancaster bombers.

I sincerely hope that I have managed to produce a fitting account that recognises the immense volumes of time and effort expended by Helen, together with her sheer determination and drive, to ensure that the seven-man Lancaster crew who perished on that night, all those years ago, are deservedly remembered and commemorated.

This is an emotional story and moving story. This is the story of that Lancaster bomber and the demise of both it and its crew. This is Helen's story.

Importantly, and given the ultimate sacrifice that was made by the JB453 crew, it did not seem appropriate that I, as the author, should make any financial gain from the sales of this book. It was, therefore, a joint agreement made between me, Helen, and the crews' descendants that, once production and publication expenses had been met, all royalties ordinarily payable to an author would be donated to the Royal Air Force Benevolent Fund charity.

Helen has always been a scientist at heart. She had studied for her A levels at school with ambitions to work at Aldermaston Forensic Laboratory, which later became part of the national Forensic Science Service. However, governmental financial cuts at the time thwarted these aims so, on leaving school, she joined ICI Pest Control as a researcher. A few years later she moved to Thames Water Sewage Treatment as a scientific analyst, taking time out at various points to raise a family. Helen worked around her commitments, taking on employments as a play group assistant, school cook, classroom assistant and night nursing auxiliary before an opportunity presented itself for her to finally get into the world of forensic science, working as a toxicologist in Lambeth, London.

John left school at 15 years old and was accepted into an apprenticeship in car mechanics, studying part time for 4 years on a college day release scheme which led to him being awarded his City and Guilds certification in Motor Vehicle Technology. He spent 31 highly successful years in this trade, before following in his Dad's footsteps working for London Underground, now Transport for London.

He spent 19 years working firstly as a train mechanic before becoming a Depot Team Leader at Northfields Depot on the Piccadilly Line from where, in the fullness of time, he retired.

Sadly, John passed in April 2024 before this book was published. Helen remains in the family home she so enjoyed with him in the rural village of Westhope, Herefordshire. They enjoyed all things from the 1930/1940's eras, most especially the music and fashion of that time. Indeed, they met each another one evening whilst dancing the Lindy Hop. John had a passion for a wide range of music. He spent many years playing the guitar and was a member of a local band called Pigs Might. A holder of a private pilot's licence, his zeal lay in building a timber framed, 1929 design, open cockpit aeroplane called a Pietenpol Air Camper in his Westhope workshop. A few years ago, I was excited to be able to watch him pilot a two-seater, single engine, canvas-bodied light aeroplane as he and Helen landed on a small grass airstrip near to my home in Devon, having taken off a short while earlier from Wiltshire. I was amazed that, even with the benefit of satellite navigation, anyone could simply find this tiny landing strip in deepest dark Devon amongst what must be many thousands of similar looking fields in the county!

When Helen wasn't out on her cherished dog walks, her spare time would often be spent woodturning alongside John in their workshop. She enjoys indulging in a variety of arts and crafts activities, dabbles in photography, loves spending time tending to her garden and is passionate in learning about local wildlife. As well as sharing a love of Lindy Hop,

Helen and John in September 2021. Photo courtesy of Helen Theron

both Helen and John enjoyed ballroom dancing and exploring the countryside.

Helen's story begins in the rural suburbs of Surrey – in Epsom Downs to be precise. In mid-2009, her mother gave her and John a small amount of money to buy themselves a "new home" gift of their own choice. They didn't know for sure what they would buy although Helen had, for a long while, wanted a weathervane, something that could sit aloft their house. Every time that Helen visited a garden centre she would keep an eye out for a suitable weathervane but, although she had sought such an item for some years, she had never found one which inspired her, or which shouted "buy me" to her. She had a close friend who often jested that, when there was a special birthday or one ending in "0", she would purchase one for her. Helen laughingly always turned down the offer, saying she would wait. Her friend told her to hurry up or else she would buy her a weathervane with a witch on it! And so it became something of a standing joke. In the back of her mind, Helen thought she would never find one although she cherished a dream of one being placed on the roof of a little rural cottage somewhere.

A short while after receiving the gift, Helen and John visited a garden centre, then known as Farm Lane Nursery in nearby Ashtead, Surrey, owned and run by a Mr Steve Popescu, where they found a salvage yard area within which they espied a metal weathervane laying, lonely and cold.

The weathervane, seemingly neglected, abandoned, and propped up in the bowels of the salvage yard was different from anything she had previously encountered. Instantly, Helen knew that this was what she had been seeking for so long. This one was special. The design was one of a World War II AVRO Lancaster heavy bomber aeroplane. It is believed – but never confirmed – that the item came from a farm in East Anglia, a region which was, of course, home to many Royal Air Force (RAF), British Commonwealth, and United States of America Air Force (USAAF) air bases during that war, most of which are no longer in existence, having been taken over by housing estates, industrial parks or, in some cases, simply by mother nature.

Steve Popescu told them that he thought the weathervane had come from an old farm in Norfolk. He added that it was likely that he bought it as part of a job lot from an auction house during one of his many family trips to the county, but evidence of this was, unfortunately, never forthcoming. The search for its origin nonetheless continues. One possibility, on the basis that some ground crews were known to have constructed similar items, was that a member of the JB453 ground crew made the vane after its demise. It appeared that, at some point in its history, the Lancaster must have been painted as there was evidence of a worn RAF roundel on the fuselage plus other faded areas of paint.

Helen and John immediately parted company with the money that Helen's mother had given her and drove off, thrilled with their quarry.

There was another reason why this purchase was clearly "meant to be". It transpired that Helen's mother, after the end of World War II, had been a member of the Women's Auxiliary Air Force (WAAF) and one of her postings had been at RAF Eval, located south-west of Padstow in

Cornwall. She had worked as a telephonist in air traffic control. She was born in 1933 so would have been in her late teens at the time.

Squadrons based at Eval during the war had a primary role to provide anti-submarine and shipping protection patrols off the south-west coast. Lancasters, or "Lancs" as they were affectionately known, were still in use at the station post-war for long-range maritime patrols before being superseded by the AVRO Lincoln and Shackleton upgrades, and it turned out that they were also the favourite aircraft of Helen's mother. She was absolutely delighted when her daughter told her of her find. Very soon, it

The Lancaster weathervane bought by Helen and John. Photo courtesy of author.

took pride of place on the roof of their house in south-east England. where it remained until, 9 years later, Helen and John decided, for a whole raft of reasons, to relocate from Surrey to rural Herefordshire. They bought a house in a tiny hamlet - Westhope - some 9 miles north of the City of Hereford. According to the 2011 Census, Westhope at that time had a population of just 266 and it was here that, having been removed from their roof in Surrey, the Lanc weathervane was destined to be "stationed". Helen was delighted that her dream was about to be realised.

Just before the move took place, the item was placed into a box with heaps of other "stuff" that tend to become a permanent fixture in one's sheds and garages. Along with many other boxes, it was taken to a builder's storage facility whilst, at their new home in the shires, an old tumbledown garage was demolished to make way for the building of a new workshop. One day after the completion of the workshop at their new home, John was with a friend, Jason, who was helping sort things out. Jason happened to see the weathervane in its box which by now had been recovered from storage. Helen was in the workshop with them at the time and heard Jason point out that there was a small inscription – JB453-F - on the side of the weathervane, something which neither Helen nor John had previously noticed. Helen thought it might be a manufacturing mark on one side of the fuselage. This meant nothing to either of them. However, never having been a person to allow curiosity an upper hand, Helen decided to carry out a little online research to see if there might be any clue as to what the inscription meant. No sooner had she pressed the "ENTER" key on search engine Google, that information flashed up onto the screen, identifying a World War II Lancaster bomber, JB453 OL-F, and its crew members, all of whom were lost when the aircraft was shot down over Berlin early in 1944. Further, later, research revealed:

"Shortly before midnight on Sunday, 02 January 1944, an AVRO Lancaster III (JB453 OL-F), from 83 Squadron, took off from airfield RAF Wyton, for a mission to Berlin in Germany. Under Bomber Command, the crew's mission was planned for the early hours of Monday, 03 January 1944. Sadly, the plane crashed at Blankenburg, Germany. All 7 crew reported dead on 03 January. They were victim of a night fighter over the Harz Mountains."

It transpired that JB453 was the serial number allocated to the aircraft at its point of manufacture. OL was the code allocated to RAF 83 Squadron and F was the sequential identifier of the aeroplane at RAF Wyton. Aircraft within the Squadron would therefore be allocated identifiers OL-A, B, C and so on. When one aircraft, in this case OL-F, was lost then that designation would be reassigned to its replacement.

To say that Helen was both amazed and astonished is probably the understatement of the century. In her own words, *"That completely and utterly gobsmacked me!"* She literally ran back into the garage and told both of the men.

Ensuing research quickly revealed the names of the seven-man crew, all of whom had perished in the crash. They were identified as:

Pilot – Flying Officer J18139 Ernest Blair STILES – Royal Canadian Air Force/Royal Air Force

Gunner – Flying Officer 151061 Ian Godfrey ALLAN – Royal Air Force

Navigator – Pilot Officer 155542 Denis Charles James McKENDRY – Royal Air Force

Flight Engineer – Flight Sergeant 614985 Patrick TRAYNOR – Royal Air Force

Wireless Operator – Sergeant 1091782 Joseph BANKS – Royal Air Force

Gunner – Sergeant 1559306 John MacIntyre DUNLOP – Royal Air Force [1]

Bombardier – Flying Officer 132869 William Horace DYKE – Royal Air Force

John later suggested to Helen, and she readily agreed, that they could perhaps mount a small plaque on the outside of their cottage in remembrance and commemoration of the crew. This was all they intended to do thinking that this would be a fitting and a permanent memorial to the

1. Some military records show Dunlop's middle name as McIntyre. The correct spelling, confirmed by his family, is MacIntyre

crew. But the information that had already been forthcoming had well and truly lit the blue touchpaper for Helen, something which would shape and influence her life, in ways she could have hardly imagined, for the best part of the following 2 years. This book tells the story of the AVRO Lancaster aircraft, operated by Bomber Command and the history of JB453 OL-F itself as part of 83 Squadron, No 8 Group (Pathfinder). It recognises and acknowledges the amazing, indeed remarkable, amounts of time and effort that Helen expended over a two-year period. Essentially though, it commemorates, honours, and celebrates the lives of the seven ordinary men who carried out extraordinary tasks, each paying the ultimate price, the JB453 OL-F crew who took off from RAF Wyton on that cold January morning.

The inscription discovered on the fuselage of the weathervane, enhanced on this image.
Photo courtesy of Helen Theron

Original graves of JB453 near Blankenburg, Germany, close to the crash site in 1944 before the crew were re-interred at the 1939-1945 British War Cemetery at Heerstrasse, Berlin in 1947. The grave of John Dunlop is thought to have been buried separately, likely because he was the only member of the crew whose body was discernible. Photo courtesy of the Dunlop family.

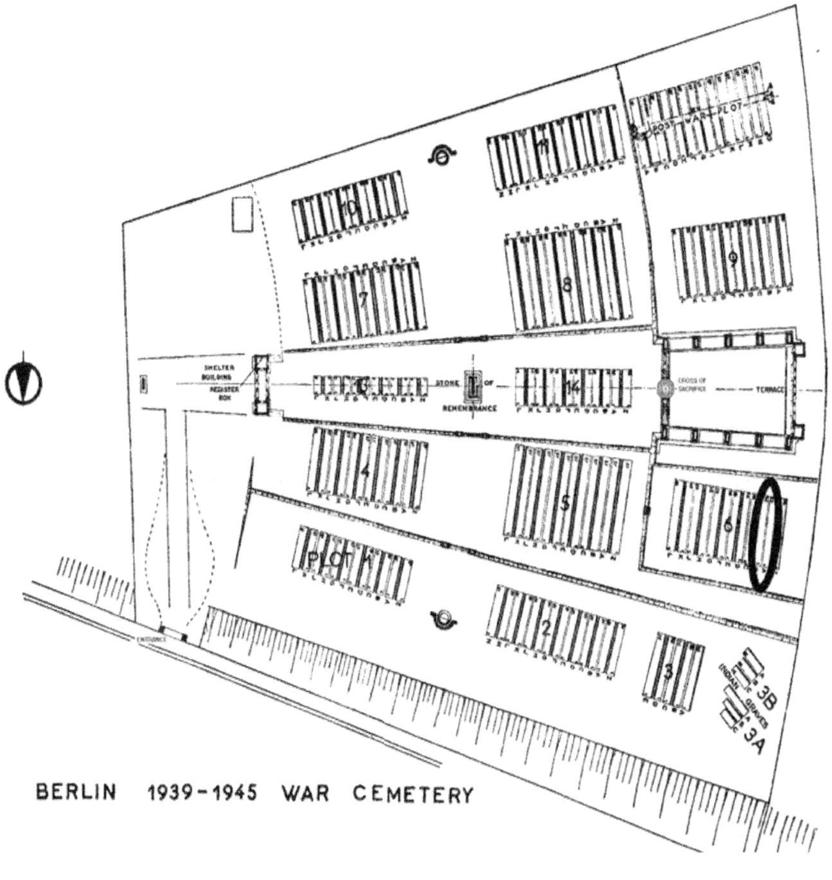

Plan of 1939-1945 British War Cemetery, Heerstrasse, Berlin indicating the location of Grave 6A 17-23, the collective graves of the JB453 crew
© Commonwealth War Graves Commission

CHAPTER 2

WE NEED A NEW BOMBER

Along with men from many nations,
We felt the pull to England's shores.
United in the face of tyranny
Born of the war, to end all wars

© Julie Wigley, *No Moon Tonight*

In reading this story it will help the reader to learn about the AVRO Lancaster heavy bomber and how it came to be regarded as the iconic bomber of World War II. The four-engine Lancaster was born, and had its origins, as a direct result of what can only be described as the abject failure of its immediate predecessor, the twin-engine AVRO Manchester. Developed in the 1930's, the Manchester, designed at A.V. Roe & Company (AVRO) by its Chief Designer Roy Chadwick, had been the British response, because of a perceived threat from an increasingly re-arming Germany, to a demand for a medium bomber. Introduced in 1941, following a period of testing at Ringway Airport, Manchester in 1939 and 1940, but apparently well before it was truly operationally ready, it very quickly became clear to crews, Bomber Command, and RAF hierarchy alike, that the Manchester was lacking in a number of vital areas. The twin Rolls Royce Vulture engines were found to be unreliable and prone to catching fire. Hydraulics systems leaked and failed. The aircraft was deemed to be

The ineffectual twin-engine AVRO Manchester from which the iconic Lancaster evolved.
Photo courtesy of BAE Systems

hugely underpowered and was incapable of flying at heights which could effectively have any real chance of avoiding enemy anti-aircraft activity or "flak". Getting the Manchester off the ground was often a hazardous and precarious operation, particularly with a full bomb payload. All of this resulted in an all-round loss of confidence in the aircraft, not great when the potential intention was for it to become the spearhead of the British wartime bombing effort. Ultimately, only 209 were built of which more than 80 were lost on operations.

The bigger, heavier, more reliable Lancaster, based in many ways upon the Manchester but which was far more positive and lighter to handle, entered service with RAF Bomber Command in December 1941, just months before its flawed and troublesome predecessor was withdrawn. With a range of over 2,500 miles carrying a maximum payload, it gave the RAF, for the first time, the capability of striking at the very heartland of Germany – Berlin. As the strategic bombing offensive in Europe developed and evolved, the Lanc very quickly became the main strike bomber of choice for Bomber Command, and for later prolonged and intensive night-time bombing raids over German cities and other strategic targets. As production of the aircraft increased apace, so it became the favoured heavy bomber not only for Bomber Command but for the RAF generally, the Royal Canadian Air Force and other British Commonwealth squadrons brought in to bolster and enhance the overall war effort. The four-engine aircraft was destined to become, arguably, the best, most effective and most popular bomber until jet power took over in later years. AVRO's main manufacturing base during the 1920s and 1930s was located in the Newton Heath area of Manchester.

However, with the winds of war and dark clouds gathering over Europe it was announced by the British government that a new, bigger, and more modern plant, specifically built in order to meet the exacting requirements of the seemingly inevitable conflict ahead, would be constructed at Chadderton, just 4 miles away. Senior figures at the company, including Roy Dobson and Chadwick himself, were of the strong opinion that this new facility should be at least twice the size of Newton Heath. They managed to persuade heads of government departments with little difficulty. The facility commenced manufacturing operations in 1939, the complex additionally housing the company's new headquarters.

The development and production of the Manchester soon followed. However, because of the aforementioned performance and reliability problems, only a little over 200 of the craft were actually produced. Although fundamentally based on the Manchester design, the Lancaster was bigger, easier to handle, and had double the number of engines, increased from two to four but, just as importantly, a different power unit was utilised. The Rolls Royce Merlin power unit, already used and proven on the Supermarine Spitfire, was incorporated into this innovative design. The game-changing Lancaster was born.

Just under 7,400 Lancs were produced during World War II. Sadly, almost half of these were fated to be lost, primarily as a result of enemy actions.

Having designed the hugely acclaimed Lancaster, it is heart-breaking to learn that, in 1947, Roy Chadwick was tragically killed during a test flight in a prototype of another of his designs, the Tudor. He is buried in the graveyard at Christ Church, Woodford, Manchester, just a short distance from the Tudor crash site.

The construction of the Lancaster bomb bay was such that it could carry the largest of bombs, up to 22,000 lbs, used by the RAF for the duration of the conflict, often in conjunction with smaller explosives and incendiary bombs. During its time in operational service, the Lancaster is thought to have delivered in excess of half a million tons of ordnance during the course of more than 150,000 missions over enemy territory. Famously, the Lancaster was chosen as the aircraft of choice for 617 Squadron, led by Wing Commander Guy Gibson VC, in May 1943, to deliver the Barnes Wallis-designed “bouncing bomb” against three dams in the Ruhr region, Germany’s industrial heartland, and immortalised in the 1955 movie, “*The Dam Busters*”. The size and shape of that bomb meant that a special jig had to be fabricated and fixed to the bomb bay for this specific operation.

AVRO Headquarters at Chadderton. Photo courtesy of BAE Systems.

Coincidentally, parts for this jig were manufactured at the High Duty Alloys factory in my hometown, Redditch, in Worcestershire.

The standard crew for a Lancaster consisted of seven men, stationed in various positions inside the fuselage, effectively little more than a metal tube with wings. The bomb aimer, at the lower front of the aircraft, had two positions to occupy. His primary location was lying face down on the floor with the bomb sighting on his left and bomb release selectors on the right. He could also use his view to assist the navigator with map reading. The aimer was also responsible for using forward weaponry, typically .303 calibre machine guns, at which he needed to stand to get into a position behind the triggers.

Lancasters under construction at Chadderton. Photo courtesy of BAE Systems.

The four-engine Lancaster entered RAF service in late 1941, replacing the troubled Manchester. Photo courtesy of BAE Systems

Grave of Roy Chadwick at Christ Church,
Woodford. Photo courtesy of Stockport Heritage Trust.

Above the bomb bay sat the pilot and flight engineer, side by side, the pilot on the port side. There were no dual controls so, by default, no co-pilot, but the flight engineer, who had a fold-down seat next to the pilot, was trained sufficiently to be able, in the event of the pilot being injured or killed, to guide the aircraft back home or to safety.

Behind the pilot and flight engineer, concealed by a curtain designed to allow him to work using a light, sat the navigator. His instrument panel showed the heading, airspeed, altitude, and other information required for accurate navigation. He had to be versatile and adaptable, the pilot being heavily reliant upon him to guide the craft to the target site and to bring both the machine and crew back home safely, sometimes in the most extreme and challenging under-fire and damaged conditions.

The wireless operator's radios were situated on a table facing the back of the aircraft. The operator sat on a seat beside these. Nearby was a window and, above him, a clear dome which had a dual function; visual signalling and for navigation by the stars.

Upper and rear gun turrets, by their very nature, meant that winds swept inside through gaps where gun barrels were located. Conditions inside a Lancaster, flying at 250 mph at altitudes approaching 25,000 ft in the middle of winter must have been horrendous. Temperatures in these areas could fall to minus 40 degrees centigrade and were not much higher in the rest of the craft, with the exception of the wireless operator’s station, immediately beneath which was the aircraft heater. This had minimal effect within the wider confines of the aircraft, but the temperature generated directly below him was such that he would often complain about being unbearably hot!

Behind him were transverse wing supports. The position of these was such that moving around the aircraft was somewhat challenging, especially for those members of the crew who were particularly tall. At the end of the bomb bay the floor dropped down, and the mid upper gunner's turret was reached. His position allowed an all-round view across the top of the aircraft. Two .303 machine guns could be fired to protect the aircraft from enemy activity above and to both sides.

Adjacent to the turret was the side crew door on the right, or starboard, side. This was the main entrance to the aircraft, which also could be used as an emergency exit. The lavatory, a rudimentary chemical toilet affair, was located near the supports for the tailplane. Known as the "Elsan" toilet, it could be likened to little more than an upturned oil barrel inside of which was a bucket. Unless urgent, it was something that the crew tried to avoid using at all costs. It was certainly not a contraption that one would want to sit upon to read a book or newspaper!

Finally, at the extreme tail-end of the fuselage, the rear gunner sat in a massively exposed tail turret, into which he entered via a pair of swing doors. This workstation was so confined that, in order to be able to move around efficiently, the occupant would have to hang his parachute on a hook near the turret hatch. Neither the mid-upper nor the rear gunner's positions were heated, so both had to wear electrically heated suits to prevent severe incapacity through extreme cold.

The Germans were fully aware of the underbelly vulnerability of the Lancaster. Subsequently, although many attacks from enemy night fighters tended to take place from the rear, they were often attempted from beneath the craft. There was little vision, or early warning, of a night fighter attacking from underneath. A rear gunner's vision to the left, right and above, was generally good but he had hardly any view of aircraft that attacked from beneath. He was often the first casualty of an attack, and invariably, because of lack of space and his parachute residing outside his pod, was unable to bale out from a fatally damaged 'plane. There were more casualties involving rear gunners than any other crew members. This was indeed a very lonely and unforgiving place in which to be stationed.

Our Lancaster, JB453 OL-F, a Mk III version, was manufactured by AVRO at Chadderton, Manchester in October 1943. It was destined to have a longevity of fewer than 3 months.

Post-completion, the craft was delivered to 156 Squadron (Pathfinder) at RAF Warboys, in what was then Huntingdonshire, on 19th October then transferred a few days later, on 24th October, to what would become its home station, 83 Squadron (Pathfinder) at RAF Wyton, Cambridgeshire. Around 25 such aircraft were manufactured by AVRO each week with the workforce working on a perpetual shift basis, 24 hours a day.

It is interesting to note that, during World War II, at least six Lancasters bore the identifier OL-F. Five are known to have crashed and one was scrapped post-war:

- R5857 - 83 Squadron. Crashed on take-off from RAF Mildenhall on 7th November 1942. Three fatalities at the crash site. One died from injuries several days later. Three survivors.
- ED312 – 83 Squadron. Attacked by an enemy night fighter and ditched into the sea in the Øresund Strait off Klagshamn, southwest of Malmö, Sweden on 21st April 1943. All crew survived. Aircraft damaged beyond repair.
- W4981 – 83 Squadron. Shot down by an enemy night fighter and crashed over The Netherlands 13th May 1943. Six crew fatalities. One survivor taken as a prisoner-of-war.
- **JB453 – 83 Squadron (subject of this book). Shot down by an enemy night fighter on 3rd January 1944 at Timmenrode near Blankenburg, south-west of Berlin. No survivors.**
- ND854 – 83 Squadron. Took off from RAF Coningsby on 14th August 1944 on a mission to attack shipping off Brest, France. Nothing was heard from the aircraft following take-off and it is believed that it crashed into the sea. No survivors.
- R5671 – 83 Squadron. Survived the war. Scrapped on 15th January 1947

Technical characteristics of the Lancaster III

- **Length:** 69 ft 4 in (21.13 m)
- **Wingspan:** 102 ft 0 in (31.09 m)

- **Height:** 20 ft 6 in (6.25 m)
- **Wing area:** 1,297 sq ft (120.5 m^2)
- **Empty weight:** 36,900 lb (16,738 kg)
- **Gross weight:** 55,000 lb (24,948 kg)
- **Max take-off weight:** 63,000 lb (28,576 kg)
- **Powerplant:** 4 × Rolls-Royce Merlin V-12 liquid-cooled piston engines, 1,280 hp (950 kW) each
- **Propellers:** 4 x 3-bladed

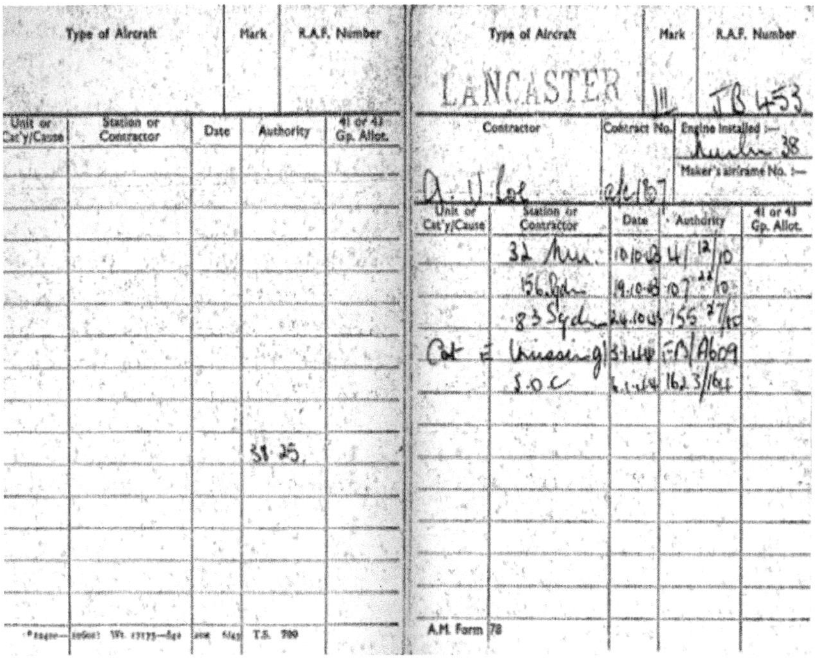

Type of Aircraft	Mark	R.A.F. Number
LANCASTER	III	JB453

Contractor	Contract No.	Engine Installed :— Merlin 38 / Maker's airframe No. :—
A. V. Roe	2/A/187	

Unit or Cat'y/Cause	Station or Contractor	Date	Authority	41 or 43 Gp. Allot.
	32 MU.	10.10.43	41 12/10	
	156 Sqdn	19.10.43	107 22/10	
	83 Sqdn	24.10.43	155 27/10	
Cat E	Missing	3.1.44	FB/A609	
	S.O.C.	6.1.44	162 3/1/44	

A.M. Form 78

Form 78 – Aircraft Movement Card for JB453. Image courtesy of BAE Systems.

Performance

- **Maximum speed:** 282 mph at 63,000 lbs
- **Cruise speed:** 200 mph
- **Range:** 2,530 miles
- **Service ceiling:** 21,400 ft at 63,000 lbs
- **Rate of climb:** 720 ft/min at 63,000 lbs

During its production years, each Lancaster aircraft cost approximately £50,000, the equivalent of just under £3 million in 2021. The 7377 Lancasters produced, therefore, cost somewhere approaching £369 million, a staggering £21.5 billion by today's standards.

CHAPTER 3

2ND/3RD JANUARY 1944

But soon this England is no longer,
We are just creatures of the void.
Above the grey miles of the North Sea,
Outbound, for towns to be destroyed

© Julie Wigley, *No Moon Tonight*

Thirteen 83 Squadron crews, a little under a hundred men, were called to the briefing room at RAF Wyton during the late afternoon of 2nd January, to learn the details of the forthcoming night's attack upon enemy-occupied Europe. The plan was for a late evening take-off for over 600 Lancasters from stations across the length and breadth of eastern England, taking a route that would traverse Northern

Europe, before crossing the Baltic coast on a heading towards the German capital, Berlin.

It was January and the weather was not expected to be anything other than what one might expect for that time of year. There had been heavy snow over the previous two days and temperatures were well below freezing. Consequently, route plans were changed with the majority of craft now instructed to take a flight path across The Netherlands before heading into Germany. A small number of aircraft were detailed to carry out attacks on other targets, as part of efforts to bluff and deceive the enemy into thinking that those were the primary targets.

Icing up made it impossible for a number of the attack force to climb successfully, being forced to abandon the operation and to ditch their bombs in the North Sea before returning to base. Crew fatigue was a major factor with over half of the flying crews likely having been on similar missions only 24 hours beforehand. They might have been expecting an evening's respite, perhaps even a night out in nearby Huntingdon or Lincoln, rather than staring at the floor to ceiling map in the briefing room and once again being directed into battle. There would be no such respite tonight.

It was commonplace for crews to be given stimulant-type drugs such as amphetamine, pre-operation, making them more alert and physically active for longer, the resulting effect of the drugs making messages zip between brain and body at lightning speed. No thought was given to the possibility of post-war dependency or addiction.

The intended target was clearly marked on the map – Berlin…..again! Hard-done-by feelings were put to one side, albeit not for the first time. They all knew that they were there to do a job, a job so important that the continued and future freedom of people throughout Europe, especially Great Britain, rested on the shoulders of servicemen such as them. They also knew that there were those sitting amongst them in the briefing room that afternoon who would never be seen alive again.

Although the Lancaster bomber was something of a huge beast, with a length of 102 feet and a wingspan of 69 feet 4 inches, room to manoeuvre inside was extremely limited. Also, many crews would follow certain "good luck" rituals before boarding. Some would say a prayer or cross themselves; others might have a mascot of some sort which would accompany them on every operation. It was not unknown for some crew members to stand and relieve themselves against one of the wheels before climbing the short ladder into the aircraft. Ground crews would have a moan about this saying that doing this repeatedly would result in tyre rubber perishing. There are, however, no recorded incidents of any aircraft failing or crashing for this reason! Crew members would often insist upon entering the aircraft in the same order for every operation. One often sees this kind of ritual in modern times. For instance, some professional footballers insist on being in the same place in the line every time the team walks out onto the pitch.

Six of the crew, that is everyone except the rear gunner, would get to the top of the ladder before stepping through the small starboard door and turning right to take up their various positions. Ian Allan, JB453's rear gunner, would be the only one to turn left before climbing into his, extremely cramped, pod. He would be unlikely to see his colleagues again for the ensuing five to seven hours. His only contact with them, normally for the duration of both outbound and inbound legs of the operation, would be via radio intercom.

Pilot Blair Stiles and Flight Engineer Patrick Traynor would have headed directly to the front of the aeroplane, manoeuvring through the restricted space, and climbing over struts. Their job right now would be to carry out all pre-flight checks. Bomb aimer, Bill Dyke, would have slid down, headfirst, into the nose section, easy to get into but more challenging when exiting, to carry out his own bomb/flare release checks – he would not be very popular if, when over the target site, the mechanisms failed. He would also have carried out checks on the twin forward-facing machine guns that he might have to use. Navigator, Denis McKendry, would by now be checking his directional instruments. His would, arguably, be the most crucial job. The plane could fly and operate with some of the engines not fully working, with malfunctioning guns, with a defunct wireless, even without a pilot as the flight engineer was trained to take the controls if necessary. Without navigation, however, the plane would be flying blind. McKendry would also require as much accurate information about the weather expected during the operation, another key part of his role. He would, for instance, need to take account of wind direction and strength, factoring these into his calculations. The weather would be a crucial aspect if it became necessary to execute navigation using the stars to establish direction. Wireless Operator, Joe Banks, would ensure that he was able to communicate with those in the control room, both with voice and Morse Code. The last member of the crew, Upper Gunner John Dunlop, would be spending this time checking his own machine guns. Although it was always in their minds, thoughts of failing to return were pushed to one side. Every crew thought… *we will never get shot down, that's something that happens to other crews, not to us…* until it does! None of the JB453 crew imagined for one minute that this would be the last time they would see England, or their families and loved ones, ever again.

The bulk of the 600+ strong attack force headed by the Pathfinder Force, one of which was JB453, headed directly on the pre-determined route towards the German capital. It was unfortunate, but often the case, that a number of aircraft would be lost en route due to enemy anti-aircraft fire or night fighters. This night was no exception and several Lancasters were witnessed as being hit and downed. Others might have had to turn back because of technical or mechanical malfunctions or icing up.

Some two and a half hours after take-off, Berlin was sighted beneath broken clouds. The Pathfinder Force leading the attack, including JB453, took control and began its approach to drop coloured flares to identify and illuminate the targets. Flak, as ever, was continuous, somewhat successful, and terrifying. Considerable numbers of attacking aircraft were either shot down or severely damaged, having been caught up in powerful searchlights.

Hauptmann (Captain) Berthold Ney, Luftwaffe

Hauptmann Berthold Ney, was born in Ukraine in 1914, coincidentally the year that World War I, or The Great War as it was initially known, began. An officer of the German Luftwaffe, he was, in 1943 and 1944, a night-time fighter pilot based at Gilze-Rijen airfield in The Netherlands, located midway between Rotterdam and Eindhoven. At the beginning of 1944, Hautmann Ney was the newly appointed Kommandeur (Commander) of III Gruppe/NJG2 – Nachtjagdgesschwader (Night-Hunting Squadron). His squadron was specifically responsible for intercepting Allied aircraft both en route to their targets or returning post-attack.

The favoured Luftwaffe night-time fighter aircraft was the twin-engine Junkers Ju88 C6, a multi-purpose aircraft with a range of some 1,200 miles and which had many applications: bomber, heavy fighter, night fighter, dive bomber and reconnaissance.

Despite a drawn-out development lasting several years, its performance and wide-ranging utility determined that the aircraft would become one of the most effective Luftwaffe aircraft. In excess of 15,000 units were built, more than any other twin-engine German aircraft of that time. Although many variants were produced, the basic design of the aircraft remained essentially the same. Each craft held a four-man crew; pilot, observer, radio operator/rear gunner, and flight engineer/waist gunner.

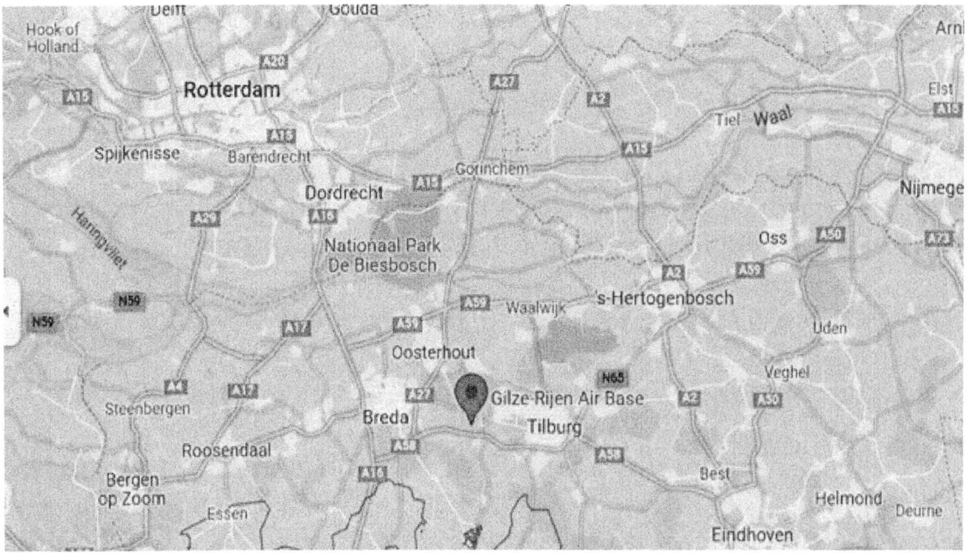

Gilze-Rijen Airfield, Netherlands, where Hautmann Berthold Ney was based in 1943/44
Map Data ©2023 Geobasis DE BKG (©2009), Google

The design of the JU88 included an upward-facing gun at the front of the craft. This meant that it was possible for approaches upon Allied aircraft could be made surreptitiously from beneath, very difficult for bomber crews to see, and fire into vulnerable underbellies.

At approximately 0310 hrs on Monday 3rd January 1944, Hautmann Ney was patrolling the skies above the Saxony-Anhalt area of Germany. It was over Timmenrode, between Blankenburg and Quedlinburg, at the foot of the Harz mountains, some 115 miles south-west of Berlin and 260 miles from his Gilze-Rijen base, that Ney claimed his first shooting-down of the night, a Lancaster thought at the time to be part of 83 Squadron. His claimed was accepted by Luftwaffe authorities in August 1944 when it was confirmed that the Lancaster Ney likely shot down was JB453 OL-F. The Lancaster was believed to be on its return to RAF Wyton, having dropped its flares payload over Berlin some half an hour earlier (see timeline below). Throughout the duration of World War II, the manner in which time was managed, because of a desire to extend daylight hours as much as possible, could differ by up to 3 hours between The Netherlands, where Bertholt Ney was stationed and from where he took off on 2nd/3rd January 1944, Germany where JB453 was downed, and Great Britain from where it took off that night. However, by early 1944, the Third Reich had standardised time throughout Germany and its occupied countries. Time in Germany, and in each occupied country, including The Netherlands, was the same, and also identical to that in Great Britain. This is confirmed by reference to Whitaker's Almanack and the Royal Observatory at Greenwich.

Below is the believed timeline of JB453 OL-F on 2nd/3rd January 1944 based upon the above time management:

- Take-off from RAF Wyton 2358 hrs 2nd January 1944
- Likely cruising speed en-route to Berlin – circa 200 mph
- Distance to Berlin 540 miles
- At this speed, arrival over Berlin would have been around 0230 hrs 3rd January

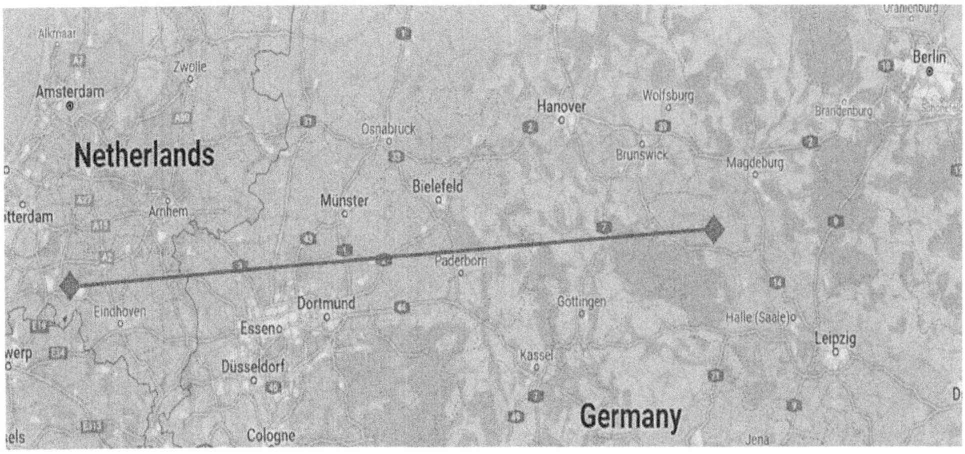

Gilze-Rijen air base to Timmenrode – a flight distance of approx. 260 miles
Map Data ©2023 Geobasis DE BKG (©2009), Google

- Records show that the aircraft was downed at 0310 hrs 3rd January over the Timmenrode region
- Distance (approx.) Berlin to Timmenrode, 100 miles – flight time approximately 30/40 minutes

This timeline supports the belief that JB453 was attacked and shot down on its return journey having already deployed its payload of flares over Berlin.

Ironically, following this operation, Ney ran out of fuel on his flight back to Gilze-Rijen whilst trying to find an airfield upon which to land. He and his three colleagues baled out safely.

The date on the RAF Loss Card for JB453 is shown as 2nd January 1944 whereas the downing of JB453 actually took place in the early hours of 3rd January. The discrepancy in date is likely to be that the aircraft was boarded for take-off in the last few minutes of 2nd January before being shot down the following morning. The loss was therefore recorded as occurring on 2nd.

On the evening of 3rd March 1945, just two months before the end of the war in Europe, Berthold Ney himself was severely injured, once again having to bale out after his aircraft sustained hits from anti-aircraft fire during a long-range intruder sortie. Ney broke his back in the process of baling out, becoming paralysed from the waist down. He was wheelchair-bound for the rest of his life and died, aged 82, on 20th February 1996. He is buried in the Lutheran Cemetery on the German Island of Borkum.

As much as Germans were the enemy as a result of the actions of its National Socialist Party (Nazi) leadership, one cannot fail to recognise that many German soldiers, sailors and airmen were never members of the Nazi Party. Ney was not a Party member. Many were young men who, like our young men, might not have chosen to fight a war but believed that they were fighting for the survival of their country. The majority had no idea of atrocities being carried out elsewhere by Nazi and SS troops, in places such as Treblinka…Belsen…Auschwitz.

So accurate is the quote attributed to ancient Greek poet, Aeschylus,

"The first casualty of war is always the truth".

CHAPTER 4

PATHFINDER FORCE (PFF)

Pathfinders flare, our bombs away now,

Among the searchlights, the flak and the shell.

We turn for home, each with his silent thoughts,

Of those below, in flames of hell.

© Julie Wigley, *No Moon Tonight*

It is recognised today that No 8 Bomber Command Pathfinder Force (PFF) played vital and dynamic roles during World War II when Allied heavy bombers were dispatched night after night through the dark skies of Europe to defined enemy targets including a prolonged operation against the German capital, and home of the Third Reich, Berlin. Multiple and protracted attacks by German bombers on London and other major British industrial conurbations in what became termed as the "Battle of Britain" between July and October 1940, only a matter of weeks after the desperate, but extraordinarily successful, evacuation of Allied troops from the beaches of Dunkirk in May and June of that year, resulted in massive damage to homes, docks and factories. Numbers of civilian casualties were high.

Even though the spirit and morale of the populous generally remained undaunted, this substantially and inevitably impacted production capacities of munitions, tanks, aircraft and many other war-related industries.

Britain's response was to conduct similar raids over enemy territory. However, during the early years of the war, its inadequately equipped and generally unsuitable aircraft, despite the bravery, grit, and determination of crews, meant that successes were few. Bombs often fell onto dummy targets deliberately laid by adversary forces. Losses were heavy. Many crews were killed as a consequence of enemy fire as aircraft fought to avoid searchlights, anti-aircraft flak and night-fighters. Hundreds more were taken as prisoners-of-war as a result of them baling out from badly stricken planes. Aircraft replacements, and parts, were slow to be delivered partly because of the enemy onslaught on home soil. There was also an increasing shortage of trained pilots. The situation was unsustainable.

It must be said that conflicting views, aspirations and objectives of senior RAF hierarchy, Government officials, ministers, scientists, and more, largely contributed to there being a lack of firm planning, both tactically and strategically. Priority targets were constantly reviewed and often subjected to last minute changes, much to the frustration and angst of RAF officers and crews in the front line.

In a little over 2 years since the beginning of the war in September 1939, there had been no fewer than 3 Commanders-in-Chief of Bomber Command; Air Marshalls Sir Edgar Ludlow-Hewitt, Sir Charles Portal and Sir Richard Peirse.

Morale amongst senior ranks of the RAF during this time was less than great but, despite a seemingly failure of top-level leadership, nothing should be taken away from the professionalism, selflessness, drive and courage shown by both air and ground crews, all of whom, day after day, night after night, worked to the very limits of their capabilities, then beyond.

It was in February 1942 that Sir Arthur Travers Harris, known immortally as "Bomber" Harris, was appointed to the role of Bomber Command Commander-in-Chief. Always outspoken but forever focussed, Harris was to transform Bomber Command from the moment he walked through the doors of its High Wycombe headquarters to the end of the war, three years later, in 1945. His philosophy was to instigate changes, previously lacking, in the chain of command from the top down, to encourage dialogue and collaboration between separate groups and departments, and for the primary efforts of Bomber Command to be directed against targets in Germany. It took until April 1943 for the Air Ministry to agree this final aspect. It is generally believed that Harris wore the Ministry down with his constant demands for support in this particular area. It finally relented, releasing a directive that year that *"Bomber Command should revert, as far as possible, to attacks upon targets in Germany".*

Earlier, in 1941 a young, already renowned, Australian Squadron Leader, recommissioned to the RAF, Donald Clifford Tyndall "Don" Bennett, was engaged for discussions with the Air Ministry. Born the son of a sheep farmer in 1910, he joined the Royal Australian Air Force in 1930 later transferring to the RAF. He left the RAF in 1935 but was re-recruited in 1941 and promoted to the rank of Wing Commander before being appointed in December 1941 to command 77 Squadron based at RAF Leeming, flying Whitley aircraft in No 4 Group, Bomber Command.

Bennett's leadership and strategic skills had already been recognised with his creation of the Atlantic Ferry Organisation, tasked with the wartime delivery of countless aircraft, manufactured in the United States of America and Canada, to the United Kingdom. Beforehand, trans-Atlantic flights were relatively rare events, but the Atlantic Ferry operation proved remarkably successful and demonstrated that, with suitable training, even relatively inexperienced pilots could safely deliver new aircraft across the North Atlantic. One of Bennett's first tasks in the RAF had been to oversee the formation of an Elementary Air Navigation School in Eastbourne, Sussex for initial training of observers, and later navigators.

In April 1942, 77 Squadron was transferred to Coastal Command and Bennett was given command of 10 Squadron, operating Handley Page Halifax aircraft, shortly afterwards notably leading a raid on the German battleship *Tirpitz.* Shot down during that raid, he evaded capture and eventually escaped to Sweden from where he was able to return to Britain. He and his co-pilot were later awarded the Distinguished Service Order (DSO), recognising their actions.

Discussions between Bennett and the Air Ministry were, to say the least, candid and open, surrounding Bennett's firmly stated views about aircraft in use at that time, and particularly challenging officials as to whether they would be prepared to climb aboard an ill-equipped aeroplane, fly for several hours over enemy territory, identify targets in the darkness whilst trying to recognise and disregard dummy targets, avoid searchlights and flak, hit targets accurately then take on the return journey when they were always at risk of attack by enemy night fighters.

In 1941, a paper known as the Butt Report, was completed and published by David Bensusan-Butt, a civil servant in the War Cabinet Secretariat. He had been tasked with reviewing and assessing over 600 post-attack target photos, comparing them with crews' claims. The results, circulated in August of that year, were shocking to many though not necessarily unexpected by RAF hierarchy who were well aware of the difficulties surrounding night navigation and target locating.

The following were some of the conclusions reached by Butt as a result of looking specifically at photographs of night-time raids taken during the early summer of 1941:

- Only one in three aircraft claiming to have successfully engaged targets got within 5 miles of the actual target.
- Over French ports, the ratio was two in three.
- Over Germany overall, one in four.
- Over the Ruhr region, the main centre of German heavy industry with coke plants, steelworks, and armaments factories, it was only one in ten.
- At full moon, the overall successful hit rate was, at best, two in five. At new moon it was down to one in fifteen.

All reviewed statistics related only to aircraft recorded as *attacking* a target. The proportion of total *sorties* which reached within 5 miles of intended targets was less than one third. The notion of forming what would become known as the Pathfinder Force (PFF), was devised and eventually agreed. An elite group of highly trained volunteer aircrew – the best of the best, especially pilots and navigators - were selected and trained to become members of the new PFF, to accurately lead squadrons of following aircraft, the main bombing force, to designated targets. It must always be remembered, however, that this was a time of war and that the term "volunteer" did not necessarily indicate a true willingness to freely step forward. It is highly likely, probable even, that many members of the PFF were "volunteered" by their commanding officers. Their brief was to identify targets using a bespoke series of differently coloured flares. This system would guide the hundreds of following aircraft and greatly increase the chances of successful outcomes.

The War Cabinet warmly welcomed this new initiative although it was initially, and fiercely, resisted by Bomber Command, firstly Peirse and then by Harris himself. Harris believed that the introduction of what could be seen as an elite force in the RAF would engender unwanted rivalry and envy with a risk of detrimentally affecting morale. Strained relations between Harris and others did little to help. It was Prime Minister Churchill himself who ultimately directed the creation of the PFF with immediate effect. In July 1942, the same year that 83 Squadron PFF made RAF Wyton its permanent home, Harris appointed Bennett as its commander. He was remarkably successful in this post, and ultimately reached the rank of Air Vice Marshal. 8 Group was re-constituted when the PFF was renamed 8 (Pathfinder Force) Group in January 1943. When new aircraft, or innovative navigational aids such as H2S and Oboe, became available, 8 Group were often the first recipients. Initially comprising 5 squadrons, 8 Group grew to a strength of 19 squadrons, over 200 aircraft. The Group was also responsible for the guiding of Light Night Striking Forces, Mosquito bombers used for harassing raids on enemy targets. 8 Group was eventually disbanded, post-war, in December 1945 although its, previously unofficial, badge and motto *"We Guide to Strike",* were subsequently authorised eight years later in 1953.

Whilst the majority of PFF personnel were from the RAF, the group also comprised many from air forces of other British Commonwealth countries, including Australia, Canada and South Africa. The PFF flew a total of 50,490 individual sorties against 3,440 targets. The cost in human lives, however, was grave. Almost 4000 members were killed on operations and 675 aircraft lost.

Early missions of the newly formed PFF, which included an initial experimental group specifically trained for the purpose, were beset with teething troubles. The first mission, in August 1942, because of changes in wind direction and strength, saw many of the 118 following aircraft drop their bomb payloads in areas up to 20 miles away from intended targets. The second mission, a few days later, was badly hampered by cloud making it impossible to identify targets. Several PFF aircraft were lost during this mission. Very soon, however, PFF came of age following several successful missions and was thereafter regarded as a highly trusted force.

PFF crews were both experienced and proven. Their role in marking targets with flares in a variety of previously agreed colours gave following bombers definitive aiming points. They then controlled and managed the progress of the mission by radio. The pilot of the lead PFF was known as the Master with the pilot of a designated following PFF craft taking on a second-in-command role, known as Deputy Master. The Deputy would be briefed to immediately take command in the event that the Master's aircraft became damaged, destroyed, or otherwise incapacitated.

The Master would be escorted by other PFF craft which would, additionally, be armed with bombs in order to be able to help protect the primary PFF's from ground attack.

The colours of flares to be used for any particular mission were agreed at the pre-mission briefing. Colours could be varied night on night which helped prevent enemy aircraft, operating covertly in likely target areas, from dropping spoof flares designed to deceive the Allied bomber force.

When escort crews had proved their worth, they would be upgraded to “backers-up”. These were distributed amongst the bombing force and provided fresh coloured flares to replace those initial flares that might be fading on the ground.

Although based for short periods at other airfields in the east of England, 8 (Pathfinder Force) Group was primarily based at RAF Wyton in Cambridgeshire. Still in existence today, RAF Wyton is a Joint Force Command Station and home to the Joint Force Intelligence Group and the National Centre for Geospatial Intelligence, both of which provide intelligence to armed forces deployed on operations around the globe.

It is interesting that a young Lancaster flight engineer, Richard “Dick” Raymond was, in the autumn of 1943, informed that his crew had been “volunteered” as Pathfinders and joined 83 Squadron at Wyton. I have dedicated a chapter of this book to Dick. Although not a member of JB453, he was part of the same squadron at the time that its crew were operational through the latter part of 1943 and into early January 1944.

I had the pleasure and privilege of interviewing Dick several times at his north Devon home during 2023. At the sprightly age of 98 years, his memory was crisp and clear, and he was able not only to tell me about his

PFF duties at Wyton, but also what day to day life was like at the station, and about socialising on operation and non-operation days. My interview with Dick provided a genuine insight into the life of a PFF crew. More of Dick later.

An operational tour for a typical bomber crew consisted of thirty, non-aborted, operational sorties. Upon completion of their tour, the crew would normally be broken up and rested, likely being assigned to various conversion or other non-operational units as instructors. It was not uncommon, however, for a rested crew member to volunteer for a second bomber tour. PFF crews were an exception to this rule. They were required to complete forty-five operations before being rested, the additional fifteen operations being added due to the high, and expensive, level of training and practice that was required in order to become specialists in target marking. However, it was often the case that Pathfinder crews continued on in the hope of reaching sixty operations, the equivalent of two full bomber tours. I mentioned that 8 PFF Group was approved in 1953 with its own badge and motto. But each individual squadron within the Group had its own version.

83 Squadron had a badge, adorned with the King's crown, recognising the reigning Monarch, with the motto *"Strike to Defend"*. The inner symbol represents the antlers of a red deer, an affinity with Scotland

where the Squadron had been founded in 1917. Having been disbanded post-World War I, the Squadron was re-formed in 1936 and based at RAF Turnhouse near Edinburgh. The six antler points represent a night in June 1918, during the latter stages of World War I, when six Distinguished Flying Crosses (DFC's) were won by the Squadron in a single action. The three top points allude to a crown of success achieved by the unit.

83 Squadron badge. Reproduced with kind permission of the UK Ministry of Defence

Pathfinders, the RAF's only World War II elite force, although Harris would never refer to it as such, was permitted another special badge, that of a gold-coloured eagle.

The PFF eagle was awarded on a discretionary basis, normally on the recommendation of the Squadron Leader and generally after the

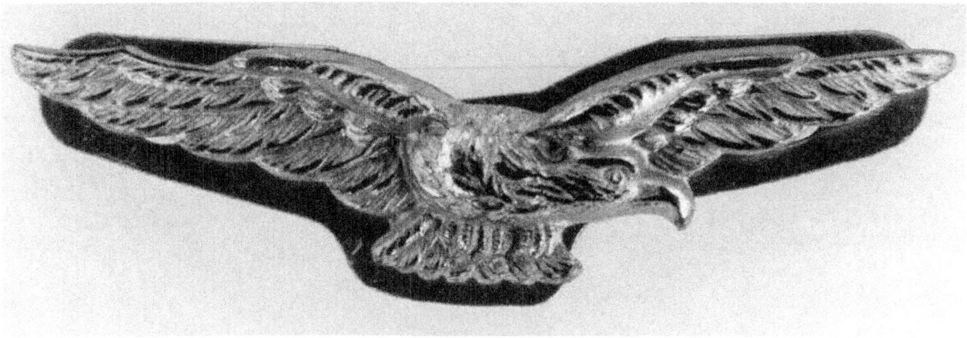

The Pathfinders gold eagle. Photo courtesy of the author

completion of six successful missions. It was worn on the left-hand breast pocket of the RAF tunic, beneath any decorations. Symbolising the unique identity of the PFF within the RAF and Bomber Command, the sign of the eagle was seen as a badge of excellence. It was initially awarded on a temporary basis and was allowed to be worn by members of the PFF after those six missions. It became permanent only on completion of the standard PFF tour of forty-five missions at which point a signed certificate was also given to the recipient.

CHAPTER 5

JB453 OL-F: THE CREW

Familiar rooms, the crews stand ready.
All battle-dressed and set to go
A cigarette, a hasty letter home,
Lest in the dawn, we do not show.

© Julie Wigley, *No Moon Tonight*

In this chapter, I have endeavoured to give readers an insight into the men who flew in the fated JB453 OL-F Lancaster in January 1944, to make it such that those readers might begin to know each crew member personally, not only during those awful war years but their lives before the conflict broke out, their families, the jobs that they had, and their personal interests. It was important, both to Helen and to me, that the crew should not be remembered, which is often the case, simply by name, rank and number, or just as seven of the fifty-five and a half thousand bomber command crew members who sacrificed their lives during World War II. They should be known, and remembered, as Blair, Joe, John, Bill, Denis known as "Jackie", Patrick known as "Willie", and Ian - family men, husbands, sons, uncles, brothers, fathers.

These were ordinary men doing extraordinary jobs; jobs that, just a few short years beforehand, they could never have imagined.

Their homes were in Canada, London, Glasgow, Ireland, Johannesburg, Cumberland (now Cumbria) and Enfield. Who could have possibly anticipated that the seven, from growing up thousands of miles apart, would be brought together as an RAF "family" by fate, coupled with the threat, then onset, of war.

Each November 11th we remember and commemorate those who fought and, in many cases died, in wars and conflicts across the globe. World War II stands alone in that, had it not been for men such as these, there is little doubt that our islands would have been invaded, and in all probability occupied, by enemy forces. Indeed, it is the case that the Channel Islands suffered from exactly that. Britain would likely have become another part of an expanding, all-powerful, German empire. If this had happened, our lives today would have been unrecognisable from those we have had the privilege of enjoying since 1945. We would never have seen Queen Elizabeth II reign for 70 years nor would we have celebrated the Coronation of King Charles III. We can do these things because of the bravery, courage, daring and heroism of these ordinary men.

Pilot - Flying Officer Ernest Blair STILES

Royal Canadian Air Force/Royal Air Force

Service Number J/18139

Photo courtesy of Stiles family

Ernest Blair Stiles, known as Blair, was born on 21st August 1921 in Apohaqui, New Brunswick, Canada to Reverend William Pierce Stiles and Jessie Annie Stiles nee Lutes.

Blair, previously employed as a dairy farmer clerk, enlisted into the Royal Canadian Air Force in mid-1941, qualifying as a radio mechanic at RCAF Yarmouth, Nova Scotia. He received his pilot's wings in August 1942 on graduating from No 8 Service Flying Training School, Monkton, New Brunswick.

Course 54 – April 1942 – No 8 Service RCAF Flying Training School, Monkton, New Brunswick, Canada

Photo courtesy of Stiles family

Three months later, Blair arrived at the RAF Personnel Reception Centre in the seaside town of Bournemouth on the south England coast, the arrival point for thousands of Commonwealth air crew. He was drafted to RAF Hixon, mid-way between Wolverhampton and Stoke-on-Trent in Staffordshire.

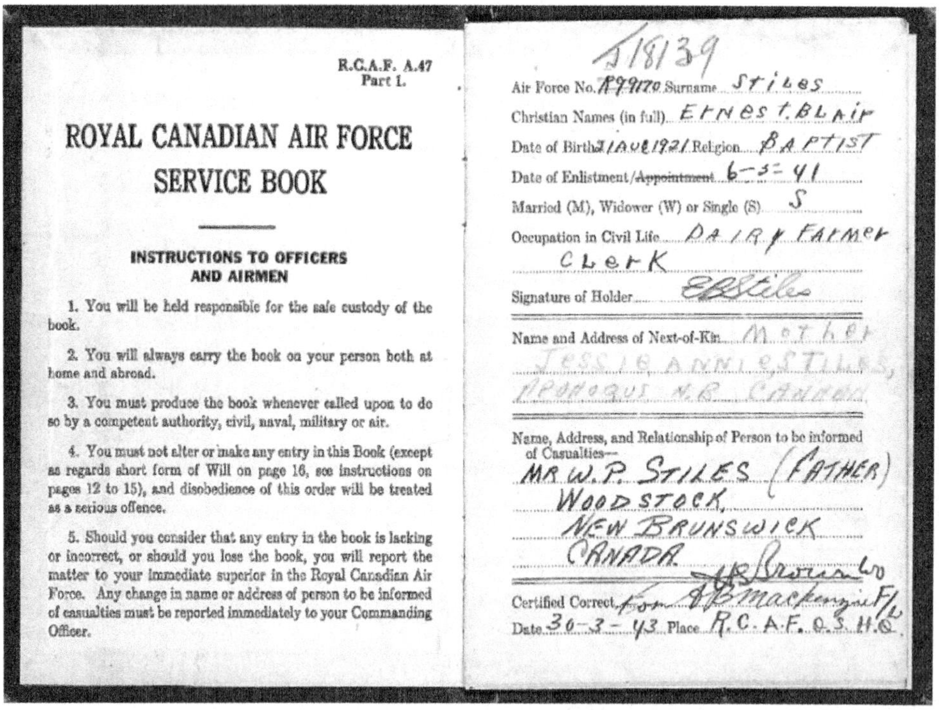

R.C.A.F. A.47
Part 1.

ROYAL CANADIAN AIR FORCE
SERVICE BOOK

INSTRUCTIONS TO OFFICERS AND AIRMEN

1. You will be held responsible for the safe custody of the book.

2. You will always carry the book on your person both at home and abroad.

3. You must produce the book whenever called upon to do so by a competent authority, civil, naval, military or air.

4. You must not alter or make any entry in this Book (except as regards short form of Will on page 16, see instructions on pages 12 to 15), and disobedience of this order will be treated as a serious offence.

5. Should you consider that any entry in the book is lacking or incorrect, or should you lose the book, you will report the matter to your immediate superior in the Royal Canadian Air Force. Any change in name or address of person to be informed of casualties must be reported immediately to your Commanding Officer.

J18139

Air Force No. R99170 Surname STILES
Christian Names (in full) ERNEST BLAIR
Date of Birth 21 AUG 1921 Religion BAPTIST
Date of Enlistment/~~Appointment~~ 6-5-41
Married (M), Widower (W) or Single (S) S
Occupation in Civil Life DAIRY FARMER CLERK
Signature of Holder E B Stiles

Name and Address of Next-of-Kin MOTHER JESSIE ANNIE STILES, APOHAQUI N.B. CANADA

Name, Address, and Relationship of Person to be informed of Casualties—
MR W. P. STILES (FATHER)
WOODSTOCK,
NEW BRUNSWICK
CANADA

Certified Correct for A B Mackenzie F/L
Date 30-3-43 Place R.C.A.F. O.S. H.Q.

Blair's RCAF Service Book - Photo courtesy of Stiles family

He must have found the broad Midlands accent somewhat challenging! In December 1942 he was trained to fly the Bristol Blenheim aeroplane, a light bomber.

The following March, Blair was posted to RAF Forres, just west of Inverness in Scotland, where he was trained to undertake operational bombing operations in the Armstrong Whitworth Whitley heavy bomber. Here, he teamed up with Sergeant Joseph Banks, blissfully unaware that they would perish together on JB453 some 10 months later.

In May 1943, a further posting saw Blair moved to RAF Winthorpe in Nottinghamshire for flight training on the highly suspect AVRO

Manchester bomber, followed by its successor, the Lancaster. Forming a crew was somewhat arbitrary, with large gatherings of trained airmen self-selecting men with whom they would fly, and perhaps die, together. These crews would become their new "family". At this point, Blair's "family" included Sergeant Joseph Banks, Sergeant John MacIntyre Dunlop, Flying Officer Ian Godfrey Allan and Flying Officer William Horace Dyke.

On 13 June 1943, Blair was formally discharged from the Royal Canadian Air Force on being appointed to a commissioned rank – Flying Officer – in the Royal Air Force. The crew left Winthorpe on 9th July 1943 to go to their new posting, RAF Wyton in Cambridgeshire.

Flying Officer Stiles is remembered on page 453 of the *Second World War Book of Remembrance* in the Canadian Virtual War Memorial (CVWM). Blair's name is also commemorated at the Canada Bomber Command Memorial at Nanton, Alberta, Canada.

One of four children born to William and Jessie Stiles, Blair, as he was known rather than Ernest or Ernie, had a younger brother Donald who was not born until 1931, an older brother, Kenneth, born in 1918, and an older sister, Annabel, with whom he was particularly close, and who was born in 1921. Kenneth married in 1931 to Mildred Ellen McAdos and died in 2011 aged 92 years. Annabel married in 1948 to Douglass Slocum Kierstead. She died in 2007 aged 85 years. They had two children, Blair –

named after her brother – and Bill. Donald married in 1954 to Marjorie Elizabeth Holmes, and died aged 88 years. They also had two children, Paul and Mark. Paul was able to forward Helen copies of many documents, including a number of personal letters between Blair and Annabel. The last letter that Annabel sent to her brother was written by her on Christmas Day 1943. Tragically, Blair was never to receive it – he was killed just 9 days later – and the letter was returned to Annabel unopened, marked "Reported missing – Return to sender".

Blair is buried in a collective grave, with his colleagues, at the 1939-1945 British War Cemetery, Heerstrasse, Berlin, Germany. He was 22 years old. The inscription on the headstone reads:

"THEY DIED THAT WE MIGHT LIVE"

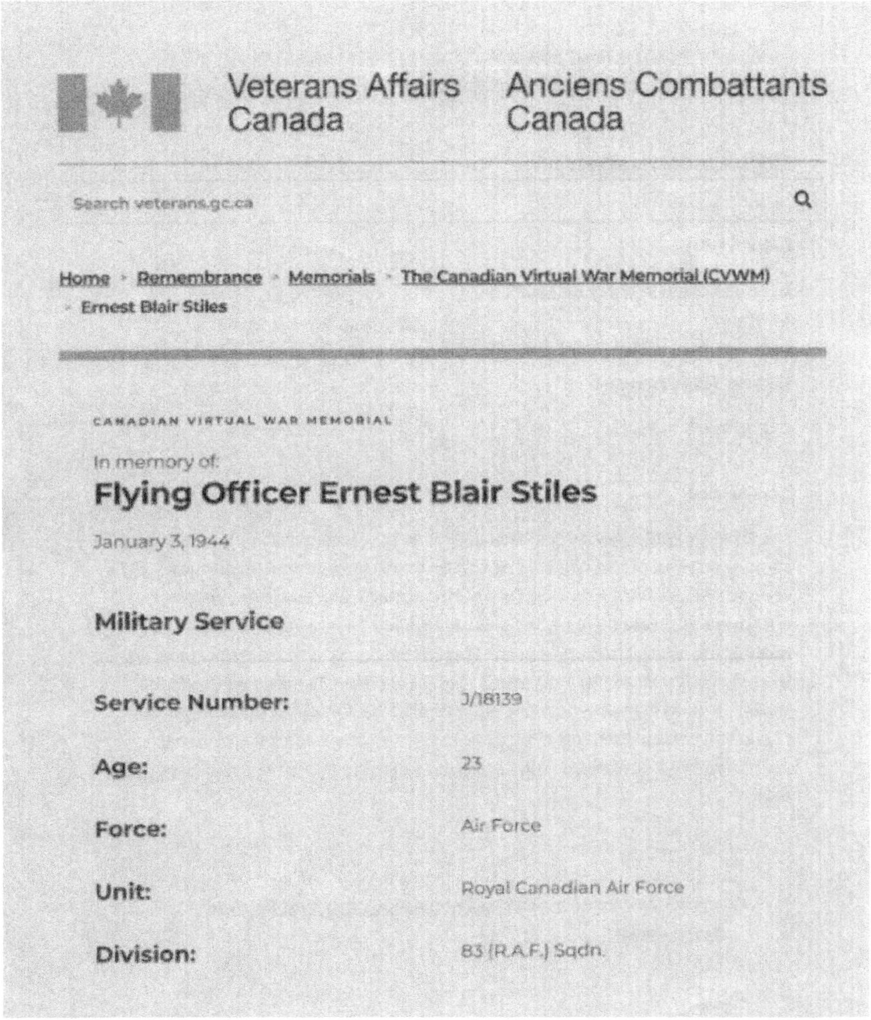

Veterans Affairs Canada | Anciens Combattants Canada

Search veterans.gc.ca

Home › Remembrance › Memorials › The Canadian Virtual War Memorial (CVWM) › Ernest Blair Stiles

CANADIAN VIRTUAL WAR MEMORIAL

In memory of:

Flying Officer Ernest Blair Stiles

January 3, 1944

Military Service

Service Number:	J/18139
Age:	23
Force:	Air Force
Unit:	Royal Canadian Air Force
Division:	83 (R.A.F.) Sqdn.

Stiles' entry in the Book of Remembrance at the Canadian Virtual War Memorial. Photo courtesy of Stiles family

Blair (centre) with Joe Banks (left) and Bill Dyke (right). Photo courtesy of Stiles family

Blair with his sister Annabel circa 1941 Blair and, now a Sergeant with pilot's wings, with his mother Jessie circa 1942. Photos courtesy of Stiles family

Wireless Operator – Sergeant Joseph Banks

Royal Air Force

Service Number 1091782

Photo courtesy of Banks family

Joseph Banks, "Joe", was born in 1921 to parents Joseph and Elizabeth Swan Banks of 48 The Gardens, Coach Road, Whitehaven, Cumberland (now Cumbria), UK. Before volunteering for the Royal Air Force at the Padgate recruitment office near Warrington in late 1939/early 1940, Joe was employed as a stereo typist at Smith Brothers, a printing company in Whitehaven. He was also renowned in local dance band circles as a tenor saxophone player and vocalist with John S. Dixon's orchestra based in nearby Egremont. Joe's great-niece, Sarah Bennett nee Banks, recalls that his Aunt Maggie had a photograph of Joe playing the saxophone in pride of place in her home. She also remembers a newspaper clipping describing that he had sung on the *"Maple Leaf Radio Matinee"* series, broadcast by the BBC. His rendition of *"Night and Day"* was particularly well received.

Following periods of initial induction and specialist wireless operator training, Joe was posted to 83 Squadron at RAF Wyton, Cambridgeshire where he became the wireless operator for JB453 OL-F. He completed 11 operations, primarily as part of the Battle of Berlin campaign, commencing in November 1943. Sgt Banks was just 22 years of age at the time that JB453 was attacked and shot down in the early hours of 3rd January 1944.

The family descendants of Banks were traced by Helen placing an article on the Facebook page of Whitehaven's Yesteryears. Several responses were received which led to her making contact with Sarah Bennett nee Banks. Joe had a brother, Charles, born in 1919 and a sister, Sarah, born in 1928. Charles married Nancy Moorhouse in Whitehaven in 1947, two years after the end of World War II. They had two sons, John, born in 1948 and Charles, born in 1950. John and his wife had a daughter, Sarah, the same Sarah with whom Helen made contact. Sarah sent Helen a series of scanned photographs, documents, and articles of, and about, Joseph which appear in various parts of this book.

In the tower of the former St Nicholas Church in the Parish of Whitehaven there is a plaque which bears the names of those 20 residents of the Parish who lost their lives during World War II. Joseph Banks was one of those and is included in the list. St Nicholas Church was destroyed by fire in 1971. The memorial plaque survived and was relocated to the church tower, the only part of the building which escaped destruction, where it resides to this day. The tower was later converted into a community café.

Joe is buried with his colleagues in the 1939-1945 British War Cemetery in Berlin. However, the original collective grave was located close to where JB453 was shot down, near Blankenburg, just north of the

Harz mountains, in what later became East Germany during the Cold War.

A reburial at Heerstrasse took place on 5 July 1947.

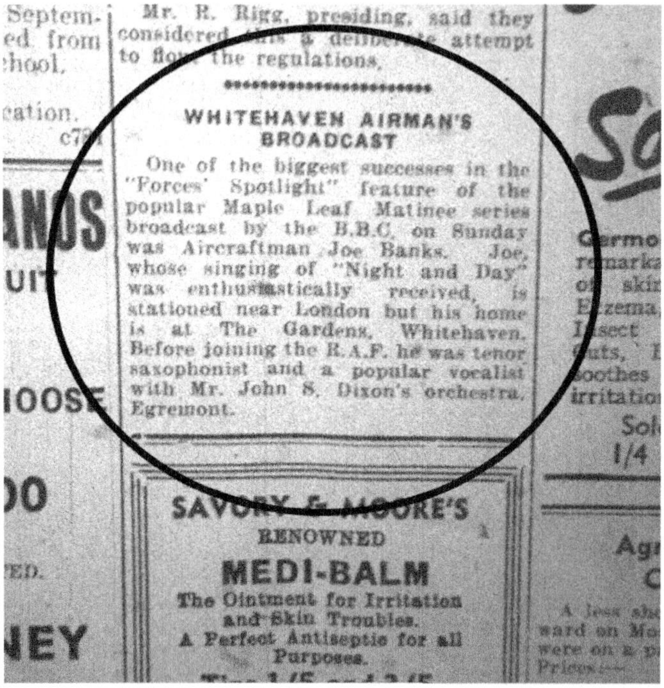

Mr. R. Rigg, presiding, said they considered this a deliberate attempt to flout the regulations.

WHITEHAVEN AIRMAN'S BROADCAST

One of the biggest successes in the "Forces' Spotlight" feature of the popular Maple Leaf Matinee series broadcast by the B.B.C. on Sunday was Aircraftman Joe Banks. Joe, whose singing of "Night and Day" was enthusiastically received, is stationed near London but his home is at The Gardens, Whitehaven. Before joining the R.A.F. he was tenor saxophonist and a popular vocalist with Mr. John S. Dixon's orchestra, Egremont.

SAVORY & MOORE'S
RENOWNED
MEDI-BALM
The Ointment for Irritation and Skin Troubles.
A Perfect Antiseptic for all Purposes.

Publicity photograph of Joe aged about 17 years and local Whitehaven newspaper article circa 1941
Photos courtesy of Banks family

Sgt Joe Banks (right) with siblings Charles and Sarah. Photo courtesy of Banks family

The inscription on his gravestone reads:

"IN DEATH…NOT DIVIDED: THEY WERE SWIFTER THAN EAGLES,

STRONGER THAN LIONS"

LOST OVER BERLIN

Now Presumed Dead

News has been received from the Air Ministry by his parents, who live at The Gardens, Whitehaven, that Sergt. Joe Banks (23), who was previously reported missing, is now presumed dead. Sergt. Banks was a wireless operator in a Lancaster which was lost during a raid over Berlin on January 3 last. He was a member of the Pathfinder force attached to Bomber Command.

Before joining the R.A.F., Sergt. Banks was a stereotyper at Smith Brothers, Whitehaven. He was well known in Whitehaven dance band circles as a tenor saxaphone player and vocalist. His only brother, Charles, who is in the Royal Corps of Signals, is serving with the 8th Army in Italy.

Media report of the presumed death of
Sgt Joseph Banks
Photo courtesy of Banks family

Joe in his RAF flying suit
Photo courtesy of Banks family

Banks, prior to joining the crew of JB453, standing, second from right, in front of what is believed to be an Armstrong Whitworth Whitley twin-engine bomber. Blair Stiles, standing third from the left is likely to be the pilot. Photo taken at RAF Forres, No 19 Operational Training Unit. Photo courtesy of Banks family

Banks' parents, Joseph snr and Elizabeth at the original grave in Blankenburg – exact date unknown but between 1945 and 1947 – Photo courtesy of Banks family.

Present-day grave at the 1939-1945 British War Cemetery, Heerstrasse, Berlin
Photo courtesy of Banks family

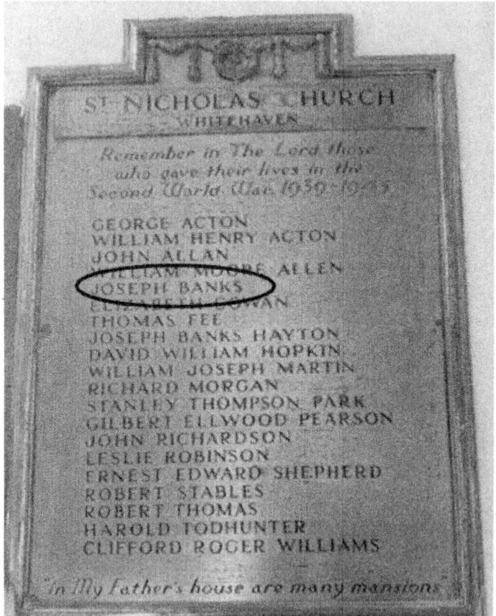

Memorial plaque in the tower of the former St Nicolas' Church, Whitehaven. Copyright – Ripley Steele, Parish of Whitehaven Archives.

Mid Upper Gunner - Sergeant John MacIntyre

DUNLOP

Royal Air Force

Service Number 1559306

Photo courtesy of Dunlop family

John MacIntyre Dunlop was born in 1922 to parents James Dunlop and Agnes Anderson MacIntyre Redmond, living south of the River Clyde in the Plantation district of Glasgow.

John joined the Royal Air Force from the RAF Volunteer Reserve. Following a standard period of basic training he was sent to an Operational Training Unit to train as a Mid Upper Gunner on Lancaster heavy bombers. Important parts of this training would be the recognition of both Allied and enemy aircraft together with gaining detailed and in-depth theoretical and practical knowledge of the Browning machine guns he would be required to use in combat. This including becoming adept in stripping down and reassembling them wearing both gloves and blindfold in order to simulate the harsh conditions likely to be experienced aboard the craft in which he would be operating.

John married Annie Millar at Admiral Street Methodist Church, Glasgow in September 1943, just 13 weeks before his life was ended. Prior to that fateful, cold January morning, John had already completed 13 operations. He was just 21 years old when he died.

Brenda Kelly, a researcher whose work helped Helen hugely through her own endeavours, was able to trace descendants of Dunlop, with the help of social media website, Facebook, and what she describes as "many kind Glaswegians". John was from a particularly large family. He was the second of 11 children borne by his mother Agnes.

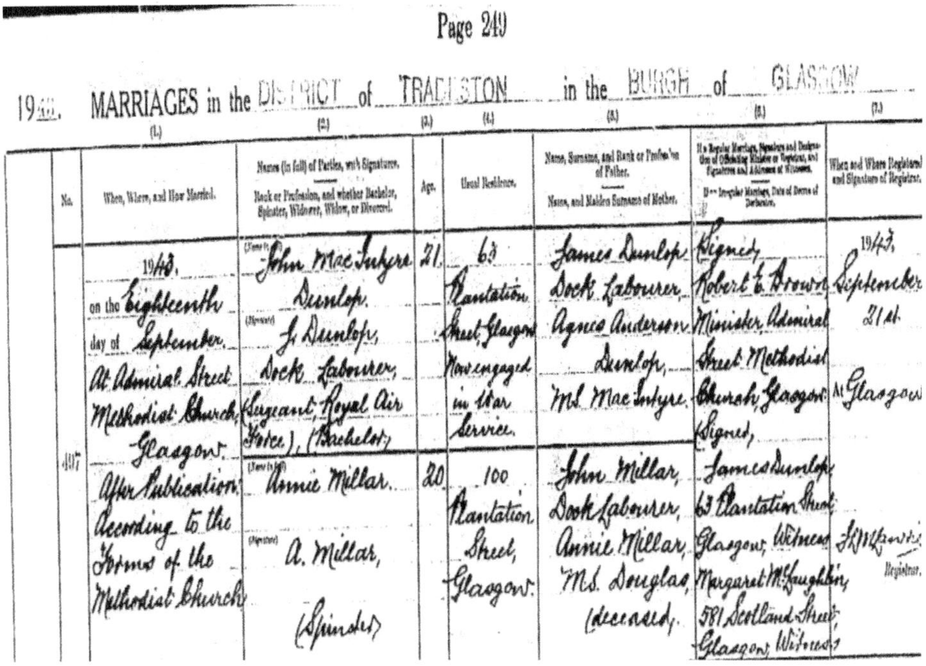
Page 249

194_. MARRIAGES in the DISTRICT of TRADESTON in the BURGH of GLASGOW

No.	(1.) When, Where, and How Married.	(2.) Name (in full) of Parties, with Signatures. Rank or Profession, and whether Bachelor, Spinster, Widower, Widow, or Divorced.	(3.) Age.	(4.) Usual Residence.	(5.) Name, Surname, and Rank or Profession of Father. Name, and Maiden Surname of Mother.	(6.) If a Regular Marriage, Signatures and Designation of Officiating Minister or Registrar, and Signatures and Addresses of Witnesses. If Irregular Marriage, Date of Decree of Declarator.	(7.) When and Where Registered and Signature of Registrar.
497	1943. on the Eighteenth day of September At Admiral Street Methodist Church, Glasgow. After Publication According to the Forms of the Methodist Church	(Signed) John MacIntyre Dunlop. (Signed) J. Dunlop, Dock Labourer, (Sergeant, Royal Air Force), (Bachelor)	21	63 Plantation Street, Glasgow. Now engaged in War Service.	James Dunlop, Dock Labourer. Agnes Anderson Dunlop, MS. MacIntyre.	(Signed) Robert E. Brown, Minister, Admiral Street Methodist Church, Glasgow.	1943. September 21st. At Glasgow
		(Signed) Annie Millar. (Signed) A. Millar, (Spinster)	20	100 Plantation Street, Glasgow.	John Millar, Dock Labourer, Annie Millar, MS. Douglas (deceased).	(Signed) James Dunlop, 63 Plantation Street, Glasgow, Witness. Margaret McLaughlin, 581 Scotland Street, Glasgow, Witness.	[illegible] Registrar.

Marriage certificate – John MacIntyre Dunlop to Annie Millar – 18 September 1943. Photo courtesy of Dunlop family

When Helen spoke with John's niece, Nancy Quinlan – Helen's main contact with the family - she was told that when they were told of his death, the family wanted, when the war was eventually over, to bring his body back from Germany to the UK so that he could be laid to rest on Scottish soil. It was his mother, Agnes, who decided that he should be left where he was, buried with his comrades.

Nancy left Glasgow in 1963, at the age of 4 years, when her parents, Redmond Iain Dunlop, brother of John, and his wife Ellen, decided to emigrate to that "land of great opportunity", Australia. They travelled on the SS Canberra as part of the *"Ten Pound Pom"* Assisted Passage Migration Scheme.

The Scheme was created in 1945 by the Australian Chifley Government and its first Minister for Immigration, Arthur Calwell, as part of the *"Populate or Perish"* policy. It was intended to substantially increase the population of Australia and to supply workers for the country's industries. The Australian government promised employment prospects, affordable housing, and a generally more optimistic lifestyle. However, upon arrival on the other side of the world, migrants were often placed in basic hostels and the expected job opportunities were not always readily available.

Adult migrants from the UK were charged only ten pounds sterling for the fare, hence the term *Ten Pound Poms*. £10 in 1945 was equivalent to just under £500 in 2022. Migrant scheme children under the age of 16 years travelled free of charge. It attracted more than a million migrants from the British Isles between 1945 and 1972. It was the last substantial scheme for preferential migration from the British Isles to Australia. In 1957 more migrants were encouraged to travel following a campaign called *"Bring out a Briton"*. The scheme reached its peak in 1969, when more than 80,000 migrants took advantage of the scheme. In 1973 the cost to migrants of the assisted passage was increased to £75, equivalent to just over £1000 in 2022. The scheme was ended in 1982.

Nancy recalls her father never being able to fully settle in the Antipodes and, years later, he returned home to the UK, sending money back to the family so that, one by one, they could all return. Nancy made the return journey on 21st September 1973, just 10 years after she had arrived.

At some point during the Cold War, Dunlop's brother, Redmond Iain, visited his brother's grave which, at that time, was on the communist side of the Berlin Wall in East Germany. John had originally been laid to rest with his crew in Blankenburg, a small town situated near to the Harz mountains where JB453 was downed, before being reburied in the 1939-1945 British War Cemetery at Heerstrasse, Berlin in 1947. He was just 21 years old.

Present-day grave at the 1939-1945 British War Cemetery, Heerstrasse, Berlin. Photo courtesy of Dunlop family

Rear Gunner - Flying Officer Ian Godfrey ALLAN

Royal Air Force

Service Number 151061

Photo courtesy of Allan family

Ian Godfrey Allan was born in 1921 to parents Robert Imrie Allan and Dorothy May Allan née Tarplée. His father, Robert, was Chief Warden for Decca Records. Along with his only sibling, sister Yvonne (affectionately known as Vonnie), they lived in Yew Tree Cottage, Worcester Park, Surrey. Vonnie died in December 1966.

Ian joined the RAF Volunteer Reserve, identified by the "VR" insignia on his tunic lapel. During his service, Ian is recorded in the London Gazette as having been promoted to Sergeant on 22nd January 1943 and to Flying Officer six months later on 22nd July.

Ian was a rear gunner on Lancaster JB453 and completed 18 operations. Rear gunners were colloquially known as "Tail-end Charlie" or "Tail-arse Charlie". The Plexiglass, or Perspex, capsule, inside which he would spend the entire mission, was small, around the size of a standard oil drum, very cramped and extremely lonely. His only communication with the crew would be via an intercom. Although named the rear gunner, the tasks of that role would not only be that of identifying and shooting down enemy aircraft that were approaching to attack from the rear. It was also to warn the pilot of an imminent attack so that instant evasive action could be taken to "corkscrew" the aircraft to port or starboard. In other words, the pilot, having heard the warning, would immediately carry out a series of ferocious manoeuvres by diving and turning sharply then equally fiercely bank and climb in an effort to lose an attacking night fighter. In many cases, the fighter would be unlikely to follow the evading heavy bomber but would more likely concentrate on finding other bombers, and there would be plenty to choose from, where the rear gunner might not be quite as alert. The British poet, Philip A Nicholson, wrote about the Rear Gunner's Job:

Alone in his transparent shell,
A speck in space,
He sits, poised in his airy kingdom;
At his back the unknown,
Before him the unfolding map
Of his journey.
Guardian of seven lives,
Taut with the concentration of survival,
He swings his turret through vigilant arcs,
Eyes straining for the fighters,
Braced for the violence of surprise.

Ian and his skipper crewmate, Blair Stiles, spent Christmas 1943 – fatefully to be their last – at the Allan family home in Worcester Park. It is a sad fact that Ian's mother, Dorothy, did not see her son that Christmas as she was away looking after her sick mother many miles away in Evesham. She was understandably devastated when her son was posted as "Missing in Action". She held out hope that he might turn up in a prisoner-of-war camp or military hospital but that was not to be. She, apparently, turned to attending seances in an effort to try and make some kind of contact, something that was fairly commonplace during the war years.

Ian with his mother, Dorothy, circa 1930. Photo courtesy of Allan family

Ian standing next to his grandmother, Alice Chamberlain. His sister Yvonne (Vonnie) is seated front left. Photo courtesy of Allan family

Helen's initial enquiries in trying to locate descendants of Ian, pointed her in the direction of Canada, despite the fact that he had been born in Worcester Park, Surrey, UK.

It was through Ian's mother's maiden name – Tarplee - from which Helen was able to obtain details of the family.

Ian's sister, Vonnie, after the end of the war, married her sweetheart, Murray Robison, a member of the Canadian forces, and later emigrated with him to Canada. It seems that she had three children, Wendy (b.1949) now living in Cowichan Bay, British Columbia, Canada, Ian (b.1955) named after his Uncle Ian and living in Coaldale, Alberta, Canada, and Elizabeth (b.1957), living in Lethbridge, Alberta, Canada. However, Vonnie actually died at quite an early age – 43 years – in December 1966 from a condition known as scleroderma which attacks the skin, internal organs, and blood vessels. Murray went on to remarry Kathryn Mae O'Mara – known as Kaye. Helen discovered, through the online listings of obituaries in Canada, that, remarkably, Kaye's grandson, Ian Robison, worked at the same funeral home that had been used for Vonnie. At the time of writing, all three children, nephew and nieces of rear gunner Ian Allan, are alive and living in the Alberta and British Columbia regions of Canada. They were all able to provide valuable information to Helen regarding their Uncle Ian, although nephew, Ian, was only 10 years old when his mother, Vonnie, died. Looking back, he feels that, at that tender age, he was too young to fully understand what had happened to his uncle.

Elizabeth (now Elizabeth McLachlan), an author in her own right, was able to confirm that her Uncle Ian, and pilot Blair Stiles, stayed at the Allan family home in Worcester Park, Surrey during the Christmas period of 1943. The following are extracts written in letters by Ian's brother-in-law, Vonnie's fiancé, Canadian Murray Robison, to his family in Lethbridge, Alberta, Canada. These were received by Helen from Elizabeth McLachlan, daughter of Vonnie and Murray, in June 2021. Elizabeth added, in her own words, "For the family of Blair Stiles, I thought it might be comforting to know that, although he was far from home, his final Christmas was spent embraced by a British family who welcomed him at their hearth for a warm, homely holiday, and that his final days were amongst friends."

December 2nd 1943

"Dear folks, it's not so long 'til Christmas now. You've no idea how much I'm looking forward to Christmas this year. My leave is all set and Vonnie is pretty certain of hers, so what could be better? Ian, her brother, may be on leave too……….. Mrs Allan dreads to hear the planes go over at night for she knows that Ian is probably in one. He is a member of the famous Pathfinder Squadron you hear so much about lately"

December 27th 1943

" Dear folks at home…..I'm sitting at the fire in Yew Tree Cottage in the lounge. I'm using a bit of "blackout" for a table across my knees. It has been a lovely Christmas….. The sad touch is that Mrs Allan is still busy nursing her very sick mother in Evesham…..Vonnie arrived home early on Wednesday. Father was already home. Ian and his friend (Stiles) *from Woodstock, New Brunswick came in early on Wednesday as well. Vonnie had gone to Evesham on Monday and stayed until Wednesday, Ian and Blair have been here for a week…. Ian and Blair had to go back to camp on*

Thursday afternoon. However, they got back for Christmas dinner on Saturday.... Vonnie turned out a super Christmas dinner for five of us – no mean task. Had to do all the shopping as well, which in these days is quite a feat what with the rationing and endless queues....here is the menu; celery soup, goose (what a lovely one too), roast potatoes, sprouts, gravy and apple sauce.... And homemade sweets. Boy, can Vonnie cook!.....gifts were opened after lunch..... "Pop" managed to get enough brandy (very scarce) for the plum pudding. And so, after dinner, in came the plum pudding garnished with holly with a blue burning light.

January 5th 1944

"....Ian, Yvonne's brother, has been reported missing. Nothing more is known about it yet. He did not return from that terrific raid on Berlin in January."

January 24th 1944

"....I took my week's kitting leave in London.....My stay in London was not really pleasant as I was all alone at Yew Tree Cottage. Mrs Allan was at Evesham, nursing her mother, and Mr Allan was at business in the Midlands. While I was at Yew Tree Cottage, the telegram came telling of Ian's (Yvonne's brother) failure to return from the raid over Berlin on Jan 2/3. By chance, Yvonne put a call through to me that night and I had to

break the news to her. Gee, she is grand – full of courage. She immediately phoned her father who in turn phoned me. It was decided not to tell Mrs Allan right then"

March 1 1944

".....news has come of Ian. It seems he died of wounds in Europe after crashing. The whole crew was lost.....

Flying Officer Ian Allan completed a total of 18 operations. He was 22 years old when he died and is buried in a collective grave at the 1939-1945 British War Cemetery, Heerstrasse, Berlin – Plot VI, Row A, Grave 23.

Flying Officer Ian Godfrey Allan headstone at 1939-1945 British War Cemetery, Heerstrasse, Berlin, Germany.
Photo courtesy of Allan family

Bomb Aimer – Flying Officer William Horace DYKE

Royal Air Force

Service Number 132869

Photo courtesy of Dyke family

William Horace Dyke, known as Bill to family and friends, was the eldest child of William and Margaret (Maggie) Dyke, nee Willets, who were married at St Peter's Church, Edmonton, Middlesex on 24th October 1920. Bill lived for many years in Enfield which, until 1965, was in Middlesex before becoming part of Greater London. He had 3 siblings, Ethel Margaret, Raymond, and Patricia, whom Bill always referred to as "the little 'un", as she was 16 or 17 years his junior. Bill attended Enfield Grammar School, from where doors were able to be opened for him to join the Royal Air Force Volunteer Reserve. His brother Raymond often spoke of his pride of Bill in achieving a Grammar School place.

Bill married Esther May Cavaye on the 17th of March 1942 in Edmonton Registry Office, Middlesex. Their respective fathers stood as witnesses to the betrothal. Bill and Esther went on to have two sons – William, who sadly died shortly before the writing of this book was started, and John who, at the time of writing, is living in north London. Both sons have previously visited their father's grave in Berlin.

Flight Officer Dyke was the bomb aimer in Lancaster, JB453. His "office" was a Plexiglass pod located at the front of the aircraft, beneath the pilot. However, official safety instructions meant that, after all of his pre-flight checks had been completed, during take-off he stood by the Wireless Operator, Sergeant Joseph Banks. Once safely in the air, he would move forward, past the navigator Pilot Officer McKendry, and down, on his belly, through the narrow entrance to the right of the pilot Stiles, re-entering his pod. Dyke would have lain on a padded board below his twin Browning machine guns in the nose of the Lancaster. His primary role was to determine when the aeroplane was in the correct position such that the payload could be successfully dispatched. For those crucial minutes, the bomb aimer was in charge, calling for the pilot to make slight moves left and right, or to remain steady, before pressing the releasing button. During his service, Bill completed 11 operations and has always been regarded as a hero in the Dyke family.

Growing up, all Bill ever wanted to do was to fly. He adored it. His mother, Maggie, when she heard the news of her son's death, said that he had often told her, *"If I have to go then I want to go doing what I love and I want to go down with my Lanc"*. Anecdotally, there is a story of Bill being reprimanded at some point for flying an aircraft under a bridge although there are no further details which might verify this alleged incident.

Bill's father, William, died in 1945, a year after his son. This must have been a harrowing time for Bill's mother, Maggie, losing both her husband and eldest son in such a short space of time.

In 1950, Bill's widow, Esther May, remarried and the young sons took on their stepfather's surname of Christie. Bill's family now live in Canada whereas John still lives in the UK.

Bill Dyke (far right) with unidentified colleagues. Photo courtesy of Dyke family

Esther reached her 100th birthday shortly before the writing of this book but has, sadly, since passed. Flying Officer Dyke is buried in a collective grave with his colleagues, at the 1939-1945 British War Cemetery, Heerstrasse in Berlin. Plot VI, Row A, He was 22 years old when he died.

The epitaph on his stone reads:-

"THOUGH TIME ROLLS ON AND YEARS PASS BY, MEMORIES OF HIM WILL NEVER DIE"

Bill Dyke (then Sergeant) receiving a medal, likely to be the Air Crew Europe Star.
Photo courtesy of Dyke family

Medals awarded to Flight Officer Dyke
(l to r) Air Crew Europe Star, War Medal 1939-1945, 1939-1945 Star
Photo courtesy of Dyke family

A very relaxed Bill – location unknown. Photo courtesy of Dyke family

Navigator - Pilot Officer Denis Charles James McKENDRY

Royal Air Force

Service Number 155542

Photo courtesy of McKendry family
Original taken at Beryl Studios, Spurriergate, York

Denis Charles James McKendry, fondly known as "Jackie" to his family, was born in South Africa on 27th April 1921 to John Harrison McKendry and Agnes Ninnie Maria McKendry nee Groth, ironically a surname of Germanic origin.

A junior clerk before enlisting, Denis had 3 siblings – Helena Deirdre, Terence Reginald, and James Fitzgerald (known as Gerald, a shortened form of his middle name). His father, John, heralded from Donegal in Ireland but moved to South Africa where he married Agnes in Port Elizabeth, Eastern Cape. Denis started life in Cape Town, later moving with the family to live in Stanhope Mansions, Plein Street, Johannesburg. As a toddler, his mother took Denis and his siblings on an extended visit to England in order to meet relatives. They returned, sailing on the SS Gloucester Castle from London to Cape Town, on 26th March 1924.

On his return to South Africa in 1924, Denis grew up in Cape Town before moving to Johannesburg where he attended one of the oldest South African schools, Parktown Boys High School. The motto of the school is simply "Arise", which, for a young man destined to join the Royal Air Force, seems entirely appropriate. Denis also spent time as a cadet on the South African Training Ship *General Botha* joining in 1937. Built in 1886, the *General Botha* was donated by philanthropist T B Davis, as a full-time association for sea training, and named after General Louis Botha, first

Prime Minister of the Union of South Africa. Davis purchased the ship from the Royal Navy in 1920 and donated it to the service in world shipping.

First name(s)	D C J
Last name	McKendry
Title	MAST
Gender	Male
Age	2
Birth year	1922
Departure year	1924
Departure day	26
Departure month	3
Departure port	London
Destination port	Cape
Destination	Cape
Country	South Africa
Destination country	South Africa
Ship name	Gloucester Castle
Ship official number	132592

SS Gloucester Castle passenger manifest entry for Denis McKendry (aged 2 years) when the family returned from London to Cape Town on 26 March 1924. Photo courtesy of McKendry family.

The following is an extract from the website of the General Botha Old Boys Association.

Denis (left) with siblings James (known as Gerald, a shortened version of his middle name, Fitzgerald) and Terry 1933. Photo courtesy of McKendry family

Cadet McKendry – South African Training Ship "General Botha" circa 1937/38, aged 16 years.
Photo courtesy of McKendry family

"McKENDRY Denis Charles James. Number 936. Born Johannesburg, 27th April 1921. Son of John Harrison McKendry, and Agnes Ninnie Maria, nee Groth. Ed, Parktown Boys' High School, Johannesburg. Cadet Draft 1937-8. In 1940 Denis James McKendry joined the RAF and was eventually posted to the position of navigator in a Lancaster bomber, 83 Squadron, as

Flying Officer. On the night of 2nd January 1944, they set out in a ninety-mile-an-hour gale on a special mission over Berlin, and having achieved their objective, were on the way home when the wireless operator sent out a message stating that they were taking ice at 8000 ft and could not make base. The last news heard of the crew was that they were ready to bale out. Death was presumed on 3rd January 1944".

The entry states that a wireless message was received from the aircraft indicating that they were taking on ice at 8000 feet. There is, however, no evidence from RAF, or other, records that this was the case, and the source of this piece of information remains unknown.

Like many wartime RAF crew members, Denis joined the Royal Air Force from the RAF Volunteer Reserve.

An operation in which Denis was involved on the night of 6th/7th July 1941 demonstrated that it was not only the enemy that could cause problems. Denis was crewed as observer on a 102 Squadron Armstrong Whitworth Whitely bomber. It took off at 2233hrs on 6th, its mission to bomb the railway station at Dortmund in the west of Germany. It released its payload at 11,000 feet then turned homewards. Shortly afterwards, it was attacked, believed from a British Wellington bomber – so-called friendly fire or, more recently, blue on blue – resulting in both the pilot and second pilot receiving leg injuries. Despite their injuries, and damage to the aircraft, a safe landing into RAF Topcliffe, Yorkshire at 0450hrs was achieved.

Denis' name appears in the London Gazette dated 24th September 1943 recognising his promotion to Pilot Officer (on probation) in July of that year, and again in January 1944, eight days after his death, confirming his promotion to Pilot Officer and recognising his further promotion to Flying Officer. The London Gazette would have gone to print before the downing of JB453 and would not have been aware of Denis' death on 3rd January. A further Gazette entry appeared on 25th January 1944 cancelling the promotion entry of 11th January.

Denis was the navigator on JB453. He was stationed at a tiny desk, upon which his charts were spread, in a position just behind the pilot, but behind a blackout curtain which served to shut out the light from his desk lamp. Occasionally, he would climb into the dome above his head to take star readings with his sextant.

Denis and his brother Terence (Terry) had always been close and stayed in touch by letter throughout World War II whilst Denis was in the RAF and Terry was serving with the South African Air Force. Although contact was initially made with McKendry's descendants in the UK on the family side of his mother Agnes, it became clear that contact with the South African McKendry arm of the family had been lost many years beforehand.

Helen turned to the press for assistance.

Sgt McKendry, far right, as a student on Observers Course in early 1940 shortly after joining the RAF - Photo courtesy of McKendry family

An article, printed in the South African People News on May 13th 2021, read:

"A search is on for the family of a South African World War II war hero, Flying Officer Denis Charles James McKendry, who will be honoured at a War Memorial unveiling ceremony in the UK later this year.

According to Helen Theron, who is researching the crew of a World War 2 Lancaster Bomber, the plane crashed on 3 January 1944 tragically killing all aboard. Helen has photos of six out of the seven crew and would like to find a photo of Denis Charles James McKendry too. She would like to also

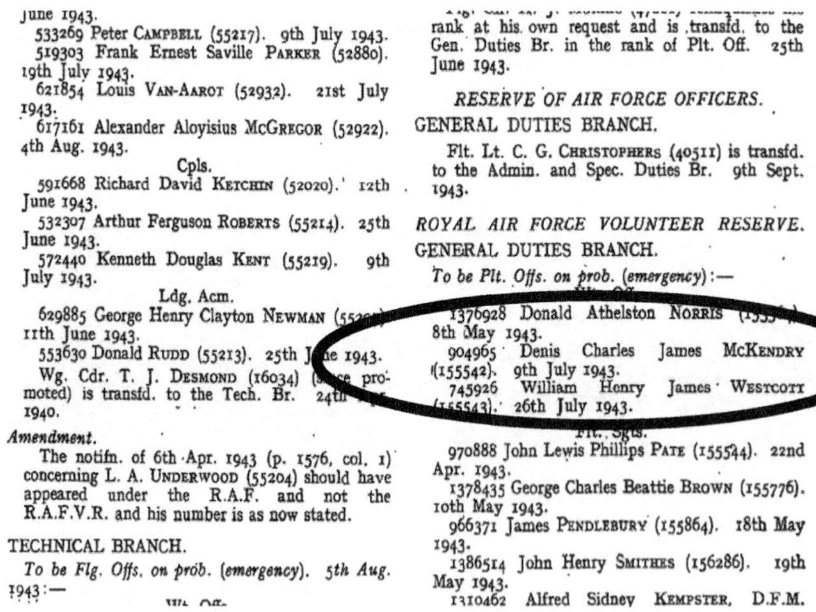

June 1943.
533269 Peter CAMPBELL (55217). 9th July 1943.
519303 Frank Ernest Saville PARKER (52880). 19th July 1943.
621854 Louis VAN-AAROT (52932). 21st July 1943.
617161 Alexander Aloyisius McGREGOR (52922). 4th Aug. 1943.

Cpls.

591668 Richard David KETCHIN (52020). 12th June 1943.
532307 Arthur Ferguson ROBERTS (55214). 25th June 1943.
572440 Kenneth Douglas KENT (55219). 9th July 1943.

Ldg. Acm.

629885 George Henry Clayton NEWMAN (55…). 11th June 1943.
553630 Donald RUDD (55213). 25th June 1943.
Wg. Cdr. T. J. DESMOND (16034) (… promoted) is transfd. to the Tech. Br. 24th … 1940.

Amendment.

The notifn. of 6th Apr. 1943 (p. 1576, col. 1) concerning L. A. UNDERWOOD (55204) should have appeared under the R.A.F. and not the R.A.F.V.R. and his number is as now stated.

TECHNICAL BRANCH.

To be Flg. Offs. on prob. (emergency). 5th Aug. 1943:—

rank at his own request and is transfd. to the Gen. Duties Br. in the rank of Plt. Off. 25th June 1943.

RESERVE OF AIR FORCE OFFICERS.

GENERAL DUTIES BRANCH.

Flt. Lt. C. G. CHRISTOPHERS (40511) is transfd. to the Admin. and Spec. Duties Br. 9th Sept. 1943.

ROYAL AIR FORCE VOLUNTEER RESERVE.

GENERAL DUTIES BRANCH.

To be Plt. Offs. on prob. (emergency):—

1376928 Donald Athelston NORRIS (155…). 8th May 1943.
904965 Denis Charles James McKENDRY (155542). 9th July 1943.
745926 William Henry James WESTCOTT (155543). 26th July 1943.

Flt. Sgts.

970888 John Lewis Phillips PATE (155544). 22nd Apr. 1943.
1378435 George Charles Beattie BROWN (155776). 10th May 1943.
966371 James PENDLEBURY (155864). 18th May 1943.
1386514 John Henry SMITHES (156286). 19th May 1943.
1310462 Alfred Sidney KEMPSTER, D.F.M.

Details of promotion to Probationary Pilot Officer on page 4 Supplement to London Gazette 28 September 1943. Photo courtesy of McKendry family

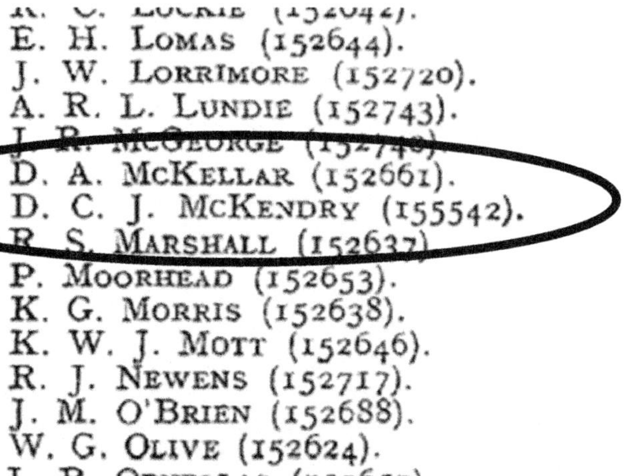

E. H. LOMAS (152644).
J. W. LORRIMORE (152720).
A. R. L. LUNDIE (152743).
J. R. McGEORGE (152740).
D. A. McKELLAR (152661).
D. C. J. McKENDRY (155542).
R. S. MARSHALL (152637).
P. MOORHEAD (152653).
K. G. MORRIS (152638).
K. W. J. MOTT (152646).
R. J. NEWENS (152717).
J. M. O'BRIEN (152688).
W. G. OLIVE (152624).
L. R. ORNELLAS (152651).
H. A. D. PALFREY (152712).

Confirmation of promotion to Pilot Officer and further promotion to probationary Flying Officer on page 3 Supplement to London Gazette 11 January 1944. The Gazette went to print several days beforehand and was not aware at that time of the death of McKendry on 3rd January 1944. The entry was withdrawn later in January. Photo courtesy of McKendry family

extend an invite to his family to attend the unveiling of the War Memorial which will commemorate these brave young men. Denis Charles James McKendry was an ex-cadet of the South African Training Ship 'General Botha' in Johannesburg. He was born in 1921, the son of John Harrison McKendry and Agnes Ninnie Maria nee Groth. Helen says they lived at Stanhope Mansions, Plein Street, Johannesburg. Denis had three siblings: Helene Deidre, Terence Reginald, and James Fitzgerald.

John McKendry (his father) died in 1961 and was last living at Andries Pretorius Street in Bloemfontein. Denis Charles James attended Parktown Boys High School in Johannesburg and joined the RAF in 1940.

Please contact Helen if you have any information on this family and in particular, Denis Charles James.

Helen herself is not South African but her husband John's grandfather was South African and John still has cousins in the country.

Helen told SA People "When we moved to Herefordshire (in the UK) we took it (the weathervane) with us and whilst it sat in a box, we noticed an inscription on it. When I Googled it, it corresponded to a real WW2 Lancaster Bomber, JB453 OL-F. I started posting info on the internet only to discover a wealth of info regarding the plane and crew.

Terry McKendry, brother of Denis, in the uniform of the South Africa Air Force
Photo courtesy of McKendry family

International Bomber Command contacted us and told us that the weathervane should be classified as a War Memorial along with a plaque to commemorate the crew. Since then, a couple of other ladies and myself have been searching for their relatives so that they could attend."

Contact with Denis' descendants in the UK was eventually made, firstly through various online genealogy sites and his mother's maiden name of Groth. Adrian Groth, a distant cousin of Denis was the initial point of contact for Helen, but this mantle was later taken up by Adrian's cousin Gillian. Unfortunately, contact with the McKendry side of the family had been lost since they left for South Africa. However, within 24 hours of the article publication by Helen in the South African People's News, Denis' nephew and Terry's son, Mike McKendry made contact with Helen from Johannesburg.

UPDATED REPORT FROM THE SOUTH AFRICAN PEOPLE'S NEWS 17 May 2021:

"We're happy to report this news from Helen: "This morning I chatted to Mike McKendry, the nephew of DCJ McKendry. He was thrilled to be in touch, and we now have a photo too. Brilliant outcome as the SA family will be coming to the unveiling, Covid permitting. A huge success. Thank you so, so much."

Coincidentally, around the same time as the news article was published, Mike had been talking with his brother about making a small replica of the aircraft that their father, Terry, had flown during World War II. This was completed and plans were made to build a model of the "Lanc" that their Uncle "Jackie" had flown. Below is the finished article.

Denis completed 30 operations as early as September 1943, 33 in total. His name appears on the WWII Memorial at City Bowl, Adderley Street at Western Cape, Cape Town and is included in the South African War Graves Project. He is buried in a collective grave with his colleagues, at the 1939-1945 British War Cemetery, Heerstrasse in Berlin. Plot Vl, Row A. He was 22 years old when he died.

Photo courtesy of McKendry family

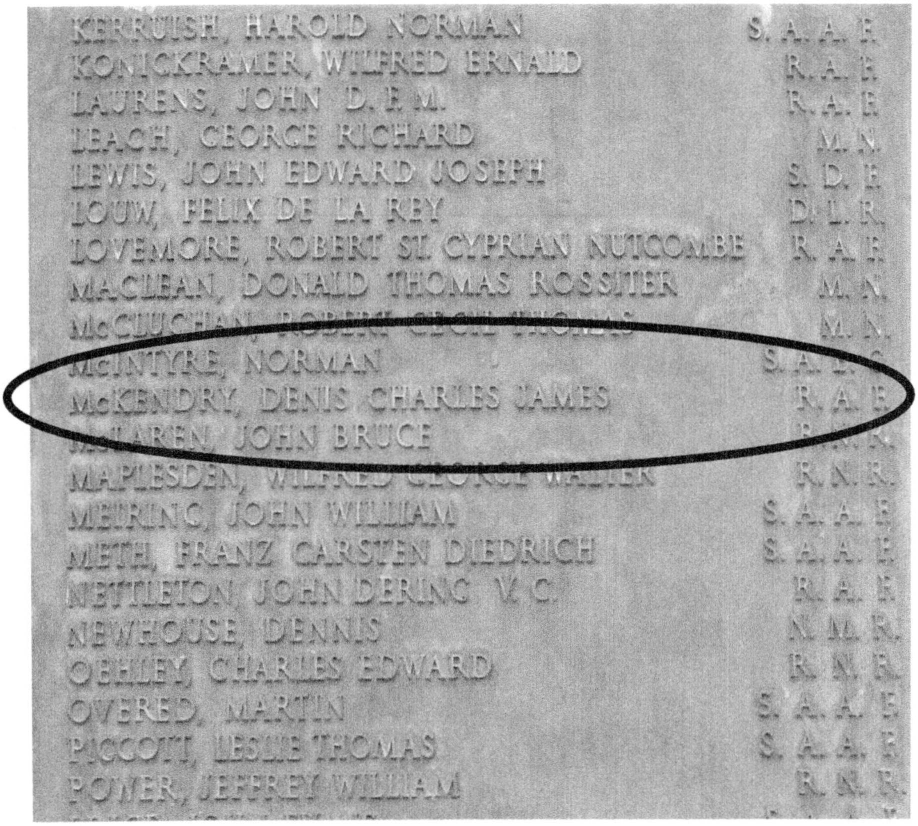

World War II Memorial, City Bowl, Adderley Street, Western Cape, Cape Town.
Photo courtesy of McKendry family

NAMES (In Full, Surname First) McKENDRY. Denis Charles James
TRADE ACH/Air Observer (Air Crew) NAV(B)
OFFICIAL NUMBER 904965

BIRTH. Date 27.4.21 Nationality British
Place: Town Johannesburg; Parish & County Johannesburg, Transvaal

RELIGION. Christian Science

CIVIL OCCUPATION Junior Clerk
Employer
Address

MARRIAGE.
Wife's Maiden Name
Date Place
Reason and date Marriage or Family Allowance ceased to be issuable.

CHILDREN. NAMES. DATE OF BIRTH.

NEXT OF KIN OR PERSON TO BE NOTIFIED OF CASUALTIES. (To be entered in pencil).
Name Mr. J. M. McKendry
Address Box 216, Bloemfontein, Orange Free State
Relationship Father

PREVIOUS ENGAGEMENTS.

Unit.	Period. From	To	Rank on Discharge

Former Service permitted :— As Service yrs. days; Qual. Service; For G.C. Badge; For Prog. Pay; Authy.

CURRENT ENGAGEMENT. D.P.E.
Date of Enlistment 17.10.39
Service Commences 17.10.39
Transferred from
Extended for
Prolonged for
Re-engaged for

Reg. Service Exp. Date. Authy.

TIME FORFEITED.

Authy.	Cause.	Dates. From	To	No. of Days.
191/42	Forfeits 1 Day Pay			

DESCRIPTION.

	Height Feet	Ins.	Chest Ins.	Hair	Eyes	Comp.	Marks, Scars, etc.
On Entry	5	5	30	Dark	Grey	Ruddy	3" scars on R. leg just above ankle.
Extn.							
Re-en.							
Transf.							

HOME ADDRESS. (To be entered in pencil).

MISCELLANEOUS.
No. 1 Selection Board "Recommended for training as an Airman Pilot." "To start at once" 17.10.39
Passed medically unfit for Pilot – fit for full Air Observer duties. 17.10.39

NATIONAL REGISTRATION IDENTIFICATION LETTER AND No. PY 9746
CARD SENT TO CENTRAL INDEX DEPARTMENT ON 30/10/39

Form 496 for training as Pilot, Rec by 20 ACSB 17.11.42.
Form 58 Medically fit for All Aircrew 17.11.42
ANNUAL FILMING SEP 1944
ANNUAL FILMING DEC

TRANSFER TO RESERVE.
Date Para. K.R.
Mobn. Stn.
Annl. Trg. Date
Recall from Reserve (Date)

DISCHARGE.
Date 8.7.43 Para. 652 (4) K.R.
Cause on appointment to a temporary Commission
Total Service 3 years. 265 days.
Qual. Service 3 " 265 "
Pension Award

Particulars of Medals, etc.	Authy. & Date	DATE Received	Despatched	Stock Bk. Ref. Page	Book

GOOD CONDUCT BADGES.

Authy.	1st, 2nd, 3rd.	A. D. B.	Date of Effect.
164/42	1st	A	17.10.42

B2A/15 11/6/45

Form 543.

XAA000271951

Service record (1) for McKendry. Provided by McKendry family

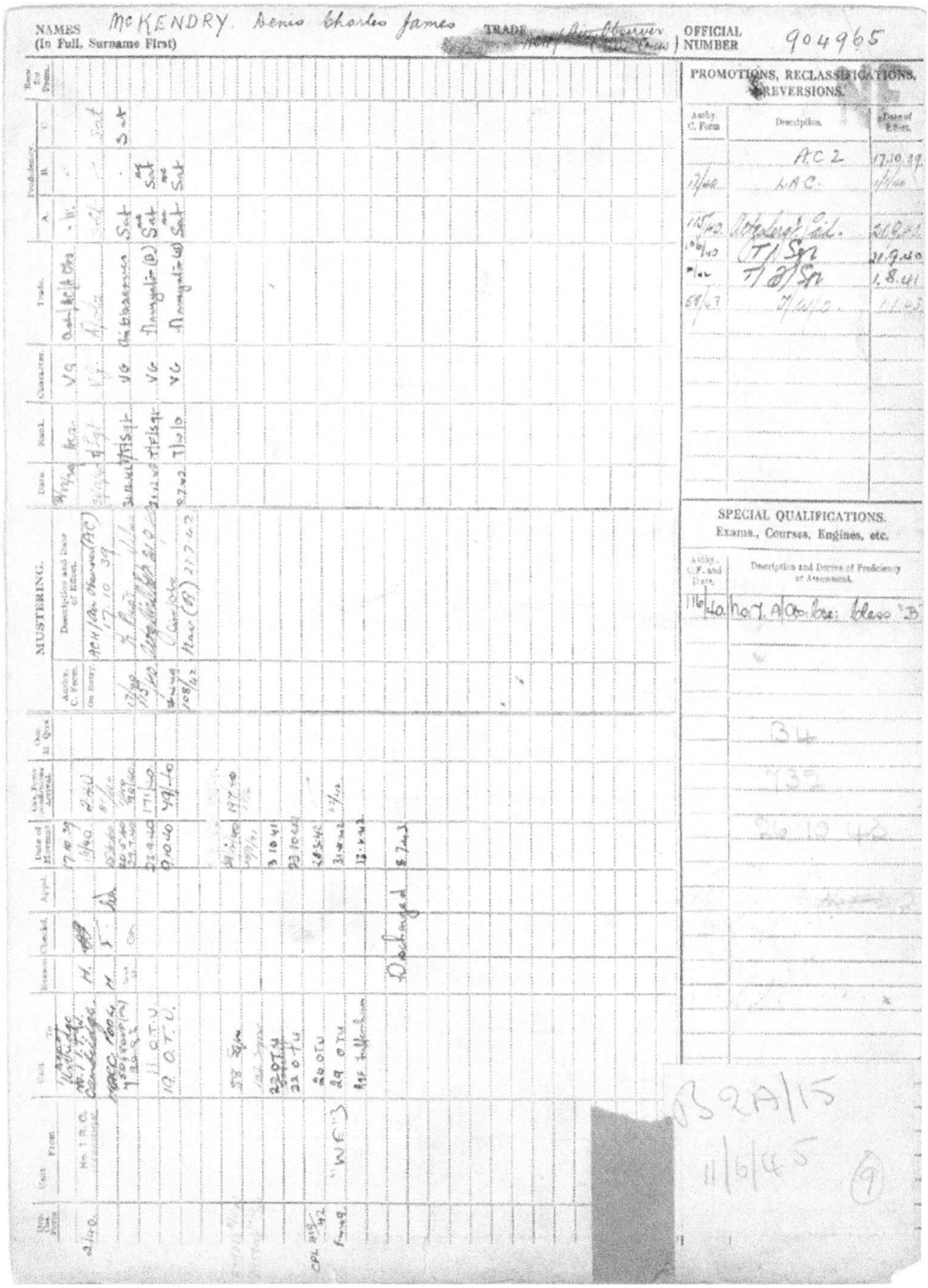
NAMES McKENDRY Denis Charles James
(In Full, Surname First)
TRADE
OFFICIAL NUMBER 904965

PROMOTIONS, RECLASSIFICATIONS, REVERSIONS.

Authy. C. Form	Description	Date of Effect.
	AC2	17.10.39
	LAC	

SPECIAL QUALIFICATIONS.
Exams., Courses, Engines, etc.

Authy., C.F. and Date.	Description and Degree of Proficiency or Assessment.

MUSTERING.

Service record (2) for McKendry. Provided by McKendry family

South African artist Terry McKendry, nephew of Denis, was so inspired by this project, that he decided to paint his own representation of Lancaster JB453, and I am delighted he has agreed for me to reproduce it below:

Flight Engineer - Flight Sergeant Patrick

TRAYNOR

Royal Air Force

Service Number 614985

Photo courtesy of Traynor family

Patrick, known as "Willie" to his family, was born in August 1919 in Portadown, Armagh, Ireland to parents, Michael Traynor and Rose Traynor nee Farrell. This was during a time of great turbulence in Ireland. At the end of 1918, whilst the country was still wholly under British rule, the republican Sinn Féin political party won a landslide electoral victory. On 21 January 1919 they formed a breakaway government (Dáil Eireann) and declared Irish independence. The self-proclaimed government was not recognised by the British Government until the formation of the Irish Free State and Northern Ireland in 1922. This was the uncertain world into which Patrick was born.

In 1938, prior to the outbreak of World War II, Patrick enlisted, originally as a civilian, at RAF Uxbridge near London. The depot was charged with managing and dispatching personnel. He remained at Uxbridge for a brief time until he transferred to RAF Halton in Buckinghamshire then, in April 1939, only 5 months before the outbreak of war, to No 6 Technical Training School at RAF Hednesford in Staffordshire. Here, he was trained in maintenance and repair of airframes and engines. Only 3 months later, Patrick was again transferred, this time to No 13 Flying Training School at RAF Drem. The Drem station was primarily responsible for the defence of Edinburgh and the shipping areas around the Firth of Forth.

In October 1939, he was sent to RAF Middle Wallop in Hampshire to continue his training. This was followed by a spell at RAF Cosford in Shropshire before joining 101 Squadron at RAF Bircham Newton in Norfolk, a station that used light bombers such as the Bristol Blenheim.

Patrick (right) with an unknown colleague circa 1938/39
Photo courtesy of Traynor family

Patrick's official training as Flight Engineer commenced at No 4 Technical Training School, RAF St Athan, South Wales where he would have received instruction as to how to take overall responsibility for aircraft mechanical smooth running and, if required, to act as a support pilot.

His training at St Athan led to his direct involvement in the RAF war effort, flying initially with 9 and 467 Squadrons. 9 Squadron was a Lancaster unit. On 15th October 1942, his bomber, W4157, was one of 289 aircraft involved in the bombing of Cologne. Two nights later, in Lancaster R5916, he was part of a successful bombing raid – Operation Robinson – in northern France, of a site that was, at that time, instrumental in improving the strength and durability of cast iron for enemy forces. Patrick flew several operations with 9 Squadron before, at the end of 1942, being posted to 467 Squadron, an Australian unit based at RAF Bottesford, Leicestershire.

The majority of Patrick's 32 operations were served with this squadron before, on 5th December 1943, he joined the 83 Pathfinder Squadron at RAF Wyton, just 4 weeks before he perished aboard JB453. Patrick, promoted to Flight Sergeant on 19 September 1943, was awarded a number of medals for his war service with the RAF, most notably that of the Bomber Command clasp, an addition to the 1939-1945 Star, but only created and approved in 2012/13, and awarded, in most cases posthumously

Squadron Leader Keith Sinclair and his Flight Engineer Sgt Patrick Traynor in the cockpit of their usual Lancaster aircraft 'Pregnant Winnie' based at RAF Bottesford 1942/43.
Photo courtesy of Traynor family

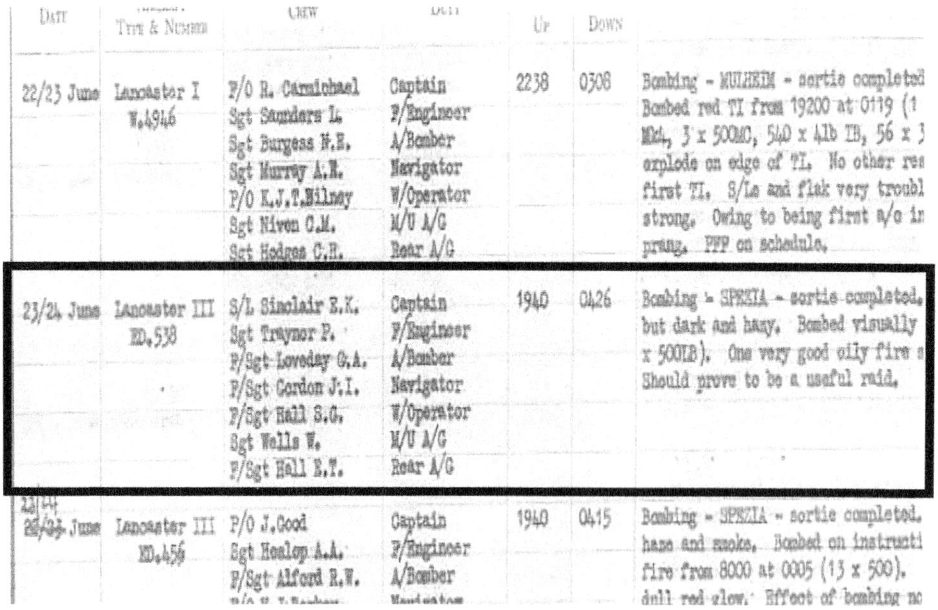

Date	Type & Number	Crew	Duty	Up	Down	
22/23 June	Lancaster I	P/O R. Carmichael	Captain	2238	0308	Bombing - MULHEIM - sortie completed
	W.4946	Sgt Saunders L.	F/Engineer			Bombed red TI from 19200 at 0119 (1
		Sgt Burgess H.E.	A/Bomber			MC4, 3 x 500MC, 540 x 4lb IB, 56 x 3
		Sgt Murray A.R.	Navigator			explode on edge of TI. No other res
		P/O K.J.T.Bilney	W/Operator			first TI. S/Ls and flak very troubl
		Sgt Niven C.M.	M/U A/G			strong. Owing to being first a/c in
		Sgt Hodges C.R.	Rear A/G			prang. PFF on schedule.
23/24 June	Lancaster III	S/L Sinclair E.K.	Captain	1940	0426	Bombing - SPEZIA - sortie completed,
	ED.538	Sgt Traynor P.	F/Engineer			but dark and hazy. Bombed visually
		F/Sgt Loveday G.A.	A/Bomber			x 500LB). One very good oily fire s
		F/Sgt Cordon J.I.	Navigator			Should prove to be a useful raid.
		F/Sgt Hall S.G.	W/Operator			
		Sgt Wells W.	M/U A/G			
		F/Sgt Hall E.T.	Rear A/G			
23/24 June	Lancaster III	P/O J.Good	Captain	1940	0415	Bombing - SPEZIA - sortie completed.
	ED.456	Sgt Heslop A.A.	F/Engineer			haze and smoke. Bombed on instructi
		F/Sgt Alford R.W.	A/Bomber			fire from 8000 at 0005 (13 x 500).
		[illegible]	Navigator			dull red glow. Effect of bombing no

Successful bombing operation report 23/24 June 1943 – Patrick as Flight Engineer
Photo courtesy of Traynor family

in recognition of the great bravery shown by those who contributed to vital operational campaigns of World War II.

Tracing his family once again proved a challenging task for Helen. She quickly, and frustratingly, found that trying to conclusively identify family members can be notoriously difficult. Several, at the time promising, lines of enquiry turned out to relate to the wrong Patrick Traynor.

Once again, Helen turned to the press for any information and the following appeared in The Derry Journal on April 30th 2021:

Friday, April 30, 2021 www.derryjournal.com

DERRY JOURNAL 13

NEWS

DERRY MAN LOST HIS LIFE ON A LANCASTER BOMBER IN WORLD WAR II

Appeal to find the descendants of Flight Sergeant Patrick Traynor

By Ciaran Lockhart
editorial@derryjournal.com
Twitter: @derryjournal

An appeal has been launched to find the local descendants of Flight Sergeant Patrick Traynor who died on January 3, 1944.

Patrick, who was a flight engineer for the Royal Air Force (RAF), lost his life in the Second World War aboard a Lancaster Bomber.

It is believed that Patrick attended the Brow of the Hill, Christian Brothers Technical school.

During his time at the school in 1939, Patrick received a prize as a result of his academic ability, that qualified him for direct entry into the RAF. At the time of his death, Patrick was flying with six other crew members, who also died after their plane was attacked over the Harz mountains in Germany. Descendants of the other crew members, have been successfully tracked down, thanks to the efforts of a dedicated team of volunteers. An unveiling ceremony for a War Memorial to the crew of the plane he died in is currently in the works, making it all the more imperative that Patrick's own descendants are found. Flight Sergeant Patrick Traynor was a member of the No. 83 Squadron which was a RAF squadron active from 1917 until 1969.

Flight Sergeant Patrick Traynor lies in rest in Berlin's War Cemetery. If you are a relative of Patrick's or have information contact: helentheron4@gmail.com

OTHER RESULTS

FEIS DOIRE COLMCILLE, 1939

Above left, an image of Patrick Traynor aboard a Lancaster Bomber, and, above right, a cutting from the Derry Journal in 1939 listing Patrick as an RAF apprentice.

Derry Journal April 2021. Photo courtesy of Traynor family

Sadly, no information was forthcoming from this article. However, a short time later Helen discovered a recent online post on the website "Wartime Memories Project" that led her to believe that information on the correct Patrick Traynor might have been found. It was finally confirmed that Patrick was part of a large family, having three brothers and eight sisters. The entry on the Memories website was traced via Facebook to a Robert Lowry. Helen contacted Robert, and he was able to confirm that Patrick had been his wife's uncle, and also that, to the family, he was indeed known as Willie. Helen sent a copy of Patrick's photograph to Robert who had no doubt that this was the correct Patrick Traynor. He added that the photograph showed that he was the image of his wife's Uncle Mick, Patrick's brother. Helen was able to contact Mark Leyden, a great nephew of Patrick through the family line of Patrick's sister Elizabeth (also known as Lily). Mark was kind enough to send Helen copies of a large number of invaluable documents, some of which are reproduced in this book, including the telegram that Patrick's father received informing him that his son was missing as a result of the operation of JB453 on 3rd January 1944, and follow-up letters from the RAF, Air Ministry and British Red Cross. At the age of just 24 years, Patrick Traynor was regarded as the old man of the JB453 crew.

He is buried in a collective grave with his colleagues, at the 1939-1945 British War Cemetery, Heerstrasse in Berlin. Plot Vl, Row A, Grave 19. An inscription, in Irish Gaelic, reads,

"AR DHEIS DE GO RAIBN A ANAM"

Translation: "May his soul be at the right hand of God"

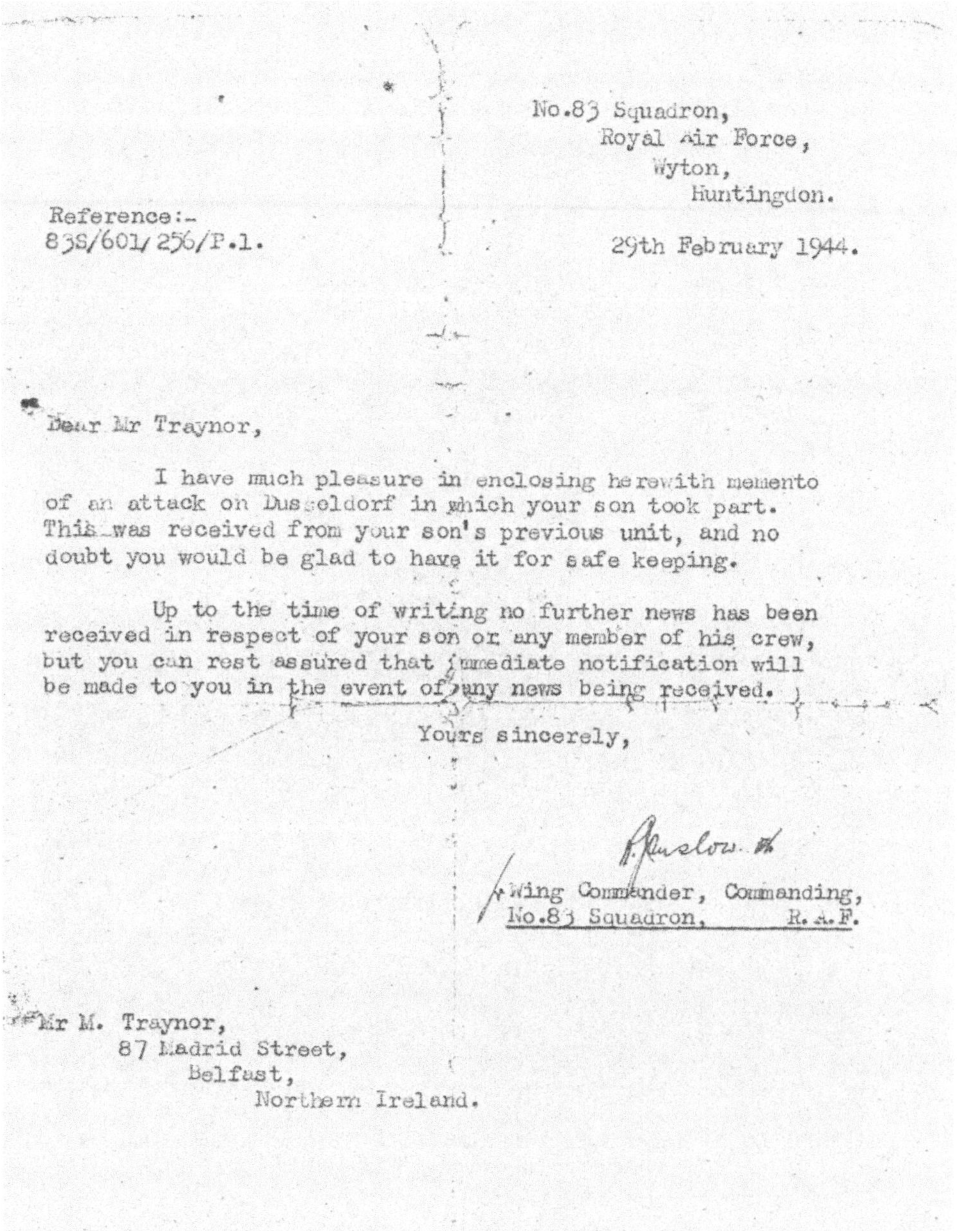

No.83 Squadron,
Royal Air Force,
Wyton,
Huntingdon.

Reference:-
83S/601/256/P.1.

29th February 1944.

Dear Mr Traynor,

I have much pleasure in enclosing herewith memento of an attack on Dusseldorf in which your son took part. This was received from your son's previous unit, and no doubt you would be glad to have it for safe keeping.

Up to the time of writing no further news has been received in respect of your son or any member of his crew, but you can rest assured that immediate notification will be made to you in the event of any news being received.

Yours sincerely,

Wing Commander, Commanding,
No.83 Squadron, R.A.F.

Mr M. Traynor,
87 Madrid Street,
Belfast,
Northern Ireland.

Letter received by Patrick's father, together with the memento below, from 83 Squadron Commanding Officer, RAF Wyton on 29th February 1944. Photo courtesy of Traynor family.

Lancaster BIII ED538 "Pregnant Winnie" and details of crew – bombing operation to Dusseldorf 11/12 June 1943 - Photo courtesy of Traynor family

Campaign Stars, Clasps and Medals

A thorough and comprehensive assessment of entitlement using the record of service has been completed. Your full and final award in recognition of service in the war of 1939-45 is enclosed.

NUMBER OF STARS, MEDALS, CLASPS OR EMBLEMS ENCLOSED	5

Order in which the awards should be set up eg for framing	Description of Ribbon	Clasp or Emblem (if awarded)
1. 1939-45 Star ✓	Dark blue, red and light blue in three equal vertical stripes. This ribbon is worn with the dark blue stripe furthest from the left shoulder.	Battle of Britain or Bomber Command ✓
2. Atlantic Star	Blue, white and sea green shaded and watered. This ribbon is worn with the blue edge furthest from the shoulder.	Air Crew Europe or France and Germany
3. Air Crew Europe Star ✓	Light blue with black edges and in addition a narrow yellow stripe on either edge.	Atlantic or France and Germany
4. Arctic Star	A central vertical stripe of white flanked on either side by a thin stripe of black and then three equal stripes of red, dark blue and light blue.	
5. Africa Star	Pale buff, with a central red stripe and two narrower stripes, one dark blue, and the other light blue. This ribbon is worn with the dark blue stripe furthest from the left shoulder.	8th Army or 1st Army or North Africa 1942-43
6. Pacific Star	Dark green with red edges, a central yellow stripe, and two narrow stripes, one dark blue and the other light. This ribbon is worn with the dark blue stripe furthest from the left shoulder.	Burma
7. Burma Star	Dark blue with a central red stripe and in addition two orange stripes.	Pacific
8. Italy Star	Five vertical stripes of equal width, one in red at either edge and one in green at the centre, the two intervening stripes being in white.	
9. France and Germany Star	Five vertical stripes of equal width, one in blue at either edge and one in red at the centre, the two intervening stripes being in white.	Atlantic
10. Defence Medal ✓	Flame coloured with green edges, upon each of which is a narrow black stripe.	Silver laurel leaves (Kings commendation for brave conduct, Civil)
11. War Medal ✓	A narrow central red stripe with a narrow white stripe on either side. A broad red stripe at either edge, and two intervening stripes in blue.	Oak Leaf

War medals awarded to Traynor. Photo courtesy of Traynor family

Medals awarded to Flight Sergeant Traynor. Top (l to r) War Medal 1939-45, Bomber Command Clasp, Defence Medal, Bottom (l to r) Air Crew Europe Star, 1939-1945 Star - Photo courtesy of Traynor family

Young Patrick "Willie" Traynor, far right during his training.
Photo courtesy of Traynor family

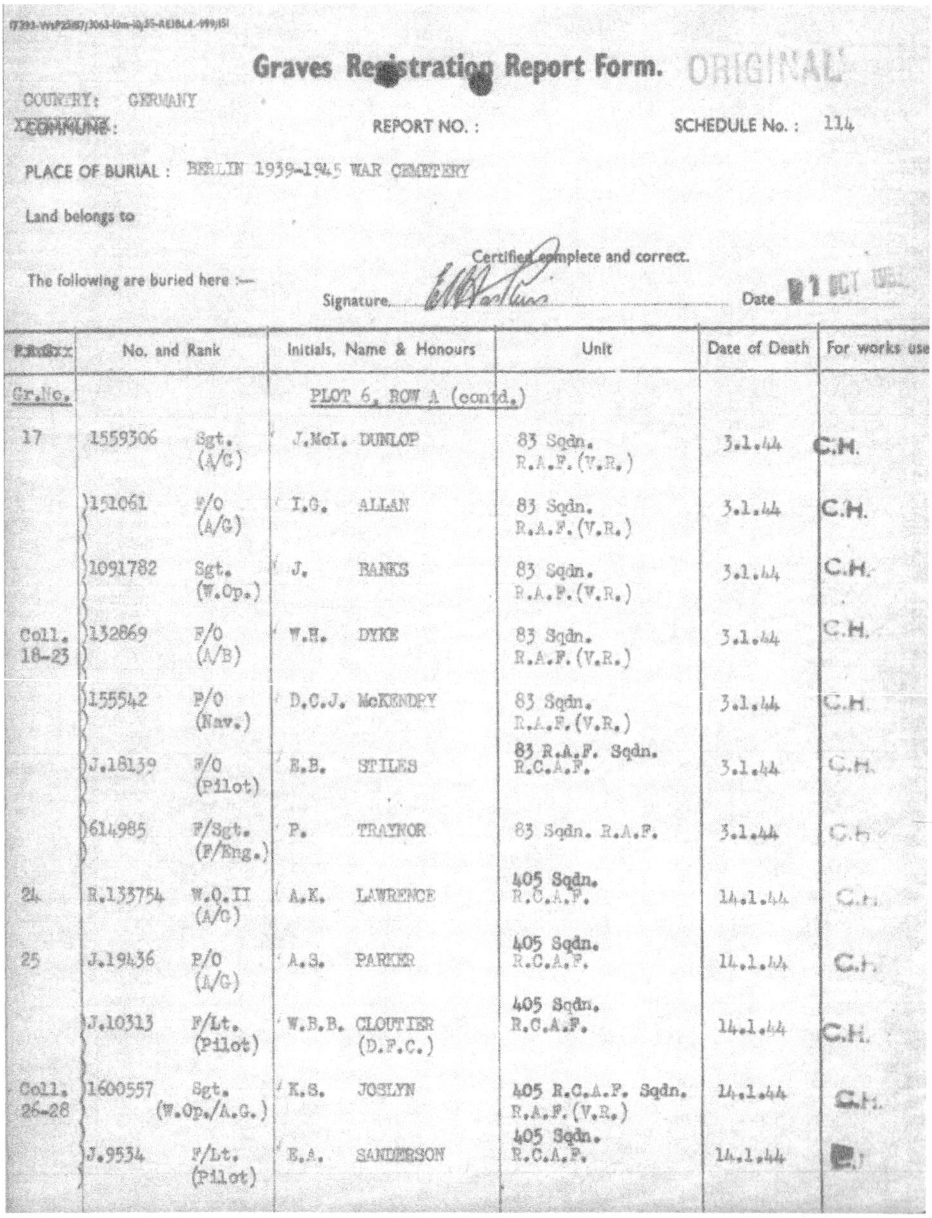

(7393-W.P25087/3063-10m-10/55-A.E.B.L.d.-999/151

Graves Registration Report Form. ORIGINAL

COUNTRY: GERMANY

~~COMMUNE~~:

REPORT NO. :

SCHEDULE No. : 114

PLACE OF BURIAL : BERLIN 1939-1945 WAR CEMETERY

Land belongs to

The following are buried here :—

Certified complete and correct.

Signature [illegible]

Date [illegible] OCT [illegible]

~~Row~~	No. and Rank		Initials, Name & Honours		Unit	Date of Death	For works use
Gr.No.			PLOT 6, ROW A (contd.)				
17	1559306	Sgt. (A/G)	J.McI.	DUNLOP	83 Sqdn. R.A.F.(V.R.)	3.1.44	C.H.
	151061	F/O (A/G)	I.G.	ALLAN	83 Sqdn. R.A.F.(V.R.)	3.1.44	C.H.
	1091782	Sgt. (W.Op.)	J.	BANKS	83 Sqdn. R.A.F.(V.R.)	3.1.44	C.H.
Coll. 18-23	132869	F/O (A/B)	W.H.	DYKE	83 Sqdn. R.A.F.(V.R.)	3.1.44	C.H.
	155542	P/O (Nav.)	D.C.J.	McKENDRY	83 Sqdn. R.A.F.(V.R.)	3.1.44	C.H.
	J.18139	F/O (Pilot)	E.B.	STILES	83 R.A.F. Sqdn. R.C.A.F.	3.1.44	C.H.
	614985	F/Sgt. (F/Eng.)	P.	TRAYNOR	83 Sqdn. R.A.F.	3.1.44	C.H.
24	R.133754	W.O.II (A/G)	A.K.	LAWRENCE	405 Sqdn. R.C.A.F.	14.1.44	C.H.
25	J.19436	P/O (A/G)	A.S.	PARKER	405 Sqdn. R.C.A.F.	14.1.44	C.H.
	J.10313	F/Lt. (Pilot)	W.B.B.	CLOUTIER (D.F.C.)	405 Sqdn. R.C.A.F.	14.1.44	C.H.
Coll. 26-28	1600557	Sgt. (W.Op./A.G.)	K.S.	JOSLYN	405 R.C.A.F. Sqdn. R.A.F.(V.R.)	14.1.44	C.H.
	J.9534	F/Lt. (Pilot)	E.A.	SANDERSON	405 Sqdn. R.C.A.F.	14.1.44	[illegible]

Copy of Graves Registration Form confirming the re-burying of the JB453 crew in the British 1939-1945 War Grave in Berlin. Photo courtesy of the Traynor family

CHAPTER 6

INTERNATIONAL BOMBER COMMAND CENTRE [IBCC] LINCOLN UK

In 2020, the world was brought almost to a standstill by the advent of the coronavirus disease, Covid-19 for short. The ensuing periods of lockdown, together with a rejuvenated mindset to discover as much as possible about the aircraft and its crew, engendered Helen to delve ever more deeply.

Uppermost in her mind was a desire that the crew should be commemorated, and that family and descendants of the crew should, in one form or another, become part of that. But how would she be able to achieve that in a sensitive and meaningful way? Where could she begin to find out the history of that fateful mission? How could she start to locate family descendants who could be living anywhere in the United Kingdom or overseas? All of these questions constantly raced through Helen's mind. She decided that, as this discovery had been revealed via the internet, then that would be a sensible starting point. This would prove to be an invaluable primary source of information and communication over the ensuing months. Websites relating to various aspects of World War II became obvious sources which Helen hoped would generate information, leads and contacts.

International Bomber Command Centre, Lincoln, UK. Photo courtesy of Helen Theron

One of the many sites she visited was *www.wwII2talk.com,* a forum designed to allow participants, often combat veterans and their families worldwide, to talk to one another, exchange information and ask questions. Helen must, at some point, have included her telephone number in her posts because she recalls an event that followed soon afterwards:

"It was a chilly spring day in 2021. John and I were in the conservatory having lunch when the 'phone rang. It was a lady, Nicky van der Drift, Chief Executive Officer of the International Bomber Command Centre in Lincoln. I had never heard of IBCC although, of course, I had heard of Bomber Command itself. When I realised who it was I immediately stood up – I almost wanted to salute! John was looking at me wondering what on earth was going on. Nicky said she had seen all of my entries on various web sites and that she would like to propose to me that the Lancaster weathervane should be classed as a World War II memorial, also that she considered it warranted a formal unveiling ceremony. I had no idea what that might entail, to be honest. She asked if I would send her some detailed information, including pictures and some history of where I had obtained the vane."

The International Bomber Command Centre (IBCC), which opened its doors to the public in January 2018, was founded to provide a world-class centre of excellence, serving as a point for recognition, remembrance, and reconciliation for Bomber Command. Lincoln was chosen as a location for the Centre, being a central point for 27 RAF and Allied air stations that earned Lincolnshire the title of 'Bomber County'.

For those returning from an operation over occupied Europe, Lincoln Cathedral would have provided a thankful and welcome landmark for crews. For those who failed to return, the Cathedral would likely have been one of the last images of home that crews ever saw. Lincolnshire accommodated over a third of all the World War II Bomber Command stations, making it the perfect location to remember and commemorate the bravery of thousands of young men of Bomber Command.

The IBCC has, arguably, become the most comprehensive guardian of Bomber Command records in the world ensuring that generations to come will be able to learn, understand, and fully value the vital and imperative roles played, which made huge contributions in ensuring the freedom we all enjoy today.

It was in 2009, coincidently the same year that Helen purchased the weathervane, that the prevailing Lord Lieutenant of the County, the late Anthony James Longmore Worth CVO, born in 1940, some 5 months after the beginning of World War II, and who died in 2017 just 2 months before the IBCC was opened to the public, created a Trust that would allow the building of a memorial to commemorate the gallantry and heroism of all those who served in Bomber Command. Also, to formally acknowledge the considerable influence of Lincolnshire and its people to the war effort, and to the ultimate outcome.

The IBCC has since evolved and grown such that the stories of all those in Bomber Command, especially those who made the ultimate sacrifice, would never be forgotten. This dream of recognition and remembrance defined the IBCC, inspired its many volunteer workers, and provided a place of solace and reconciliation for many thousands of visitors.

When she put the handset down, Helen turned to John, who of course had only heard one half of the conversation, and who was by now most intrigued as to what had just transpired. Helen, who readily admits to becoming a little over-zealous at times, was by now full of excitement and related the conversation she had just had. She felt as though it was completely unreal and couldn't believe what had just occurred. Nicky had suggested to Helen that contact with the Royal British Legion might be made so that it could take part in any ceremony, whatever form that might take. One of Helen's initial decisions was that no ceremony should take place unless as many as possible of crews' family descendants were located, contacted, and invited to attend. Helen couldn't imagine having a ceremony without family representation. For her, this project had just become a full-on, all-consuming, mission which would drive her through the following months of 2021, and well beyond.

Lincoln Cathedral behind a field of poppies.
Oil painting reproduced with kind permission of amateur artist, Olive Lacey, Dorset

CHAPTER 7

THREE REMARKABLE RESEARCHERS

Back, ever mindful of the fighters,
Their trails as chalk against the night.
At last, through morning mist,
We glimpse eternal green

© Julie Wigley, *No Moon Tonight*

Mid to late Spring in 2021 was an exceptionally busy time for Helen. She describes her laptop as "almost going into meltdown!". She expended immeasurable numbers of hours through days and nights in her attempts to locate families of the crew. She engaged the assistance of two ladies – Di Ablewhite and Brenda Kelly – without whom Helen says she would not have been able to achieve such success. Di, describes herself, amongst other things, as an Amateur

Historical Researcher. Her work with Helen was, however, as professional as any researcher who carries out that type of work as a full-time career. Both Di and Brenda's input turned out to be invaluable.

Di was the subject of an article written in 2020 by Nicky van der Drift, in which she is described as "The Reluctant Researcher".

In the article Di says:

"My main hobby was amateur archaeology, and our local area seemed to have quite a lot of both known and still to be discovered Roman

activity. I'd been involved in several local projects exploring and recording Roman sites. So, when one of my regular clients, an elderly farmer, announced he had boxes of fragments of Roman pottery he had amassed over a period of 50 years stored in his barn, and would I like to take a look, I couldn't wait to get out there!

True to his word, there were several large boxes of different size shards of amazing pottery. I was in my element, but he was more interested in a piece of metal on top of one of the boxes which looked like a bit of old tractor to me!

He kept coming back to this piece of metal which, in the end, distracted my attention away from the pottery. The village in which he lived wanted to hold a millennium exhibition in the Church to mark historic events and he felt this piece of metal was important to its history. Could I research it for him?

He told me that it was it was part of wreckage from a WW2 accident, possibly involving a Wellington bomber, on one of his fields. He had no idea of the date, just that it was winter, dark and very cold. He knew that there were several men killed as he'd had the terrible job of assisting the recovery team.

With so little information to go on my only option was to read Chorley's Bomber Command Loss books page by page...all of them...twice...as my first reading showed no Wellington's lost there. Newark Air Museum was able to confirm that the piece of wreckage was actually part of a Lancaster, not a Wellington. I can't describe the emotions I experienced reading through those books, page after page of names, I was shocked at my total ignorance and humbled by many of the stories.

Along with a couple of others we unpicked the full story of Lancaster W4270 QR-T, although it took 11 years to find relatives for all the crew. We built a memorial, and recorded a short film to tell their story, and I remember saying in the voiceover how we wished all could be commemorated in such a similar way.

From that time barely a day goes by when I don't receive a request for help. Sadly, the most common request is for photos and, as fellow researchers will testify, they are often the most difficult to find. I always hope that we can trace other crew members relatives who may just have one. So, from not really being at all interested in Bomber Command research it is now very much part of my daily life, but still with probably only a 50% success rate, but after hundreds, if not thousands, of various searches, like many other researchers, I now know some of the first places to look!"

The second researcher, Brenda Kelly, similarly gave Helen essential assistance. A former member of WRAF, Brenda gives the following biographical information:

Di with Helen on a visit to the International Bomber Command Centre
Photo courtesy of Helen Theron

"I am ex WRAF although I was a Dental Surgery Assistant during the early 1970s. I am also a member of the Royal Air Forces Association and the Royal British Legion. At 69, I am happily married and retired. My hobbies include researching my family history, travelling in our motorhome around the UK and Europe, music, swimming, walking and dancing. I completed my family tree about 15 years ago, although I regularly re-visit

it to add any new information. I have written books for my two sons, Andrew and Christopher, in which I documented their lives from their birth, through to their days with the RAF in Germany and RAF Leuchars in Scotland. The books end on the day they left home to go to Manchester University. It was very rewarding to be able to give my sons a personal keepsake, full of happy

memories and photographs of their young lives. My involvement with Helen and the weathervane project began on the 28 February 2020 when I read a Facebook post on the Royal Air Force and Families Group. Helen was seeking help to try and trace families of the JB453 crew members. I was intrigued by the story, so I contacted the International Bomber Command Centre in Lincoln to offer my help in locating the families of these brave warriors. I had recently successfully completed, with several other volunteers, two similar searches for two people from The Netherlands. Working with Helen and Di Ablewhite was an absolute privilege. We worked so well together, with emails literally being exchanged at all hours of the day and night. It was an amazing feeling when I traced the first family for Helen, who was overjoyed. Each step of our journey was about uncovering clues, sharing facts, photographs, telephone numbers and more. When we finally contacted the last family there were feelings of overwhelming jubilation. The rest of the story is Helen's. I am now helping other people in The Netherlands and France to find their own brave heroes' families. I think I have signed up to a lifetime of World War II searches and, as my husband, Mike, says, 'It keeps Brenda quiet…' "

Finally, of course, there is Helen herself. The initial meeting with her at my Devon home was quickly followed by a three-hour session midway between her home and mine at a delightful pub, The Little Harp Inn, on the English side of the Severn estuary at Clevedon near Bristol. Her enthusiasm was unbelievably infectious to the point where I had to tell her to slow down so that I could take notes. I took a valuable lesson from this, investing in a small digital dictation gadget that I used extensively for recording ensuing online and face-to-face meetings. For our Clevedon meeting, Helen had brought with her a small library of files, books, pamphlets, newspaper cuttings, and a whole raft of associated paraphernalia, all of which I couldn't wait to trawl through, and which would ultimately form the basis of this book. These were all transported back to Devon in three large, reuseable, Sainsbury shopping bags.

On its own, what Helen referred to as her master file comprised hundreds of documents, papers, email prints and photographs within a lever-arch folder. I actually measured the depth of the documentation in the file – five and a half inches – a great deal of reading which would take me the winter and spring of 2021/2022 to go through several times, digest and fully comprehend, allowing me to make copious volumes of notes. Some of the most difficult choices I had to make over many months were not so much in deciding what to use in the book but determining that which I could afford to omit without detracting from the value and importance of the narrative.

The distance between Helen's home and mine, a return road journey of over 300 miles, meant that wide use was made of video conferencing technology, mainly Zoom, a medium that became a primary source of communication for hundreds of thousands of people during the global

Covid 19 pandemic between 2020 and 2023. Zoom, together with large volumes of email exchanges, proved vital.

Helen's energy and passion continued to be indefatigable. As a resource, researcher, investigator, and friend, she proved to be second to none. From the moment the results of the weathervane inscription had flashed onto her laptop screen months beforehand she became an unstoppable driving force. Everything that followed, all the progress, discoveries and revelations, manifested only because of her.

CHAPTER 8

BOMBING OF BERLIN CAMPAIGN 1943-44

How many kits lie packed this morning?
Whose bed an empty iron frame?
How many more, friends and companions,
Still to be lost in freedom's name?

The German capital city and operational home of the Third Reich, Berlin, was, between 1943 and 1944, a primary target of 363 individual daytime and nighttime air raids by RAF Bomber Command and the USAAF 8th Air Force, involving many thousands of aircraft, as part of an intensive strategic campaign. From the onset of World War II in 1939, Franklin D Roosevelt, President of the, then neutral, United

States of America, made a request to the Allied forces to restrict their air raids to military targets only. The French and the British agreed to this request, but with a proviso that this was *"upon the understanding that these same rules of warfare will be scrupulously observed by all of their opponents"*.

Great Britain was already adhering to its existing strategy of using aerial bombing specifically against military targets but also against infrastructure targets such as ports and railways which were of direct military significance to the ongoing supply of goods and weaponry to enemy forces. While it was always acknowledged that the aerial bombing of Germany would unavoidably, and inevitably, cause civilian casualties, Britain routinely avoided the deliberate bombing of civilian targets outside combat zones. This policy was, however, abandoned in May 1940, when, following a German air attack on Rotterdam, the RAF was directed to attack targets in the heavy industrial heart of Ruhr in western Germany, including oil plants and other civilian industrial targets that aided the German war effort.

The so-called Battle for Berlin was commenced by Air Chief Marshall and Commander-in-Chief of Bomber Command, Arthur *"Bomber"* Harris, following his protracted and vociferous campaign to the War Ministry and RAF hierarchy . In November 1943, a concentrated air campaign against the German capital, and other cities, unfolded. Harris believed that such a strategy would be central to destroying German endurance and morale, bringing about the end of the war in a shorter time. *"It will cost us between 400 and 500 aircraft",* he said. *"But it will cost Germany the war."* Given that each Lancaster bomber, the main aircraft of choice, had a crew of 7, simple mathematics dictates that Harris was prepared to lose circa 3500 airmen. At this time, he had the capability to deploy over 800 long-range bombers for any single operation. Between November 1943 and March 1944, Bomber Command carried out multiple mass attacks on Berlin and other German cities.

The first such attack was made on the night of 18/19 November 1943. Berlin was the main target and was attacked by 440 Lancasters with the assistance of de Havilland Mosquitos. Berlin that night was shrouded in cloud. Consequently, damage was not severe. A second operation, 4 nights later was far more effective and resulted in extensive damage to the Ministry of Munitions, the barracks of the Imperial Guard, the Waffen SS College, and several arms factories as well as a number of residential areas west of the city centre.

These raids caused massive destruction and loss of life. An attack on 22 November alone killed 2,000 Berliners and made 175,000 homeless. The following night a further 1,000 were killed and 100,000 made homeless. During December and January, bombing missions killed hundreds of people each night and rendered between 20,000 and 80,000 homeless each time. In all, over 4,000 people, mainly civilian, were killed, 10,000 injured and 450,000 made homeless.

On 17 December 1943, widespread destruction was caused to Berlin’s railway system. By this time, the overall effect of the bombing strategy had resulted in greater than a quarter of the city's total living accommodation being destroyed or at least being rendered unhabitable. Further attacks in January and February 1944 resulted in Berlin's western and southern districts being targeted in intensely focussed raids. Raids continued until March 1944.

Despite these prolonged and intensive attacks, however, this strategy failed to realise Harris’ objectives, aspirations and beliefs. Similar to that shown by British civilians during the blitz upon London, German civilian morale did not break. The city's defences and essential services were disrupted, but maintained, with war production resuming after short periods of recovery and repair.

In total, the nighttime raids on Germany cost Bomber Command more than five hundred aircraft and over three thousand air crew. Another one thousand crew, predominantly those who had parachuted from incapacitated bombers, were captured and became prisoners of war.

It has long since been the subject of much debate as to whether the bombing of cities such as Berlin, Dresden, Hamburg, and others, resulting in the deaths of many thousands of civilians should have been treated, then or now, as war crimes committed by Allied forces. It would be remiss of me to not make mention of this aspect. Arguments for and against have been vehemently proffered, not only regarding Allied raids on enemy targets but also against the Luftwaffe for its extensive bombing campaigns including those on Great Britain, Poland, and The Netherlands. Written accounts of Allied bombing campaigns help to fill libraries and the internet across the world, with the exception of Germany where such writings are far scarcer. There is a quote, often attributed to Churchill, which says that *"history is mainly written by the victors"*. The quote implies that history records might not necessarily always be supported by facts but more sustained by the victor's interpretation of those facts. Some historians argue that documented accounts created since the end of the war, of bombing campaigns carried out by Allied forces during the conflict, would seem to support this quote.

To this day, the prolonged campaign of bombings between 1939 and 1945, by Allied and Axis forces alike, where it is clear beforehand that large numbers of civilians might be killed or injured, engenders fierce debate and controversy, especially when one adds the atomic and plutonium bomb attacks on Hiroshima and Nagasaki into the mix when an estimated 200,000 civilians were killed.

It has oft been argued that no specific international law with respect to aerial warfare existed before or during World War II, although the Hague Convention refers to the bombing of "undefended" cities. The interpretation of "undefended" tends to open up a plethora of diverse beliefs and opinions. It is a fact that no Japanese or German leaders were ever prosecuted at later war crime trials for their respective aerial campaigns which resulted in the death or injury to enormous numbers of civilian populations.

This book is not intended to answer such political arguments that have been made for or against treating such campaigns, on either side, as war crimes. However, no opinions expressed during the course of these debates should ever take anything away from the courage, bravery, daring and resolution of those air crews, such as the crew of JB453, who night after night, day after day, put their lives on the line, many paying the ultimate price, as part of the overall effort to ensure that Hitler and his regime were doomed to failure, and that the world could return to a state of peace and freedom.

CHAPTER 9

FLIGHT ENGINEER RICHARD "DICK" RAYMOND 83 (PATHFINDER) SQUADRON – RAF WYTON 1943-45

Then sweet relief, the fog descends now.
We're free to take the bus and paint the town.
To court and dance and drink, as no tomorrow,
And sing our bawdy songs around.

© Julie Wigley, *No Moon Tonight*

A 20-year-old Lancaster flight engineer, Richard "Dick" Raymond, was, in the autumn of 1943, informed that his crew had been "volunteered" as Pathfinders and were to join 83

Squadron at RAF Wyton. Although not a member of JB453, he was a member of 83 (Pathfinder) Squadron at the same time that its crew were operational through the latter part of 1943 and into early January 1944.

I interviewed Dick several times during 2023, firstly in January, then again in June, this time with Jacquelin Magnay, European correspondent of The Australian newspaper who was researching for an assignment about the loss of an Australian Lancaster crew from RAF Wyton in 1944. My third interview took place in August that year with Janine Jensen from BBC TV Spotlight, home of south-west news, who filmed an article about Dick. At an amazing age of 98 years Dick was able not only to tell us about his Pathfinder exploits at Wyton, but also extremely articulate at relating what day to day life was like at the station, and about socialising on operational and non-operational days. My interviews with Dick provided a genuine, first-hand, insight into the life of a Pathfinder crew. His stories, many of which could take pride of place in any wartime fiction story, provided a real gold nuggets that, purely because of the passage of time, are becoming increasingly rare from those who were there, during those years of bloody conflict.

For instance, he tells of the time when his Lancaster exploded on the ground at RAF Wyton in the autumn of 1943. Fifteen of Dick's crewmates and ground crew were killed. He survived but was hospitalised for several weeks.

On one of his operations, two out of the four Lancaster Merlin engines were destroyed, and a third damaged, by enemy fire resulting in him and the pilot, Ken Lane, struggling to get the plane home. As Flight Engineer, Dick was able to get the damaged engine running and they managed to nurse the craft home, landing at the first airbase they came across once over England. This was an American airbase, but it seemed that our brothers from across the pond were more concerned that the crippled Lancaster had landed and blocked their runway rather than being too worried about the welfare of the crew!

On another operation, Dick's plane was attacked by enemy night fighters causing the crew to have to bale out over The Netherlands. Dick was captured by German forces and spent the remaining months of the conflict as a Prisoner of War in Stalag 8 on the Polish border. As 1944 went into early 1945, the Germans increasingly realised that they were not destined to win this war. Then came what became known as the Long March. During January and February 1945, as Russian forces reclaimed massive areas of land across Poland, upwards of 30,000 PoW's, servicemen from a whole raft of nations, were marched for hundreds of miles in blizzards and freezing conditions from outlying camps towards Berlin. Dick was one of those and survived when many around him died. Eventually incarcerated in Stalag 3A, a camp near to the capital, they were eventually discovered by Russian forces, the German prison masters having disappeared. But therein manifested another problem. The Russians refused to release PoW's due to difficulties with the ongoing Yalta talks between Prime Minister Churchill, US President Roosevelt, and Russian President Stalin. Dick took matters into his own hands and, with several others, escaped from the Russians, eventually turning up at an American base near Berlin before being repatriated back to England. A remarkable man and a true hero.

My interview with him lasted over 2 hours but what follows is a first-hand account from Dick of what day to day life was like at RAF Wyton during those dark times, especially on the day preceding a night-time mission. The feelings he describes would have mirrored exactly those of the JB453 crew. I asked Dick what led him to join the RAF:

"I spent six years in the Royal Air Force, three in wartime and three in peace. I was aged 15 when war broke out in 1939 and attended a Grammar school in Barnstaple where they tried to educate me. My father ran a local bakery business. Up until that time he had two delivery men, but they had both gone off to fight. Father took me out of school to take over this job. I couldn't drive a van, but I could handle a horse and cart. I didn't enjoy the job one little bit. My father realised this and eventually found another delivery hand. He knew I was mechanically minded and managed to get me an apprenticeship at a Barnstaple garage. I was well paid. I got five shillings a week for 54 hours of work. I was deducted one penny to go to the Red Cross, and I used to queue up weekly to collect my four shillings and eleven pence. Incidentally, Lilian Prowse worked in the garage pay office. She later became renowned as the political agent of Liberal party leader Jeremy Thorpe.

I was a member of the Boy Scouts, the finest organisation for boys that ever existed. I progressed from the Scouts to the Air Training Corps, the ATC, and when I was old enough I volunteered for the RAF. All kinds of silly things happened including failing the medical and being turned down. Eventually, I got into the RAF but not as air crew, which I badly wanted. I was accepted as an Aircraft Hand (General Duties) with additional training as a Flight Mechanic (Engines and Air Frames).

I did my initial training, square bashing we called it, at Blackpool. God, I hated that place. I have never been back and if I could ever find my landlady, I'd ring her bloody neck! I had to collect my kit from Penarth in Wales. Do you know, when I went there I thought I was going abroad. I had never been out of Devon, and I had to change trains at Taunton! My God, I'd never been anywhere! Anyway, off we all went, all of us recruits, to Blackpool and when we got there we were looking forward to a good meal. Well, they lined us up in the school hall and these men gave us two injections in one arm and a vaccination in the other, all in one go, and not gently. People were dropping like flies!

They put us in civilian billets and these landladies, they were being paid so much per head, and they would just cram as many in as they could. More heads meant more money. It was unbelievable, and terrible. After passing out from training, I was posted to RAF Locking in Weston-Super-Mare for a flight mechanic course. I was told that if you failed the course then you would end up in the RAF Regiment. By God, they worked us hard. I certainly didn't want to be in the bloody RAF Regiment. They were little more than odd bods who would carry out tasks such as protecting airfields and recovering downed pilots. That was not for me! I managed to pass the course near the top of the class and got posted to RAF Halton in Buckinghamshire"

I asked Dick how he became a flight engineer:

"I hadn't been there long when a notice went up. Volunteers wanted for flight engineer. I thought why not. I'll have a go. I volunteered and got sent to London for a medical. My health hadn't changed since I failed my initial medical, but I thought they must be desperate for flight engineers

Dick Raymond, front row far left kneeling, RAF Locking Flight Mechanic Course. Photo courtesy of Dick Raymond.

because I sailed through. I was in!

I was posted immediately to RAF St Athan in South Wales to complete a six-week conversion course for heavy bombers. I passed and left there proudly wearing my sergeant stripes. I was just nineteen years old. I was posted to RAF Wigsley at Newark. God, that was another dump!

That said, I was very lucky because I missed the last AVRO Manchester bomber course. The Manchester was an awful thing to fly. I ended up with a Wellington bomber crew. That was a baptism of fire. All the rest of the crew had completed about 100 hours each on Wellingtons. I had nothing. Definitely a baptism of fire alright!

After we had finished our heavy conversion training we were told we were going to be part of the Pathfinders. No-one was really listening, and we had no idea what they were. Pathfinders? What the hell was all that about?

We discovered that Pathfinders were supposed to be the elite of crews. Having said that, my view is that the pilot and navigator were the ones that had to be elite, particularly the navigator. He was the one who would accurately guide the aircraft over the target so that flares could be dropped for the main force bombers to home in on."

We went on to talk about Dick's time at RAF Wyton:

"I was posted to RAF Wyton in September 1943. My first two ops were bombing missions over Berlin. On 26th November that year we had been briefed for another op and we went out to the aircraft, a Lancaster, to carry out our checks inside and outside. Just as I got out of the plane the whole thing blew up. How I escaped God only knows because fifteen ground and air crew were killed. I ended up in the RAF hospital at Ely in

Cambridgeshire. Although not seriously wounded, some of my injuries turned septic so I was there for a while. When I was discharged I had another stroke of luck. Lucky must have been my middle name. When I got back to Wyton I wanted to know nothing about aeroplanes. Even the smell of one would turn my stomach, all because of the explosion. I just sat there and did very little. It was terrible, the worst time I ever had in the RAF. If you experienced something like I had, they are supposed to get you back in the air quickly but that never happened to me. I was simply left to stew.

*Then a pilot came up to me and asked me to identify myself. I did. He told me his name was Ken Lane and that 'you are flying with me tonight!'. I joined Ken who, in my view, was the best of pilots and we became long-standing friends. After the war in 1945 I was his best man and in 1950 he was mine. Ken was a Warrant Officer and finished up as a Flight Lieutenant DFC. Ken got the DFC (*Distinguished Flying Cross*) when we were sent to bomb Munich. Our Lanc became coned in searchlights. We lost 2 engines through enemy fire but luckily, one on either side. A third engine failed but I managed to get it going again. Ken put us into such a deep dive to escape the lights that it's a wonder we didn't disintegrate. How we got out of it I don't know. It took us 5 hours to get back and, for this, Ken was awarded the DFC."*

This operation took place during the late evening of 24th April 1944 with Ken Lane piloting Lancaster ND467, 83 Squadron. Their mission into the following morning was to bomb strategic targets in and around Munich. Whilst over the city, festooned by searchlights and unceasingly subjected to massive anti-aircraft flak, the Lanc suddenly became brightly illuminated. In short, it became a sitting duck for enemy fire. Inevitably, it was hit several times, causing two engines, one port and one starboard, to catch fire. Fuel supplies to both engines were cut, and the crew were able to shut both down.

A lack of two engines for such a heavy bomber as the Lancaster was critical and everything that could be thrown out was ditched or jettisoned in order to reduce the weight of the craft and to give pilot Lane a chance of getting the Lanc home.

A combination of Lane's skill, heavily assisted by Dick, who managed to get the third malfunctioning engine working again, together with the sheer robustness of the magnificent Lancaster, made it possible for it to limp home, and for Lane to make a successful emergency landing at RAF Lashenden in Kent, just 25 miles inland from the English Channel. It is unlikely that the aircraft could have flown much further in its crippled

Dick Raymond (far right) and Ken Lane (third from left) pictured at RAF Wyton 1944. Photo courtesy of Dick Raymond.

condition. RAF Lashenden at that time was home to elements of the United States of America Air Force. Dick recalls that:

Ken Lane and Dick Raymond's Lancaster following the emergency landing at RAF Lashenden on 25th April 1944. Photo courtesy of Dick Raymond.

"The Americans were not happy with the fact that blocking their runway was a Lancaster that had about 40 bullet holes and only two engines, not happy at all in fact. But at least they fed us!"

We spoke about the crew of JB453 and how they had been shot down. I knew that Dick had survived, a few months after the Lashenden incident, having his Lancaster suffer a catastrophic hit from a German fighter, and having to bale out over The Netherlands. I asked if he would tell me about this incident.

"We got hit on a mission. We had the order to bale out. I did everything wrong but somehow still got away with it. Lucky again! Actually, I didn't bale out. I got blown out. Up until that point, because we were flying at about 23,000 feet, I had been wearing an oxygen mask. All of a sudden I was thrown into the sky without any oxygen. At that height there is very little oxygen in the air. Do you know, it took over ten minutes for me to parachute down to the ground. And all I remember is thinking, bloody hell, I'm supposed to be Ken's best man when he gets married on Saturday! You see, because of a lack of oxygen, I was hallucinating. As I was thrown out of the plane, I felt it explode. I thought Ken had died but to my delight, he had set off his parachute and it threw him through the roof. The only bad thing that happened to him was his flying boots fell off. I landed in a field in The Netherlands. A farmer, or more accurately a peat

digger, looked after me. He took me to his home and was kind enough to feed me. We had goats' milk and black bread. I stayed there for the night. The next morning the farmer said he was sorry, the Germans knew I was there, and he would have to hand me in, otherwise he and his family were likely to get shot.

He had contacted a local doctor who came to see to my injuries. The doctor then took me on his two-stroke motorcycle to the local police station. I loved that short journey. The farmer's wife and two daughters, in their night attire, came to see me off. It was a wonderful moment for me when, at the police station, Ken Lane was brought in. Then this goon came in, stuck a rifle in my ribs and said, 'Don't try to escape, you're my prisoner'. *I felt like saying, you bloody fool, do you think I am going to run away with a gun in my ribs!?"*

Four of the Lancaster crew survived, including Dick, but three of the seven were killed and are buried at Emmen, Drenthe, The Netherlands.

"By various routes, mainly by train, we were taken to Frankfurt. The boys had just bombed it so you can imagine, us in RAF uniform, we were not very well received. The Germans had to make a ring around us to keep the civilians from attacking us. They were shouting things like swine, baby killers, murderers. Eventually, we ended up at Stalagluft 8, a PoW camp in Silesia, then in Germany but now part of Bakow in Poland."

This purpose-built camp was opened on 6th June 1944, coincidently the same day as the D-Day landings in Normandy, specifically for RAF flying crews. By mid-year almost 250 PoW's were incarcerated there. Six months later, at the beginning of 1945, this number had swelled to over 1500 comprising many different nationalities including British, Australian, Canadian, New Zealanders, American, Polish, and South African.

"We were there until, I can't remember the exact date, but it was January 1945 [author note - 19th January 1945]. *Germany knew they were losing the war by then. The Russians were closing in from the east, so we were marched out. Well, we didn't march. We shuffled. It became known as the Long March, or the Death March. We had three weeks on the road in the worst winter they had had for years. Some nights it was minus 10 or minus 15. We literally had no food. We ate raw potatoes, raw sugar beet, anything we could steal. You'd put it in your pocket but when you took it out it was frozen and that's how we ate it. One night we slept in a pigsty, in between two large sows. It was so warm. Then the farmer came in and threatened to shoot us if we didn't get out. We got out alright, pretty fast, but we soon came back in through another door ten minutes later. That was the best night's sleep we had, and the pigs didn't mind at all! We finished up at another camp, Stalag 3A in Luckenwalde, about 35 miles south of Berlin. There must have been over 30,000 PoWs there, every*

nationality under the sun. You'd never believe it. The Russians were the worst treated. If we had Red Cross parcels we would scrape out the tins then throw them to the Russians for them to have whatever was left. The Germans would stand and laugh at them. Three weeks we were on the road. They call it a march but as I said, it wasn't a march, it was a shuffle. You just followed the person in front. You could easily have escaped but you would just have frozen to death. There was a foot of snow on the ground, and we had blizzards. Many died on route but there was nothing you could do about that. You just kept trudging along. Eventually the Russians liberated us, but even they wouldn't let us go because of the Yalta conference and difficulties in the talks between Stalin, Churchill, and Roosevelt over the carving up of Europe after the war.

After a while some of us decided we had had enough so one night some of us escaped. There was an incident I think is worth remembering as we made our way away from the camp. As we were walking through a pine forest, out of the trees came several Russian soldiers. I thought, oh my God, not now. I was convinced I would be shot. But one of them came up to me and pointed to the crowns on my battle dress. He obviously wanted them so I took them off as quickly as I could and gave them to him. In return, he gave me a packet from his pocket. It was some horse meat wrapped in paper. We shook hands, he went east, and I went west. It was clear that he didn't want to stand and fight any more than I did. Anyway, we eventually crossed the Rhine at the Truman Bridge and met up with the Yanks just north of Magdeburg about 150 miles west of Berlin. They took us to Brunswick then flew us to Brussels. Then the RAF flew us home."

The Long March/Death March January/February 1945 – Photograph courtesy of Dick Raymond

Having shown Dick pictures of each JB453 crew member, the only one he had a recollection of was Patrick Traynor. He thought he probably met him during one or more flight engineer training courses.

"It was very difficult to get to know other crews. Often they would come in, put their kit on the bed and then they died that night. There was

a constant flow of crews coming and going. I didn't fly in any JB series Lancasters. I never flew main force, always Pathfinders. Seventeen ops in all."

Because he had completed a sufficient number of operations, Dick was awarded the Pathfinders Golden Eagle clasp, the badge of excellence. During 2013 he was presented with the newly authorised Bomber Command clasp as an addition to his 1939-1945 War Star. The clasp was approved by HM Queen Elizabeth II in 2012 and announced by the Ministry of Defence in 2013. It was granted to the aircrew of Bomber Command who served for at least sixty days, or completed a tour of operations, on a Bomber Command operational unit and flew at least one operational sortie on a Bomber Command operational unit between 3 September 1939 and 8 May 1945. Additionally, Dick was awarded the Caterpillar clasp. This was awarded to those who had had their lives saved by parachuting from their aircraft. Created by what became known as the Caterpillar Club, the significance of the caterpillar refers to the silk threads from which parachutes were originally made, thus recognising the debt owed to the silkworm.

I asked what day to day life was like at RAF Wyton.

"If we were flying that night, how would we spend the day? That's a good question. There was a snooker table in the mess and card games.

Anything to take your mind off the night's job. First thing in the morning you would look at the list and ask, 'are we on for tonight?' We'd think, oh my God, here we go again. And then your stomach started turning over. When we went in the briefing room, you talk about smoking. There was so much smoke you could have cut it with a knife. Then the CO would walk in, and we would stand up. Sit down he would say and then he would draw the curtains back. There would be moans and groans and 'here we go

The author with Dick Raymond and a copy of The Pathfinders by Will Iredale, in which Dick appears.
Photo courtesy of the author

again'. But the time up to when you knew where you were going was the worst time of all. Because the loss rate was so high, you'd think, which night will I get it, will it be tonight? It was awful. You had to convince yourself that you were going to get through, but it was very difficult. It was not a time that I would wish on anybody. We got looked after – we had eggs and bacon before we took off. When, if, we got back we had all kinds of things. We even had a steak occasionally. You would come back and you would be debriefed by an officer. They would give you hot tea, sometimes even with some brandy in it. Yes, we were well looked after when we got back but it was a question of whether you would actually make it back or not.

Would days when we were not scheduled for operations – would they be any different? Well, we always flew, if we were not on ops we would be training.

Did we ever get off the base and socialise in any of the nearby towns? Yes, we used to go into Lincoln into the Saracens Head."

The Saracens Head was a hotel situated at 298 High Street in Lincoln. This grade-II listed building closed in 1959, the site now used for shops and offices. It would no doubt have been one of the favoured hostelries used by the crew of JB453.

"It was a standing joke – if you wanted to know if someone was on ops or not then ask at the Saracens Head. They would know! If there was no flying that night the base would put on 3 or 4 coaches from the MT (Mechanical Transport) *section, and they would take you wherever you wanted to go, into Huntingdon, Lincoln or Cambridge but you should have seen the condition of those buses on the way back to the base!"*

Plaque on the wall of the building which used to be the Saracen's Head at 298 High Street, Lincoln.
Photo courtesy of author.

Helen was able to meet with Dick in 2021 and it was she who pointed me in his direction.

Thank you, Dick, for allowing me into that world, for the lengthy conversations we had and for agreeing for me to audio record the interviews.

Helen with Dick Raymond 2021. Photo courtesy of Helen Theron

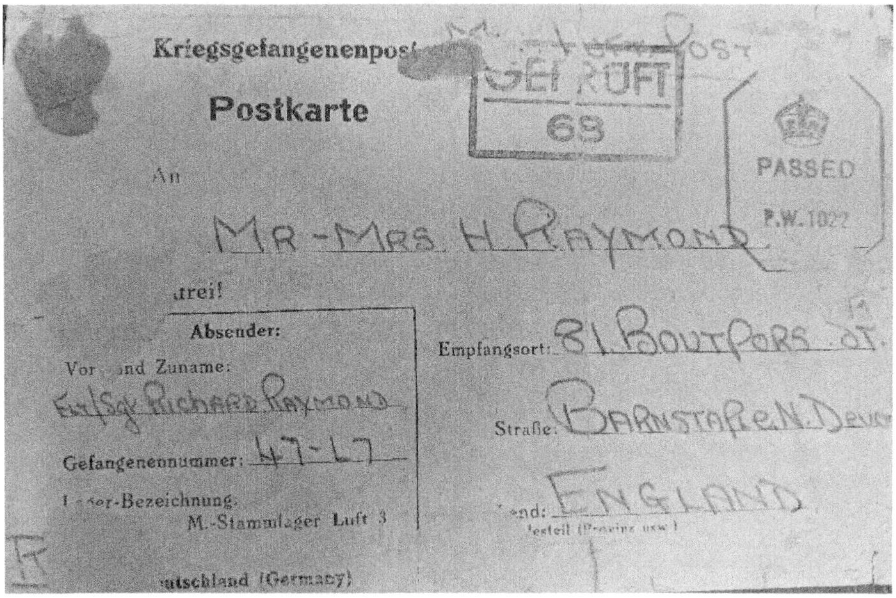

Christmas card sent home by Dick from Stalagluft 8 Christmas 1944 . Photo courtesy of Dick Raymond

Dick being interviewed by BBC Spotlight, wearing the medals and clasps he was awarded including the Bomber Command clasp, an addition to the 1939-1945 War Star created and awarded in 2012/13, and the Caterpillar clasp. Photos courtesy of the author.

CHAPTER 10

LETTERS AND CORRESPONDENCE

The runway soon will be in sight
And village folk can now sleep easy.
As engines throb and shake their walls,
By luck, or skill, we live another day,
Safe 'til the cloak of evening falls

© Julie Wigley, *No Moon Tonight*

Seeing and reading letters and documents that were sent almost 80 years ago, some across thousands of miles, was a truly humbling experience. Documentation of this nature is such a rarity. In writing this book, I am so grateful and fortunate to be able to share a number of these that have been kept and preserved by some of the JB453 crews' descendants. Some were sent between crew and family, others by the Ministry of War, RAF and British Red Cross, to families following the sad news of the aircraft loss, and in the years immediately following the end of the war. These letters provide real context, especially regarding the relationships between crew members and their loved ones. In this chapter I have reproduced copies and/or transcripts of documents that have been kindly provided by descendants and I thank them all for allowing me to include them in the book.

All spelling and grammar are as per original letters.

STILES – All letters and documents courtesy of Stiles family

Letter from Stiles to sister Annabel dated 10 November 1942 on his arrival from Canada to Bournemouth, UK

To: Miss Annabel
138 Bromley Ave
Moncton
New Brunswick
Canada

Field Post Office
Senders Address: Sgt. Stiles E B
RCAF Overseas

Dear Annabel

Just a line now letting you know I arrived safely and had a swell trip over. Like it fine so far, a great country and wonderful people. We have good amenities, staying in a hotel, previously a summer resort. The food is good but not many sweets. Lots of good-looking girls and good chances to meet nice ones . No doubt you know the boat we came over in, was a wonderful one. I wasn't a bit seasick, and we had no bad weather but was glad to see land. Will write an ordinary letter soon, hoping to receive lots from you, so don't forget to write often. Send me interesting clippings from Observer. I'm here with Bear now, ready to go for supper so will close. Remember me to all.

Love

Blair

Letter from Stiles to sister Annabel dated 15 December 1942

Dec 15/42

RCAF Overseas

Attached RAF

Dear Sister Annabel

This is the third letter tonight so don't be surprised if I cut it short. I have rather neglected in writing as I was on a 48 to London then sent up here to start flying so I am just getting settled nicely.

I received your parcel today and couldn't resist the temptation so opened it and it sure tasted good, of course there's still lots left, thanks so very much Annabel and I hope you have a very nice Xmas. Also hope you will be able to get home, by the look of things we don't get any time off.

I also received three more parcels today, two from Ken and one from home so I won't go hungry for a while, also got two from home a week ago today. I haven't any letters from you but hope to one of these days.

I lost my Eversharp pencil two days ago and didn't know what I was going to do for one but now I am OK, very thoughtful sister I have, alas I ran out of envelopes last night so just got your parcel on time, things appear to happen at the right moment.

Excuse this writing, my pen don't seem to be feeding right. I filled it with ink from one here. I guess that's the main trouble.

This is not a bad station. RAF of course and flying twin engine plane just like starting over again, we don't have any choice, just go where they want you or need you. Second is my Coastal Command. I don't know what I fly from here. No snow here yet and quite warm and as usual lots of rain and not much sun. Archie is still in the hospital and expects to go back to Canada after Xmas. The eats are not too bad here, we get 4 meals a day, the Englishman has to have his tea around 4 or 5 o'clock then supper at 8, but tea is the last meal here. The people go in and buy a cup of tea here just the same as we go in at home and buy a Coca-Cola and no doubt more often. There is a show in the Sgt's mess tonight so will go over for a while . I was on a 4 hour route march this morning so might fall asleep at any time. On my 48hr leave in London I saw Max Lipsett. Sure glad to see someone from home, we had quite a talk. I was also through Westminster Abbey and St. Pauls Cathedral. I saw Buckingham Palace and Big Ben and heard it strike. It sounds about the same over the radio, also was over Westminster Bridge and as the poet writes (you know his name , I just can't remember) Ships towers domes theatres temples lie, he's about right I guess. You didn't know I could quote poetry, I didn't study during high school for nothing, for hard strenuous hours I put in studying did me good. I just started to read this letter and couldn't make it out so I guess I better quit because you will be tired by the time you get this far. So will close for tonight wishing you a Very Merry Xmas and a Happy New Year.

Lots of Love   Remember me to all

Blair

Letter from Stiles to Annabel dated 22 January 1943

Jan 22/43

R.C.A.F Attached R.A.F

Dear Annabel

Again, I am rather late in writing you, but probably I intend to slow down on my letter writing as it is so old when you receive it and (ILLEGIBLE) *if I keep on getting letters myself, that's the main thing so don't stop writing. Do you think I better change my mind, or do you think it's a good idea, after all I write a lot of letters as it is.*

First I must thank you for doing my Xmas shopping for me, hope you don't go in debt, everyone I get a letter from tells me how busy you were shopping for the both of us so thanks again, by the way, are you getting my mail, you never answer any of the questions I ask you. I got a letter from Murray a few days ago, he expects to get leave soon, so he wondered if we couldn't see each other, but since I have been moved to another section for a week or two so I can't see him unless he don't get leave 'til I get back. He is a Flight Lieutenant now equivalent to a Captain in the army.

It seems funny the middle of January and no snow. I guess Herb Mallory is over here now. I hear he is at Moncton now, is he at no.8 or no.5? H, also as you told me Clarence Hickson is there too, he is a mechanic isn't he?

Some fellows are lucky, where is Bhissal Lutes now. I received Alice's Xmas card, or did I tell you before?

I was down to London 2 weeks ago and saw Beverly Baytes, he gave a talk at the Beaver Club. I also met a fellow who graduated with Best. I met him at Halifax and had quite a talk with him. I also saw the show Yankee Doodle Dandy. It was a good show. There are sure some nice theatres in London. Also have nice shows. Theatres are called cinemas over here. A theatre is a place where they have stage shows.

I haven't received your parcel that you mentioned in your last letter, or did you change your mind and send it to Montreal. Sure would like to get in that 4-chocolate box, they wouldn't last long believe me. I received a 2-chocolate box from home about two weeks ago, not quite that long ago and given because I still have some left. I got some handkerchiefs, a pair of gloves and a pair of socks from the Canadian Red Cross again this week so I'm not doing too bad. Surprised to hear of Frederick stepping out with the girls but I suppose it is about time. I guess you started before he did, of course they never bothered Blair!

Archie is feeling better, he is getting up a while each day now but guess he will never fly again, over here anyway.

I suppose you read of the train wreck around Xmas time at Almonte Ont. Well, a fellow on our class is from there and he came down here with me and we are rooming together. He graduated at Moncton, two classes after I did. He was only in Halifax three days.

Glad to hear you got a new job and better money, a little hard work will do you good, probably make you go to bed early. I can't remember now what you told me you were doing so better tell me again. Are you kind of the boss or just senior, better give me the details again.

I think I have said enough for this time so will close, hope you can make this writing out.

Love

Blair

Letter from Stiles to Annabel dated 18 March 1943

March 18/43

RCAF Overseas

Attached RAF

Dear Annabel

It's 11.20 pm so won't finish this letter tonight but will give it a start. I wrote to Ken tonight, had to mail it home as I lost his address. I'm on 14 days leave now, only 6 more days left but am having a wonderful time for now at Joe's home, he sure has wonderful people and very nice and sociable and makes oneself feel at home.

Since I went to O.T.U I sure have had a good time over here. I liked Scotland pretty well, had a good time up there anyway but likely have seen the last of Scotland for a while. I met a Corporal W.A.A.F. up there, probably that's why I had a good time of course. She was stationed 30 miles away but saw her on my day off which gave me two nights. Her home is in London so am going to see her on her next leave.

We don't get up 12 o'clock every day unless there is something important on the list for the day. We go out for a bike ride most every afternoon, that is quite a sport over here, I enjoy it myself, she and I and a couple of girls were out for a ride tonight, the weather has sure been grand here lately.

Tomorrow morning we are going through an aircraft factory, so will have to get up early.

Yesterday morning we were down in a coal mine, 1,700 ft down and 3½ mile under the sea, it sure was interesting, no job for me, I would always be thinking of the thing caving in. They're sure welcome to their job.

I only expected to stay here for the first few days of my leave then go to London, but they wouldn't hear of it. Said I knew nobody in London so why go down there all alone, well that's right but I don't like to impose on good nature.

This is a nice little town. 30,000 people I believe, 2 theatres, they are trying to learn me to dance.

I received a letter from you last week, you can tell me what happened when you left Eatons. What difference does it make anyway. You got a mind of your own. Nothing to Eatons. Very glad to hear you like your new job.
Glad you got my air mail letter. I wanted a Wireless Air Gunner badge, a badge with W.A.G. printed on the front, not just A.G. If you can't get it write to Ken and he will be able to. Also send me some films 616. I still want that badge too, in case you didn't get that letter.
I finished O.T.U. going on 4 engine planes now, don't know how long I will be learning to fly them. I had good assessments when I finished. There were 4 pilots and their crews on a flight, 3 were officers and myself. On leaving one of the officers and myself were assessed as above average, the other two officers were only average, so I felt pretty good beating 2 officers and being as good as the other one, hope I continue that way. I think I had the best crew, anyway as good as the others, we had the best practice bombing results. I was on Whitleys.
Did Frederick get my letter I wrote to him? Also did Daisy? I got a couple of letters from Archie so I will have to write him. I believe Ferguson is still in Dartmouth. He is a Flight Sgt. now, going to put in for myself at the next station, was going to apply for a commission but changed my mind, have a lot better time this way. I have two officers in my crew so that will do. My Bomb Aimer was entertained at a Mrs Henryetta Lutes in High St. when he

was in Moncton. I think 38a was that. High St. of course could be wrong. She is a widow probably have her first name spelt wrong.

Let me know if you received this letter (written March 18th) This 7-page letter will be quite a shock to you so want to know if you get it.

I'm just listening to the midnight news; it just said the Americans shot down 121 fighters in the last 3 days. Believe what they say, the war would be over here then. They might of saw that many, 121 fighters, that's a joke.

If you can send me some gum. I have taken quite a few pictures lately so I will send them home and then they can send them to you, don't forget the films also a box of chocolates, don't get any ideas there for myself.

Well I will close for tonight, I hope you congratulate me on this letter, after your recovery from the shock. Good night.

Joe sends his love.

Your loving Brother

Blair

Letter from Stiles to Annabel dated 6 April 1943

April 6/43

RCAF Overseas

Attached RAF

8pm

Dear Annabel

I sure will have to write you tonight and thank you very much for the nice parcel I received today. Everything in it was OK and just what I wanted. Couldn't of been any better. I guess I have a very thoughtful sister so again "thank you". I also received your letters today written March 1st, also on Feb 15. I received 9 letters yesterday and 4 letters and 2 parcels today, so I will be busy for a while, the other parcel being from home, it was one with the Noxzema Avlis hangers and hankies in it. I thought it must have got lost on the way but finally reached here. It was mailed Feb15th. It had been nearly

4 weeks since I had received any mail, so I was glad to get some. I received the one from Alice also, thank her for what she sent and tell her I will write and thank her very soon. Also, one from Frederick, he had quite an argument with his teacher, he also told me what kind of records you told him to buy but he said he didn't like that kind.

The house must look like new now, you don't know how lucky you really are, I sure miss having some place to get like while I was at Moncton. Quite a display of Charles Harmer & Co in that magazine you sent me. That is sure a good picture of George, in fact George looks good in all of them. I don't think I ever saw Harmer in person.

I think I told you I have all my crew now, my Wireless Air Gunner and I are in the room here with a nice fire, both writing letters. When I finish here, I am going down to his place for a week, a few days anyway. He is a real nice fellow and quiet i.e. like myself. We are having a good feed night now. I showed him your picture, so he wants to be remembered to you. He says he just shaved so he looks alright now. I have an all-English crew. I am always telling them about Canada's War Effort etc. but kind of spoiled it today receiving two parcels. Now they tell me Canada doesn't know there is a war going on, that's why I can get these nice parcels. If they get the best of me I just say remember Dieppe and they have no answer for that, they're a real nice bunch though my rear gunner talks all the time.

By the way JB can play the saxophone, used to play in a band, also he can sing, he has a wonderful voice.

The weather up here is terrible lately. Of course no snow but what a wind, shakes every building. Dorine says she doubts she will pass probation; she says if she doesn't there will be lots of gossip in J'Ville.

I just told Joe when he came, to get some coal for the fire so he just left to get some, he thought it was alright to go get it but when he left I said if anyone asks you any questions, tell them you didn't get any coal ration this week, so I hope he gets back in one piece. He said to tell you that your brother had him out stealing coal, he just took a little can with him. I used to take a wheelbarrow with us. (He has just come back and made out alright.)

It is 9 o'clock now, just an hour writing this so better close. We are 5 hours ahead of you now, so I suppose you are still at work, to tell you the truth I am thinking about going to bed. I was glad to get the hankies and envelopes.

Ps I will thank you again for everything, the sweets are sure appreciated.

Hoping to hear from you again soon

Excuse writing

Love (your) Blair

Letter from Stiles to Annabel dated 26 May 1943

May 26/43

R.C.A.F Overseas

Attached R.A.F

7.15pm

Dear Annabel

Here I am in the canteen with 3 of my crew having a cup of tea so will also write some letters. My leave finished Monday so now I am back at work. I spent all my leave with Joe at his home and did I ever have a good time. The best time since I came over here. I enjoyed every minute of it. I took some pictures, sent some home so you can get them from home to have a look. In the next parcel you can send me some films 6/6. Joe had a brother away in the army and I wore his civvy suit, it fit me perfectly. I intended to go to London for a while on my leave, but they wanted me to stay so I did as I sure was having a good time. I was down in a coal mine 1700ft deep and 3½ miles under the sea, it sure was a wonderful sight, but that is one place I wouldn't work. I also was through an aircraft factory, met the boss stereographer and was to her home one night to see her, made a date to go for a bike ride with her the next Sunday afternoon but cancelled it as I was going with another one, 4 of us, and guess it was for the better. I've finished OTU now, glad it's over with, they say if you get through that you've got half a chance. In the flight I was in there were 4 pilots and their crews, 3 of the pilots were officers and myself, when we left the pilots were assessed as to their flying abilities. One officer and myself were above average and the other two officers were only average, so I sure felt good about that, only hope I do as good on 4 engine aircraft. Did Frederick receive the letter I wrote to him. It's not bad to be captain of an aircraft, if anything happens it's me that catches hell, but I wouldn't want to be over here as anything else but a pilot.

I was going to pay in for my commission but changed my mind. I'm having too good a time so am putting in for my Flight Sergeant.

I'm doing awful at letter writing lately, can't seem to sit down long enough to write even 1 letter.

You know Annabel, I don't even write to Dorine very often, about as often as I do you and you know how often that is. I don't suppose I should write this to you but will get it off my mind. I thought I was in love with her but since I came over here I sometimes wonder. I guess she's not my type, probably it's because I don't see her, after all when I was home there was no one else to take out, at least and have a good time, but I'll never write to her and tell her as I may be sorry afterwards especially when I see her again. I don't think I would ever marry her. Also I have changed my mind about Englishwomen. I met a couple that was really nice, and I don't mean maybe they had everything, personality, looks and even figure. Too bad I told Mother I'd come home alone. I lost Ken's address so will send his letter home 'til I get it. Glad to hear you like your new job so well. Don't forget that Wireless AG badge. I told you to get in previous two letters. This pen don't work very good so will close for tonight.

Love

Blair

The following, and last, letter was written by Annabel to Stiles on the evening of Christmas Day 1943. He never received it, his plane, JB453, having been shot down in the early hours of 3rd January 1944. The letter was returned to her in mid-January 1944 marked “Reported Missing”. A typed transcript follows this copy of the original letter:

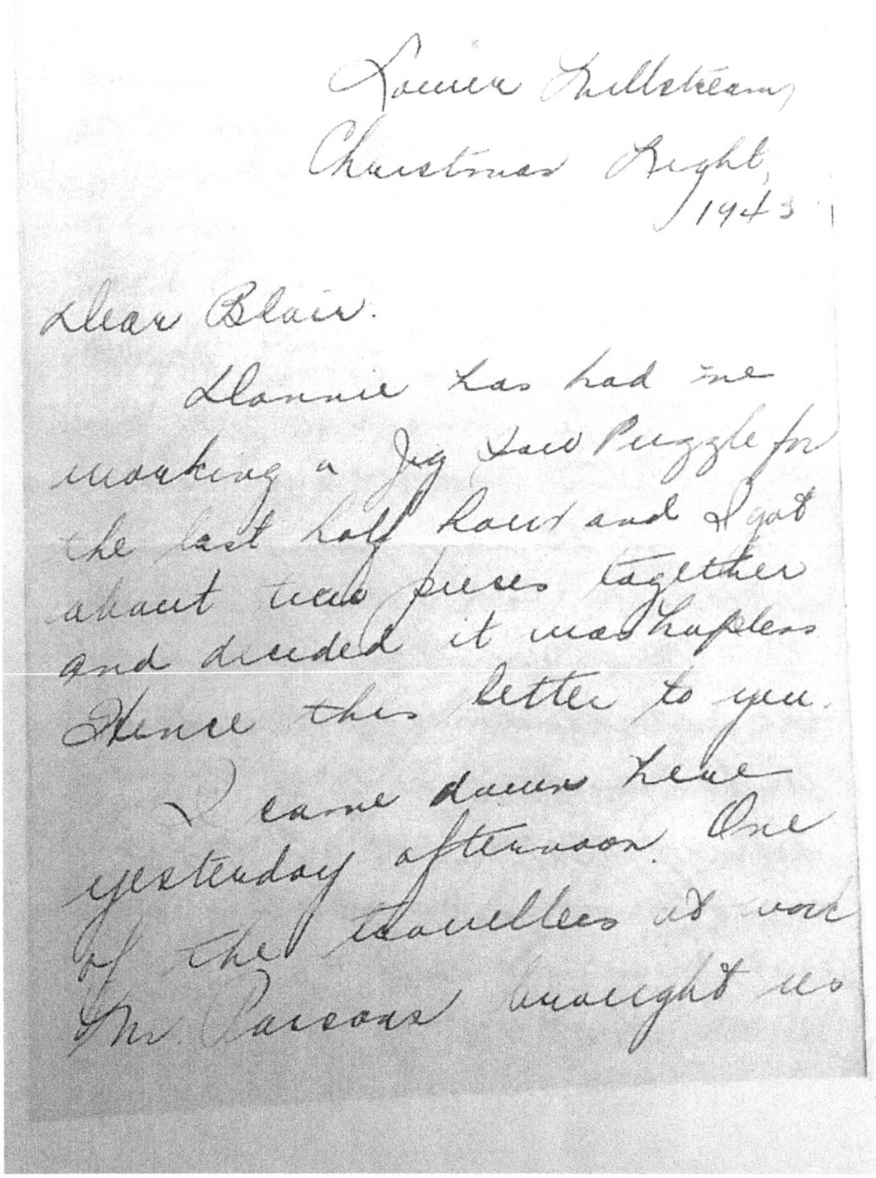

Lower Millstream,
Christmas Night,
1943

Dear Blair:

Donnie has had me working a Jig Saw Puzzle for the last half hour and I got about two pieces together and decided it was hopeless. Hence this letter to you.

I came down here yesterday afternoon. One of the travellers at work Mr. Parsons brought us

2.

down by car. Mr. Maclean from work, his wife and mother came down to Sussex for Xmas, so we all came together.

Things are very quiet down here. Dorothy Holmes from next door was over this afternoon, she's very nice, a bit younger than I. Then I went over to her place to see her gifts. They wanted me to stay to supper but I came home.

I will make a list of what I received for Xmas.

3.

Ski Boots from Blair
Thanks very much, I love them. (sweet & what I wanted)
Gold Ear Rings from Lorne
Slip from Mum
Kid Gloves from Dad
Silk Pyjamas – Ken & Mildred.
Stationary – Lonnie
Slip (rose taffeta) from Irene Thompson at work
Revlon nail polish & lipstick from Margaret Weldon at work.
Charles & Vera's photo from Vera.
White skating socks from Bev.
Evening in Paris Talcum Powder and Toilet water from Alice

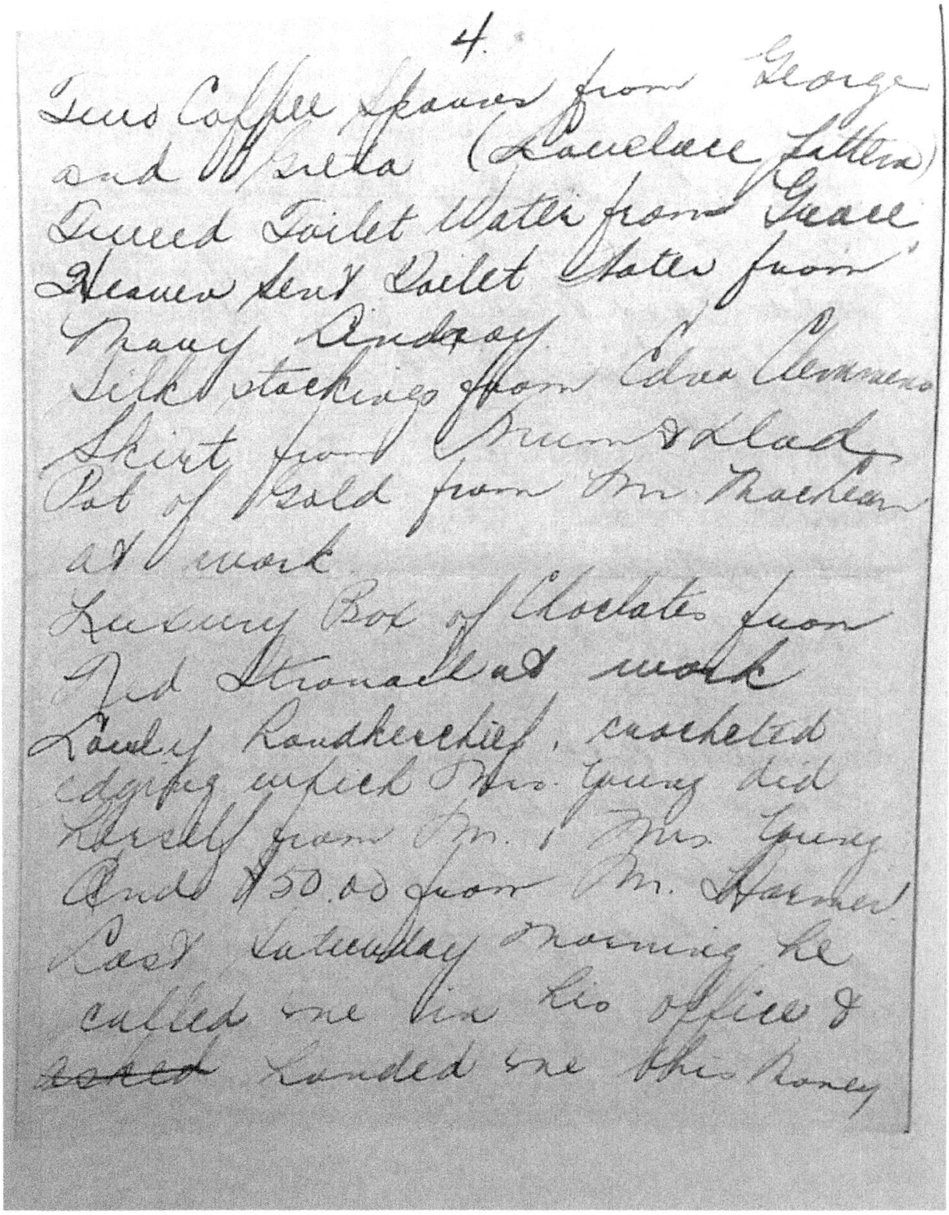

4.

Tens Coffee Spoons from George
and Greta (Lovelace pattern)
Tweed Toilet Water from Grace
Heaven Sent Toilet Water from
Mary Lindsay
Silk stockings from Edna Clemmens
Skirt from Mum & Dad
Pot of Gold from Mr. MacLean
at work
Luxury Box of Chocolates from
Ted Stronach at work
Lovely handkerchief, crocheted
edging which Mrs. Young did
herself from Mr. & Mrs. Young
And $50.00 from Mr. Harmer
Last Saturday morning he
called me in his office &
~~asked~~ handed me this money

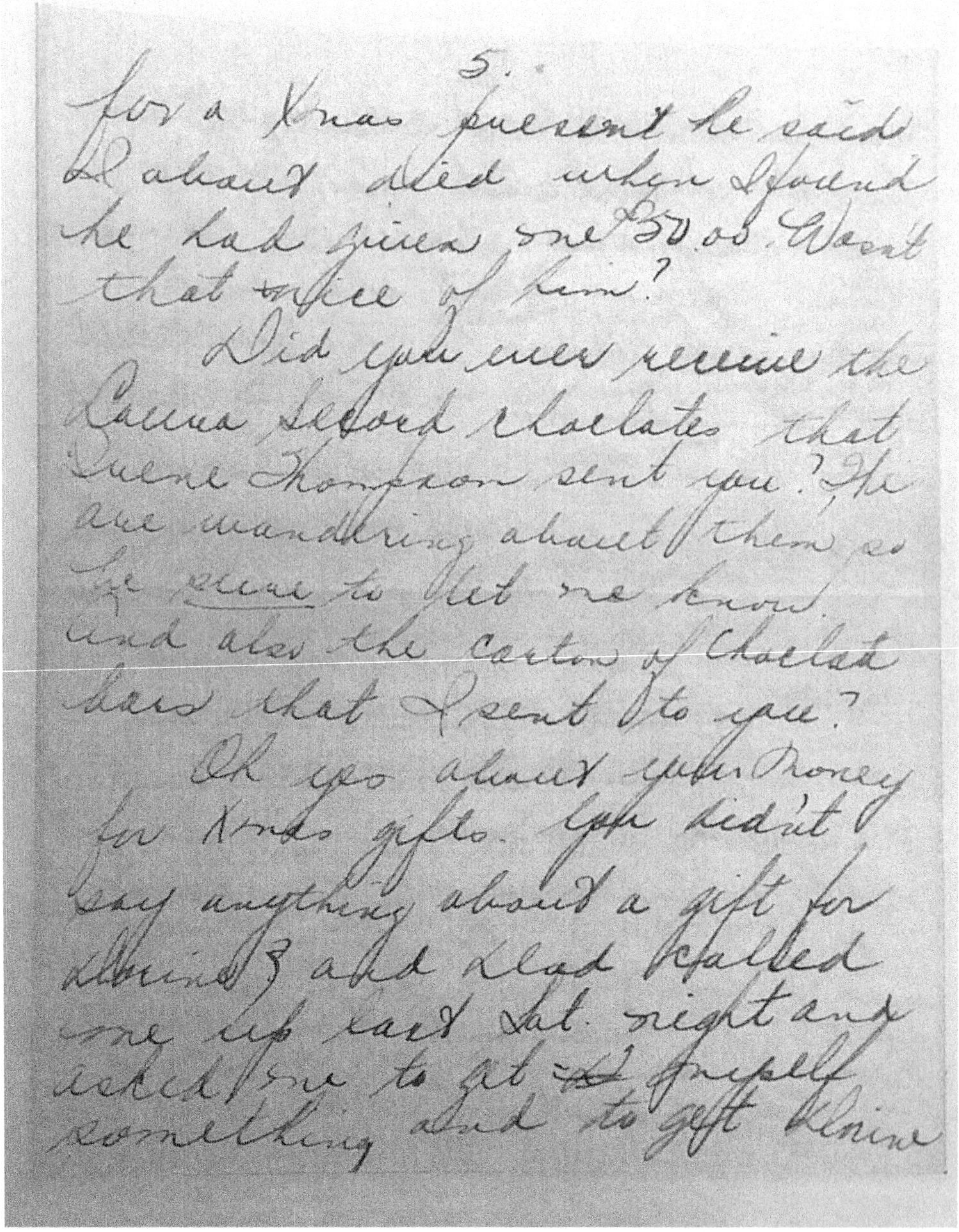
5.

for a Xmas present he said
I almost died when I found
he had given me $50.00. Wasn't
that nice of him?

Did you ever receive the
Laura Secord chocolates that
Irene Thompson sent you? We
are wondering about them so
be sure to let me know.
And also the carton of chocolate
bars that I sent to you?

Oh yes about your money
for Xmas gifts. You didn't
say anything about a gift for
Elaine ? and Dad called
me up last Sat. night and
asked me to get myself
something and to gift Elaine

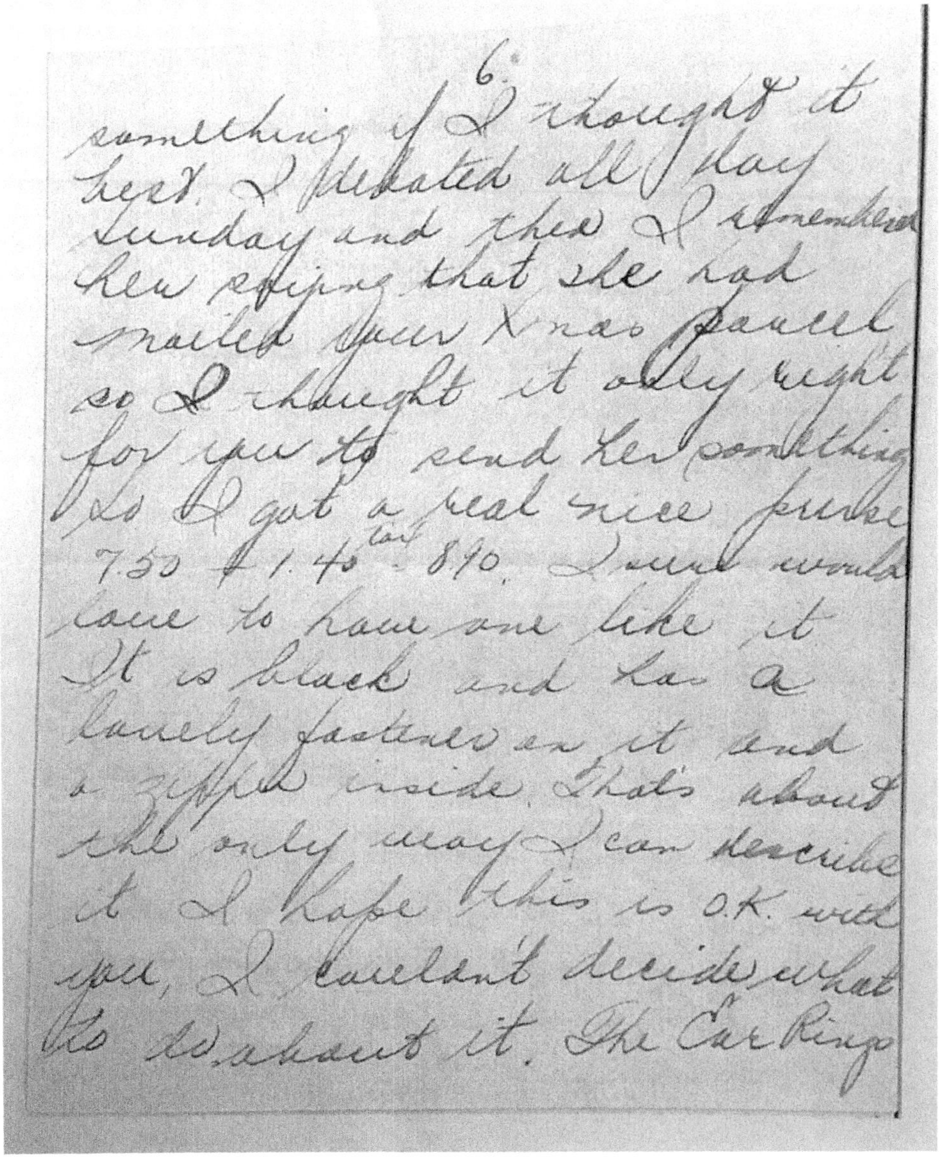

6.

something if I thought it
best. I debated all day
Sunday and then I remembered
her saying that she had
mailed your Xmas parcel
so I thought it only right
for you to send her something
So I got a real nice purse
7.50 + 1.40 tax = 8.90. I sure would
love to have one like it
It is black and has a
lovely fastener on it and
a zipper inside. That's about
the only way I can describe
it I hope this is O.K. with
you, I couldn't decide what
to do about it. The Ear Rings

7.

she sent me a nice sweet, shaped like wings, not like the kind you wear, more the shape of an observer's wings. I sent her a blue plaid scarf. I sent ~~Aloa~~ to Vera a red scarf.

Oh yes. I got two dickies to wear under my sweaters to make collars from Isabel. They were very nice.

I want to get a new brown ski suit when I go back to Moncton. I have to go back Monday night to be to work Tuesday A.M.

8.

Last Sunday night we
went to Church at First
Baptist and then to the
sing song afterwards. Gordon
Landon sat with Alice and
me and walked home with
us afterwards. And who was
at the sing song but Rev. Master
Wilson. You know he had
been a Prisoner of the Japanese
and was released. It was
wonderful seeing him again
and he remembered Gordon
and me and was asking
about "my Brothers". Imagine
that!

4

I haven't heard from you
for nearly a month.

There is a re-broadcast of
the King's Speech on the radio
now.

We had a card from
Bev. Martin. It was exactly
the same kind of card as
Jim's, from 408 Squadron.
So we found out they
are in the same Squadron
over there.

I haven't heard from
Cracker since I saw him
I guess I owe him a letter

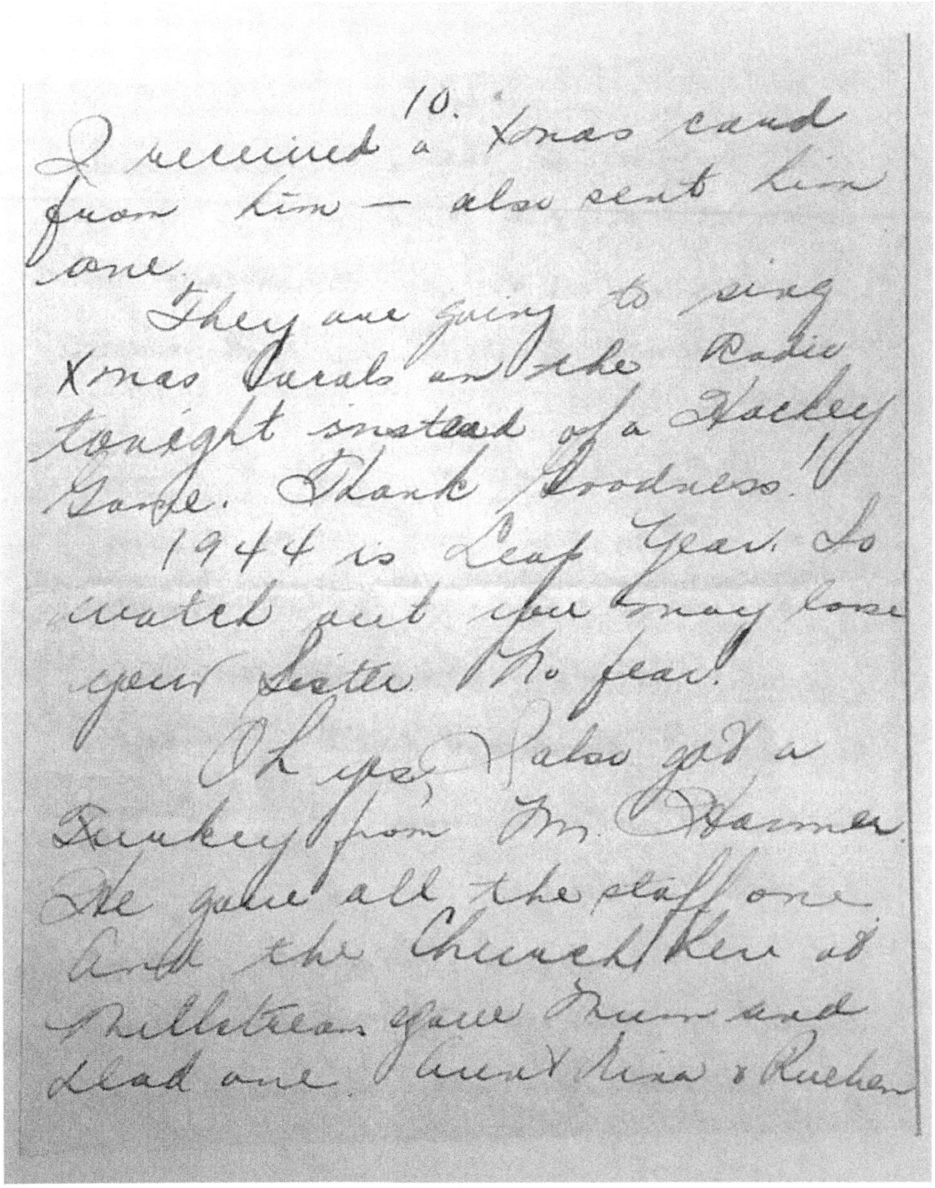

I received a 10. Xmas card from him — also sent him one.
They are going to sing Xmas Carols on the Radio tonight instead of a Hockey Game. Thank Goodness!
1944 is Leap Year. So watch out you may lose your Sister. No fear.
Oh yes, I also got a Turkey from Mr. Harmer. He gave all the staff one. And the Church here at Millstream gave Mum and Dad one. Aunt Nina & Reuben

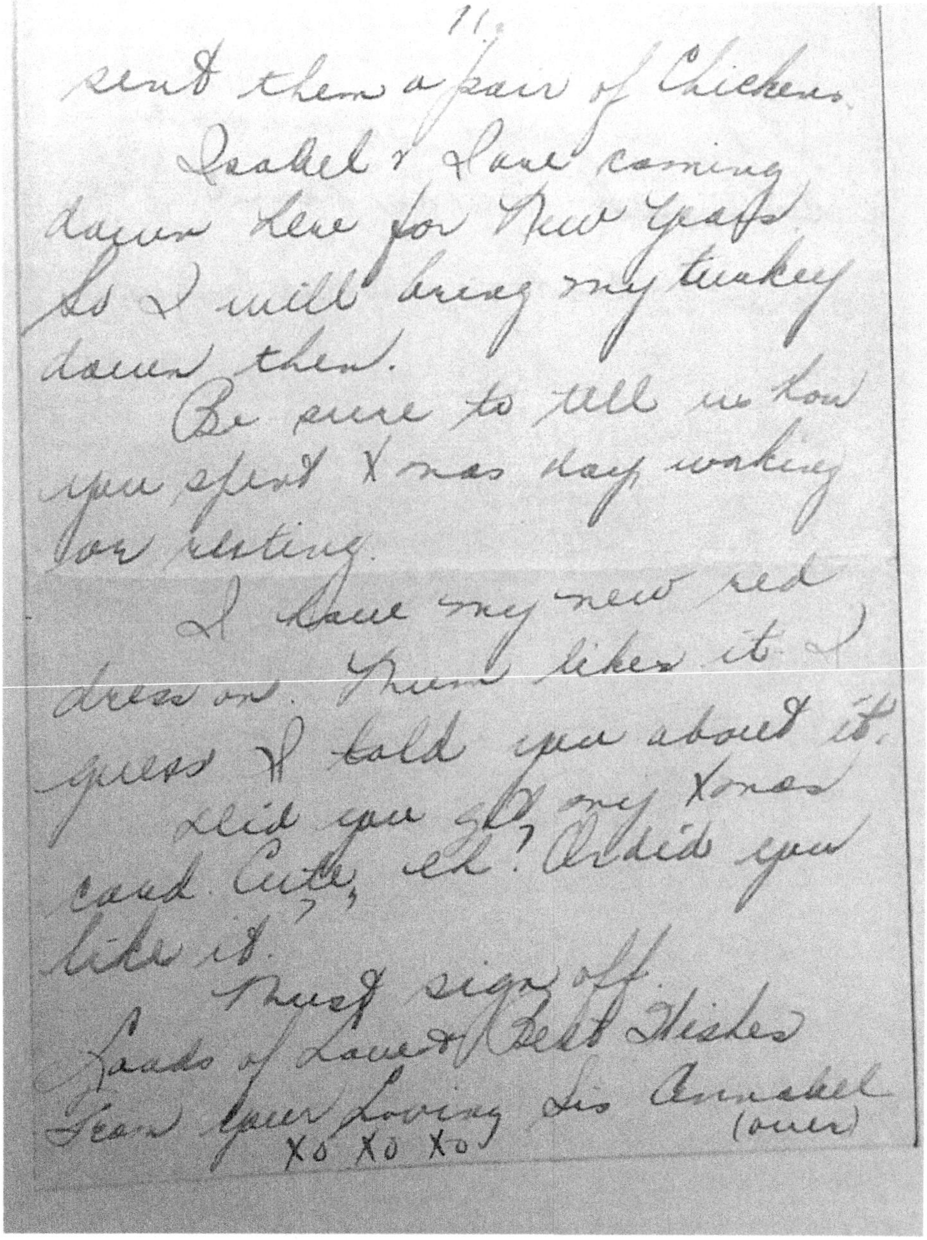

11.

sent them a pair of Chickens.

Isabel & Dave coming down here for New Years. So I will bring my turkey down then.

Be sure to tell us how you spent Xmas day working or resting.

I have my new red dress on. Mum likes it I guess I told you about it.

Did you get my Xmas card. Cute, eh? Or did you like it.

Must sign off.
Loads of Love & Best Wishes
From Your Loving Sis Annabel
XO XO XO
(over)

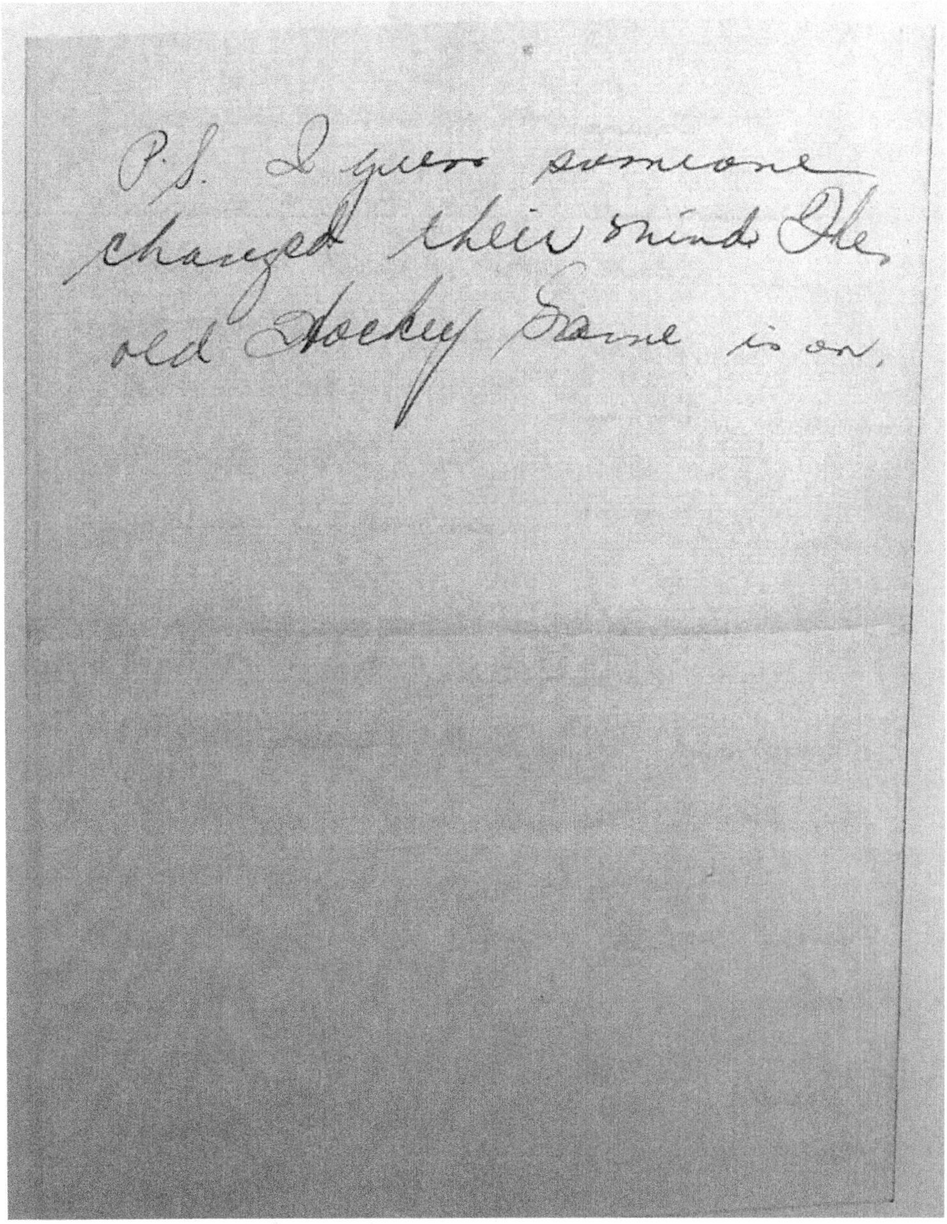

P.S. I guess someone changed their mind. The old Hockey Game is on.

Transcript of above letter

Millstream

Christmas night

1943

Dear Blair

Dannie has had me making a jigsaw puzzle for the last half hour and I got about two pieces together and decided it was hopeless. Hence this letter to you. I came down here yesterday afternoon. One of the travellers at work Mr Parsons brought us down by car. Mr MacLean from work, his wife and mother came down to Sussex for Xmas, so we all came together.

Things are very quiet down here. Dorothy Holmes from next door was over this afternoon. She's very nice, a bit younger than I. Then I went over to her place to see her gifts. She wanted me to stay to supper, but I came home.

I will make a list of what I received for Xmas

Hi-Boots from Blair. Thanks very much. I love them.

Gold earrings from Dorine (just what I wanted)

Slip from Mum

Kid gloves from Dad

Silk Pyjamas - Ken & Mildred

Stationary - Dannie

Slip (real taffeta) from Irene Thompson at work

Revlon nail polish and lipstick from Margaret Wildon at work

(?) & Vera's photo from Vera

White skating socks from Beau

Evening in Paris talcum powder and Toilet water from Alice

Two coffee scarves from George and Gita (Lovelace letters)

Tweed Toilet Water from Grace

Heaven Sent Toilet water from Mary Audrey

Silk Stockings from Edna Clemens

Skirt from Mum and Dad

Pot of Gold from Mr MacLean at work

Luxury Box of Chocolates from Sid Stranacht at work

Lovely handkerchiefs, crocheted edging which Mrs Young did herself from Mr and Mrs Young

And £50.00 from Mr. Harmer.

Last Saturday morning he called me into his office & handed me this money for a Xmas present. He said I about died when I found he had given me £50.00. Wasn't that nice of him?

Did you ever receive the Launa Second chocolates that Quene Thompson sent you? She is wondering about them so be sure to let me know and also the carton of chocolate bars I sent you?

Oh yes, about your money for Xmas gifts. You didn't say anything about a gift for Dorine. Mum and Dad called me up last night and asked me to get myself something and to get Dorine something if I thought it best. I debated all day Sunday and then I remembered her saying that she had mailed your Xmas parcel so I thought it only right for you to send her something so I got a real nice purse - 7.50 + 1.40 tax - 8.90. I sure would love to have one like it. It is black and has a lovely fastener on it and a zipper inside. That's about the only way I can describe it. I hope this is OK with you. I couldn't decide what to do about it. The earrings she sent me are sweet, shaped like wings, not like the kind you wear. more the shape of an observer's wings. I sent her a blue plaid scarf. I sent Vera a red scarf. Oh yes, I got two dickies to wear under my sweaters to make collars from Mabel. They were very nice. I want to get a new brown Ski suit when I go back to Moncton. I have to go back Monday night, to be at work Tuesday A/M. Last Sunday night we went to Church at Baptist and then to the Sing Song afterwards. Gordon London sat with Alice and me and walked home with me afterwards.

And who was at the Sing Song but Rev. Diantec Wilson, you knew he had been a prisoner of the Japanese and was released. It was wonderful seeing him again and he remembered Gordon and me and was asking about my brothers. Imagine that !

I haven't heard from you for nearly a month. There is a re-broadcast of the King's speech on the radio now.

We had a card from Bev. Martin. It was exactly the same kind of card as Jim's, from 408 Squadron. So we found out that they are in the same Squadron over there.

I haven't heard from Crocker since I saw him. I guess I owe him a letter. I received a Xmas card from him- also sent him one.

They are going to sing Xmas Carols on the radio tonight instead of a Hockey game. Thank Goodness!!

1944 is leap year. So watch out you may lose your sister. No fear!

Oh yes, I also got a turkey from Mrs Harmer. She gave all the staff one and the church Rev Millstream gave Mum and Dad one, and Nina & Reuben sent them a pair of chickens.

Isobel and I are coming down here for New Year so I will bring my turkey down then.

Be sure to tell me how you spent Xmas day, working or resting.

I have my new red dress on. Mum likes it. I guess I told you about it.

Did you get my Xmas card, cute eh? And did you like it?

Must sign off

Loads of love & best wishes

Your Ever loving Sis Annabel

XO XO XO (over)

I guess someone changed their mind. The Hockey Game is on.

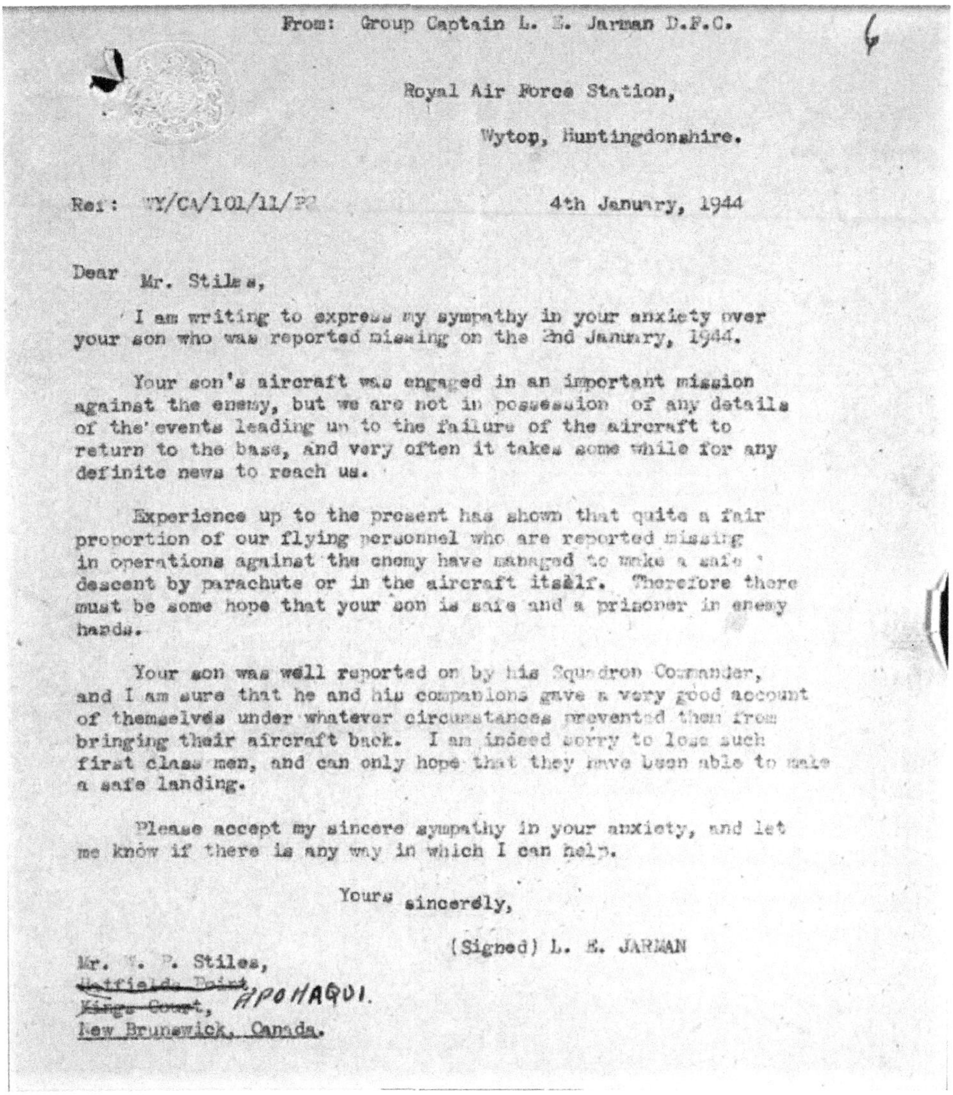

From: Group Captain L. E. Jarman D.F.C.

6

Royal Air Force Station,

Wytop, Huntingdonshire.

Ref: WY/CA/101/11/P

4th January, 1944

Dear Mr. Stiles,

I am writing to express my sympathy in your anxiety over your son who was reported missing on the 2nd January, 1944.

Your son's aircraft was engaged in an important mission against the enemy, but we are not in possession of any details of the events leading up to the failure of the aircraft to return to the base, and very often it takes some while for any definite news to reach us.

Experience up to the present has shown that quite a fair proportion of our flying personnel who are reported missing in operations against the enemy have managed to make a safe descent by parachute or in the aircraft itself. Therefore there must be some hope that your son is safe and a prisoner in enemy hands.

Your son was well reported on by his Squadron Commander, and I am sure that he and his companions gave a very good account of themselves under whatever circumstances prevented them from bringing their aircraft back. I am indeed sorry to lose such first class men, and can only hope that they have been able to make a safe landing.

Please accept my sincere sympathy in your anxiety, and let me know if there is any way in which I can help.

Yours sincerely,

(Signed) L. E. JARMAN

Mr. W. P. Stiles,
~~Hatfields Point~~
~~Kings Court~~, APOHAQUI.
New Brunswick, Canada.

Letter of condolence from Group Captain Jarman DFC, RAF Wyton to Stiles' father dated 4 January 1944

F/O. Stiles E.B. Copy to Ottawa 14/1/44

P.412291

No. 83 Squadron,
Royal Air Force,
Wyton,
Huntingdon.

Reference:
83S/601/256/P.1.

8th January, 1944.

LANCASTER MK.III J.B.353 - MISSING NIGHT 2/3RD JANUARY, 1944

Can.J.18139	P/O.	E.B.Stiles	Pilot
614985	F/Sgt.	Traynor P.	F/Engineer
155542	P/O.	D.C.J.McKendry	Navigator
1091782	Sgt.	Banks J.	W/Operator
132869	F/O.	W.H.Dyke	A/Bomber
1559306	Sgt.	Dunlop J.M.	M.U.Gunner
151061	F/O.	I.G.Allen	Rear Gunner

Sir,

I have the honour to refer to my signal A.609 dated 3rd January, 1944, and to submit the following report.

This aircraft was detailed to carry out an attack on Berlin, on the night of the 2/3rd January, 1944, and after leaving base at 00.10 hours nothing more was heard of the aircraft and the cause of its failure to return is unknown.

The crew as a whole was quite experienced to operations. The Captain having completed 14 operational trips, the Air Bomber and Wireless Operator had each completed 11 sorties, whilst the Navigator, Flight Engineer, M.U.Gunner and Rear Gunner had each completed 33, 32, 13 and 18 trips respectively.

The crew were quite reliable, and would be capable of taking the correct action in the face of any emergency.

I have the honour to be,
Sir,
Your obedient Servant

Sgd: T.Deane,
Wing Commander, Commanding,
No.83 Squadron, P.F.F. R.A.F.

The Under Secretary of State,
Air Ministry, P.4.Cas.
73/77 Oxford Street,
London, W.1.

Copy to: Headquarters,
Path Finder Force.

Letter from Wing Commander Dean, 83 Squadron, RAF Wyton to Under Secretary of State, Air Ministry, dated 8 January 1944

In March 1944 Margaret Banks, wrote the following letter to Blair's sister, Annabel, 3 months after the loss,

48 The Gardens

Whitehaven

Cumberland

March 8th

PS Would Like to hear from you soon.

Did you receive my last A.G telling you of the sad news?

My Dear Annabel

Thank you so much for your very nice letter I received on Saturday. I was very pleased to hear from you and to receive the clipping of Blair. Blair showed us the snap when he was on leave, and we thought it was very good. Well, by now you will have received the sad news of the boys. There doesn't seem to be much hope does there, but it isn't official and there have been mistakes made. We are hoping and praying that this is a mistake.

We wish you were here in England, so that we could talk to you. We went to Glasgow to see Jock Dunlop's wife (The mid-upper gunner). She was awfully nice, but she didn't know any more than we did.

Joe was to be married at Easter you know, and I was to be bridesmaid and

Blair best man. Anne (Joe's fiancé) does not believe Joe or the other four have been killed. Besides all this trouble, Anne's wedding dress has been destroyed at her home in London, and her people have been bombed out.

But I shall be boring you with all our troubles, so I'll tell you something that may interest you; we heard of someone being reported missing, and then officially reported killed. Nine months after this, his people heard from him, saying that he was a prisoner-of-war. So you see, mistakes are made.

What I can't understand is, that they could identify McKendry and Allan and not the other five. Jock at least should have been identified he wore so many clothes, and it was very strange that the navigator and tail gunner were identified, when the navigator sits next to Joe and Blair. It really is very queer isn't it? All we can do is pray for more definite and better news.

Mother and Father are quite broken-hearted, and I can quite understand what your parents will be like. Mother does nothing but talk of the happy times we had together when Blair and Joe came on leave. We adopted Blair for the duration of the war. I treat him as a brother and Mother and Dad treat him as a son.

We can only hope and trust in God that those five are alive. Although if it is true what the German Authorities say, they cannot be brought back to life.

I liked the few lines of poetry enclosed very much and am enclosing some too and I wish this could happen.

Well I should have to draw to a close now, as it is rather late, and I should have to get as much sleep as possible, just now, because I'm sitting a big exam soon, to see if I'm 'brainy' enough to sit my school certificate. I believe your equivalent to our S.C is Graduation, and you don't take it until you are 18years old. Ours is an extremely 'stiff' exam, the average age of taking it is 16 years and I won't be 16 until April 24 so I shall be lucky if I pass.

Give my love to your father and mother and tell them to have hope, I'm sorry to say Mother has none although Dad has. Lots of love to yourself.

Yours very sincerely

Margaret Banks

Our file J18139(R.O.)

ROYAL CANADIAN AIR FORCE

OTTAWA, Canada, 12th June, 1947.

R.C.A.F. Casualty Liaison Officer,
Casualty Branch,
Air Ministry,
2 Seville St.,
Knightsbridge,
London, S.W.1,
England.

J18139 F/O E.B. Stiles

1. A communication has been received from the next-of-kin of the above noted officer which states that they have received a letter from Mr. J. Banks, father of Sergeant Banks, a member of this crew which states:

> The air ministry have advised that
> "Examination of captured German documents has disclosed that the members of your son's aircraft are laid to rest in Graves 2 - 8 Group 192 in the general cemetery Blankenburg, Germany. It is disclosed that their Lancaster Aircraft was shot down between Timmenrode, three miles east south east of Blankenburg and Wanstedt two miles east of Limmonede."

2. The next-of-kin of F/O Stiles have requested confirmation of this information. May the latest information on this crew be forwarded to these Headquarters.

77

(W.A. Dicks)
Wing Commander,
for Chief of the Air Staff.

FFF:GB

Letter from RCAF Chief of the Air Staff to RCAF Casualty Liaison Officer dated 12 June 1946

J18139 (RO)

Ottawa, Canada, October 24th, 1947.

Mr. W.F. Stiles,
Opahaqui,
New Brunswick.

Dear Mr. Stiles:

Further to our letter of June 12th, 1947, a report has been received from our Missing Research and Enquiry Service concerning your son, Flying Officer Ernest Blair Stiles and his crew. Investigating Officers of this Service ascertained that your son's aircraft crashed east of Timmenrod, approximately 4 miles from Blankenburg. Blankenburg is approximately 46 miles northeast of Muhlhausen. The cause of the crash was not known, but it was noticed that night that fighters had been active in the area.

The remains of the crew were recovered and taken to Blankenburg by the police where they were placed in coffins and buried in a collective grave in the town cemetery. As no cross was erected and no records of the grave kept, exhumation is being carried out in an effort to effect individual identification. The remains of the crew will then be re-interred in a permanent British Military Cemetery in Germany, in accordance with existing policy. On receipt of this information, you will be further advised.

Yours sincerely,

R.C.A.F. Casualty Officer,
for Chief of the Air Staff.

FFF:JJF

Letter from RCAF Chief of the Air Staff to Stiles' father dated 24 October 1947

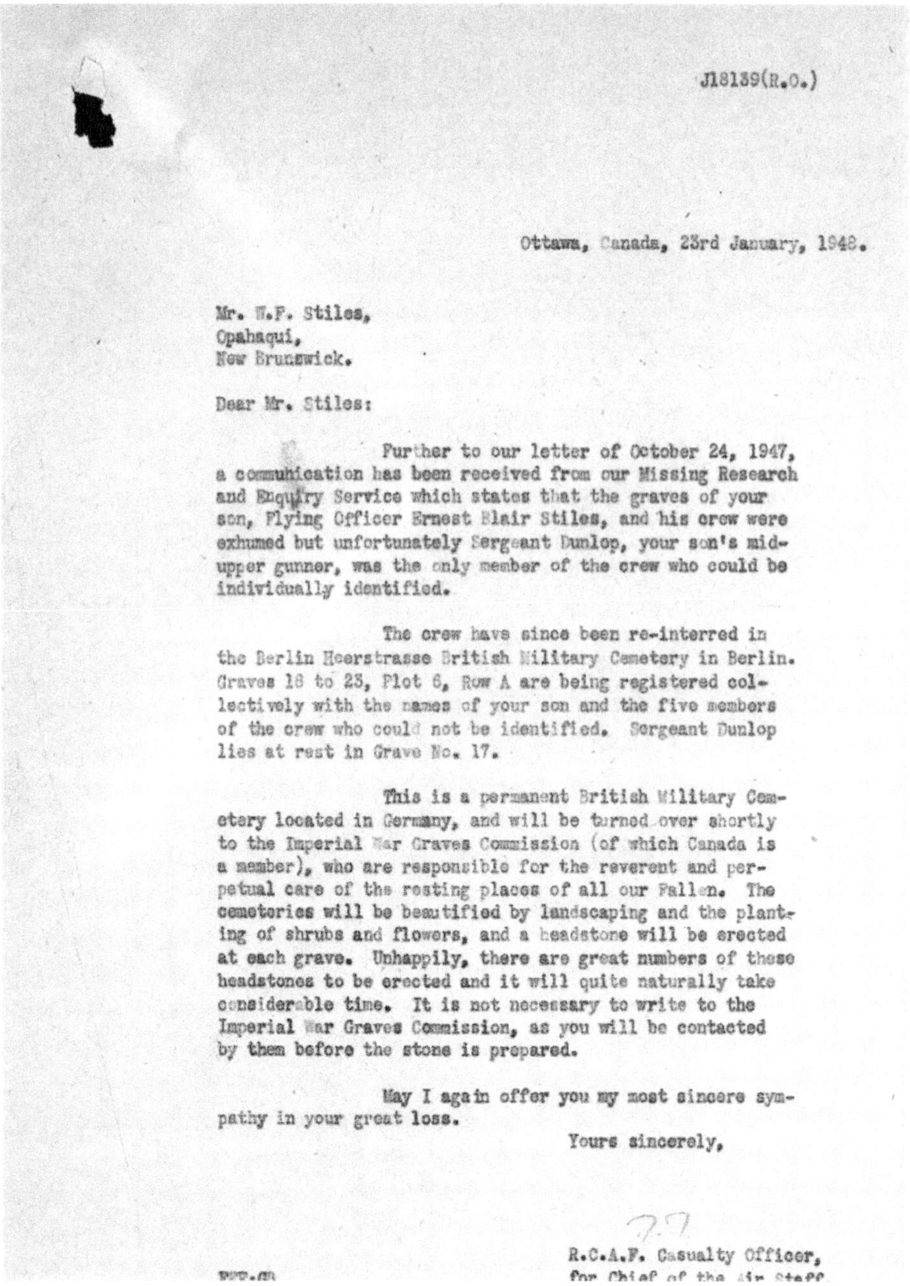

J18139(R.O.)

Ottawa, Canada, 23rd January, 1948.

Mr. W.F. Stiles,
Opahaqui,
New Brunswick.

Dear Mr. Stiles:

Further to our letter of October 24, 1947, a communication has been received from our Missing Research and Enquiry Service which states that the graves of your son, Flying Officer Ernest Blair Stiles, and his crew were exhumed but unfortunately Sergeant Dunlop, your son's mid-upper gunner, was the only member of the crew who could be individually identified.

The crew have since been re-interred in the Berlin Heerstrasse British Military Cemetery in Berlin. Graves 18 to 23, Plot 6, Row A are being registered collectively with the names of your son and the five members of the crew who could not be identified. Sergeant Dunlop lies at rest in Grave No. 17.

This is a permanent British Military Cemetery located in Germany, and will be turned over shortly to the Imperial War Graves Commission (of which Canada is a member), who are responsible for the reverent and perpetual care of the resting places of all our Fallen. The cemeteries will be beautified by landscaping and the planting of shrubs and flowers, and a headstone will be erected at each grave. Unhappily, there are great numbers of these headstones to be erected and it will quite naturally take considerable time. It is not necessary to write to the Imperial War Graves Commission, as you will be contacted by them before the stone is prepared.

May I again offer you my most sincere sympathy in your great loss.

Yours sincerely,

R.C.A.F. Casualty Officer,
for Chief of the Air Staff.

Letter from RCAF Casualty Officer to Stiles' father dated 23 January 1948 – Reburial to the British Military Cemetery in Berlin

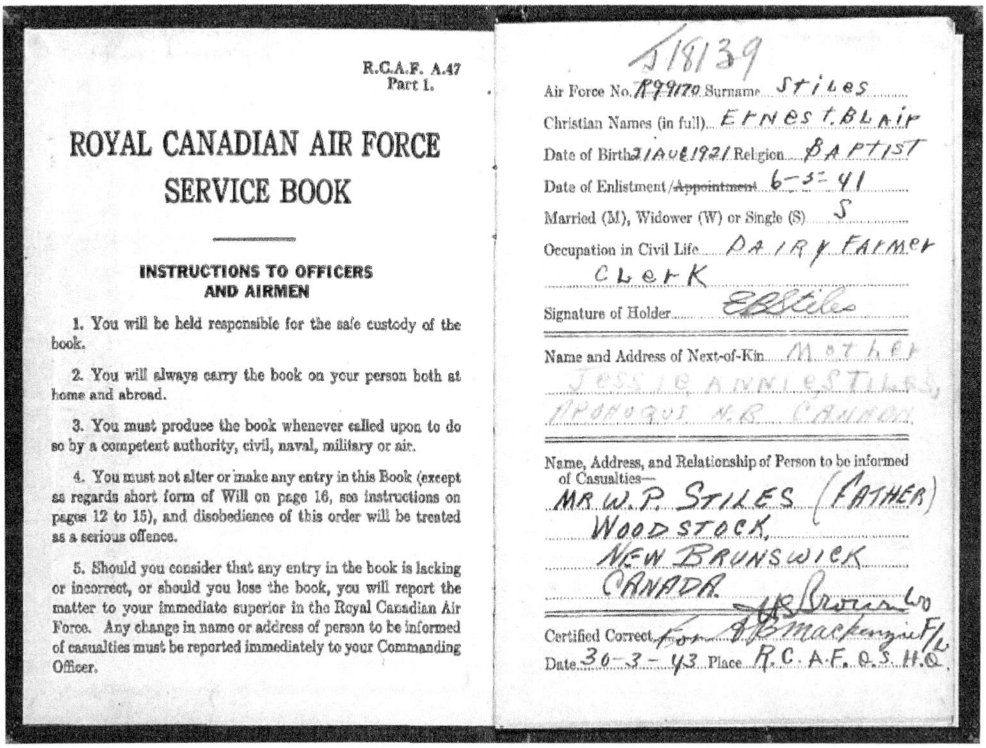

R.C.A.F. A.47
Part 1.

ROYAL CANADIAN AIR FORCE
SERVICE BOOK

INSTRUCTIONS TO OFFICERS AND AIRMEN

1. You will be held responsible for the safe custody of the book.

2. You will always carry the book on your person both at home and abroad.

3. You must produce the book whenever called upon to do so by a competent authority, civil, naval, military or air.

4. You must not alter or make any entry in this Book (except as regards short form of Will on page 16, see instructions on pages 12 to 15), and disobedience of this order will be treated as a serious offence.

5. Should you consider that any entry in the book is lacking or incorrect, or should you lose the book, you will report the matter to your immediate superior in the Royal Canadian Air Force. Any change in name or address of person to be informed of casualties must be reported immediately to your Commanding Officer.

J18139

Air Force No. R99170 Surname STILES

Christian Names (in full) ERNEST BLAIR

Date of Birth 21 AUG 1921 Religion BAPTIST

Date of Enlistment/~~Appointment~~ 6-3-41

Married (M), Widower (W) or Single (S) S

Occupation in Civil Life DAIRY FARMER CLERK

Signature of Holder E B Stiles

Name and Address of Next-of-Kin MOTHER JESSIE ANNIE STILES, APOHAQUI N.B. CANADA

Name, Address, and Relationship of Person to be informed of Casualties—
MR W.P. STILES (FATHER)
WOODSTOCK,
NEW BRUNSWICK
CANADA

Certified Correct for A.B. Mackenzie F/L

Date 30-3-43 Place R.C.A.F. O.S. H.Q.

Stiles' RCAF Service Book

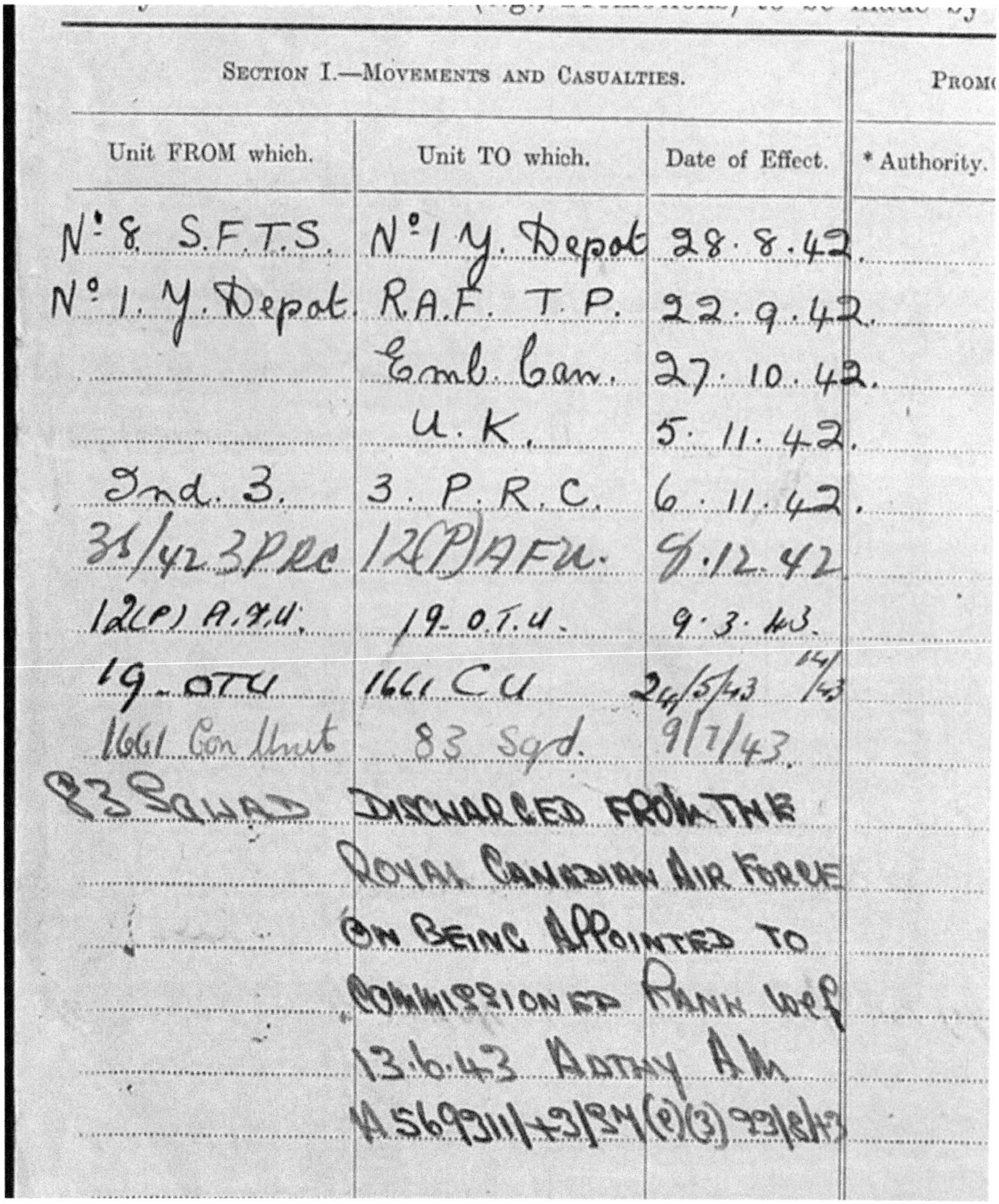

SECTION I.—MOVEMENTS AND CASUALTIES.

Unit FROM which.	Unit TO which.	Date of Effect.	* Authority.
No. 8 S.F.T.S.	No. 1 Y. Depot	28.8.42.	
No. 1. Y. Depot	R.A.F. T.P.	22.9.42.	
	Emb Can.	27.10.42.	
	U.K.	5.11.42.	
Ind. 3.	3. P.R.C.	6.11.42.	
31/42 3PRC	12(P)AFU.	8.12.42	
12(P) A.F.U.	19 O.T.U.	9.3.43.	
19 OTU	1661 CU	24/5/43 14/7/43	
1661 Con Unit	83 Sqd.	9/7/43.	
83 SQUAD	DISCHARGED FROM THE ROYAL CANADIAN AIR FORCE ON BEING APPOINTED TO COMMISSIONED RANK wef 13.6.43 AUTHY AM A569311/43/SM(P)(3) 23/8/43		

Stiles' movements with RCAF until his appointment to RAF on 13 June 1943

EXHUMATION REPORT

2. LANDKREIS BLANKENBURG

No. - RANK - NAME - UNIT -

CEMETERY OR PLACE OF BURIAL Town Cemetery BLANKENBURG, M.52/D.2259
(Map reference if isolated)

PLOT 19A ROW 1 GRAVE (Collective) 2/8

DESCRIPTION OF BODY: Smashed and decomposed, few remains.

HEIGHT:
(short, medium, tall)

BUILD
(thin, broad, etc.)

HAIR:

TEETH:
(Use chart if man might be Dominion personnel)

	LEFT								RIGHT								
	1	2	3	4	5	6	7	8	8	7	6	5	4	3	2	1	Upper
	1	2	3	4	5	6	7	8	8	7	6	5	4	3	2	1	Lower

FINGERS AND HANDS:

IDENTITY DISC:
(or identifying articles)

DOCUMENTS OR LETTERS: OR RELICS:

CLOTHING:

TUNIC R.A.F. B/D.

TROUSERS

SHIRT R.C.A.F. other ranks issue shirt, laundry mark P056.

UNDERWEAR Issue underpants

SWEATER White flying

SOCKS

BOOTS

MISCELLANEOUS

EQUIPMENT: Electrically heated flying suit.

DATE OF DEATH: 2/3.1.44

CROSS SHOWS: None

CEMETERY RECORD: None

REMARKS: Reburied at British Military Cemetery HEERSTRASSE, BERLIN
Plot: VI Row: A Grave: 18

DATE EXHUMED 1.7.47 EXHUMATION DONE BY Capt. J.H.M. LOWENSTEIN

R.A.F. OFFICER WITNESSING F/O R.P. HUNTER

PSS (B) 4509/10m/5.47

Stiles' Exhumation Report dated 1 July 1947

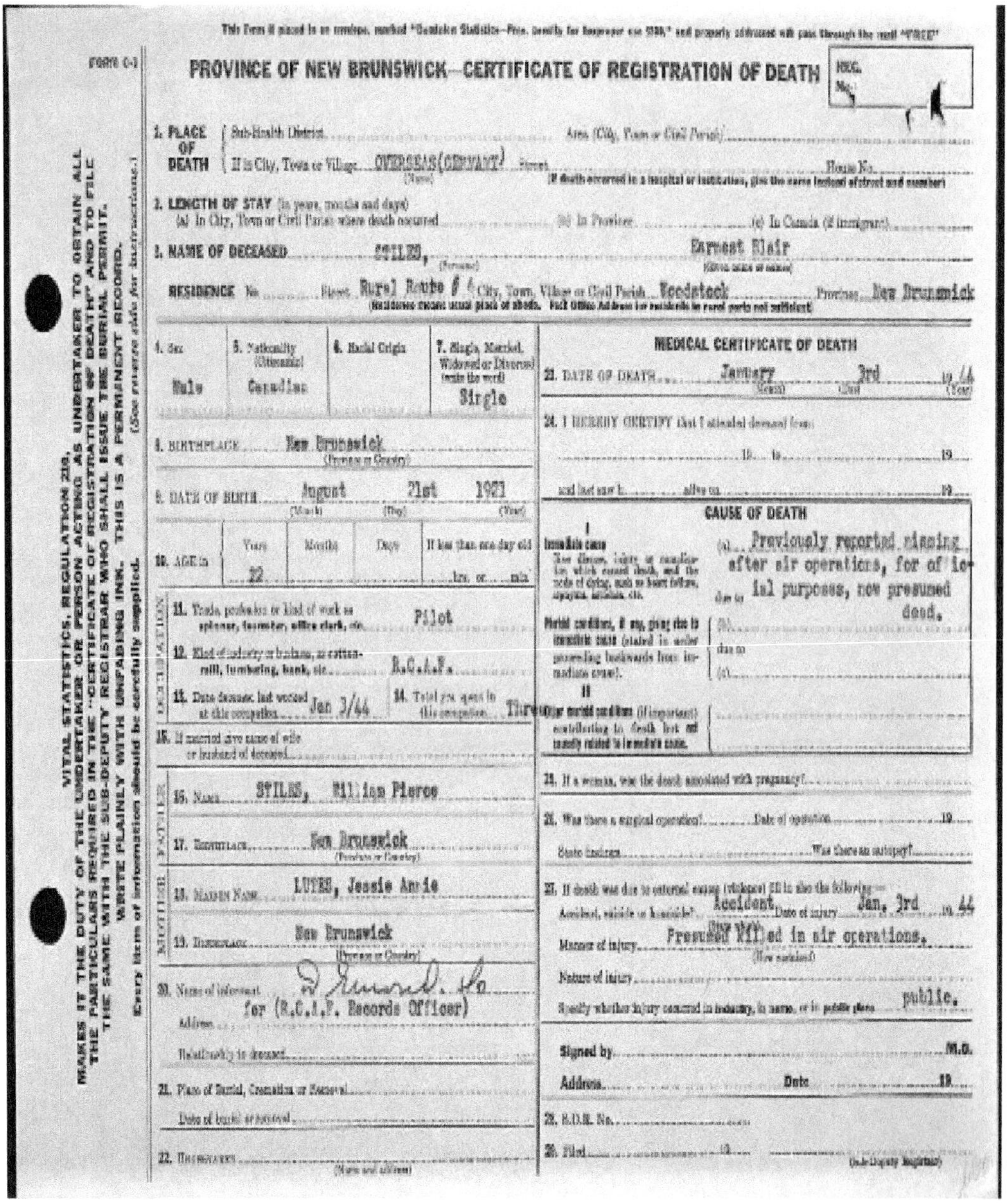

FORM C-1

VITAL STATISTICS, REGULATION 219, MAKES IT THE DUTY OF THE UNDERTAKER OR PERSON ACTING AS UNDERTAKER TO OBTAIN ALL THE PARTICULARS REQUIRED IN THE "CERTIFICATE OF REGISTRATION OF DEATH" AND TO FILE THE SAME WITH THE SUB-DEPUTY REGISTRAR WHO SHALL ISSUE THE BURIAL PERMIT. WRITE PLAINLY WITH UNFADING INK. THIS IS A PERMANENT RECORD. Every item of information should be carefully supplied. (See reverse side for instructions.)

PROVINCE OF NEW BRUNSWICK—CERTIFICATE OF REGISTRATION OF DEATH

REG. No.

1. PLACE OF DEATH — Sub-Health District; Area (City, Town or Civil Parish); If in City, Town or Village: OVERSEAS (GERMANY); Street; House No.

2. LENGTH OF STAY (in years, months and days) (a) In City, Town or Civil Parish where death occurred; (b) In Province; (c) In Canada (if immigrant)

3. NAME OF DECEASED: STILES, (Surname) Earnest Blair (Given name or names)

RESIDENCE: Street: Rural Route # 4; City, Town, Village or Civil Parish: Woodstock; Province: New Brunswick

4. Sex: Male
5. Nationality (Citizenship): Canadian
6. Racial Origin:
7. Single, Married, Widowed or Divorced (write the word): Single
8. BIRTHPLACE: New Brunswick (Province or Country)
9. DATE OF BIRTH: August (Month) 21st (Day) 1921 (Year)
10. AGE in Years: 22
11. Trade, profession or kind of work: Pilot
12. Kind of industry or business: R.C.A.F.
13. Date deceased last worked at this occupation: Jan 3/44
14. Total yrs. spent in this occupation: Three
15. If married give name of wife or husband of deceased:

FATHER
16. Name: STILES, William Pierce
17. Birthplace: New Brunswick (Province or Country)

MOTHER
18. Maiden Name: LUTES, Jessie Annie
19. Birthplace: New Brunswick (Province or Country)

20. Name of informant: D. [signature] for (R.C.A.F. Records Officer)
Address:
Relationship to deceased:
21. Place of Burial, Cremation or Removal:
Date of burial or removal:
22. Undertaker: (Name and address)

MEDICAL CERTIFICATE OF DEATH

23. DATE OF DEATH: January (Month) 3rd (Day) 19 44 (Year)

24. I HEREBY CERTIFY that I attended deceased from 19 to 19, and last saw h... alive on 19

CAUSE OF DEATH

I Immediate cause: (a) Previously reported missing after air operations, for official purposes, now presumed dead.

II Other morbid conditions (if important) contributing to death but not causally related to immediate cause.

25. If a woman, was the death associated with pregnancy?

26. Was there a surgical operation? Date of operation 19. State findings. Was there an autopsy?

27. If death was due to external causes (violence) fill in also the following — Accident, suicide or homicide? Accident. Date of injury: Jan. 3rd 19 44. Manner of injury: Presumed killed in air operations. (How sustained) Nature of injury: Specify whether injury occurred in industry, in home, or in public place: public.

Signed by M.D.
Address. Date 19.
28. S.D.R. No.
29. Filed 19 (Sub-Deputy Registrar)

Registration of Stiles' death with Province of New Brunswick, Canada

TRAYNOR - All letters and documents courtesy of the Traynor family

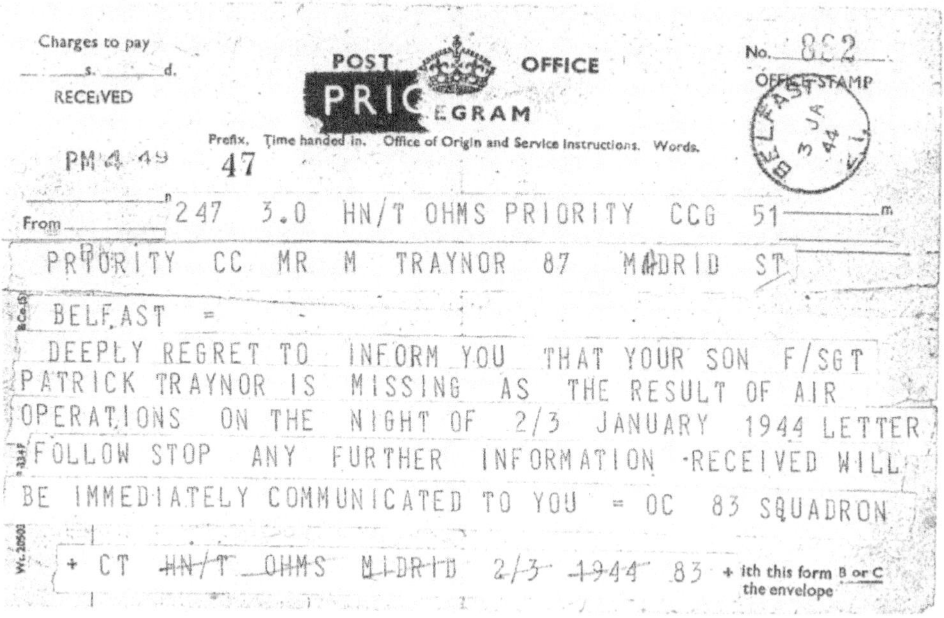
Charges to pay
s. d.
RECEIVED
POST OFFICE
PRIC EGRAM
No. 862
OFFICE STAMP
BELFAST 3 JA 44
Prefix. Time handed in. Office of Origin and Service Instructions. Words.
PM 4 49 47
From 247 3.0 HN/T OHMS PRIORITY CCG 51
PRIORITY CC MR M TRAYNOR 87 MADRID ST
BELFAST =
DEEPLY REGRET TO INFORM YOU THAT YOUR SON F/SGT
PATRICK TRAYNOR IS MISSING AS THE RESULT OF AIR
OPERATIONS ON THE NIGHT OF 2/3 JANUARY 1944 LETTER
FOLLOW STOP ANY FURTHER INFORMATION RECEIVED WILL
BE IMMEDIATELY COMMUNICATED TO YOU = OC 83 SQUADRON
+ CT HN/T OHMS MADRID 2/3 1944 83 + ith this form B or C the envelope

Telegram dated 3 January 1944 – the day of the crash - to Patrick's father informing that his son was missing

From: Group Captain L. E. Jarman D.F.C.

Royal Air Force Station,

Wyton, Huntingdonshire.

Ref: WY/CA/101/11/P2

4th January, 1944

Dear Mr Traynor.

I am writing to express my sympathy in your anxiety over your son who was reported missing on the 2nd January, 1944.

Your son's aircraft was engaged in an important mission against the enemy, but we are not in possession of any details of the events leading up to the failure of the aircraft to return to the base, and very often it takes some while for any definite news to reach us.

Experience up to the present has shown that quite a fair proportion of our flying personnel who are reported missing in operations against the enemy have managed to make a safe descent by parachute or in the aircraft itself. Therefore there must be some hope that your son is safe and a prisoner in enemy hands.

Your son was well reported on by his Squadron Commander, and I am sure that he and his companions gave a very good account of themselves under whatever circumstances prevented them from bringing their aircraft back. I am indeed sorry to lose such first class men, and can only hope that they have been able to make a safe landing.

Please accept my sincere sympathy in your anxiety, and let me know if there is any way in which I can help.

Yours sincerely

L E Jarman

M. Traynor Esq.,
87 Madrid Street,
Belfast,
Northern Ireland.

Letter from Group Captain Jarman DFC to Traynor's father dated 4 January 1944

No.83 Squadron,
Royal Air Force,
Wyton,
Huntingdon.

Reference:-
83S/601/256/P.1.

5th January 1944.

Dear Traynor,

Please accept my deep sympathy and that of the squadron over the news that your son, F/Sgt. Traynor failed to return from an operational flight. He was the Flight Engineer of an aircraft detailed to carry out an attack on Berlin on the night of the 2nd/3rd January 1944, and since leaving base nothing further has been heard of them.

It is to be hoped that they may have had an opportunity of baling out or making a forced landing in enemy territory, and if this is the case any further news must now come from the British Red Cross Society, the address of which I am enclosing, together with a list of addresses of next of kin of the other members of the crew in case you wish to communicate with them.

Your son had carried out many operational flights, and although he had only been with this squadron since the 16th December 1943 had shown a great keenness to operate. His loss will be keenly felt. Should there be any further news, I promise to let you know immediately.

Yours Sincerely

Deane.

Wing Commander, Commanding,
No.83 Squadron, R.A.F.

Mr H. Traynor,
87 Madrid Street,
Belfast,
Northern Ireland.

Letter from Wing Commander, Commanding, RAF Wyton to Traynor's father dated 5 January 1944

Gerrard 9234.

Casualty Branch,
77, Oxford Street,
London, W.1.

P.412291/1/44/P.4.A.2.B.

9 January, 1944.

Sir,

I am commanded by the Air Council to express to you their great regret on learning that your son, Flight Sergeant Patrick Traynor, Royal Air Force, is missing as the result of air operations on the night of 2nd/3rd January, 1944, when a Lancaster aircraft in which he was flying as flight engineer set out for action over Berlin and was not heard from again.

This does not necessarily mean that he is killed or wounded, and if he is a prisoner of war he should be able to communicate with you in due course. Meanwhile enquiries are being made through the International Red Cross Committee and as soon as any definite news is received you will be at once informed.

If any information regarding your son is received by you from any source you are requested to be kind enough to communicate it immediately to the Air Ministry.

The Air Council desire me to convey to you their sympathy in your present anxiety.

I am, Sir,
Your obedient Servant,

Charles Evans.

H. Traynor, Esq.,
87, Madrid Street,
Belfast,

Letter from RAF Casualty Branch to Traynor's father dated 9 January 1944

Committee of Adjustment,

Royal Air Force Station,

Wyton, Huntingdonshire.

Ref: WY/CA/201/15/P3

8th January, 1944

Dear Mr. Traynor,

As the officer supervising the disposal of your son's effects, may I be permitted to offer you my sincere sympathy.

In accordance with Air Ministry instructions his efffects assembled at this Station will shortly be forwarded to the Standing Committee of Adjustment, Central Depository, R.A.F. Colnbrook, Slough, Bucks., who will communicate with you at their earliest opportunity, and to whom all future correspondence should be addressed. His effects, however, cannot be released until the requirements of the Regimental Debts Act have been complied with.

A civilian clothing book, A.527549, holders registration number UAJD/903/2, which was found amongst F/Sgt. Traynor's effects, has been forwarded to Air Ministry, Dept. Accounts 13, Worcester, for their attention.

Yours sincerely,

Committee of Adjustment
R.A.F. Station, Wyton, Hunts.

M. Traynor Esq.,
87 Madrid Street,
Belfast, Northern Ireland.

Letter from Committee of Adjustment RAF Wyton to Traynor's father dated 8 January 1944

WAR ORGANISATION
OF THE
BRITISH RED CROSS SOCIETY and ORDER OF ST. JOHN OF JERUSALEM

RAF/A.2.

President :
HER MAJESTY THE QUEEN

Grand Prior :
H.R.H. THE DUKE OF GLOUCESTER, K.G.

WOUNDED, MISSING AND RELATIVES DEPARTMENT

Chairman : THE DOWAGER LADY AMPTHILL, C.I., G.B.E.

Telephone No.
SLOANE 9696

In replying please quote reference
PB/DL
RAF/L.21026

7 BELGRAVE SQUARE,
LONDON, S.W.1

18th January, 1944.

Dear Mrs. Traynor,

We have received your enquiry in which you ask for news of your son, Flight Sergeant P. Traynor, No.614985, Royal Air Force.

We are so sorry to tell you that no information has been received about him up to the present, but all possible enquiries are being made. Any news which may be forthcoming from the International Red Cross Committee at Geneva or from any other source, will be passed to you immediately. If, however, you are the registered next-of-kin, your first notification will come from the Air Ministry.

Yours sincerely,

Margaret Ampthill

Chairman.

Mrs. Traynor,
87 Madrid Street,
Belfast, N.I.

Letter from British Red Cross Society/Order of St John of Jerusalem to Traynor's mother dated 18 January 1944

TELEPHONE: GERRARD 9234
Extn. 3802

Any communications on the subject of this letter should be addressed to:—
THE UNDER SECRETARY OF STATE,
and the following number quoted:— P. 412291/1/44/P.4. Cas. B. 4.
Your Ref. ....

AIR MINISTRY
(Casualty Branch),
73, OXFORD STREET,
W.1.

28th January 1944.

Sir,

I am directed to refer to your letter dated 19th January 1944, regarding your son, No. 614985 Flight Sergeant P. Traynor, Royal Air Force.

I am to state, with deep regret, that no news has as yet been received of your son or any of the other members of his crew. I am to assure you that enquiries are being made of all possible sources and should any news be received of your son or his crew it will be passed to you without delay.

In writing this, I am to add an expression of the sincere sympathy of the Department with you in your anxiety.

I am, Sir,
Your obedient Servant,

E Cowan

for Director of Personal Services.

M. Traynor Esq.,
87 Madrid Street,
Belfast,
NORTHERN IRELAND.

Letter dated 28 January 1944 from Air Ministry Personal Service to Traynor's father

TELEPHONE: GERRARD 9234
Extn. 3802

Any communications on the subject of this letter should be addressed to:—
THE UNDER SECRETARY OF STATE,
and the following number quoted:— P.412291/1/44/P.4.Cas.B.4.
Your Ref. ....

AIR MINISTRY
(Casualty Branch),
73, OXFORD STREET,
W.1.

22nd February, 1944.

Sir,

I am directed to refer to this Department's letter dated the 9th January, 1944 notifying you that your son, No.614985 Flight Sergeant P. Traynor, Royal Air Force, was reported missing as the result of air operations on the night of the 2nd/3rd January, 1944 and to inform you, with deep regret, that a report has been received from the International Red Cross Committee, quoting German information, stating that Pilot Officer D.C.J. McKendry, Flying Officer I.G. Allan and five unknown members of the crew of this Lancaster aircraft lost their lives on the 3rd January, 1944.

Although it would appear from this report that the whole of the crew, which consisted of seven members, has been accounted for, no action to reclassify those referred to as 'unknown' will be taken until confirmatory evidence of death is received, or until, in the absence of such evidence it becomes necessary, owing to lapse of time, to presume, for official purposes, that death has occurred. A further notification would be sent you when this action was about to be taken.

In conveying the above information I am to extend to you the Department's very deep sympathy in your grave anxiety.

I am, Sir,
Your obedient Servant,

Jordan

for Director of Personal Services.

M. Traynor Esq.,
87 Madrid Street,
Belfast,
Northern Ireland.

Letter from Air Ministry Casualty Branch to Patrick's father informing him of indications that Traynor may have lost his life dated 22 February 1944

Telephone No:-
COLNBROOK 231/232/233.

In reply please quote
reference:-
CD/FV.43828.

Central Depository,
Royal Air Force,
Colnbrook,
Slough, Bucks.

8th February, 1944.

614985 F/Sgt. Traynor P.

Dear Sir,

The personal effects of the above named as listed on the attached inventory, have been received from the Unit, and are held at the Central Depository in safe custody.

Should you desire these effects to be sent to you and will kindly return to this office, duly signed and witnessed, the enclosed form of indemnity, arrangements will be made accordingly. A prepaid addressed label is enclosed for your reply.

May I be permitted to express my sympathy with you in this period of anxiety.

Yours faithfully,

Squadron Leader, Commanding,
R.A.F. Central Depository.

M. Traynor Esq.,
87, Madrid Street,
Belfast,
N. Ireland.

Letter dated 8 February 1944 from Central Depository, RAF Colnbrook to Traynor's father

WAR ORGANISATION
OF THE
BRITISH RED CROSS SOCIETY and ORDER OF ST. JOHN OF JERUSALEM

President: HER MAJESTY THE QUEEN | *Grand Prior:* H.R.H. THE DUKE OF GLOUCESTER, K.G.

WOUNDED, MISSING AND RELATIVES DEPARTMENT

Chairman: THE DOWAGER LADY AMPTHILL, C.I., G.B.E.

Telephone No. SLOANE 9696

In replying please quote reference: S/MFE/RAF/C.10489

7 BELGRAVE SQUARE,
LONDON, S.W.1

22nd February, 1944.

Dear Mrs. Traynor,

We very much regret to have to tell you that no information has come through attached to the name of your son, Flight Sergeant P. Traynor, No.614985, although full enquiries are being made on your behalf. We feel it is only right however, that you should be informed of the grievous report which has reached us through the International Red Cross Committee at Geneva, concerning the crew of which your son was a member, for although the information which this contains can but add most deeply to your already great anxiety, we believe that you would not wish it to be withheld.

A telegram from the Organisation at Geneva reports that according to the official German Authorities Pilot Officer D.C.J. McKendry and Flying Officer I.G. Allan lost their lives on the 3rd January, 1944 and also five airmen whose identity it has not yet been possible to establish. On receipt of this tragic news the Air Ministry has posted the above two named airmen as "Missing, believed Killed in Action", but we fear that until further information is forthcoming, no official action can be taken about the other five airmen. Therefore, your son, and the four remaining members of the crew must still remain classified as "Missing".

P.T.O.

-2-

We realise what this report will mean to you, and we wish you to know that every effort is being made in order to clarify this distressing situation. Please understand that whenever further information comes to light you will be notified immediately, and we ask you to accept meanwhile our sympathy in your suspense.

Yours sincerely,

Margaret Ampthill
pp

Chairman.

Mrs. Traynor,
87, Madrid Street,
Belfast, N.I.

Letter, written on very thin paper, dated 22 February 1944 from British Red Cross to Traynor's mother informing her that, from German records, information appeared to confirm the deaths of all JB453 crew

Telephone No:-
Colnbrook 231/232/233.

In reply please
quote reference:-
CD/FV-43828.

Central Depository,
Royal Air Force,
Colnbrook,
Slough, Bucks.

24th. February. 1944.

614985. F/Sgt. Traynor, P.

Dear Sir,

I thank you for returning the Form of Indemnity duly signed and would inform you that the effects of the above named will be forwarded to you as soon as possible.

I will, of course, advise you of the actual date of despatch.

Yours faithfully,

W. C. Warden W/O

Squadron Leader, Commanding,
R.A.F. Central Depository.

M. Traynor, Esq.,
87 Madrid Street,
Belfast.
N. Ireland.

Letter dated 24 February 1944 from Central Depository, RAF Colnbrook to Traynor's father

No.83 Squadron,
Royal Air Force,
Wyton,
Huntingdon.

Reference:-
83S/601/256/P.1.

29th February 1944.

Dear Mr Traynor,

I have much pleasure in enclosing herewith memento of an attack on Dusseldorf in which your son took part. This was received from your son's previous unit, and no doubt you would be glad to have it for safe keeping.

Up to the time of writing no further news has been received in respect of your son or any member of his crew, but you can rest assured that immediate notification will be made to you in the event of any news being received.

Yours sincerely,

Wing Commander, Commanding,
No.83 Squadron, R.A.F.

Mr M. Traynor,
87 Madrid Street,
Belfast,
Northern Ireland.

Letter from Wing Commander, Commanding, 83 Squadron, RAF Wyton to Traynor's father dated 29 February 1944

In May 1944, 4 months after the crash, Traynor's mother received a letter from the mother, in South Africa, of navigator Denis McKendry, Typed transcript is included after the letter.

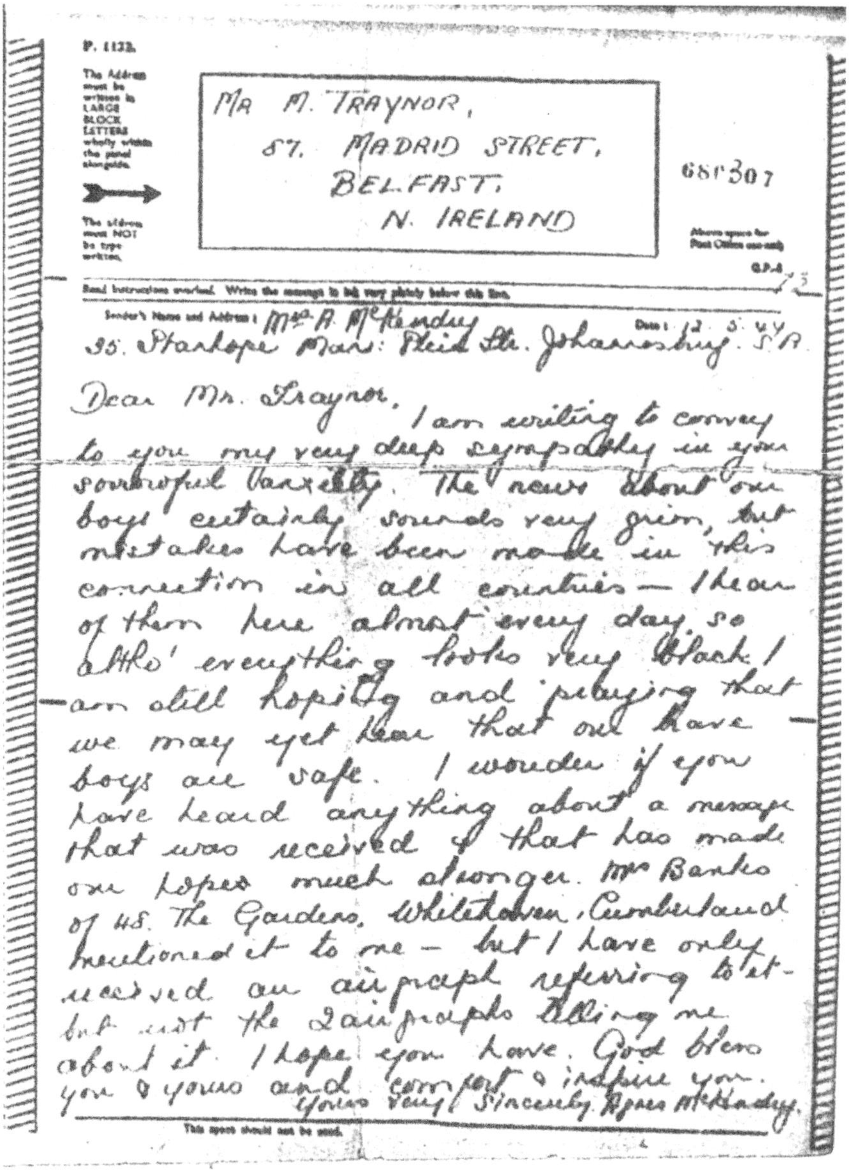
P. 1132.

MR M. TRAYNOR,
57. MADRID STREET,
BELFAST,
N. IRELAND

68P307

Sender's Name and Address: Mrs A. McKendry
35. Stanhope Mans: Pleid Str. Johannesburg. S.A.
Date: 12. 5. 44

Dear Mrs. Traynor,
I am writing to convey to you my very deep sympathy in your sorrowful anxiety. The news about our boys certainly sounds very grim, but mistakes have been made in this connection in all countries – I hear of them here almost every day so altho' everything looks very black I am still hoping and praying that we may yet hear that our brave boys are safe. I wonder if you have heard anything about a message that was received & that has made our hopes much stronger. Mrs Banks of 45. The Gardens, Whitehaven, Cumberland mentioned it to me – but I have only received an airgraph referring to it – but not the 2 airgraphs telling me about it. I hope you have. God bless you & yours and comfort & inspire you.
Yours very sincerely, Agnes McKendry.

This space should not be used.

Mrs M Traynor

87 Madrid Street

Belfast

N. Ireland

12/5/44

From Mrs A McKendry, 32 Stanhope Mansions, Plein Street, Johannesburg SA

Dear Mrs Traynor,

I am writing to convey to you my very deep sympathy in your sorrowful anxiety. The news about our boys certainly sounds very grim but mistakes have been made in this connection in all countries. I hear about them every day so altho' things look very black I am hoping and praying that we may hear yet that our boys are safe. I wonder if you have heard anything about a message that was received and that has made ones hopes much stronger. Mrs Banks of 48 The Gardens, Whitehaven, Cumberland mentioned it to me, but I have only received an air graph referring to it but not the 2 air graphs telling me about it. I hope you have.

God bless you and yours and comfort and inspire you.

Yours very sincerely

Agnes McKendry

Tel. No.
GERRARD 9234, Ext. ....

Correspondence on the subject of this letter should be addressed to
THE UNDER-SECRETARY OF STATE,
AIR MINISTRY (P.4(Cas.)),
and should quote the reference
P.412291/1/P.4.(B.6.)

Your Ref. ....

AIR MINISTRY,
73-77, OXFORD STREET,
LONDON, W.I.

18 October 1944

Sir,

I am directed to refer to this Department's letter of the 7th September 1944, and to request that you will be good enough formally to confirm that you have received no evidence of the survival of your son, 614985 Flight Sergeant P. Traynor.

I am to explain that this confirmation is necessary to enable the Department to proceed with the presumption of death for official purposes, to facilitate the settlement of his service estate and, if any personal effects are held in Air Force custody, to permit of their release.

Presumption of death does not in any way imply the cessation of enquiries by the International Red Cross Committee and I am to assure you that should any news become available it will be at once conveyed to you.

An addressed label, which need not be stamped, is enclosed for your reply.

I am,
Sir,
Your obedient Servant,

for Director of Personal Services.

M. Traynor Esq.,
87 Madrid Street,
Belfast,
NORTHERN IRELAND.

Letter from Air Ministry Personal Services to Traynor's father dated 18 October 1944

Telephone : Worcester 3411.

Extn................

Any communications on the subject of this letter should be addressed to :—
THE UNDER SECRETARY OF STATE,
and the following number quoted :—

FF.316434/44/Accts.13.

AIR MINISTRY,
WHITTINGTON ROAD,
WORCESTER.

[illegible] May, 1945.

Sir,

The late Flight Sergeant P. Traynor.

I am directed to inform you that the out-turn of the Service Estate of your son is as detailed hereunder:-

	£	s.	d.
Service Gratuity	6	0	0
Balance of pay and allowances....................	15	14	9
Service Post War Credit	18	6	0
Cash in effects	8	0	0
Refund of Income Tax on Service Emoluments ..	3	0	3
	£51	1	0

A Payable Order, therefore, for this amount in your favour is being forwarded to you under separate cover and should reach you in the course of the next few days.

I am, Sir,
Your obedient Servant,

for Director of Accounts.

M. Traynor, Esq.,
87, Madrid Street,
BELFAST.

Letter dated 23 May 1945 (after the end of the war in Europe) from Air Ministry Director of Accounts to Patrick's father. £51.00 in 1944 is the equivalent of just under £3000 in 2023

BNT

P.412291/44/S.14 Cas(a)
Ref. No........................

The ***Under Secretary of State for Air*** *presents his compliments to*
.............M. Traynor, Esq.,...........*and begs to forward herewith photographs*
of cross marking the grave of No....614985....., ...Flight Sergeant......... *(rank)*
........................Patrick.TRAYNOR........................ *(full name).*
These have been received from the Army Graves Service, who are responsible for the temporary marking of war graves.

Temporary crosses will be replaced in due course by permanent headstones to be erected by the Imperial War Graves Commission. Details of the inscription on the temporary cross will be carefully checked at that stage and any errors rectified before the permanent headstone is erected.

Air Ministry, London, S.W.1 *Date*.....22nd..August,..1949.

Notification from Under Secretary of State for Air dated 22 August 1949 regarding Traynor's grave at the British Military Cemetery in Berlin

With Loving Wishes

Loving Xmas Wishes.
Each day may joys awake,
Good Fortune be your guide
With all that goes to make
A happy Christmastide.
To Willie from
Mother with
Love X

Birthday and Christmas cards sent to Traynor from his mother whilst he was serving in the RAF

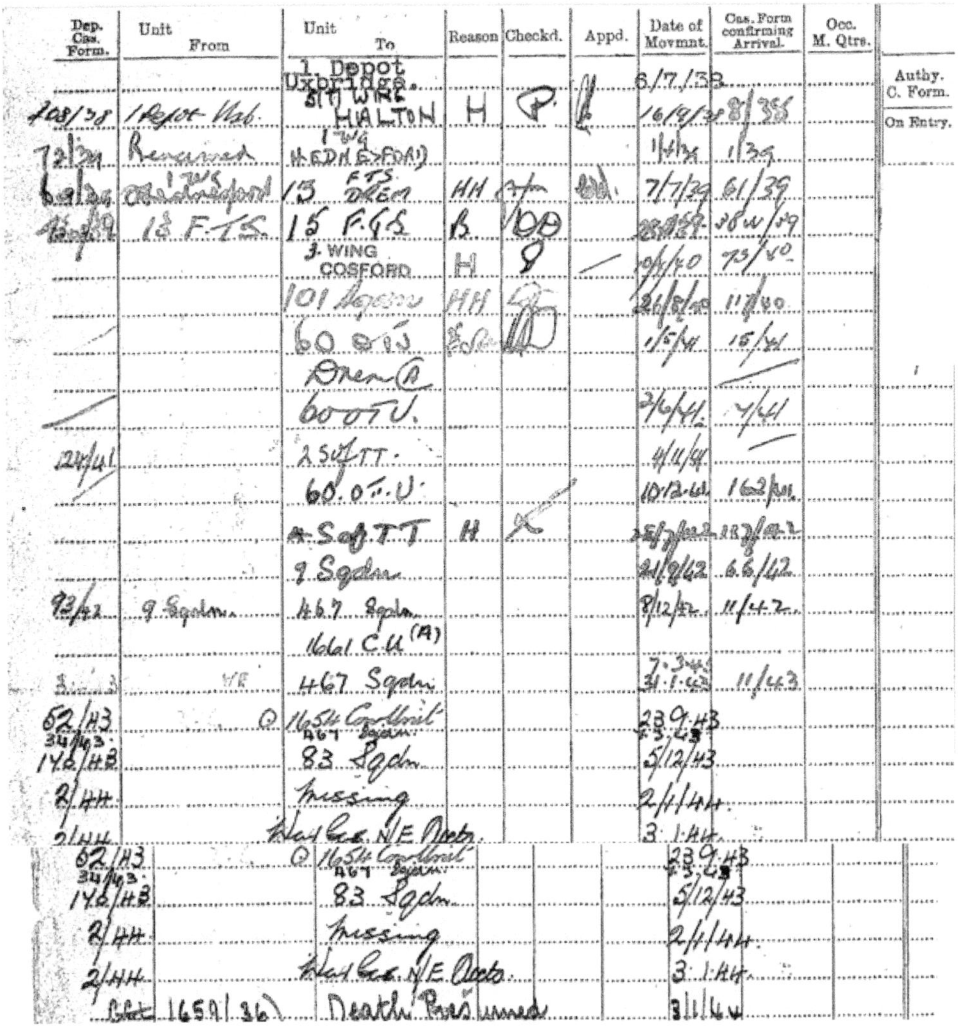

Dep. Cas. Form.	Unit From	Unit To	Reason	Checkd.	Appd.	Date of Movmnt.	Cas. Form confirming Arrival.	Occ. M. Qtrs.	Authy. C. Form. On Entry.
		1 Depot Uxbridge.				6/7/38			
108/38	1 Depot Uxb.	1(T) Wing HALTON	H	P.	[illegible]	16/9/38	8/38		
72/39	Remustered	1 Wg HEDNESFORD				1/1/39	1/39		
6/39	1 Wg Hednesford	13 FTS Drem	HH	[illegible]	[illegible]	7/7/39	61/39		
[illegible]	13 F.T.S.	15 F.T.S.	B.	[illegible]		[illegible]	38w/39		
		3 Wing Cosford	H	[illegible]		[illegible]/40	73/40		
		101 Sqdn	HH	[illegible]		26/8/40	11/40		
		60 OTU	[illegible]	[illegible]		1/5/41	15/41		
		Drem (A)							
		60 OTU.				2/6/41	7/41		
124/41		25 OTT.				4/11/41			
		60. O.T.U.				10/12/41	162/41		
		A. S of T.T	H	[illegible]		25/7/42	187/42		
		9 Sqdn				21/9/42	66/42		
93/42	9 Sqdn.	467 Sqdn				8/12/42	11/42		
		1661 C.U (A)							
[illegible]	[illegible]	467 Sqdn				7.3.43 31.1.43	11/43		
62/43		1654 Con Unit				23.9.43			
34/43		467 Sqdn				[illegible]			
146/43		83 Sqdn				5/12/43			
2/44		Missing				2/1/44			
2/44		War Cas. N/E Notn.				3.1.44			
62/43		1654 Con Unit				23.9.43			
34/43		467 Sqdn				[illegible]			
146/43		83 Sqdn				5/12/43			
2/44		Missing				2/1/44			
2/44		War Cas. N/E Notn.				3.1.44			
	Cert 1659/36	Death Presumed				3/11/44			

Traynor's Service Record 1938-1944

McKENDRY - All letters and documents courtesy of the McKendry family

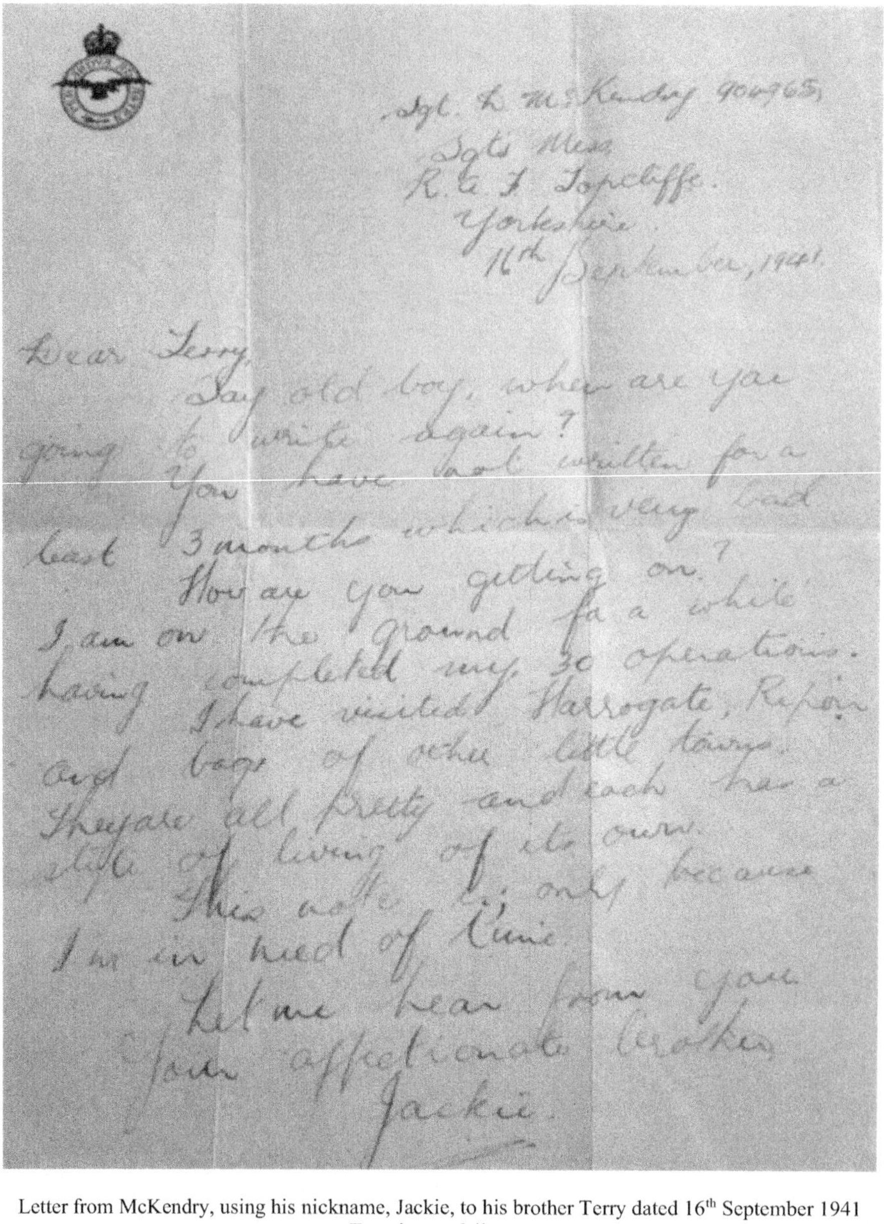

Sgt. L. McKendry 904965,
Sgts Mess
R.A.F. Topcliffe.
Yorkshire.
16th September, 1941.

Dear Terry,
Say old boy, when are you going to write again?
You have not written for a least 3 months which is very bad.
How are you getting on?
I am on the ground for a while having completed my 30 operations.
I have visited Harrogate, Ripon and bags of other little towns.
They are all pretty and each has a style of living of its own.
This note is only because I'm in need of time.
Let me hear from you
Your affectionate brother
Jackie.

Letter from McKendry, using his nickname, Jackie, to his brother Terry dated 16th September 1941
Typed copy follows.

Sgt. D McKendry

Sgt's Mess

RAF Topcliffe

Yorkshire

16th September 1941

Dear Terry

Say old boy, when are you going to write again? You have not written for at least 3 months which is very bad. How are you getting on? I am on the ground for a while having completed my 30 operations. I have visited Harrogate, Ripon and bags of little towns. They are all pretty and each has a style of living of its own.

This note is only because I'm in need of time.

Let me hear from you

Your affectionate brother

Jackie

DENIS CHARLES JAMES McKENDRY Deceased. Notice is hereby given that after the expiration of eight days APPLICATION will be made in the Principal Probate Registry of the High Court of Justice for the SEALING of the LETTERS of ADMINISTRATION of the personal estate of DENIS CHARLES JAMES McKENDRY late of Stanhope Mansions, Plein Street, Johannesburg, South Africa deceased granted by the Orange Free State Provincial Division of the Supreme Court of South Africa at Bloemfontein on the 14th day of February 1946.

25·10·1946

BIRCHAM & CO. Solicitors for Leonard Danvers Smith, of 100 Old Broad Street, London, E.C.2, the lawful Attorney of John Harrison McKendry, the Executor Dative.

Entry in South African press dated 25/10/1946

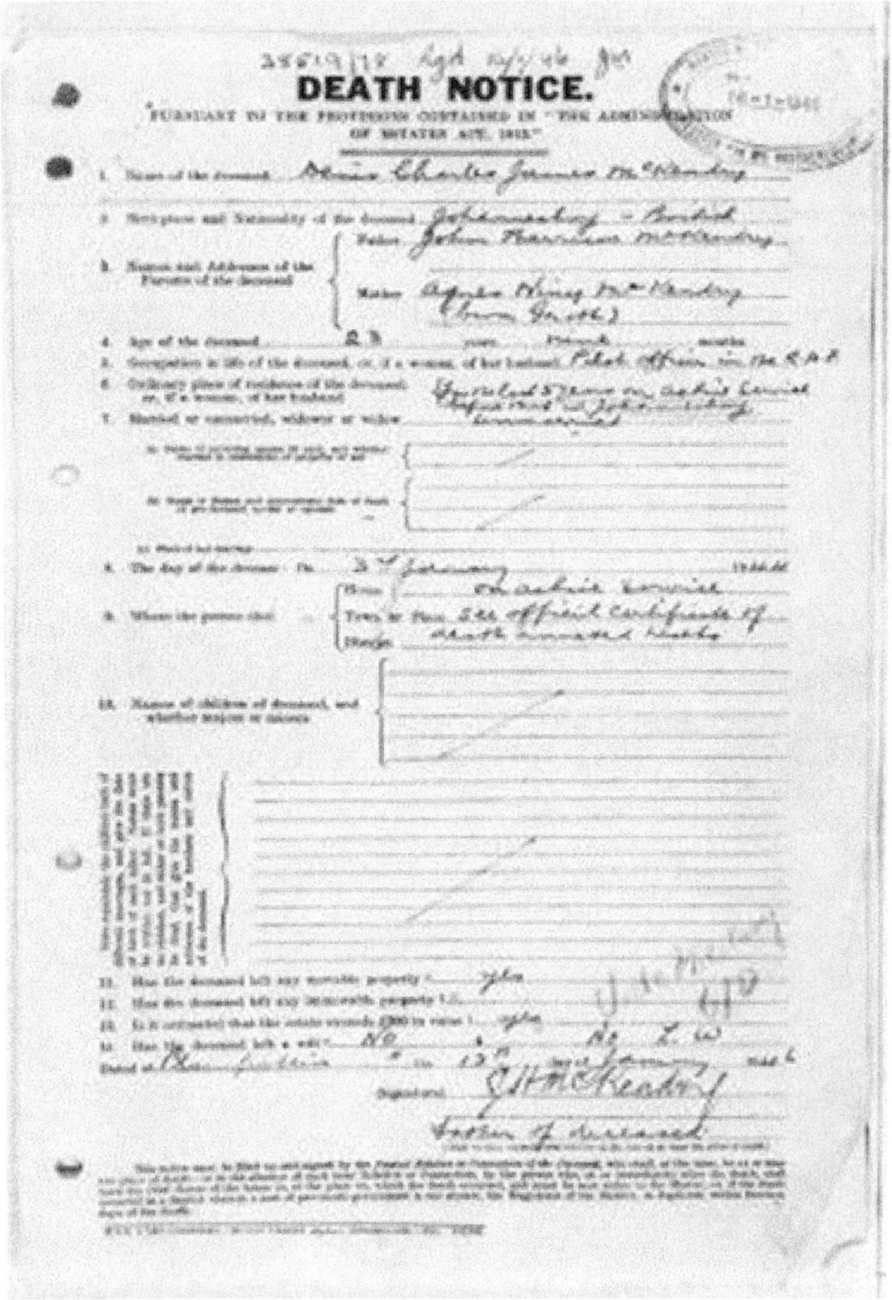
DEATH NOTICE.

McKendry's death registered in Johannesburg, South Africa

Memorial at Ely Cathedral

In the autumn of 1955, those families of Bomber Command crews who had lost their lives during World War II were sent letters by the Pathfinder Association inviting them to the formal unveiling of a memorial to No 8 Group Pathfinder Force to take place at Ely Cathedral on 6th November that year.

THE PATHFINDER ASSOCIATION
LTD.
115 & 116, MOUNT STREET, BERKELEY SQUARE,
LONDON, W.1

President: Dr. J. C. MacGown, D.F.C.
Vice-Presidents: G/Cpt. J. M. Birkin, D.S.O., O.B.E., D.F.C., A.F.C.; L. G. Johnson, D.F.C.

Telephones: GROsvenor 3382; MAYfair 5982 (Residential Annexe)
Patron: Air Vice-Marshal D. C. T. Bennett, C.B., C.B.E., D.S.O.

Secretary-General: G. A. Thorne, D.S.O., D.F.C.

Dear Sir or Madam,

Unveiling of Bomber Command Memorial
to Nos. 2, 3, 8 and 100 Groups —
Ely Cathedral – 6 NOV 1955

Although announcements have already been made in the national press the Council of the Pathfinder Association feel it their duty, to those of No. 8 Group Pathfinder Force Bomber Command whose names will appear in the Book of Remembrance which will be part of the Memorial in Ely Cathedral, to ensure that a personal notification regarding the unveiling of the Memorial is sent to their next-of-kin. The only addresses available are those appearing in the official records, but it is hoped that where they have been changed this communication will be forwarded.

The Memorial will be a stained-glass window with four lights or panels installed in the north side of the Nave. The right-centre light portrays St. George and the Dragon above the badge of No. 8 Group, which has just been approved by Her Majesty The Queen.

In the tracery at the top of the window are displayed the badges of the Royal Air Force, Royal New Zealand Air Force, and Bomber Command, together with the emblems of the various Allied Forces who fought with Bomber Command. At the bottom of the two centre lights is written "In honour and memory of the members of Nos. 2, 3, 8 and 100 Groups who served in the Ely district during the Second World War, 1939-45." The Rolls of Honour of each Group will be dedicated in the Cathedral during the Unveiling Ceremony and will be housed in a cabinet of light oak and glass below the window.

If you would like to be present at the unveiling ceremony in Ely Cathedral you should apply immediately to The Precentor, 32, High Street, Ely, Cambs., enclosing a stamped addressed envelope and mentioning this advice from The Pathfinder Association.

You will be interested to know that the Council of this Association has decided to prepare and install in a specially designed alcove in our premises at 115 Mount Street, London, a duplicate of the No. 8 Group Book of Remembrance which will be permanently on view, and to which relatives will be able to refer to particular entries, by arrangement with the Secretary. The cost of the duplicate Book of Remembrance will be met by private subscriptions from all those interested in the project.

Yours truly,

Alex Thorne

Secretary.

Stained glass memorial window at Ely Cathedral

CHAPTER 11

BOMBER COMMAND GROUNDCREWS

Shall we have safe return, or perish in this sky?

No moon tonight.

© Julie Wigley, *No Moon Tonight*

An extensive team of dedicated, skilled men on the ground was essential in keeping a Lancaster fully operational and airworthy. It would not be unusual for there to be upwards of 2000 personnel based on a wartime Bomber Command station, yet only around 10% would have been actual aircrew. Many more were required to prepare each Lancaster, and other aircraft, such that they were ready to take on that night's operation and to give respective flight crews the greatest confidence in the performance of the metal tube that would project them through the sky into enemy territory and, hopefully, back again. These ground crews, affectionately known as "erks", were highly respected and appreciated by flight crews, not least when the craft in which they were flying had been damaged as a result of enemy fire and was having to limp home.

Often exposed to the elements at dispersal points, conditions, especially through the winter, could be atrocious. Airfields are, by their very nature, based in open and little-sheltered areas of the countryside with scant respite against freezing temperatures, high winds, driving rain or heavy snow.

The hard work, efforts, and sheer determination of ground crews cannot be understated. Individual crews took huge pride in what they termed to be *their* aircraft, often joking with flight crews that they were merely "*borrowing*" the craft on the understanding they *"would not break it!"* Typically, a team of ground crews would be responsible for the maintenance and repair of a "Flight", normally between six and nine aircraft. Ideally, one crew would be responsible for one aircraft. However, the demands of war meant that, often, a ground crew would find themselves tending two, even three, aeroplanes.

It is difficult to imagine the thoughts running through the minds of ground crews as they watched *their* bombers fade into the night sky on take-off, not knowing if they would ever see men or machine again. They would be delighted to see them land, however crippled they might be, many hours later. Others would experience the intense sadness of loss once realisation set in that neither aircraft nor crew would not be returning. It was something they would never get used to.

The term "erks" is an old RAF nickname believed to have derived, during World War I, from the pronunciation, possibly of East London cockney origin, of aircraftsman as "airk". It was, and probably still is, used to describe any low or basic rank individual, especially a raw recruit. During World War II it was commonly used as a term of endearment for ground crews, who were proud to have that designation.

Those erks assigned to work on specific bombers would not have a fixed shift pattern, other than on paper. More, they would work as required, whenever it was necessary, day or night, sometimes both, and for however many hours it took, to ensure that *their* craft was fit for operations. Indeed, without these selfless groups of bodies, it is likely that Bomber Command would have very quickly ceased to have been a major force during the war. These lowly ranked "erks" were fundamental, but essential, elements to all airborne operations. The informal, and unauthorised, motto of erks was *"Ubendum – Wemendum!"*

Erks came in a variety of guises, ranging from fitters who were generally responsible for the engines and other mechanical parts of aircraft, to riggers – a legacy term from the days of World War I relating to wire-braced bi-planes – responsible for the airframe and related matters, and everything in between.

Preparations for operations would generally culminate with a flying test which would be carried out by the crew designated to fly that night's operation, in order to identify any last-minute glitches or snags.

Fuelling heavy bombers was often a balancing act between ensuring that the craft had sufficient fuel for the entire operation, including extra for unforeseen manoeuvres and change of flight paths, but at the same time making sure that, taking account of that night's bomb payload, the aircraft was not so heavy as to affect its ability to take off and achieve optimum performance. There were also many seemingly minor tasks jobs carried out by the ground crew which, while seeming menial, were absolutely essential. For instance, all plexiglass surfaces were highly polished. It would be easy, mid-operation with adrenalin running at maximum levels, for a gunner to mistake a speck of dirt for an enemy night fighter. On the other side of the coin, it could prove fatal to dismiss an approaching night fighter as a discolouration or dust spot. Anti-freezing fluid for the front and side cockpit windscreens was an absolute necessity, especially during the winter, at heights exceeding 20,000 feet. The fluid tank therefore had to be topped up and the pump checked. All lights had to be checked as well as checking emergency equipment that might determine whether some, or all, of the aircrew lived or died.

The starting of each engine was overseen by the ground crew Chief and the pilot. An erk would operate a starting battery in order for this to be achieved. The last task of the ground crew would be to remove the wheel chocks enabling the aircraft to join the taxying queue of operational bombers heading towards the runway and the dark, foreboding, skies of Europe.

Only then would the erks permit themselves the comparative luxury of a hot meal, sweetened tea, and broken sleep whilst they waited for the hours to pass before the cycle started once again, hoping – too often forlornly – that all of their bombers, and crews, would return. It was indeed a rarity for every aircraft that had, only a few hours previously taken off, to return safely. The faces of many aircrews that the erks had helped board their bomber would end up as little more than a memory of a bad dream, to be replaced by a new aircraft and crew – but who knew how long *they* would last?

Crews working on the ground can often be identified by the fact that they were *rarely* identified. Unsung heroes. And yet, night after night, the heavy bomber crews would put their total faith into the work that the ground crew, working around, and against, the clock, had carried out. History would dictate that individual flying officers, or squadrons, or battles, would be recorded and remembered. The names of ground crew, notwithstanding the crucial work that they undertook under the most stressful of conditions, would seldom roll off the tongue as easily.

CHAPTER 12

BOMBER COMMAND – A TYPICAL DAY

During 1943 there were over 50 Bomber Command stations based in the counties of eastern England primarily because of the flat topography, making it ideal for the operation of heavy bombers, together with the close proximity to enemy territory, just a short hop across the North Sea. Lincolnshire contained the lion's share of bases and became known as Bomber County. Many of these bases, after the end of World War II, were demolished ready for the land to be used for badly needed new housing estates. Others were sold off and the buildings used for industrial purposes. A small number, and RAF Wyton is a prime example, were retained and developed into modern, world class, RAF stations. If one looks carefully near to disused or developed airfields, one can often still find evidence of abandoned runways and control towers, their decaying reinforced concrete walls crumbling and frequently graffiti ridden. What one can never see, but can nonetheless often sense when standing alone in those empty, window-less, former centres of air control, are the wartime ghosts of yesteryear; the officers, the WAAFs, the technical geniuses of that period and more, all working towards a long term goal of victory, but more concerned in the immediacy of trying to ensure that all of

A typical disused and dilapidated World War II RAF control tower.

the bombers that had gone out on that night's operation, received the best possible ground and radio support giving them the greatest chance of returning unscathed. The reality, of course, was that many didn't.

At RAF Wyton, for 83 (Pathfinder) Squadron, the heavy bombing aircraft of choice was, of course, the Lancaster, with its powerful, and highly effective Merlin engines. The engines were the beating heart of these vast machines. Aeroplanes could continue to fly having sustained damage to many parts; wings, fuselage, radio, hydraulics; but without working engines they were crippled.

Every day would begin in the same way. Aircraft that had, luckily, returned from the previous night's mission were subject to a hive of activity; damaged engines replaced, bullet-ridden fuselage panels repaired; broken, and often bloodstained, Perspex or Plexiglass gunner position cowlings swapped for shiny new units. Some planes would have to remain grounded for several days before they would be declared fully airworthy once more. The operational life expectancy of a Lancaster crew member averaged only 40 hours flying time. Every one of them who attended a mission briefing wondered if they would ever see another one.

Whilst work was being carried out on repairing aircraft, groups of analytic specialists in the Photographic Section would pour over photographs taken from bomber aircraft, of the previous night's operation. It would, despite sometimes wild and inaccurate claims of success from debriefed crews, be their informed and collective judgements that would form comprehensive reports which would influence commanding officers as to whether targets, because of identified failures of a mission, should be revisited and retargeted that night, or whether the earlier operation was deemed to have been successful and new targets chosen.

Having rested and recovered, at least in part, from the previous night's mission, flight crews would check noticeboards to see if they were due to be operational again that night or not. Those whose names were on the list would be called to the briefing room during the afternoon when the intended enemy target or targets would be revealed.

RAF stations, by their very nature, occupied huge swathes of land. With some holding upwards of 3000 military and civilian personnel, they could fill 500 acres with ease. Getting around the base therefore provided its own challenges. The simple, but quintessential and ubiquitous, bicycle came into its own with many hundreds being utilised daily.

In the Briefing Room, once the formalities of acknowledging the presence of senior officers in the room, crews would sit, many taking copious notes for later reference. Cigarette smoke would cast a grey swirling fog that managed to find, and fill, every conceivable space. All eyes would be on the full-wall curtains behind which lay the map detailing that night's mission. As the curtain was drawn back, and the targets revealed, there would be some exclamations or groans from those seated but, by and large, the discipline drilled into them led them to stay silent and simply accept what they were looking at. In any event, they couldn't change it. Each operational briefing would be split into several parts and delivered simultaneously at each of the 50 or so squadron stations involved in that mission. Crews would be briefed upon the weather that was likely to be experienced that night over England, the sea, and across European nations along the agreed flight path. Bearing in mind that the Battle for Berlin began in the late autumn of 1943 and ran virtually nightly through the winter and into the spring of 1944, the obvious issues would be those of rain, snow, ice, and fog on the ground as well as the risks of icing up at altitude. Pilots and navigators in particular needed to be fully aware of what they could expect, when and where.

The Flying Control Officer at each airfield would then talk about his responsibility to ensure that the 40 or 50 aircraft under his control, through engine start-up and taxying, were all able to take off safely with split second timing without wasting their precious fuel. And all this to be achieved without any radio communications so as to avoid giving enemy listeners any clues about the forthcoming mission targets. Once airborne, the aircraft would join several hundred similar aircraft from other Squadrons to form the main bombing force.

Then would come the Intelligence Officer who would give useful information gained from a variety of sources; photographs, codebreakers, Special Operations Executives in the field, Resistance Groups, and informants. Location details where concentrated anti-aircraft flak could be expected would be briefed together with likely locations of enemy night fighters. The crews, each of which were likely to have been flying over Germany at least once, maybe twice, in the past week, would be armed with as much valuable and useful information as possible.

The Squadron Commander would then brief about the specific targets for that night, flight routes, alternative flight paths and the identification of targets. 83 Squadron would be responsible for dropping flares once the target had been positively identified. The main bombing force would then release their payloads to follow the agreed colour of the PFF flares. The colours would often be changed to minimise the chances of being misled by enemy decoy flares. Main force crews were additionally, for the same attempted deception reasons, instructed to bomb only on those agreed colours, not on any fires that might be seen. Given that there could be many hundreds of bombers all heading towards similar target areas, it was vital that precise altitudes, speed, and distances were maintained in order to minimise the risk of mid-air collisions. Notwithstanding this, such collisions periodically and inevitably occurred, as did aircraft being hit by bombs released from colleagues flying at a greater altitude.

Whilst the briefing was taking place, ordnance payloads would be transported to, and loaded onto, the aircraft, including 5,000lb and 10,000lb bombs together with incendiary bombs and those designed to either explode on or just before impact or where fuses were programmed to detonate hours, even days, after impact in order to maximise disruption to the enemy.

The Lancaster was an extremely versatile beast. It could even be modified to take the 22,000lb Grand Slam "earthquake" bomb, 25 feet long and 4 feet in diameter. Tractors pulling trolleys of bombs would trundle out to dispersal areas where they would be primed and prepared before being loaded by chain winch.

Fuel bowsers would pump sufficient fuel into the wing fuel tanks to ensure that each aircraft had enough for the entire mission plus extra to cater for unforeseen events. A Lancaster heading into the depths of Germany would use virtually the whole of its 2,100 gallons – over 9,500 litres – capacity during the operation.

Once the briefing was complete, the pilots would go away to brief the remaining members of their respective crews; radio operators, flight engineers and gunners.

Eventually, the crews drew their flying kit – parachutes, life jackets, whistles – and their personal flying gear. Even during this stressful pre-op period, military humour was commonplace. One of the favourites, often heard in supplies stores, related to parachutes,

"If it doesn't work, don't worry, sir. Just bring it back and we'll give you another one!"

A little over an hour remained until they were driven out to their aircraft which they boarded, carried out all of the necessary checks and prepared for take-off. Once in the air, the fully laden Lancaster would take over 40 minutes to reach its operating height of 20,000 to 25,000 feet.

It would be a minimum of another 6 hours before those lucky ones returned. The ground crews would await the return of each aircraft well into the early hours. The daily routine started over.

CHAPTER 13

LOCATING AND VISITING THE CRASH SITE

Establishing precisely where JB453 crashed was always going to be an important aspect of the story, but it was far from certain as to whether or not this could ever be positively ascertained. There are many websites dedicated to establishing where World War II aircraft perished, both in the UK and overseas. Many hours were expended going through these sites but nothing definitive was ever found.

Official papers indicated that the Lancaster had crashed at the base of the Harz mountains near to the town of Blankenburg, some 100 miles south-west of Berlin. Other sources spoke of the crew's initial burial place at Quedlinburg, described as being "close to the crash site", it being situated only 10 miles from Blankenburg but unfolding an area of approximately 80 square miles where the aircraft could have crashed.

Logically, and particularly because of the extremely detailed and accurate records that were kept by German authorities during the war, it seemed that enquiries made directly with local history and archive authorities in those towns might provide some answers. However, despite prolonged searches being made by staff in Mayors' offices and archivists in Blankenburg and Quedlinburg, it seemed that nothing positive would ever be forthcoming. It was clear that if this mystery were ever to be solved, more detailed information would be required.

Many crews' descendants, via Helen, had provided me with a great number of official documents and so I decided to once more trawl through them to see if any clues could be uncovered.

It was the family of pilot, Blair Stiles, who provided the answer. Amongst the vast number of papers they had sent was a copy of the RAF Investigation Report into the crash, compiled in July 1947 by the Berlin Detachment No.4 MR and EU RAF (Germany) then forwarded to the Air Ministry in London. It identified the Search Officer as Flying Officer R P Hunter. Rather an apt name for a searcher! More importantly, included in the report was a map reference of the crash site. There was no reason to suppose that this reference was anything other than fairly accurate.

The map reference shown for the crash site on the report was M52/D.2557 at a place called Timmenrode near Blankenburg. Therein lay the next challenge. Yes, I had a map reference but that was of scant use without being able to plot it on an actual map. I returned to the internet to see if I could discover even a little information. Quite quickly, I discovered that M52 was the number allocated to a War Office Army/Air map of the Halle region of Germany. A road atlas search revealed that, in that region, lay the towns of Blankenburg, Quedlinburg, and Timmenrode, a small village with a population of under 1500. I was on the right track!

Even so, I still needed a copy of the map which might reveal what the second part of the reference – D.2557 – meant. Were the four numbers search vectors, similar to six figure map references used by the Ordnance Survey office?

With few expectations, I set about searching online to see if anyone had a copy of the M52 map for sale, or at least one that I could refer to. Imagine my amazement when, within minutes, I found an original War Ministry copy for sale on the shopping site, Ebay. This was just too good to be true and I swiftly parted with £25.00 to secure it. It dropped through my letterbox a few days later.

The map was issued by the War Ministry in 1943 and is marked up as a first edition. It was a relatively large-scale map, 1:250000, or approximately 4 miles to 1 inch. Hopes of success escalated at the same rate as fears of failure.

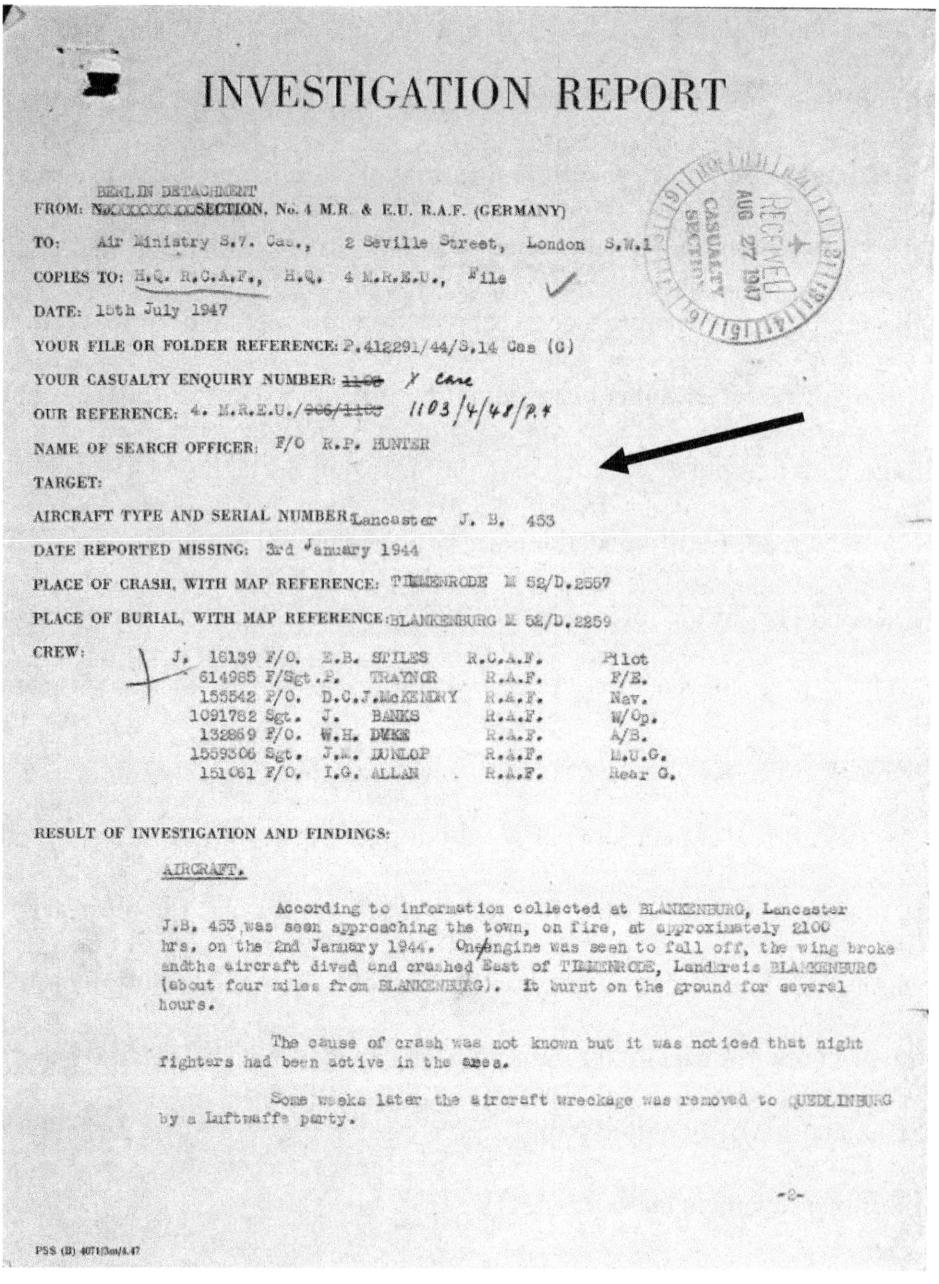

INVESTIGATION REPORT

FROM: ~~No. XXXXXXXXX~~ SECTION, No. 4 M.R. & E.U. R.A.F. (GERMANY) BERLIN DETACHMENT

TO: Air Ministry S.7. Cas., 2 Seville Street, London S.W.1

COPIES TO: H.Q. R.C.A.F., H.Q. 4 M.R.E.U., File ✓

DATE: 15th July 1947

YOUR FILE OR FOLDER REFERENCE: P.412291/44/S.14 Cas (C)

YOUR CASUALTY ENQUIRY NUMBER: ~~1103~~ X case

OUR REFERENCE: 4. M.R.E.U./~~906/1103~~ 1103/4/48/P.4

NAME OF SEARCH OFFICER: F/O R.P. HUNTER

TARGET:

AIRCRAFT TYPE AND SERIAL NUMBER: Lancaster J. B. 453

DATE REPORTED MISSING: 3rd January 1944

PLACE OF CRASH, WITH MAP REFERENCE: TIMMENRODE M 52/D.2557

PLACE OF BURIAL, WITH MAP REFERENCE: BLANKENBURG M 52/D.2259

CREW:

J. 18139	F/O.	E.B.	STILES	R.C.A.F.	Pilot
614985	F/Sgt.	P.	TRAYNOR	R.A.F.	F/E.
155542	P/O.	D.C.J.	McKENRY	R.A.F.	Nav.
1091782	Sgt.	J.	BANKS	R.A.F.	W/Op.
132869	F/O.	W.H.	DYKE	R.A.F.	A/B.
1559306	Sgt.	J.M.	DUNLOP	R.A.F.	M.U.G.
151061	F/O.	I.G.	ALLAN	R.A.F.	Rear G.

RESULT OF INVESTIGATION AND FINDINGS:

AIRCRAFT.

According to information collected at BLANKENBURG, Lancaster J.B. 453 was seen approaching the town, on fire, at approximately 2100 hrs. on the 2nd January 1944. One engine was seen to fall off, the wing broke andthe aircraft dived and crashed East of TIMMENRODE, Landkreis BLANKENBURG (about four miles from BLANKENBURG). It burnt on the ground for several hours.

The cause of crash was not known but it was noticed that night fighters had been active in the area.

Some weeks later the aircraft wreckage was removed to QUEDLINBURG by a Luftwaffe party.

-2-

PSS (B) 4071/3m/4.47

Copy of investigation report dated 15th July 1947

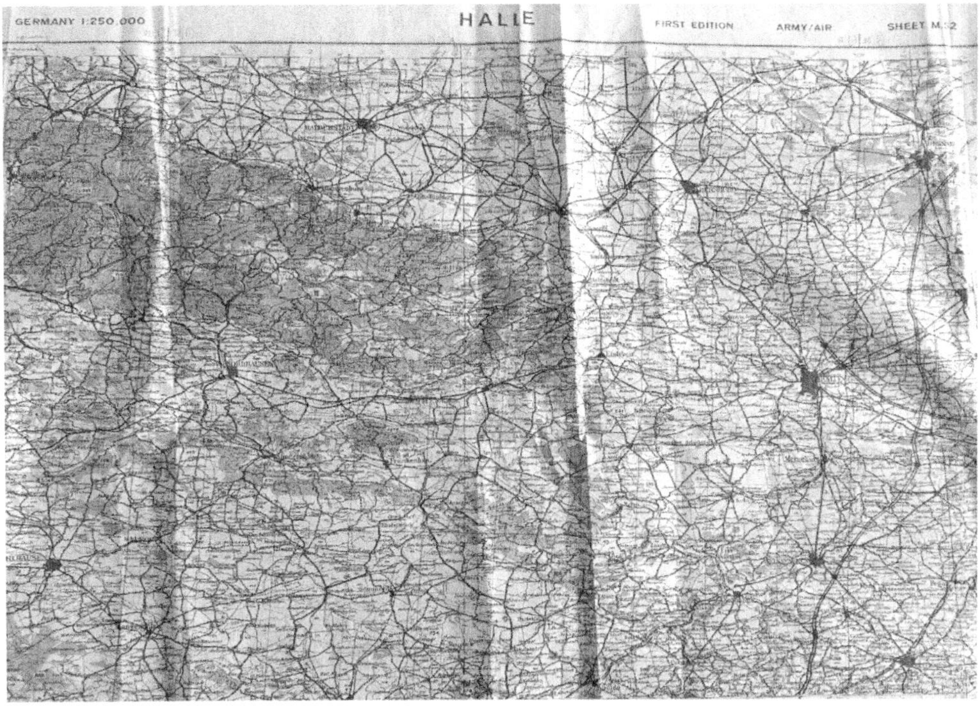

The map was divided into large square areas – C, D, E and H, J, K. D! I had found D. I was left with the numbers 2557. I found smaller squares, again seemingly identical to the system used by OS, marked up west to east and south to north. I pencilled in straight lines from 25 going across the map and 57 going down. I was overjoyed to see the crosshair lines intersect over Timmenrode. Assuming that the location information on the Investigation Report was accurate, and there were no reasons to believe that it was anything but, I had at last found the crash site.

Allowing for slight margins of error, both in the accuracy of the reference and of the map itself, JB453 had crashed within a few hundred metres of the centre of Timmenrode. The Investigation Report indicated that the aircraft had been seen approaching the town, on fire, before it lost an engine and crashed into the ground. The timing on the report is questionable – it states that the sighting of the crash was at 2100 hrs on 2nd January 1944. Bomber Command records confirm that JB453 did not take off from RAF Wyton until shortly before midnight on 2nd and would not have reached the target area until approximately 2.30am on 3rd.

The tiny village of Timmenrode today. Photo courtesy of the author

There is no question, however, that the aircraft seen to crash was JB453 as the report identifies the crew. German records confirm that the aeroplane was shot down at 0310hrs on 3rd, in all likelihood by Hauptmann Ney's JU88 night fighter, which aligns with all other written records. There is no explanation as to why the timing on the report is so wrong.

Incidentally, there was a lovely, albeit faded, pencil sketch of a US Army Jeep in the margins of the map I had acquired. I will never know who drew it, but it is yet another unique piece of wartime history.

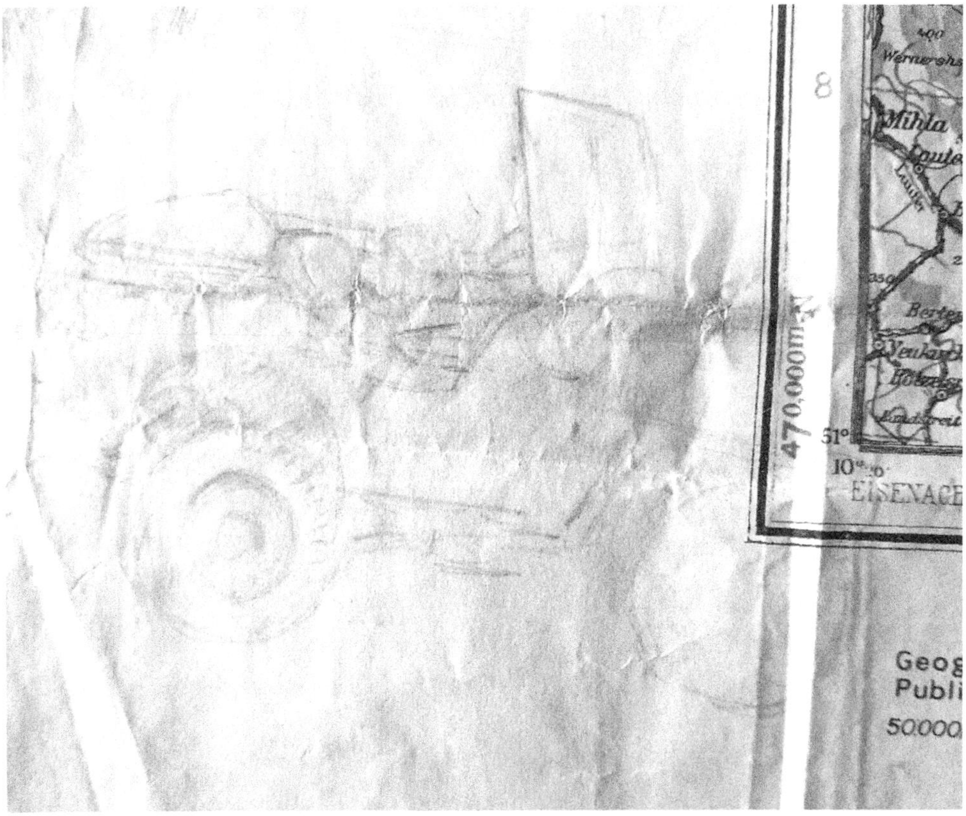

I sent details of the crash site to my contacts in Germany to see if any records existed, anecdotes or, indeed, any aircraft parts remained, which might provide additional evidence or verification. I heard nothing for several weeks but then, a reply was received from Lothar Wiegmann, Ortschronist (Archivist and Chronicler), in Timmenrode. I could not believe what I was reading after I had translated his message into English.

Lothar stated that it was known from eyewitness accounts at the time that on January 3rd, 1944, between three and four o'clock in the morning, a burning British four-engine bomber flew over the Teufelsmauer towards Timmenrode. The Teufelsmauer is a rock formation in the district of Harz in Saxony-Anhalt, a few hundred yards northwest of Timmenrode. The wreckage, together with seven bloody and partially charred bodies, was found nearby. The remains were placed in coffins in the local cemetery and transported to Blankenburg. The wreckage was removed by authorities and taken away. Apparently though, debris could still be found buried deeper in the soil.

Lothar also provided details of a journal, made at the time by a local church cleric, Pastor Müller, of these events:

"Monday, January 3 (1944) *early in the dark between 3:00 and 4:00 a.m. a burning four-engine enemy bomber flew over the Teufelsmauer toward our location. Below the train station to the left of the* (River) *Jordan, an engine was thrown into the field. The rest of the wreck made a turn to the right of the Jordan and then fell as well. At first no one could approach, since potentially exploding ammunition meant serious danger. Soon, however, the police and teams from Quedlinburg Airport were there and cordoned off. Municipal servant Hermann Görlitz guarded the ejected*

Lothar Wiegmann, Timmenrode archivist

engine. Two bloody and five badly charred corpses were driven to the local cemetery around noon by the farmer Karl Nabert, who was working near the crash site, and, after being designated by the master carpenter Louis Niewerth and gravedigger Karl Henneberg, after a few days to Blankenburg by the farmer Otto Rasehorn, where the funeral took place."

After expending so much time and effort in attempting to elicit information to definitively identify the crash site, not only was I now in possession of this information, but I also had details of named individuals who, in the hours immediately following the crash, played important roles in protecting the sites and recovering the remains of the crew.

In September 2023, together with my ever-supportive wife, Kay, I drove to Germany to meet with Lothar. I must make mention of a somewhat extraordinary moment that occurred as we drove eastwards along the A38 autobahn with the Harz mountains clearly visible on our left. I had, over a prolonged period, put together a playlist on the digital music service, Spotify. My, highly eclectic, list comprises over 2500 tracks. We had been listening to songs, set to random selection, for most of the journey. However, as we drove past the mountain range, a most surreal experience occurred. Through the car loudspeakers came the unmistakeable voice of our dear friend, Katie Ashby, and her premier wartime singing act, the D-Day Darlings, singing *"Comin' in on a Wing and a Prayer"*. I looked over at Kay and I could see the emotion in her eyes, as she could in mine. This was an intense, wholly unexpected, and overwhelming moment that was clearly meant to be. As we listened to the poignant lyrics of this song, which bizarrely seemed both highly appropriate and inappropriate in equal measures, in our mind's eye we could almost see our Lanc struggling to stay in the air over these very mountains before it succumbed to its unthinkable, but inevitable, fate.

"Comin' in on a wing and a prayer
Comin' in on a wing and a prayer
With our one motor gone
We can still carry on
Comin' in on a wing and a prayer

What a show, what a fight
Boys, we really hit our target for tonight
How we sing as we limp through the air
Look below, there's our field over there
With our one motor gone
We can still carry on
Comin' in on a wing and a prayer

Comin' in on a wing and a prayer
Comin' in on a wing and a prayer
With our full crew on board
And our trust in the Lord
We're comin' in on a wing and a prayer"

Written by Jimmy McHugh and Harold Adamson 1943

Timmenrode railway station, now a private residence, near to which the burning JB453 was seen to lose an engine. Photos courtesy of Lothar Wiegmann

We were warmly welcomed by Lothar and his wife, Viola, at their home in Timmenrode before Lothar took us to the crash site, just a short drive away.

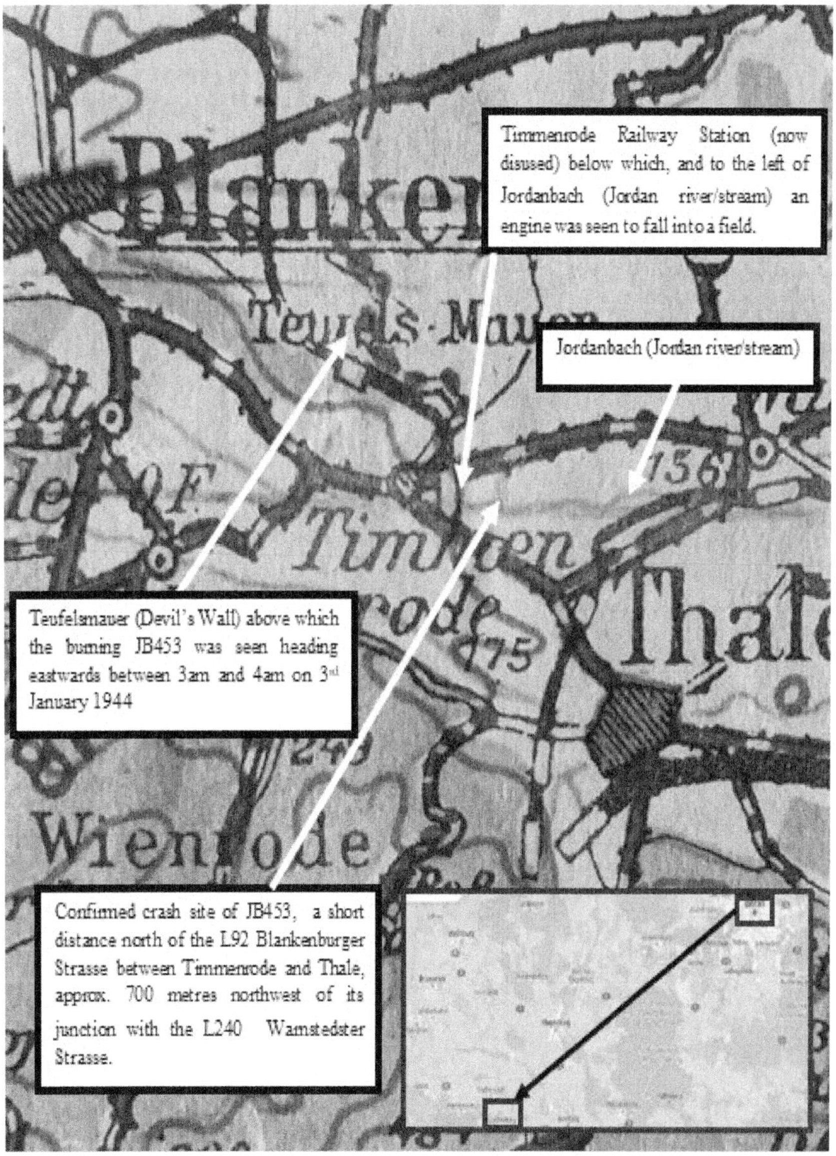

Crash site of JB453 as described by eyewitnesses, marked by the author on original War Office map.
Inset - Map Data ©2023 Geobasis DE BKG (©2009), Google showing proximity to Berlin, a flight distance of circa 100 miles

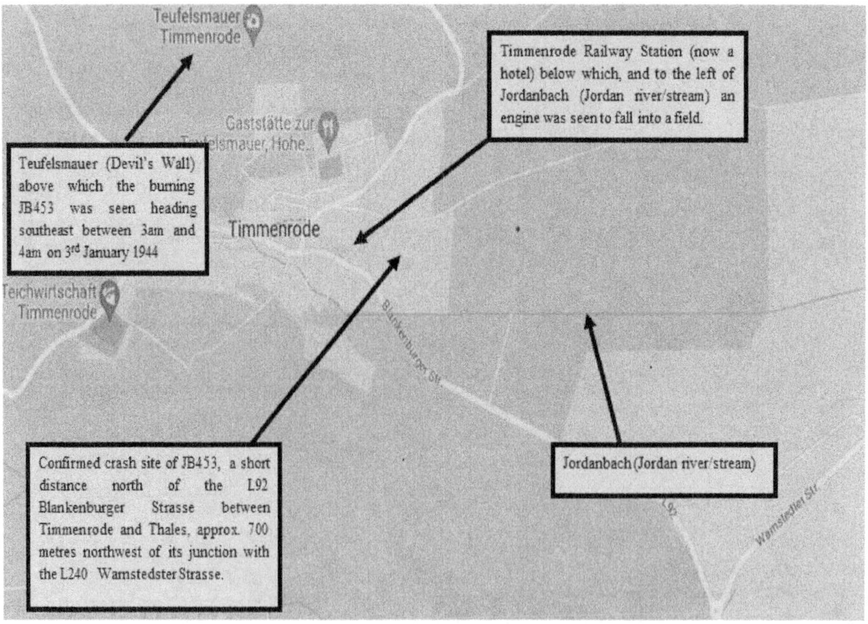

Crash site of JB453 as described by eyewitnesses, marked by the author on modern map.
Map Data ©2023 Geobasis DE BKG (©2009), Google

Today, as on 3rd January 1944, the site is a farmer's field on the eastern extremity of the village. However, from the eyewitness accounts discovered by Lothar, I was able to plot the last moments of the fated Lanc and its crew as pilot Stiles appeared to be attempting to regain control.

Lothar told me that he knew of no photographs that were taken of the crash site nor of any wreckage parts that might have been found and kept as souvenirs by local residents. His research indicated that the whole area had been cordoned off by German forces and that all traces of the aircraft and its crew were removed over the following days.

Confirmed crash site of JB453 at Timmenrode. Photo courtesy of author.

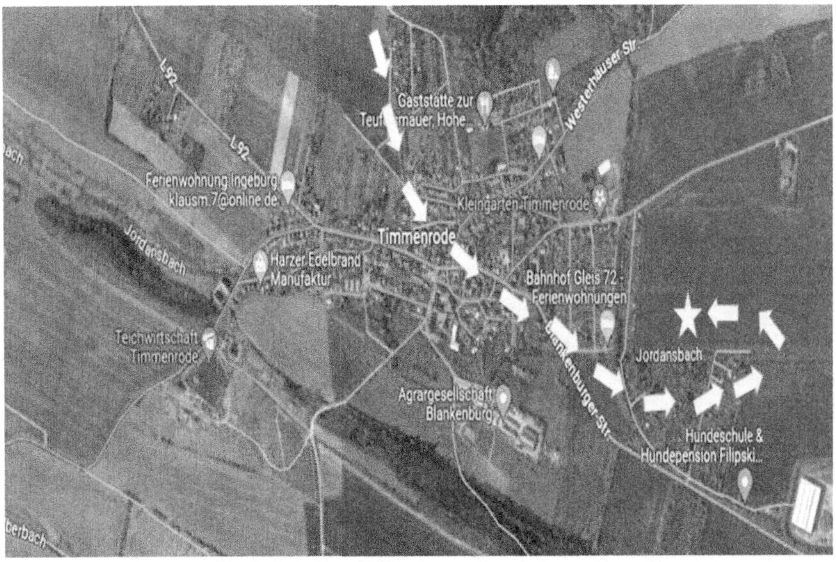

Final flight path of JB453 as described by eyewitnesses.
Map Data ©2023 Geobasis DE BKG (©2009), Google

Last moments of JB453, as described by eyewitnesses, superimposed onto photo of crash site by the author. Photo courtesy of author.

Lothar (left) and the author at the crash site – September 2023. Photo courtesy of author.

CHAPTER 14

FLYING THE LANC TODAY

In the world today, of the 7,377 Lancaster bombers that were built to support activities in World War II, there are just two that remain airworthy.

The first is PA474, owned by the Royal Air Force and which is regularly flown throughout the spring and summer months each year as part of the Battle of Britain Memorial Flight (BBMF).

The other is FM213 VR-A, known as VeRA, owned by the Canada Warplane Heritage Museum at the John C. Munro Hamilton International Airport in Mount Hope, Ontario.

A third Lancaster NX611, "Just Jane", is currently undergoing restoration to flight readiness at the Lincolnshire Aviation Heritage Centre.

To assist in funding this project, the Centre offers runway taxy rides in the aircraft. It will be wonderful to see "Just Jane" back in the air in due course.

It is rare indeed to see both airworthy aircraft flying together. However, in 2014, FM213 was flown across the Atlantic Ocean to the UK, landing at RAF Coningsby, to tour with PA474 as part of the BBMF programme.

In 2023 I was introduced to Mike Osborne by his daughter, BBC TV presenter Alex Osborne. Mike had been fortunate enough to be invited to fly on board FM213 in 2014 and was able to tell me, from his personal experience, what it was like to fly in this iconic aircraft today.

"In 2014 I had been following the Canadian Lancaster all over the country. The crew would come over to spectators to chat, so over two or three weeks I got to know them quite well and they would recognise me. I said one day that I would love to fly in a Lancaster. The pilot told me that if I ever went over to Canada, I could. I asked how that worked and he said that the aircraft was part of the Canadian Memorial Association (CMA) *and that the rules and regulations over there are less stringent than they are in the UK. I said that was a long way to go but the pilot said to give him my telephone number and we would keep in touch. He was really nice. Anyway, two weeks later I had a 'phone call from the CMA. I was asked,*

'What are you doing next Tuesday?'. I was due to go to London with work. The Lanc was in Coningsby and was coming into Humberside. Did I fancy a trip? Apparently, the pilot had organised it that he could take some personal friends for a flight on VeRA and asked to take me. I thought…WOW! I couldn't believe it. He said I would have to sign some documents but providing everything was OK, he would be there around eleven o' clock in the morning. I went to my boss and told him that I needed a day's holiday. He replied that, you've got no chance. It will have to be something really important like a hospital appointment or something. I told him I had an offer to fly in a Lancaster bomber. Tony, my boss, who was out of the army said, no, don't give me that, tell me the truth. I said, that is the truth. Anyway, he let me have the day off and I thought, great, we're off. On the morning, we went to Humberside Airport in the car. It is only half an hour away. There were two other guys there who were both pilots with Virgin Atlantic. They had had the same offer of a flight. So the three of us sat there and waited for the Lancaster to come in from Coningsby. It got to eleven o'clock. We were then told that there had been a bit of a technical problem in Coningsby, and it wasn't certain whether VeRA would be able to get to Humberside. I thought, oh no! It got to three o'clock when we were updated that they had got the engines running but that we need to be ready as soon as it arrived because when it does land it won't be stopping. It will

be touch down and then off again. We waited on the tarmac then watched, and heard, the iconic Lanc come in. I'd got my video camera there, as it was in those days, and I was taking photos. The pilot got down and told us it would be a hot take-off. I asked him what this was. He said that we would be boarding with the Merlin engines running. I walked up to the ladder to board to discover that the power coming out of those engines was unbelievable. It was literally blowing us backwards.

FM213 VeRA on the tarmac at Humberside. Photo courtesy of Mike Osborne

Anyway, we clambered on board. We were told to sit wherever we could which we did. A sign was then pointed out to us which told us that this plane does not meet British CAA standards, but we were also assured that this

was nothing to worry about! Even so, we entered at our own risk. We were handed a piece of paper and told, if you still want to come you have to sign this. The paper, in as many words, said that flying in the plane was totally at my own risk. I thought, well, if you have flown all the way from Canada, I'll take that risk.

Mike with FM213 VeRA. Photo courtesy of Mike Osborne.

There were two or three seats on the left-hand side, so we sat in those. For such a big and heavy bomber, it was very small and uncomfortable inside. I couldn't stand up fully. We fastened a seat belt of sorts and when we started moving off the whole aircraft shook unbelievably. It was actually quite frightening. Sometimes, when you go on an aeroplane you look around and think, this doesn't look very safe, but the Lanc, and it was quite a windy day, was rocking and rolling all over the place. It taxyed out to the back of the runway. All you could hear, apart from the engines, was the

Mike at the Wireless Operator's station. Photo courtesy of Mike Osborne.

noise of levers and pulleys. There were few hydraulics. It was clunk, clunk, clunk all the time. It was so noisy, and the smell – it was a mixture of all the gasoline and the oils. It was really quite noxious. It was also very dark. You couldn't see very much. Then we were off down the runway and into the air. The Lanc was shaking all the time.

After a few minutes the pilot came on the radio to say that we could get up and walk around wherever we wanted. He added to be careful if we went into the rear tail gunner pod because if we turned it, we could fall out! If the rear gunner had to bale out, the first thing he would have to do was to turn around and get his parachute which was on a hook because there wasn't enough room to wear it inside his turret. But to actually leave the aircraft, he would have to rotate the turret left or right and literally fall out the hole. The pilot said that everything in that rear turret, and in the rest of the plane for that matter, was as it was eighty years ago, so not to press any buttons!

I went into the turret through two swing doors, and it felt really weird. I felt completely isolated and alone, in a different world. All I could see were the two machine guns, and when I looked around it was difficult to see anything.

Of course, many rear gunners would remove part of the Perspex from the turret so that they could better see what they were doing. Also, I was flying backwards which in itself felt strange. And although we were only seven or eight thousand feet high, and it was the summer, it felt really icy cold. You can't imagine what it must have been like flying at twenty-five thousand feet, at night, in the middle of winter. Trying to see night fighters,

Looking backwards towards the twin swing doors and the rear gunner turret. Photo courtesy of Mike Osborne.

let alone hit them, must have been nigh on impossible, and what must it have been like if the pilot had to corkscrew, goodness only knows! Immediately behind the rear turret was the Elsan toilet and, said the pilot, that often came off its haunches with its contents spreading all over the plane. I sat in the turret for about ten minutes in awe thinking I was on a bit of a jolly whereas the guys that were here, in this seat, during the war, never knew whether they would get back on any given night. It must have been horrendous. Then I went to the upper gunner position and that was so difficult to get into. I climbed up and squeezed onto this little bench. Again, one of the crew said not to touch anything. The machine guns were still loaded with bullets, although they had been welded together. It was, like the rear turret, as it would have been during operational missions. After this I went forwards and stood just behind the pilots, chatting away. I asked what it was like to fly. The pilot said it's brilliant to fly but the worst thing he'd encountered was turbulence if he was flying behind another Lancaster. He said, in Canada, you go up on your own and you don't witness it. But, he said, imagine what it must have been like going up on an operation with up to a thousand other Lancs, Wellingtons, Stirlings and Mosquitos, at night, when you can't see where you are going. Risks from turbulence and air to air collisions were ever present. Then you would have flown into occupied Europe, and you started getting shot at. I asked how they would have navigated. He spoke about the navigator's table and said that was all you had, and if your navigator got shot then you had no chance. You wouldn't know where you were or where you were going. If the navigator got lost, or even just dropped his pencil, then he would have to navigate by looking at the stars from a Perspex dome above his head. It makes you realise just how brave these young men were, doing this night after night. A standard bombing tour was thirty operations, but crews never knew if they would survive just one! The only protection a pilot had was a small piece of steel behind his head, and that was it. Everything else around him was Perspex and aluminium. You could almost have punched your hand through the fuselage. The pilot then asked if I wanted to feel the aircraft. I said yes. He

View from the upper gun turret. Photo courtesy of Mike Osborne.

told me to lean over, and the plane was really steady at that point. He said, just pull it back a bit so I pulled and, really, it was like trying to pull a donkey backwards that didn't want to move! So difficult.

I was invited to climb into the bomb aimer's position in the front. It was alright getting in because you were crawling forwards but once you were in laying on your stomach, you could hardly move to get out. So there the bomber would have been, likely being shot at by night fighters or surrounded by exploding flak and, often, all he would hear on the radio was 'DROP THOSE BLOODY BOMBS!'.

The crews must have been terrified up there. We flew for about an hour before landing. When we landed, our crew were exhausted and delighted that the engine, that had an earlier fault, had performed well. So was I! If it hadn't then we may have had to make an emergency landing as happened a few weeks later when an engine caught fire! When I got out, my legs were trembling. The pilots were the same. They said it is very, very hard keeping control of a Lancaster, even in peace time with no-one shooting at you. But for me, this had been a once-in-lifetime chance and I had had an amazing, never to be forgotten, experience in what was really a pleasure flight. Nobody can fully realise or appreciate what the, essentially volunteer, Bomber Command crews went through to give us what we have today. And we have to remember that over fifty-five thousand never came home. We must never forget them".

It was quite clear from Mike's experience that, being a crew member in a Lanc in a time of war, was far from easy. It was tough, it was frightening, it was perilous and at times horrendous, but the comradery, bravery and determination shown by those young men cannot be overstated. Mike's experience gives just a flavour of what those Bomber Command crews went through, and I am hugely grateful to him for sharing his thoughts and recollections with me.

FM213 VeRA cockpit. Note the modern satellite navigation device which was fully utilised in flying the Lanc from Canada to the UK.
Photo courtesy of Mike Osborne.

CHAPTER 15

DEDICATION OF THE WEATHERVANE AND MEMORIAL SERVICE SUNDAY 19TH SEPTEMBER 2021

Earlier, I wrote about how Helen had received a call from Nicky van der Drift, CEO at the International Bomber Command Centre. When Helen began her research into JB453 and its crew, she had no intentions of taking her efforts any further than seeking permission to erect a memorial plaque at her and John's cottage such that anyone who wanted to, could come along, see the memorial, and pay their respects.

The call from Nicky changed all of this and Helen tried to take on board the enormity of what could be a full-on ceremonial event. Having never before arranged such a high-profile occasion, she turned for advice to her good friend and researcher, Di Ablewhite, whom she knew had arranged such things. Di proved to be an enormous help in many ways but her first suggestion was for Helen to contact the local branch of the Royal British Legion. She spoke with the Chair of Herefordshire RBL, Barbara Leeson, someone else with whom, through this project, Helen has become close friends. Barbara was able to provide a list people that Helen could consider inviting. This included the Mayor of Hereford and HM Queen's representative, the Lord Lieutenant of Herefordshire, although there would be a protocol to observe and numerous forms to complete. Barbara was able to recommend a bugle player to play *The Last Post* and a Legion standard bearer. She also recommended that RAF Cadets at Lucton School and Hereford Cathedral School be involved in the event. She considered, and Helen agreed, that this was an important move because the young members of the Cadet Force would be amongst those responsible for ensuring that the memories of those who fought in World War II, especially those who made the ultimate sacrifice, live on.

The next stage was for Helen to arrange for a member of the clergy who would be able to preside over a religious service at the event. Sunday September 19th 2021 had been provisionally set for the commemoration and dedication event. However, Helen's local church vicar was not going to be available on that day and she was directed to Reverend Paul Roberts. He readily agreed to preside on the day and also offered to create and produce an Order of Service at no cost to Helen. Paul was assisted on the day by local curate, David Wyatt.

Another friend, Adam Buckley who was originally from Westhope, agreed to take on responsibility for the provision of audio and video facilities as it was planned that there should be a live feed of the event online. He was also tasked, along with another local resident, Nigel Pullen-Warner, with taking photographs on the day. Nigel additionally assisted with setting up a memorial display at the cottage.

When it came to issuing invitations, Di was able to supply a template from a prior event that Helen was thankful to use.

Helen contacted a local newspaper, the Hereford Times, together with BBC Radio Hereford & Worcester, both of which readily agreed to cover the event. An article even appeared in the pages of The Times and Daily Telegraph national newspapers.

Helen took delivery of a memorial plaque which had been designed and created to an exacting commission by Yellow Farm Workshops in High Bickington, Devon – coincidently only a short distance away from my home – and which was ready to be placed.

The preceding weeks and months had seen many of the JB453 crews' descendants beginning their own explorations into their family histories, delving into local archives and rooting out dusty boxes containing old photographs and documents, many of which have been reproduced in this book. Everything that could be prepared and arranged was completed. The only thing that Helen had no control over was the weather. She prayed for a dry day.

After months in planning, the day had finally arrived. Helen and John were naturally feeling very nervous and keen that the day should unfold seamlessly. They woke up to a mixture of cloud and sunshine, the latest forecast indicating the possibility of rain later in the day. Fingers were well and truly crossed.

That final week had whizzed by. Helen had written a day-by-day summary of tasks that needed completing and it was thrilling for her to tick each one off as they were accomplished. Earlier that week, on the Tuesday, there had been a practice run-through of the order of ceremony with the Chairperson from the Royal British Legion. Wednesday saw a final rehearsal, in front of a small audience, for four ladies, including Helen, and two men, who had formed a singing troupe especially for the event – The Andrews Dusters - in the style of the famous wartime close-harmony group, The Andrews Sisters.

In the final days leading up to the ceremony, village residents cheerfully and gladly joined together to help in erecting a large marquee, bake cakes, collect or deliver chairs, tables, crockery and to create signage.

You are cordially invited to attend the unveiling of the memorial
to the crew of
Avro Lancaster III JB453 OL-F

at 3.30pm,

on Sunday 19th September 2021,

at Holly Lodge, Westhope, Hereford, UK, HR4 8BL

and to stay for refreshments afterwards.

Please RSVP by 31st August 2021
with numbers attending.

Feel free to bring wreaths or floral tributes.

Please note this will be a formal event.

Parking will be available.

Nigel and his partner Jacky had put together a fabulous display in a retro tin garden shed showing the crew's working positions in the Lancaster, a brief resume on each of the crew members, a succinct history of AVRO and its production line of planes, along with a handmade model of Lancaster JB453 OL-F. On Saturday evening prior to the event the following day, Helen and John went to meet a group of descendants from air gunner, John

MacIntyre Dunlop, who were staying in Hereford. If they hadn't known beforehand, they very quickly realised just how excited the crews' families

Retro shed at Holly Lodge which housed the JB453 display. Photo courtesy of Mark Errington

were to be coming to the ceremony.

Gratitude poured out from them. It was quite overwhelming and emotional for all of them. Amongst the group was Phyliss, John Dunlop's sister-in-law. She had flown from Glasgow to attend, having never flown alone before. Nothing was going to prevent her from attending.

As daylight dawned on Sunday the 19th, it was all hands-on-deck to put everything into correct positions. The garden was snipped and clipped.

Holly Lodge was festooned with bunting and the Union Flag flew proudly in a gentle breeze, together with the national Maple Leaf flag of Canada.

Part of the retro shed display showing the positions of each crew member relative to a model of JB453
Photo courtesy of Nigel Pullen-Warner

More friends, Rob and Trish Edden, arrived early to set up the sound system for The Andrews Duster's party piece. The weather appeared to be kind. Helen and John were quietly confident that the gods were looking favourably down on them.

Soon after midday, after eating lunch on the hoof, it was time for both of them to don their outfits for the day. Fittingly, they chose 1940s-style attire. Then, disaster struck, the heavens opened introducing torrents of rain. Once more, it was all hands to the pump to rescue everything that was in imminent peril of being ruined. The Springfield band, who were to provide period music during the event had just arrived and were anxiously trying to set up beneath the marquee whilst trying to avoid their instruments from getting wet.

Car park attendants became drenched as guests started to arrive. Many wisely chose to stay in their cars whilst the worst of the weather passed over. By 2.30pm, only an hour before the service was due to begin, it seemed as though the clouds had emptied themselves and the weather, thankfully, improved for the rest of the day. Chairs were dried off and umbrellas were put aside. Once inside, guests were welcomed with beaming smiles and each of the family 43 descendants given a badge indicating to which crew member they were related. After this joyous meet and greet, they all mingled, some having contact with other members of their own families for the very first time. It was truly heart-warming for Helen and John to be able to put faces to those people they had only, until now, encountered by post, telephone and email.

Local residents of Westhope provided enormous support to Helen and John, not least of which was guiding cars to a temporary car park at a nearby orchard and directing other cars to use own private driveways.

There were nieces and nephews, great-nieces and great-nephews, sisters and sisters-in-law, with many more watching a live feed from the comforts of their own homes as far away as Canada and South Africa. Families of five out of the crew of seven were present on the day. Large groups of local residents gathered around the garden wall, looking on at the spectacle that was about to unfold. This was history in the making.

At 3pm, the warning moan of an air raid siren signalled everyone to take their places. The garden very quickly filled to capacity leaving standing

Helen and John, both attired in period dress, on ceremony day.
Photo courtesy of Helen Theron.

room only. 3.30pm arrived and John asked all to be upstanding as Helen escorted The Queen's representative, Lord Lieutenant of Herefordshire, Mr. Edward Harley OBE, and Mrs. Harley to their seats. They had driven in earnest to attend the ceremony having earlier attended an official engagement at Windsor Castle with Her Majesty. Curate David Wyatt welcomed all to the event, followed by the entrance of Royal British Legion Standard Bearers and very proud-looking RAF Cadets, marching to the music of the Dam Busters. The Service of Dedication opened with prayers followed by The Airman's Hymn, connecting everyone emotionally to the essence of the occasion. John read the first poem, *"Lie in the Dark and Listen"* by Noel Coward. The poem is a touching tribute to the crews of Bomber Command in World War II.

Lie in the dark and listen,
It's clear tonight so they're flying high
Hundreds of them, thousands perhaps,
Riding the icy, moonlight sky.
Men, materials, bombs and maps
Altimeters and guns and charts
Coffee, sandwiches, fleece-lined boots
Bones and muscles and minds and hearts
English saplings with English roots
Deep in the earth they've left below
Lie in the dark and let them go

THE BOMBER AND THE WEATHERVANE

Lie in the dark and listen,
They're going over in waves and waves
High above villages, hills and streams
Country churches and little graves
And little citizen's worried dreams.
Very soon they'll have reached the sea
And far below them will lie the bays
And coves and sands where they used to be
Taken for summer holidays.
Lie in the dark and let them go
Lie in the dark and listen.

Lie in the dark and listen
City magnates and steel contractors,
Factory workers and politicians
Soft hysterical little actors Ballet dancers,
'reserved' musicians,
Safe in your warm civilian beds
Count your profits and count your sheep
Life is flying above your heads
Just turn over and try to sleep.
Lie in the dark and let them go
Theirs is a world you'll never know
Lie in the dark and listen.

Order of Service booklet. Photo courtesy of Helen Theron.

The Commemoration Service at Holly Lodge – Photo courtesy of Adam Buckley

Cadets from Hereford Cathedral School Combined Cadet Force RAF
L-R Cadet Flight Sergeant Alexander Campbell, Cadet Warrant Officer Olivia Anderssen and Cadet Sergeant Anna Finlay. Photo courtesy of Adam Buckley

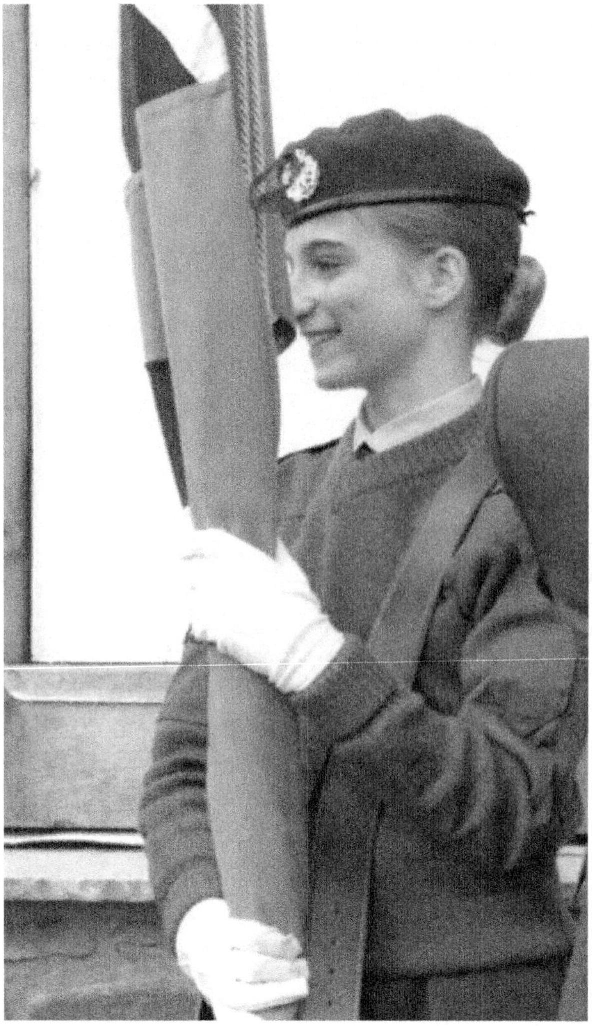

RAF Cadet Standard-bearer Amy-Rose Stevens
Combined Cadet Force Lucton School. Photo courtesy of Adam Buckley

Family members then stepped up to read passion-filled tributes to their lost crewman. A recorded tribute to Flying Officer Ian Allan, made in Canada by a family member who was unable to attend in person, was played.

Hearing a voice from Canada, speaking so heartfeltly, added an additional dimension to proceedings. The emotion of the occasion was palpable.

Clair Donetta-Yates – Dyke family
Photo courtesy of Nigel Pullen-Warner

David Dunlop – Dunlop family.
Photo courtesy of Nigel Pullen-Warner

Wing Commander (Retd) P J Hereford OBE
Photo courtesy of Nigel Pullen-Warner

A Bible reading, Isaiah 40:25 – 31, followed:

Youths may faint and grow weary, and young men stumble and fall
but those who wait on the Lord will find new strength.
They will rise up high on wings like eagles.
They will run and not grow weary. They will walk and not faint.

A second poem, High Flight, written by John Gillespie Magee, was narrated by Wing Commander (Retd) PJ Hereford OBE. Magee was an Anglo-American aviator and poet who served in the Royal Canadian Air

Force, joining before the USA entered the war. He died in a mid-air collision over Lincolnshire in 1941.

Oh! I have slipped the surly bonds of Earth
And danced the skies on laughter-silvered wings;
Sunward I've climbed, and joined the tumbling mirth
of sun-split clouds,—and done a hundred things
You have not dreamed of—wheeled and soared and swung
High in the sunlit silence. Hov'ring there,
I've chased the shouting wind along, and flung
My eager craft through footless halls of air ....
Up, up the long, delirious, burning blue
I've topped the wind-swept heights with easy grace
Where never lark nor ever eagle flew—
And, while with silent lifting mind I've trod
The high untrespassed sanctity of space,
Put out my hand and touched the face of God.

The Lord Lieutenant gave a most poignant speech of well-received words before unveiling the memorial plaque by removing the RAF ensign flag that until now had been shrouding it. Curate David Wyatt dedicated the Weathervane and Memorial, in solemn remembrance of the seven men who died in the cause of freedom.

Reverend Paul Roberts led prayers that followed. The names of each member of the JB453 OL-F crew were read out by Air Vice Marshal

Mr Edward Harley OBE – Lord Lieutenant of Herefordshire
Photo courtesy of Nigel Pullen-Warner

(Ret'd) Michael D Smart OBE which he followed with the Exhortation.

"They shall grow not old, as we that are left grow old,

Age shall not weary them, nor the years condemn.

At the going down of the sun, and in the morning,

We will remember them."

JB453 OL-F Memorial Plaque. Photo courtesy of author

Bugler, Kelvyn Jenkins, sounded the Last Post, and two minutes silence was observed by all. The Last Post is played at military funerals and commemorative services as a final farewell and symbolises that the duty of the dead is over and that they can rest in peace. A bugle is used as it was during the war. The end of the silence heralded the Reveille which, traditionally, calls soldiers' spirits to rise and prepare for another day.

The Kohima Epitaph was read by Mrs. Barbara Leeson, Chair of Herefordshire Royal British Legion.

"When you go home, tell them of us and say:

For your tomorrow, we gave our today"

Thirteen wreaths were laid. One, laid by Patricia Donetta, the sister of Bomb Aimer Flying Officer Dyke, bore some dried slices of orange amongst the flowers. This was in remembrance of when her brother brought her oranges from his time spent training in Canada. She had never held nor tasted one before. Another wreath, laid by The Right Worshipful Mayor of Hereford, Councillor Paul Stevens, senior Mayor of England, bore, for the first time ever at such an occasion, the coat of arms of the City of Hereford. The floral display was magnificent and intensely moving. The National Anthems of Canada and United Kingdom were sung enthusiastically and with immense pride. Curate Wyatt gave the final Blessing. The service had been remarkably moving, impressive, poignant, and stirring. It was exactly what Helen and John had envisaged and proved an exceptionally fitting way in which to commemorate and remember the brave young men who lost their lives on that cold January morning in 1944. As the service ended, an Isaac Spitfire flew low, twice, over the cottage before returning back to its

The Last Post by bugler Kelvyn Jenkins. Photo courtesy of Adam Buckley

Base. This was a home build, flown by Alan James, which provided a sublime finale. Everyone waved and cheered as the iconic aircraft with its instantly recognisable elliptical wing shape flew overhead.

This event was the last official engagement of AVM (Retd) Michael Smart and Lord Lieutenant Harley delivered a few words to thank him for his incredible service to the county of Hereford, presenting him with a certificate of thanks.

Following the fly-past, the Standard bearers led the way for all to walk into the walled garden for refreshments. Local residents provided a magnificent spread.

Attendees mingled whilst The Springfield Band filled the air with golden tunes from the wartime era. Later in the afternoon, The Andrews Dusters, including Helen, joyfully sang their much rehearsed songs of the time. Many sang along to *"Boogie Woogie Bugle Boy"* and *"The White Cliffs of Dover."* There was hardly a dry eye left as the Dusters rendition of the song made famous by the late Dame Vera Lynn, *"We'll Meet Again"*, flowed through the garden. During the afternoon's proceedings, file ledgers containing copies of all the information gathered during the project were presented to family representatives of each crew member. These historical documents are there to be handed down through future generations, keeping these brave young men's memories alive.

Flypast of the Isaac Spitfire over the weathervane. Photo courtesy of Helen Theron

Family descendants mingling in the garden of Holly Lodge. Photo courtesy of Adam Buckley

Christopher and Rebecca Oliver – Traynor family
Photo courtesy of Helen Theron

Joanne and Bill Deehan, Deidre Oliver and Tony Earley – Traynor family
Photo courtesy of Helen Theron

A full garden at Holly Lodge during the ceremony. Photo courtesy of Adam Buckley.

Sarah Bennett representing the Banks family. Photo courtesy of Nigel Pullen-Warner.

Gill Moriarty representing the McKendry family. Photo courtesy of Nigel Pullen-Warner.

Dunlop family descendants . Photo courtesy of Adam Buckley

The commemoration service bestowed a fitting finale to what had been an incredible and prodigious journey that Helen and John had undertaken. Little did they know, on the day they discovered the Lancaster weathervane buried away in a Surrey salvage yard, just where it would lead.

Their relentless and all-consuming efforts over the preceding months made many people tremendously proud and thankful. Chris Oliver, family descendant of Flight Engineer Patrick Traynor wrote to them:

"I/we would like to thank you and the rest of the team, for putting on such an absolutely amazing day yesterday. You should all be very proud of what you achieved, it really was unlike anything that we have been to before or are likely to be at again. From start to finish we were made to feel so

welcome, and the day was one that will remain in our thoughts forever. I could think of no better tribute for the crew of JB453 OL-F."

This event was extraordinarily special and unique. It remembered and commemorated the loss of seven courageous, young, crew members of Lancaster JB453 who perished on that fateful January night over Germany 80 years ago. It is vital that we remember these, and every other airman, sailor, soldier, and civilian who were killed or injured during the six years of this cruel and vicious conflict. Part of this lies in the education of young people both now and for the future. It was reassuring and welcoming that a group of young RAF Combined Cadets Force were present at the commemoration event. They, and youngsters like them, are the future. They are the ones who must carry the memories forward such that their children, grandchildren, and generations to follow never forget the sacrifices that were made in their name, sacrifices that allow them, and will continue to allow them, the freedom to live in peace and to make their own life choices.

Just over 2 years later, on 5th November 2023, Helen, John and I met with more descendants of the Traynor family at Holly Lodge. They had contacted Helen a few weeks beforehand having only just learned of the JB453 project. More family members that we knew very little about!

Gavin and Kay Traynor had travelled from their home in Northern Ireland especially to meet us. The other family members had travelled from their home in Cheshire. They were able to give a great deal of information about the Traynor family history and dynamics. They said that they had only got to know about the project when Ryan, who was celebrating his 21st birthday on the day we all met, had been carrying out some research of his own online and had stumbled across some of Helen's posts. Soon afterwards, the family contacted Helen and the meeting was arranged. The family were able to provide documents that neither Helen nor I had previously seen. It was wonderful to see Ryan clearly so proud of his

The Andrews Dusters. Photo courtesy of Adam Buckley

The Springfield Band. Photo courtesy of Adam Buckley

Helen and John at the end of a unique and memorable day. Photo courtesy of Hazel Maidman

great-great uncle. This was a wonderful example of a young person who would carry the flag of Patrick's memory forward for future generations to appreciate and remember. Indeed, Ryan was delighted to be able to show off a tattoo on his arm, depicting a soldier standing in a field of poppies beneath an overflying Lancaster. As a thank-you for seeking and finding the information that led to this visit, and to celebrate his 21st birthday, Helen gifted Ryan a complete ledger file of the JB453 project. She even managed to somehow conjure up some cakes topped with candles for him!

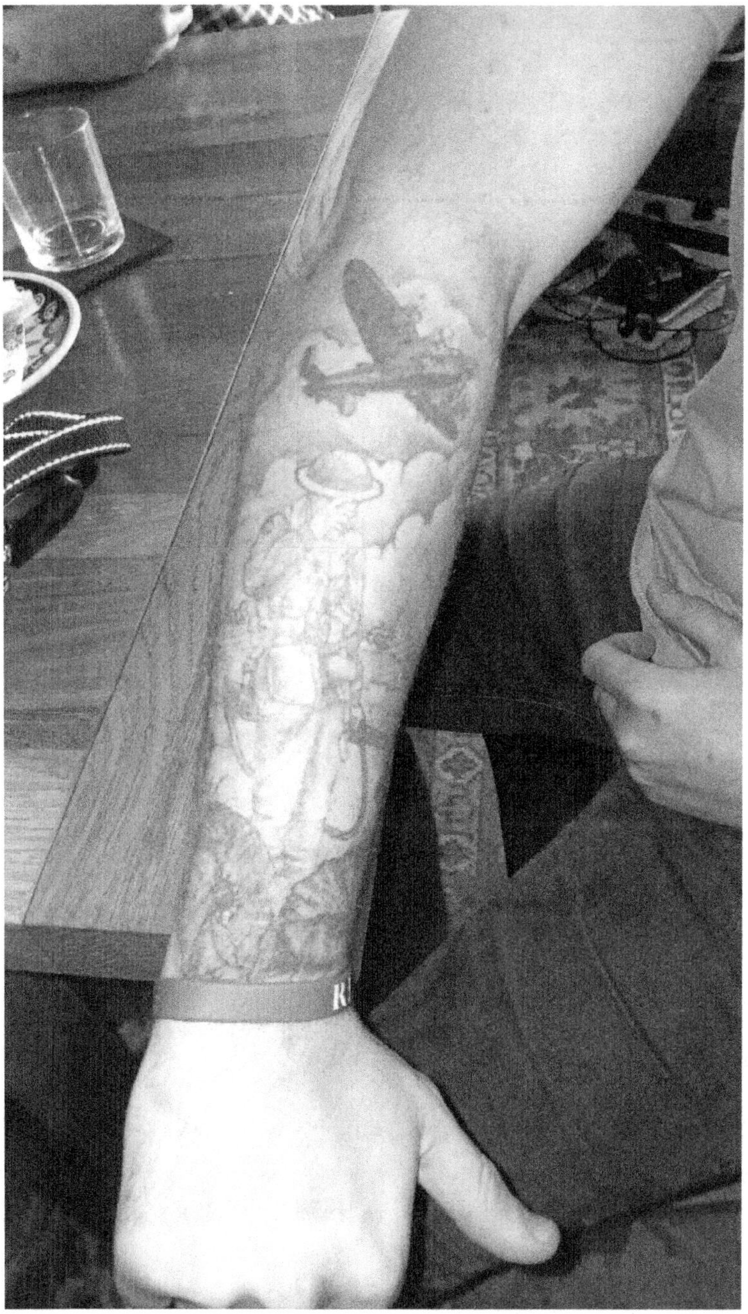

Ryan Traynor's arm tattoo. Photo courtesy of the author.

In front of the memorial plaque at Holly Lodge. L-R Ryan Traynor, great-great nephew of Patrick Traynor, Kay Traynor, Gavin Traynor, husband of Kay and great nephew of Patrick, Angie Lawler nee Traynor, great niece of Patrick and Chris Lawler, husband of Angie. Photo courtesy of author.

In May 2024, Mike McKendry, nephew of Pilot Officer and navigator of JB453, Denis "Jackie" McKendry, and brother of Terry McKendry whose painting of the Lancaster appears earlier in this book, travelled from his home in Johannesburg, South Africa for a vacation around the UK and Ireland. Mike's father was Terry McKendry, brother of Denis. Helen and I were delighted to meet with him at Holly Lodge and spent a wonderful afternoon discussing his uncle and his family. A pilot of a light aircraft himself in South Africa, it was clear that Mike was extremely proud of his uncle. It was he who commissioned the building of a replica model of Lancaster JB453, a picture of which is shown in Chapter 5.

Mike McKendry at Holly Lodge holding a copy of the JB453 dossier presented to him by Helen.
Photo courtesy of Helen Theron

Helen was pleased to be able to present Mike with a complete dossier of the JB453 project.

The author, Helen, and Mike McKendry beneath the weathervane and memorial plaque at Holly Lodge.
Photo courtesy of Helen Theron

CHAPTER 16

WHERE THE STORY ENDS (OR DOES IT?)

For the future, in September 2024, Kay and I will join Helen, together with family descendants of the JB453 crew in a memorial service at the crew's graves at the British 1939-1945 War Graves Cemetery in Berlin, with the support of the Royal British Legion, International Bomber Command Centre, the British Embassy in Berlin and the Commonwealth Graves Commission, together with other individuals and organisations. The following day a visit has been arranged for the families to travel to the crash site at Timmenrode where a memorial plaque commemorating the crew, commissioned by Blankenburg and Timmenrode authorities, will be unveiled by Helen and the region's Mayor, and a tree planted. Local archivist Lothar Wiegmann and local dignitaries will attend to meet with the families.

On Armistice Day, Saturday November 11th 2023, Kay and I were thrilled to attend the 100th Festival of Remembrance, hosted as ever by the Royal British Legion, at the Royal Albert Hall in London. This annual event is always exceptionally emotional and thought-provoking, focussing on, and honouring, veterans from past wars, some of whom, now in their 80s and 90s, were present, service men and women who were destined never to return from battle, and those who suffered the most horrendous of physical or mental traumas, in many cases both. Those included families who had lost loved ones in latter day conflicts across the globe.

Towards the end of the evening, representatives from all armed and civilian services mustered together. As the RAF marched in to their famous March Past music, their flag was displayed on giant screens. As they stood to attention, in my mind, I read out each member of the fated JB453 crew, and again during the two minutes of silence as poppies fluttered down from the roof;

Blair Stiles, Ian Allan, Denis McKendry, Patrick Traynor, Joe Banks, Bill Dyke, John Dunlop.

100th Festival of Remembrance 2023, Royal Albert Hall as RAF officers muster together.
Photo courtesy of the author.

150 miles away in Westhope, Herefordshire, Helen and John performed their own private ceremony, raising the Union and Canadian flags, before placing wreaths and poppy cross tributes beneath the memorial plaque.

It seems an age since that first meeting with Helen and John in my Devon home late in 2021. Much of the ensuing two years was spent with fingers rivetted to my laptop keyboard. My writing saw the Covid crisis come and go, the Coronation of King Charles III following the passing of our beloved Queen Elizabeth II, ongoing combats between Russia and Ukraine, as well as continuing difficulties in the Middle East, previously unimaginable global weather events, massive rises in the cost of living and much more.

It would have been wonderful to have found the origin of the weathervane. Sadly, thus far, this has not materialised. However, who knows what might

Armistice Day 2023 at Westhope, Herefordshire. Photos courtesy of Helen Theron.

transpire in the months and years to come. Indeed, as I write, specialists from the RAF Museum at East Kirkby have stated that the metal used for the weathervane did not appear to be original metal used on Lancaster builds but could have been metal used for repair work.

Suffice to say that everyone who has been involved in this story, from the purchase of the weathervane all those years ago, discovering the inscription that led to the identification of the stricken aircraft and crew, locating family descendants, interviewing Dick Raymond, the dedication of the vane as a formal war memorial, locating and visiting the crash site, and writing this book, have all contributed in no small way to uncovering incredibly important pieces of history from within that long and brutal world war.

DEDICATION EVENT ATTENDEES

Approaching 100 people attended this exceptional event, including:

Mr Edward Harley OBE – Lord Lieutenant of Herefordshire representing HM The Queen, and Mrs Harley

Helen and John Theron

Air Vice Marshall (Retd) Michael D Smart OBE DL

Wing Commander (Retd) P J Hereford OBE and Mrs Hereford

The Right Worshipful Mayor of Hereford, Cllr Paul Stevens and Mayoress Mrs Stevens

Lieutenant Colonel Christopher Barnard, Royal Canadian Air Force

Rear Commander Philip Wilcocks

Sebastian Bowen

Barbara Leeson (RBL County Chairperson) & Rob Leeson (RBL Standard Bearer), Hereford Royal British Legion

Kelvyn & Helen Jenkins

Rev. Paul Roberts and Mrs Roberts

Rev. David Wyatt

Alexander Campbell, Olivia Anderssen & Anna Finlay (RAF Cadets)

Deborah House (RAF Cadet Lead)

Ray Farmer (RAF Cadet Standard Bearer)

Amy-Rose Stevens (RAF Standard Bearer)

Brenda Kelly

The Springfield Band

Jacky and Nigel Pullen-Warner

Hazel Maidman and Mark Errington

Adam and Jo Buckley

Rob and Trish Edden

Andrews Dusters

Judy Anderson

Jackie and Ian Watson

The Ladies from Westhope

STILES Family

Represented by Lieutenant Colonel Christopher Barnard, Royal Canadian Air Force

ALLAN Family

Nell Hackney unable to attend but sent a pre-recorded tribute

BANKS Family

Sarah & Stephen Bennett

DUNLOP Family

Stuart & Alison Dunlop

David & Theresa Dunlop

Carole Benson

Phyliss Hannah

Carlene & Daniel Phillips

John & Sally Nesbit

Bill & Karen Nesbit

Lesley McAuley

Chris Humer

Mina Bradford

Martin Bean

Nancy & Phil Quinlan

Cosette & Agatha Dunlop

Jordan Potter

Sid Dunlop

Lizzy Dodd

DYKE Family

Clair Donetta-Yates

Paul Donetta

Tom & Jamie Yates

Patricia & Raymond Donetta

McKENDRY Family

Gill Moriarty

TRAYNOR Family

Joanne & Bill Deehan

Deidre & Gerry Oliver

Tony & Maire Earley

Christopher & Rebecca Oliver

Kevin & Rani Oliver

BIBLIOGRAPHY

Title	Author	Publisher
83 Squadron 1917-1969	Ronald G Low/Frank E Harper	Compaid Graphics
Lancaster	John Nichol	Simon & Schuster UK
Lancaster at War 4: Pathfinder Squadron	Alex Thorne	Ian Allan Ltd
The Pyonear magazine volunteers Articles - various editions representing the villages of Birley, Bush Bank, Canon Pyon, King's Pyon, Ledgemoor and Westhope, Herefordshire	Helen Theron	Pyonear
And In the Morning 83 Squadron Royal Air Force	Barry Hope	Barry Hope
83 Squadron	Chris Ward	Mention the War Ltd
Lancaster	Christopher Chant	Parragon
Bomber Command:	Steve Bond, Linzee Druce	Fighting High Ltd
Failed to Return II	Steve Darlow, Sean Feast Julian Evan-Hart, Andrew MacDonald	
The Pathfinders	Will Iredale	W H Allen
Pathfinder – A War	Air Vice-Marshall DCT Bennett	Goodall Publications Ltd
AVRO Lancaster	Mike Spick	Anness Publishing Ltd
The Lancaster Story	Peter R March	The History Press

Mother Worked at AVRO	Gerald Myers	Compaid Graphics

https://www.baesystems.com/en/heritage/chadderton

www.wwII2talk.com

www.uploads-ssl.webflow.com

www.wartimememories.co.uk

https://generalbotha.co.za

ALSO BY TONY ASTON

REDDITCH - From the Chip Shop to the Batchley

Published by Brewin Books Ltd

Tony grew up in Redditch, a short bus ride from Birmingham, during the 1950s and 60s at a time when the town, like hundreds of other towns and cities throughout the UK, were striving to repair, rebuild and re-invent themselves after World War II. He was born in 1953, a year when Winston Churchill was Prime Minister, the coronation of Queen Elizabeth II had taken place and Mount Everest had been conquered for the first time. Tony recalls day to day life in Redditch, a small 25,000 population town, globally famous for its needles and fishing tackle, before much of it was demolished to make way for Redditch Development Corporation to build a New Town. He talks about his personal recollections of friends and family, high days and holidays, Christmas, food and drink, incidents and accidents, the big freeze of 1962/63, radio and television, all intertwined with significant national and international events.

www.tonyastonauthor.com **info.tonyastonauthor@gmail.com**

Printed in Great Britain
by Amazon

44185592R00196

PATRICK BRUEL
TOUR 95
On s'était dit
Patrick Bruel Lequel de nous
DANS L'OEIL ENFOIRÉS
CW01653753
PATRICK BRUEL
Casser la voix
Noël Ensemble
2006
LE VILLAGE DES ENFOIRÉS
En concierto
PATRICK BRUEL
Marre de cette nana-là
LIVE
BRUEL 2014
Les Enfoirés
AU GRAND REX
CE SOIR ON SORT...
PATRICK BRUEL
Patrick Bruel
Plaza de los Heroes
CARRAPICHO
TIC TIC TAC
2CD
TOUR 95
BRUEL
On s'était dit
patrick bruel juste avant
2012
LE BAL DES ENFOIRÉS
Patrick Bruel
des souvenirs devant
BRUEL
Si ce soir...
VOL.1
ENTRE DEUX
À L'OLYMPIA
PATRICK BRUEL
LES ESSENTIELS
PATRICK BRUEL
CASSER LA VOIX • ALORS REGARDE • MARRE DE CETTE NANA LÀ
PATRICK BRUEL
ALORS REGARDE
bruel
décalé
PATRICK BRUEL
CASSER LA VOIX
la soirée des Enfoirés 96
Patrick Bruel
vide
PatrickBruelive
juste avant
2009
LES ENFOIRÉS
CINÉMA
PATRICK BRUEL
EN CONCERT
OLYMPIA 87
BRUEL
LIVE
des souvenirs... ensemble
PATRICK BRUEL
LEQUEL DE NOUS
Bruel
Combien de murs...
DE FACE

LA VÉRITABLE HISTOIRE DES CHANSONS DE
PATRICK BRUEL

Un livre édité par Hervé Desinge
Direction littéraire : Laurent Abrial
Direction artistique : Jef Cortes
Iconographie : Damien Ferdel, PIXL

34-36, rue La Pérouse, 75116 - Paris
www.hugoetcie.fr

ISBN : 9782755684636

Dépôt légal : octobre 2020

FABIEN LECŒUVRE

LA VÉRITABLE HISTOIRE DES CHANSONS DE PATRICK BRUEL

Hugo Image

AVANT-PROPOS

Patrick Bruel,

Un séducteur dans le cœur des Français

Patrick Bruel est un artiste universel qui est depuis toujours guidé par la curiosité et l'envie. En près de quarante ans de carrière, il a su traverser le temps avec un riche parcours musical, théâtral, mais aussi cinématographique. En alternant cinéma et chansons, Patrick Bruel est entré dans la vie des Français comme un personnage de la famille, quelqu'un qu'on ne perd jamais de vue parce qu'il est toujours là, quelque part.

Dès son deuxième album, *Alors regarde*, sorti le même jour que la chute du mur de Berlin, le 9 novembre 1989, Patrick Bruel a rencontré son public et a enchaîné les tubes, qui lui ont ouvert les portes des plus grandes scènes françaises et internationales.
Avec des chansons parfois engagées, parfois intimes, mais dans lesquelles chacun de nous retrouve toujours un peu de son histoire, de son quotidien, Patrick Bruel est entré dans la vie et le cœur de millions de Français. Une belle preuve d'amour pour ce garçon abandonné tout petit par son père et élevé seul par sa mère, Augusta, qui lui fait découvrir des artistes de qualité qu'elle apprécie comme Barbara ou Serge Reggiani et l'a initié très jeune à la culture artistique. Grâce à une éducation humaniste et respectueuse des autres, sans jamais rien renier, mais en allant toujours de l'avant, le petit garçon s'est forgé un destin sans jamais cesser de croire en ses rêves.

De Tlemcem à Argenteuil

L'histoire de Patrick Bruel commence en Algérie, à Tlemcen, une ville de l'Ouest oranais dont on a longtemps dit qu'elle était la cité « des beaux cavaliers, de l'air et du feu ».
Elle est située à huit cents mètres d'altitude, les hivers y sont froids et les printemps précoces, qui transforment cerisiers et pêchers en un océan de pétales immaculés.
Patrick Benguigui y voit le jour, le 14 mai 1959, dans une famille de juifs berbères devenus français par décret. Sa mère, Augusta Kammoun, est institutrice. C'est la deuxième d'une famille de cinq enfants. En 1958, elle a épousé Pierre Benguigui, lui aussi instituteur. Ils sont très jeunes et se rencontrent dans le cadre de leur métier en emmenant des enfants se faire vacciner dans un centre. Ils tombent amoureux et ont un enfant qui, vingt ans après, deviendra un phénomène de la chanson française sous le nom de Patrick Bruel.
En attendant, le petit Patrick joue sous les oliviers centenaires de Tlemcen et plisse les yeux sous le soleil qui gifle les murs blancs. Il respire un air qui a le parfum des oranges, de la grenade et du térébinthe.
Ce riche terreau, il saura s'en inspirer et le respirer au moment de jouer dans son premier film, *Le Coup de sirocco*, mis en scène par Alexandre Arcady. Le bonheur est là, à la portée de ses petits doigts, et pourtant, sans le savoir, il vit au cœur de la pire des tragédies.
Cinq ans plus tôt, à peine la guerre d'Indochine terminée, le sang s'est mis à couler en Algérie. Jusqu'alors, indigènes et pieds-noirs d'origine européenne se côtoyaient sans heurts, mais aux Algériens musulmans qui ont aidé à libérer la France du joug nazi, Paris a fait des promesses qui n'ont pas été tenues. Les nationalistes ont fait leur lit de l'injustice et de l'ingratitude de la métropole, et d'attentats en représailles, de massacres en carnages, ce qu'on s'obstine encore à considérer comme de malheureux « événements » a fini par dégénérer en une vraie guerre.
Il n'y a pas seulement des riches colons chez les pieds-noirs, mais essentiellement de modestes travailleurs, de petits commerçants et des fonctionnaires enracinés à cette terre à la fois âpre et généreuse. En Algérie, les juifs forment une communauté soudée. Tlemcen a été longtemps surnommée « la Jérusalem du Maghreb », car Arabes et Juifs y gardaient leur lieu saint.
Patrick naît donc dans un pays en guerre. Bientôt, ce seront les barricades d'Alger, puis le putsch des généraux,

les massacres d'Algériens dans les rues de Paris, et enfin le cessez-le-feu négocié à Évian. Aux derniers soubresauts de l'OAS succédera la proclamation de l'indépendance algérienne, le 3 juillet 1963.

Après Tlemcen, Augusta Benguigui est mutée avec son mari à Colomb-Béchar. Ils se séparent au bout d'un an et elle revient à Tlemcen, où son père, Élie, un socialiste convaincu, est secrétaire général à la Mairie.

En 1962, la famille doit quitter précipitamment Tlemcen car Élie, au courant d'un projet d'embuscade, a prévenu les soldats français pour éviter un massacre, ce qui a fortement déplu au FLN.

Augusta et son fils de trois ans prennent alors l'avion pour rejoindre la France.

À l'instar de deux millions d'apatrides, le petit garçon de Tlemcen va devoir se refaire une vie sous un autre ciel, dans un autre climat, loin de l'odeur de l'Algérie, de ses couleurs et de sa douceur.

En 1962, Patrick s'installe donc avec sa mère, à Argenteuil, dans le Val d'Oise, en banlieue parisienne. Comme elle est institutrice, ils habitent dans des logements de fonction dans les deux écoles où elle travaille. Pour combler l'absence du père de Patrick, Augusta s'est mise en quatre pour remplacer cet amour-là par un amour deux fois plus fort. Patrick a appris à vivre sans appeler « Papa ! », il a grandi sans qu'une grosse voix lui indique le chemin.

Mais quel petit garçon peut se passer durablement de modèle, d'idole et d'adversaire ?

À qui s'identifier, se comparer, et comment aimer quand on n'a pas été aimé ?

Patrick n'est pas orphelin, il est abandonné : en un sens, c'est pire.

Il leur faut à tous les deux beaucoup de courage et de dignité pour porter cette marque au front et au cœur, dans ces années 60, dans un milieu où tout se voit, se sait et se répète.

Miracle de l'enfance : le petit Benguigui devient en quelques semaines un banlieusard dégourdi. Il a cinq ans, tout l'étonne, tout le ravit, tout le questionne. Bientôt, il se fait ses premiers copains, compose sa première bande.

Il sympathise alors très vite en classe ou en jouant au foot avec des garçons de son âge, dont les parents travaillent sur les chantiers, chez Renault à Boulogne-Billancourt où à Gennevilliers sur le Port. Des polonais , des portugais, des turcs, des espagnols, des marocains.

Argenteuil, quand on a sept ans, quand on a huit ans, quand on a tout son temps, c'est un paradis qui fait penser irrésistiblement aux photos de Doisneau. Il y fait bon vivre, et il fait bon être le fils de l'institutrice...

Position privilégiée entre toutes : il est près du Savoir, au centre du Pouvoir. L'école est à lui, c'est sa maison. Il peut s'enorgueillir de tutoyer les maîtres et les maîtresses de l'école et, en cachette, il recopie les notes des copies corrigées par sa mère pour les donner aux copains. Le samedi et le dimanche, il tape le ballon dans la cour déserte, il joue aux petites autos dans les classes qui sentent bon la craie et l'encre violette, et il chante à tue-tête dans le réfectoire vide.

Comme il chante bien, mon Patrick ! s'extasie Augusta. Elle est à mille lieues de se douter de ce que son fils fera de ce talent particulier. Chanteur, pour elle, ce n'est pas un métier, c'est un destin.

Il faut être Maurice Chevalier, Charles Trenet ou André Claveau pour vivre en chantant. Les autres, le public, fredonnent « Cerisiers roses et pommiers blancs », esquissent un pas de cha-cha-cha sur « Si tu vas à Rio » de Dario Moreno, ou répètent sous leur douche « Scoubidou-bidou, ha ! », le tube qui a lancé le neveu de Ray Ventura, Sacha Distel.

Patrick aime la musique, toutes les musiques. À l'âge de six ans, sa mère lui offre le 45 tours des Beatles, *Michelle*, et celui des Stones, *Satisfaction*, et à huit ans, elle lui fait découvrir sa chanteuse préférée, Barbara, ainsi que Jacques Brel. Elle l'emmène aussi au cinéma voir le film de Jacques Tati, *Playtime*, sorti le 16 décembre 1967.

Le tout premier concert auquel assiste Patrick Bruel, c'est celui de Johnny Hallyday, à Pietroso, en Corse, au cours de l'été 1965. Ce soir-là, il se retrouve sur les genoux de Sylvie Vartan !

Augusta l'emmènera aussi voir l'opéra *Aïda* dans les arènes de Vérone, en 1967, et même la *Tosca*, aux thermes de Caracalla, à Rome, l'année suivante.

En 1969, après sept ans passés à Argenteuil, Augusta est nommée à Paris, dans le 5e arrondissement. Comme elle souhaite reprendre des études de lettres, elle se rapproche de la faculté de Censier.

Cette année-là, avec sa mère, Patrick Bruel assiste à un concert de Serge Reggiani à Bobino. Un moment inoubliable pour le jeune garçon de dix ans.

Patrick aime la musique mais aussi le cinéma et le football. Il se verrait bien devenir footballeur professionnel.

"Le tout premier concert auquel assiste Patrick Bruel, c'est celui de Johnny Hallyday en 1965. Ce soir-là, il se retrouve sur les genoux de Sylvie Vartan !"

Une nouvelle vie à Paris

Devenu parisien, Patrick Bruel va en classe de CM2, rue Rollin, dans une école située près de la place de la Contrescarpe. Il fréquente ensuite le lycée Henri-IV, où il se fait de nouveaux amis.

En 1970, Augusta, après avoir mis sa vie sentimentale entre parenthèses pour élever son fils, se remarie avec Philippe Moreau, un artiste peintre et brillant architecte-décorateur, fils d'un grand médecin de Niort, qu'elle a rencontré en Corse en 1966.

Le jeune Patrick découvre alors une nouvelle vie avec de nouveaux codes, ceux de la bourgeoisie catholique des Deux-Sèvres. Il va aussi régulièrement à Megève, dans le chalet familial. Le petit garçon s'entend très bien avec le père de Philippe, le docteur René Moreau, un grand médecin qui lui apprend à jouer au poker, au bridge et aux échecs et à apprécier les grands vins millésimés. Avec son second mari, Augusta a deux enfants : David-François Moreau, en 1972, et Fabrice Moreau, en 1975.

La famille recomposée s'installe dans le 13e arrondissement de Paris. Patrick fait sa quatrième, puis sa troisième et sa seconde à Henri-IV. Le lycéen Patrick a souvent l'impression de rétrograder, voire de patiner, mais il est en train d'avancer. Sans s'en rendre compte, il respire l'air du temps, il joue toujours au foot et rêve plus que jamais de devenir professionnel. On lui propose d'aller à l'Institut national du football, mais sa famille au grand complet refuse !

Patrick est un grand fan du joueur néerlandais Johan Cruijff, qui porte le numéro 14 et joue à l'Ajax d'Amsterdam. Patrick tapisse les murs de sa chambre de posters de Cruijff et de numéros 14. Comme sa tante vit aux Pays-Bas, il réussit à avoir le même maillot que son idole, avec le numéro 14 dans le dos.

Patrick adore aussi le cinéma. Il est impressionné par Piccoli dans *Les Choses de la vie*, le très beau film de Claude Sautet. Comment pourrait-il alors songer que, dans une vingtaine d'années, il lui donnerait la réplique dans un film d'Agnès Varda ?

La musique prend aussi de plus en plus de place dans la vie de Patrick Bruel. Il aime Jimmy Hendrix, Eric Clapton, Jeff Beck. Le 20 janvier 1975, Patrick Bruel se rend dans une boutique pour acheter des places pour le match de rugby France/ pays de Galles. Hélas, lorsqu'il arrive dans la boutique du boulevard des Capucines, on lui annonce que le stade est plein et qu'il n'y a plus de billet à vendre. Patrick est très déçu. Il déambule alors sur le boulevard quand un homme l'aborde et lui propose de lui vendre, pour la somme de vingt francs, une place pour l'Olympia. Patrick regarde alors le fronton de la salle et constate que c'est Michel Sardou qui est à l'affiche. Cet artiste n'est pas trop la tasse de thé du jeune Patrick, mais par curiosité, il décide d'aller le voir sur scène et achète donc la place. Il se retrouve au dernier rang du balcon. Et là, pendant les deux heures du concert, Patrick est totalement subjugué par le charisme de Sardou. Ce 20 janvier 1975, Patrick éprouve un sentiment très étrange. À la fin du spectacle, il reste vingt minutes seul, à regarder la scène et la salle, tout en se disant que, lui aussi, un jour, il pourrait se produire sur cette même scène. Ce jour-là, à l'issue du concert, Patrick Bruel est conforté dans son désir de devenir chanteur. Dès lors, il va tout faire pour concrétiser son ambition et il va y parvenir puisque, douze ans et quatre mois plus tard, le 5 mai 1987, il se retrouve lui-même à l'affiche de l'Olympia.

Mais pour l'instant, c'est encore le temps des boums, des copains et des copines. Toutes les filles craquent pour ce beau garçon aux grands yeux noisette et au sourire éblouissant. Le lycée Henri-IV qu'il fréquente n'est pas encore mixte. En revanche, il y a des filles au lycée Claude-Monet, situé en face de chez lui, dans le 13e arrondissement. Aussi, Patrick Bruel adore aller promener son petit frère David dans le square en bas de chez lui, en face du lycée Claude-Monet. C'est ainsi l'occasion de rencontrer de nouveaux amis comme Marion Suffert, la fille du célèbre journaliste Georges Suffert, Éric Jacquet, Pascale, Philippe, mais aussi ses premières amoureuses, Patricia et Laurence.

Après la seconde à Henri-IV, Patrick Bruel change de lycée pour préparer un bac économique. Il se retrouve au lycée François-Villon, dans le 14e arrondissement. À la différence d'Henri-IV, l'ambiance est plus populaire, plus libre. Patrick se fait de nouveaux amis chez qui il se retrouve après les cours et avec lesquels il joue des chansons de Dylan, de Cat Stevens ou de John Lennon.

En juin 1978, Patrick Bruel passe son bac.

> ***“Patrick adore aussi le cinéma. Il est impressionné par Michel Piccoli dans* Les Choses de la vie, *de Claude Sautet. Comment pourrait-il alors penser que, dans une vingtaine d'années, il lui donnerait la réplique ?”***

Hollywood

Les premières chansons et les débuts au cinéma

En attendant les résultats du baccalauréat, le jeune Patrick Bruel ne sait pas trop quoi faire. C'est alors qu'un de ses amis repère une petite annonce dans le quotidien *France-Soir*. Un jeune réalisateur pas encore très connu, Alexandre Arcady, recherche de jeunes garçons à l'accent pied-noir pour son premier long métrage. Comme Patrick s'amuse souvent à imiter cet accent, son ami lui suggère de répondre à l'annonce. Mais Patrick hésite. Deux ans plus tôt, il avait failli tourner dans *L'Hôtel de la plage*, et après plusieurs castings, il n'avait pas été retenu. Son copain insiste, et finalement, le 18 juin 1978, Patrick Bruel répond à cette annonce de casting. Quelques jours plus tard, il est convoqué à une audition qui se déroule au 38, rue des Saules, à Montmartre.

Patrick s'y rend très décontracté, sans se faire d'illusions, d'autant qu'ils sont une centaine à tenter leur chance.

Quelque temps après, le jour des résultats du bac, qu'il n'obtient pas, Patrick Bruel reçoit un coup de téléphone du Club Méditerranée pour lui annoncer que sa candidature pour être GO à Cancun a été retenue. Faute d'avoir le bac, Patrick va donc partir travailler six mois au Mexique en tant que chanteur et animateur. Il signe son contrat le 10 juillet et doit partir le 18. Mais le 17 au soir, il reçoit un appel d'Alexandre Arcady pour lui annoncer qu'il est retenu pour jouer le rôle de Paulo Narboni, aux côtés de Roger Hanin et de Marthe Villalonga, dans *Le Coup de sirocco*. Patrick explique alors au réalisateur qu'il a déjà un engagement avec le Club Med et qu'il doit partir le lendemain à Cancun. Mais Alexandre Arcady va réussir à le faire changer d'avis. Il intervient auprès du Club Med pour reporter l'engagement de Patrick après le tournage de son film.

Ainsi, Patrick Bruel tourne dans *Le Coup de sirocco* jusqu'au mois de novembre 1978 et enchaîne ensuite avec quatre mois à Cancun.

Le film *Le Coup de sirocco* sort dans les salles obscures le 18 avril 1979, et c'est un grand succès.

Dans l'intervalle, Patrick Benguigui est devenu Patrick Bruel. Bruel, c'est comme Brel, avec une lettre en plus,

"Bruel, c'est comme Brel, avec une lettre en plus, ce 'grand Jacques' qui a disparu le 9 octobre 1978 à quarante-neuf ans, loin de ses chères Marquises…"

ce « grand Jacques » qui a disparu le 9 octobre 1978, à quarante-neuf ans, loin de ses chères Marquises...
Pour Patrick, c'est une seconde naissance. Un nouveau nom, pour ne rien devoir à son passé, mais le petit Benguigui sera toujours là, riche de ses trésors d'enfance, explique-t-il à Augusta. Du jour au lendemain, le jeune Bruel devient la coqueluche des médias.
En juin 1979, il repasse le bac mais en candidat libre. Cette fois, il l'obtient avec Mention bien. Il s'inscrit alors à la fac de Tolbiac, en sciences éco, pour la rentrée universitaire de 1979. Mais avant de reprendre les cours, en octobre, il décide de partir à New York rejoindre sa copine Patricia, d'origine brésilienne, dont la mère, qui est diplomate, a été mutée là-bas. Il passe alors trois semaines avec elle au cours de l'été 1979, avant de rentrer à Paris pour commencer la fac. Très vite, Patricia lui manque. En plus, les cours l'ennuient et il n'a qu'une idée en tête : retourner à New York.
Ce qu'il fait dès le mois de novembre. Il a vingt ans, il est libre, il en profite. Il file aux États-Unis...
Seulement, quand la mère de Patricia le voit revenir, elle n'apprécie pas du tout et lui explique que sa fille, qui a juste seize ans, ne peut pas construire une histoire d'amour avec lui. Bref, poliment mais fermement, Patrick Bruel est éconduit. Après une nuit passée dans le canapé du salon, il se retrouve au petit matin à errer dans les rues de New York. Il appelle alors un ami à Paris qui travaille dans une agence de voyages pour lui demander s'il ne connaît pas quelqu'un à New York qui pourrait l'héberger. Cet ami l'oriente vers un certain Philippe Bénichou, un élève comédien dans une école d'art dramatique new-yorkaise.
Patrick et Philippe sympathisent. Ils sont tous les deux originaires de la même ville algérienne de Tlemcen, ils ont à peu près le même âge et tous les deux rêvent d'une carrière artistique. Pendant plusieurs mois, Patrick s'installe dans l'appartement que Philippe partage avec son frère Pascal, un jeune danseur qui rêve lui aussi de gloire. Pour gagner un peu d'argent, ils s'improvisent photographes et réalisent des books pour de jeunes acteurs comme eux. Patrick Bruel reste à New York jusqu'au mois de mars 1980. Pendant cette période, chez Philippe Bénichou, il rencontre un certain Gérard Presgurvic, un jeune musicien qui étudie aussi le cinéma à New York. Très vite, Patrick et Gérard deviennent amis et s'aperçoivent qu'ils partagent la même passion pour la chanson. Patrick aime beaucoup les textes de Gérard, qui mélangent habilement poésie et une certaine violence. Leurs rêves se ressemblent, ils rentrent ensemble en France.
Patrick démarche des agents. Il est repéré par une directrice de casting, Margot Capelier, qu'il avait aidée à retrouver son chemin, un an plus tôt, dans les couloirs du Palais des Festivals, à Cannes. Cette grande dame des castings, à la voix gouailleuse, propose à Patrick de rencontrer Pierrette Bruno, qui cherche des jeunes acteurs avec du caractère pour sa nouvelle pièce, *Le Charimari.*
Patrick Bruel est alors retenu pour tenir le rôle drôle de Martin. Le spectacle démarre le 4 septembre 1981, au théâtre Saint-Georges, et va se jouer 480 fois sur deux saisons. Dans le même temps, Patrick fait son Service militaire en journée, à Fontainebleau, et en chantant avec son pote Florent Pagny, après le théâtre, au *Vin aux Halles*, un restaurant de nuit.
Si le métier d'acteur et l'armée occupent alors le temps de Patrick Bruel, la chanson reste sa priorité.
Il est toujours en contact avec Gérard Presgurvic, rencontré à New York. Ils se voient souvent et travaillent ensemble sur des chansons. C'est avec l'une d'elles, intitulée « Vide », que Patrick Bruel enregistre son premier 45 tours

Entre le 8 juillet et le 24 août 1985, Patrick Bruel fait une tournée d'été en première partie de Patrick Sébastien.

chez Barclay. Avec un titre comme celui-ci et des paroles déprimantes, le disque ne peut que passer inaperçu, et ça ne manque pas.
Cette même année 1982, Patrick Bruel tourne dans *Les Diplômés du dernier rang*, un film de Christian Gion qui se laisse aisément oublier. Il y croise Michel Galabru, immense acteur. Il passe aussi le casting pour un rôle dans *La Boum 2*, de Claude Pinoteau, pour tenir le rôle de Philippe Berthier, mais on lui préférera l'acteur Pierre Cosso.
Et après, il joue dans *Le Bâtard*, de Bertrand Van Effenterre, avec la belle Julie Jézéquiel, puis retour chez Arcady pour *Le Grand Carnaval*, qui sort dans les salles le 7 décembre 1983.
Patrick Bruel tourne aussi dans des spots publicitaires diffusés en Belgique.
En 1984, Patrick Bruel connaît son premier succès en chanson avec « Marre de cette nana-là », une chanson co-écrite avec son copain Gérard Presgurvic quelques années plus tôt à New York. Le titre devient un important succès radio et permet à Patrick Bruel de participer à d'importantes émissions de télévision comme *La Chance aux chansons*, présentée par Pascal Sevran, le 16 janvier 1984 et *Champs-Élysées*, de Michel Drucker, le 10 mars 1984.
L'année suivante, en 1985, les planètes s'alignent bien pour le jeune artiste. Non seulement sa nouvelle chanson, « Comment ça va pour vous », toujours écrite avec Gérard Presgurvic, devient l'un des tubes de l'été 1985, mais de plus, la comédie *P.R.O.F.S.*, de Patrick Schulmann, dans laquelle il tient le rôle de Frédéric Game, un jeune prof de lycée, aux côtés de Fabrice Luchini, fait un triomphe au mois de septembre, avec plus de 3 millions de spectateurs.
Entre le 8 juillet et le 24 août, Patrick Bruel a fait une tournée d'été avec Patrick Sébastien, dont il assure la Première partie avec les trois chansons qu'il a à son répertoire, dont « Comment ça va pour vous ? », qui chaque soir est acclamée par les foules de vacanciers. Des choix judicieux, des interprétations épatantes, ce garçon a décidément tous les dons, dont celui de sortir par la porte du cinéma pour entrer par la fenêtre de la chanson, et inversement.
Ce n'est pourtant pas si évident.
Chanter, c'est facile, se disent beaucoup d'acteurs, qui nantis en tout et pour tout de leur notoriété et d'un filet de voix, ne résistent pas au plaisir de pousser une chansonnette insipide sur des arrangements d'hier. Passons sur les noms… Idem pour les chanteurs : la tentation est grande de passer devant la caméra, sous le prétexte qu'ils connaissent déjà les feux de la rampe.
Ça n'a pas si mal réussi à Montand, Dutronc, Brel, Souchon… mais beaucoup moins à d'autres !
Patrick, lui, a passé la ligne. De comédien, il est devenu chanteur, puis de chanteur il est redevenu comédien, avec

“Avec Claude Lelouch, Patrick intègre une seconde famille, chaleureuse, soudée, peuplée de femmes étourdissantes, les deux hommes sont sur la même longueur d'onde.”

la même aisance. Comme Jeanne Moreau, Serge Reggiani, Jane Birkin, Eddy Mitchell, Vanessa Paradis... Il réussira même à tel point qu'on peut se demander s'il était d'abord un acteur ou essentiellement un chanteur. Il aura, en tout cas, réuni autant de spectateurs que d'auditeurs en quarante ans de carrière.

En 1986, Patrick retourne au théâtre dans *On m'appelle Émilie*, de Maria Pacôme. Puis il tourne trois films coup sur coup, *Champagne amer*, de Ridha Béhi (qu'il retrouvera l'année suivante pour tourner *La Mémoire tatouée* avec deux partenaires prestigieux : Ben Gazzara et Julie Christie) ; *Suivez mon regard*, de Jean Curtelin, avec Stéphane Audran ; enfin, *Attention bandits !* qui voit le début de sa collaboration avec Claude Lelouch.

Lelouch, c'est plus qu'un cinéaste, c'est un chef de tribu. Avec lui, Patrick intègre une seconde famille, chaleureuse, soudée, peuplée de femmes étourdissantes. Les deux hommes sont sur la même longueur d'onde.

La même année, Patrick Bruel enregistre son premier album, *De face (2 faces)*. Il l'a écrit avec Presgurvic, bien sûr. L'une des dix chansons de ce disque, « Tout le monde peut se tromper », servira de générique au film de Claude Lelouch.

Acteur, chanteur, Patrick doit gérer maintenant un agenda surchargé, répondre aux innombrables sollicitations, tout cela en satisfaisant sa passion pour les matchs de foot (c'est un inconditionnel du Paris Saint-Germain), le tennis, les voitures et les demoiselles...

Même si son premier album ne se vend qu'à 20 000 exemplaires, Patrick Bruel fait son premier Olympia entre le 5 et le 8 mai 1987. Son nom s'étale en lettres énormes sur le fronton du célèbre music-hall du boulevard des Capucines, à Paris. Un moment fort et émouvant pour le gamin qui avait tant rêvé d'être lui aussi un jour sur cette scène.

Le soir de la première, le 5 mai 1987, Patrick Bruel reçoit un formidable accueil. Dès sa première chanson, « Comment ça va pour vous ? », le public chante avec lui et ça continue presque sans interruption pendant près de deux heures.

Dans le spectacle, entre deux chansons, Patrick s'amuse à faire des sketchs ou des imitations et crée une véritable interactivité avec le public. On sent déjà l'homme de scène qu'il est. Quand il reprend « Amsterdam », de Brel, la salle l'écoute religieusement. Il termine son concert avec « À tout à l'heure », une belle chanson de sortie de scène dans laquelle il fait une belle déclaration d'amour à son public en lui promettant de le revoir bientôt.

Quelques mois après, le 5 août 1987, le film *Attention bandits !* de Lelouch arrive dans les salles. Parmi les spectateurs, à la première séance de 14 heures, il y a Georges Lautner, le célèbre réalisateur des *Tontons flingueurs* et de *La Route de Salina*. Après avoir vu Patrick Bruel dans *Attention bandits !*, Lautner appelle Patrick Bruel et lui propose un rôle dans son prochain film, *La Maison assassinée*, d'après le roman de Pierre Magnan. Après avoir lu le scénario, très vite, Patrick Bruel accepte le rôle de Séraphin Monge, qui revient dans son village natal de Haute-Provence, après la Première Guerre mondiale, pour élucider le mystère de sa famille assassinée alors qu'il n'était qu'un bébé. Dans ce film en tenue d'époque qui est à l'affiche le 3 février 1988, Patrick Bruel a pour partenaire la comédienne Anne Brochet.

L'année suivante est également une année importante sur le plan cinématographique pour Patrick Bruel, avec deux films : *L'Union sacrée*, d'Alexandre Arcady, aux côtés de Richard Berry, qui sort le 15 mars 1989, et *Force majeure*, de Pierre Jolivet, avec François Cluzet et Kristin Scott Thomas, qui est dans les salles de cinéma le 5 avril 1989.

Michel Drucker a toujours soutenu la carrière de Patrick Bruel.

Fender

La consécration et la Bruelmania

La fin des années 80 est pour Patrick Bruel le temps de la consécration aussi bien au cinéma que dans la chanson. Il change de maison de disques et signe avec BMG Ariola. Le président de ce groupe, Bernard Carbonez, attend beaucoup de cette nouvelle signature, et pour se donner toutes les chances de réussite, il demande à Mick Lanaro, une référence, de produire le disque de Patrick Bruel.

L'album *Alors regarde* est enregistré durant l'été 1989, d'abord au Studio Polygone, en banlieue de Toulouse, puis au Studio Hit & Sounds, à New York.

Au total, onze chansons sont réalisées, dont plus de la moitié vont devenir des immenses succès. Le disque paraît le 9 novembre 1989.

Dès la sortie du premier extrait, « Casser la voix », au début du mois précédent, c'est un véritable raz-de-marée. Dès le 25 novembre, la chanson entre au Top 50 et va y rester 19 semaines, pour se retrouver à la 3e place du classement des meilleures ventes, le 1er janvier 1990.

“Ce sont les filles qui ont plébiscité Patrick, elles l'ont choisi pour incarner leur idéal masculin, il est plus que leur chanteur favori : il est l'amour, l'ami, l'amant, le confident.”

Ce titre est incontestablement le détonateur à ce qui va devenir le « phénomène Bruel ». La critique est unanime pour saluer la qualité de ce disque. Michel Drucker consacre un spécial *Champs-Élysées* à Patrick Bruel, qui est invité aussi à *Sacrée Soirée* sur TF1, le 16 mai 1990.

L'artiste se retrouve en une de tous les magazines. Ce succès immédiat, disproportionné, monumental, il l'avait peut-être espéré, mais il ne l'avait pas prévu. Et surtout, il n'avait pas pensé qu'il cesserait d'être un homme pour devenir un dieu vivant pour des jeunes filles romanesques.

Car ce sont les filles qui ont plébiscité Patrick. Elles l'ont choisi, lui et pas un autre, pour incarner leur idéal masculin.

Il est plus que leur chanteur favori : il est l'amour, l'ami, l'amant, le confident.

Patrick Bruel est LE succès des années 1989 et 1990. Il n'y a rien eu de semblable en France depuis Bécaud, Hallyday et Claude François.

On campe en bas de chez lui, on embrasse sa voiture, les paparazzi le traquent impitoyablement, et jour et nuit résonne le fameux cri d'hystérie « Patriiiiick !!! » poussé par des adolescentes qui tournent de l'œil en le voyant. Il va devenir le sujet de toutes les conversations, l'objet de centaines d'articles et de débats savants, mais aussi la cible privilégiée des humoristes, à commencer par ceux de Canal+ avec des sketchs parfois plus méchants que drôles.

À tout juste trente ans, Patrick Bruel se retrouve au cœur d'un véritable phénomène de société. La gloire, quand on ne l'a pas, vous éblouit. Quand vous l'avez, elle vous plombe. Vos amis, vos amours, votre famille, vos vices et vos vertus, ce que vous faites de votre temps et ce que vous faites de votre argent, tout est passé au crible.

Vous appartenez au public qui vous a sacré, vous êtes le roi et vous êtes l'esclave, à la fois responsable de tout et de rien. On ne vous voit pas, on vous imagine. On l'a mis sur un piédestal du jour au lendemain, et des millions de bouches répètent ses refrains comme si c'était le miel de la terre. Mais, au milieu de ces foules en délire, Patrick ne peut compter que sur ses proches, ses amis, son clan.

Après « Casser la voix », les extraits de l'album se succèdent et deviennent tous des tubes très bien classés au Top 50. « J'te l'dis quand même » sort le 2 mars 1990, « Alors regarde » le 3 septembre et devient N° 1, « Place des grands hommes » le 4 février 1991, et « Décalé » le 4 juillet 1991. Avec cette succession de tubes, les ventes de l'album s'envolent et finiront par atteindre près de 3 millions d'exemplaires.

Ce disque phénomène conduit tout logiquement Patrick Bruel à partir en tournée à la rencontre de son public. Au départ, seulement 30 dates avaient été prévues, mais finalement, Patrick Bruel fera 130 concerts, dont 14 Zénith de Paris, entre le 4 octobre 1990 à Évry et le 18 août 1991 à Annecy, totalisant un million de spectateurs. Les places s'arrachent et des dates doivent être doublées, voire triplées. En Belgique, Patrick Bruel remplit cinq fois le fameux Forest National.

Chaque soir, des milliers de briquets s'allument, des milliers de mains se tendent, et Patrick mesure sa popularité. Dans les interviews de l'époque, l'artiste n'hésite pas à comparer ses concerts à des rendez-vous d'amour avec la même attente, puis la même découverte.

En arrivant sur scène, vêtu d'un long manteau noir de chez Armani et d'un bandana autour du cou, dès qu'il entonne « Alors regarde », les salles sont en ébullition et chantent en même temps que lui.

“En 1992, Patrick Bruel obtient enfin la Victoire de la Musique du meilleur interprète masculin, lors de la cérémonie qui se tient le 1er février, en direct du Palais des Congrès de Paris.”

Au Zénith, le tout-Paris accourt pour se rendre compte de ce qu'on appelle déjà la Bruelmania. Dans les coulisses, on croise Johnny Hallyday, Catherine Deneuve, Francis Huster, Michel Berger et beaucoup d'autres. À l'évidence, Patrick Bruel est en train de se faire une place parmi les plus grands.
Pendant cette tournée, Patrick crée sur scène une chanson inédite qui avait été écartée de l'album. Elle a pour titre « Qui a le droit » et parle d'un sujet qui lui tient à cœur : l'absence d'un père.
Alors qu'il hésitait à la chanter, sa mère, Augusta, lui a conseillé de le faire, et il a eu raison de l'écouter, car la chanson devient un immense succès. Elle fera d'ailleurs partie du double album live de cette éblouissante tournée, intitulée *Si ce soir*, qui paraît en novembre 1991 et se vend à un million d'exemplaires. « Qui a le droit » est la chanson qui soutient cet album live qui se vendra à un million d'exemplaires. Elle entre au Top 50 le 2 novembre 1991 et va y rester jusqu'au 18 avril 1992, dont 7 semaines à la première place.
Si la Bruelmania a ses avantages, elle a aussi ses inconvénients. Un jour, alors qu'il prend un café, à 17 heures, avec son ami Alexandre Arcady, dans l'arrière-salle de la pizzeria *Café di Roma*, sur les Champs-Élysées, Patrick est reconnu par une jeune fille qui prévient immédiatement toutes ses copines, et très vite, plus de mille personnes se rassemblent devant le restaurant. Le chanteur, qui est attendu ce soir-là pour un dîner de famille chez sa mère, doit être évacué dans un fourgon de police. Rapidement, toute la presse se fait l'écho de cet incident et certains journalistes malintentionnés se servent de cela pour ridiculiser le public de l'artiste et le réduire à une armée d'hystériques à la limite de la folie. Même le magazine d'informations *Envoyé spécial*, diffusé à l'époque sur France 2, fait un reportage sous cet angle lors d'un concert NRJ.
Cette caricature facile et injuste blesse beaucoup Patrick Bruel, qui ne supporte pas que son public soit résumé à quelques allumées ! Il n'apprécie pas non plus que l'on catalogue son succès comme un phénomène de société sans vraiment souligner les qualités artistiques de ses chansons ou de ses concerts. Le 2 août 1990, le magazine *L'Express* en remet une couche dans la même lignée, en consacrant sa couverture et un important article titré : « La folie Bruel ».
Si la presse n'est pas tendre avec lui, les Victoires de la musique ne le sont pas non plus. Lors de la sixième cérémonie des Victoires de la musique qui se tient au Zénith de Paris, le 2 février 1991, Patrick Bruel, nommé dans trois catégories, n'en remporte aucune alors qu'il est incontestablement l'artiste du moment, avec un album et une tournée qui battent tous les records !!! Patrick Bruel vit mal cette injustice et ce mépris de la profession. Patrick est blessé, mais il ne le montre pas.
Il lui suffit qu'au *Printemps de Bourges*, en mai de l'année suivante, 89 000 billets soient vendus sur son nom en quelques heures. Que ses chansons soient dans tous les charts européens et canadiens. Qu'on lui donne le prix Vincent Scotto en juin 1991, et qu'en novembre il ait vendu 2,5 millions de son album pour comprendre que la seule victoire qui compte est celle que lui donne le public à chacun de ses concerts.

Au-delà d'être un chanteur fédérateur de toute une jeunesse, Patrick Bruel est aussi un citoyen engagé, très concerné par les problèmes de son époque. Sollicité depuis plusieurs mois pour participer à l'émission *7 sur 7*, présentée par Anne Sinclair sur TF1, le chanteur finit par accepter. Cette émission d'information, très suivie, est un enjeu très important pour celui que trop de journalistes regardent alors avec condescendance. Pour bien préparer sa participation à cette émission, Patrick se fait conseiller par Guy Carcassonne, un éminent spécialiste de droit constitutionnel et enseignant à l'université de Paris-X Nanterre, mari de la célèbre dessinatrice Claire Bretécher. Patrick Bruel a rencontré Guy Carcassonne lors d'un déjeuner, en 1989, avec le Premier ministre Michel Rocard, dont il était un des conseillers. Entre le juriste et le chanteur qui sont tous les deux nés un 14 mai, une vraie et durable amitié s'est installée.
Le dimanche 24 novembre 1991, Patrick Bruel est donc l'invité d'Anne Sinclair sur TF1. Pendant cette émission, il aborde tous les sujets d'actualité auxquels il est sensible, comme le processus de paix au Proche-Orient et la montée de l'antisémitisme en même temps que celle du Front National. Pour stopper justement la progression de Jean-Marie Le Pen aux prochaines élections régionales et éviter

Fender
Gibson

un important taux d'abstention, le chanteur encourage les téléspectateurs à aller voter.
Et son message va être entendu puisque, le 22 mars 1992, jour du scrutin, la participation est importante et l'abstention moindre que prévu.
Quelque temps après l'élection, Patrick Bruel déjeune à l'Élysée avec le président François Mitterrand et quelques invités triés sur le volet. L'un d'eux félicite Patrick pour sa participation à l'émission *7 sur 7* dans laquelle il l'a trouvé formidable. Une remarque que le président François Mitterrand rectifie en disant qu'elle n'avait pas été formidable mais beaucoup plus que cela, elle avait été déterminante !
Cette même année 1992, Patrick Bruel obtient enfin la Victoire de la musique du meilleur interprète masculin, lors de la cérémonie qui se tient le 1er février 1992, en direct du Palais des Congrès de Paris. Il ne lui manquait que cette reconnaissance de ses pairs, celle de ses consœurs et de ses confrères, ces femmes et ces hommes qui savent de quelles souffrances se paye une vocation d'artiste dans ce monde voué au matérialisme et à la consommation.
En 1992, le succès de Patrick Bruel dépasse largement nos frontières. À partir du 15 avril, il part chanter à Québec, puis à Montréal, puis Sherbrooke. Une tournée canadienne qu'il reprend au mois de novembre suivant avec deux concerts au Forum de Montréal. Lors des World Music Awards qui se déroulent dans la salle des Étoiles, à Monaco, Patrick Bruel reçoit une récompense pour être le Français qui a vendu le plus de disques. Il enregistre aussi des versions espagnoles et italiennes de ses tubes et se produit avec grand succès à Rotterdam, en Hollande, et en Tunisie également.

Cette même année, Patrick Bruel fait l'acquisition d'un vaste appartement sur plusieurs niveaux, à Neuilly-sur-Seine, avec une terrasse donnant sur le bois de Boulogne.
Même si Patrick Bruel savoure sa réussite et ce succès international, il sait qu'il est attendu au tournant pour son prochain album et que personne ne lui fera de cadeaux. En attendant de créer de nouvelles chansons, il décide de faire une pause musicale de quelques mois pour se remettre de son épuisant marathon et redescendre sur terre. Sans le dire, Patrick attend que l'hystérie retombe : il ne veut pas rester éternellement ce chanteur qui fait tourner la tête aux minettes. Cette caricature, cette image réductrice que certains médias et humoristes lui ont collée, Patrick Bruel va s'employer à la faire oublier patiemment pour laisser apparaître ce qu'il est vraiment : un musicien passionné guidé par l'envie.

La reconquête

Tous les artistes le savent bien. Il n'est jamais facile d'enchaîner après un immense succès et une sur-médiatisation. Patrick Bruel sait bien qu'après le triomphe de son album *Alors regarde*, une certaine pression pèse sur ses épaules. Il le confie d'ailleurs à son ami Nagui, dans l'émission *Taratata* diffusée le 25 mars 1993. Après deux ans de tournée, l'artiste sait aussi dans quelle direction musicale il veut aller. Ce qui est certain, c'est qu'il veut faire mieux tout en se faisant plaisir.
En attendant de sortir un nouveau disque, Patrick Bruel revient à son autre grande passion, le cinéma. Après avoir tourné aux côtés de Jacques Dutronc et de Mathilda May, sous la direction de Michel Deville, dans le film *Toutes peines confondues*, sorti le 8 avril 1992, il a enchaîné avec le polar de Claude Zidi, *Profil bas*, dans lequel il tient le rôle de l'inspecteur Julien Segal, qui a perdu la foi en son métier. Sorti le mercredi 8 décembre 1993, le film ne rassemble qu'un peu plus de 600 000 spectateurs dans toute la France.
Retour à la chanson, le 26 avril 1994, avec un troisième album studio intitulé *Bruel*, tout simplement parce qu'il ne trouve pas une chanson qui le résume sans être restrictive. Six ans plus tard, il le rebaptisera *3*. Le disque a été produit comme le précédent, avec Mick Lanaro, et enregistré au Studio Power Station de New York et dans un studio à Bordeaux. Il comprend quatorze nouvelles chansons (chiffre porte-bonheur du chanteur), dont « Bouge », qui est le premier extrait.
Le 22 mai 1994, Patrick Bruel vient présenter son nouveau disque dans l'émission *Taratata* animée par Nagui, sur France 2.
La tonalité générale de ce nouvel album est plus rock, comme pour mieux casser cette image de chanteur romantique qui lui colle trop à la peau. Le disque reçoit

un bon accueil de la presse, mais en revanche, les radios sont plus réticentes à le programmer. L'enthousiasme des radios à l'égard du chanteur n'est plus là. Mais Patrick Bruel garde le cap et il sait que personne ne pourra l'empêcher de maintenir ce lien qu'il a établi avec son public. Pour cette raison, il décide très vite de remonter sur scène.

Dès le 9 septembre 1994, il retrouve son public au Sportica de Gravelines, puis à Amiens et Laval, avant d'attaquer Bercy, à Paris, pour cinq soirs, entre le 16 et le 20 septembre 1994. Lokua Kanza fait la première partie. Même si l'hystérie est moins expressive que lors de la tournée précédente de 1990, l'ambiance est toujours là, n'en déplaise au journaliste du *Monde*, qui titre : « Bruel, c'est fini ! Les gens ne chantent plus dans la salle ! » Un journaliste qui en plus n'avait même pas assisté au concert à Bercy ! Un manque de professionnalisme et de déontologie qui, hélas !, va avoir une influence sur l'accueil des médias et qui a beaucoup touché et attristé l'artiste, d'autant que ce n'était pas vrai.

La tournée se poursuit jusqu'au 18 décembre 1994 avec un passage au Bataclan, à Paris.

Côté cinéma, Patrick Bruel a été pressenti pour tenir le rôle d'Henri de Navarre dans le film de Patrice Chéreau, *La Reine Margot*. Il a même fait des essais. Mais finalement, on lui a préféré Daniel Auteuil. Pour Patrick, son image de chanteur adulé était alors trop forte et trop connotée et avait certainement effrayé les producteurs de ce film.

En revanche, il tourne dans le nouveau film d'Agnès Varda, *Les Cent et Une Nuits de Simon Cinéma*, une comédie aux côtés de deux figures du septième art : Michel Piccoli et Marcello Mastroianni.

Au mois de mai de cette même année 1995, Patrick Bruel part chanter en Allemagne. Le 3 mai, il est à Berlin, le 4 à Hambourg, le 5 à Cologne, le 8 à Munich et le 9 à Mayence. La tournée française, interrompue en décembre, reprend à Martigues, le 12 juillet 1995, et passe le 16 juillet par l'esplanade Saint-Jean-d'Acre, à La Rochelle. À l'initiative de Jean-Louis Foulquier, le maître d'œuvre des *Francofolies*,

"Lors des World Music Awards qui se déroulent dans la Salle des Étoiles à Monaco, Patrick Bruel reçoit la récompense du Français qui a vendu le plus de disques."

Patrick Bruel, Youssou N'Dour, Khaled, un Juif, un Africain et un Arabe, reprennent symboliquement la chanson québécoise « Quand les hommes vivront d'amour ». Un très beau moment de fraternité et de tolérance.
Cet été-là, la guerre civile déchire l'ancienne Yougoslavie, Jacques Chirac devient président de la République, et l'ONU fête ses cinquante ans. Le monde est toujours conduit par l'appétit de pouvoir et les sombres démons de l'intolérance et de la convoitise.
Patrick Bruel a ses idées sur ce monde-là. Patrick l'étend à toutes les luttes qui servent la dignité humaine, du

Téléthon et des Restos du Cœur à l'Initiative pour la paix de Genève – une idée pour laquelle il s'engage à fond aux côtés de sommités intellectuelles ou politiques comme Bernard-Henri Lévy, Marek Halter, Shimon Peres ou Hubert Védrine. L'urgence d'une solution politique à l'interminable et sanglant conflit entre Israéliens et Palestiniens s'impose à tous. On verra, hélas, par la suite, qu'une tragédie ne s'arrête pas parce que des hommes de cœur l'ont ardemment désiré. Au moins auront-ils essayé, de toutes leurs faibles forces…
La tournée 1995 se poursuit tout l'été. Patrick Bruel est acclamé à Alès, à Vaison-la-Romaine, à Palavas-les-Flots, à Juan-les-Pins, à Genève… Il refuse en revanche de se produire dans des villes comme Marignane ou Orange, administrées par le Front National, dont il méprise l'idéologie xénophobe.
Un album live de ce Tour 95 intitulé *On s'était dit…* est publié à la fin de l'année. On y retrouve les seize chansons des concerts avec la reprise de la chanson de Jacques Brel, « Fernand », mais aussi de « Pour exister », chanson que Patrick Bruel avait écrite et composée pour Johnny Hallyday, en 1991. C'est d'ailleurs avec ce titre qu'il fait la promotion de cet album qui est relativement boudé par le public. Contrairement au précédent, il se vend à peine à 200 000 exemplaires.
Patrick Bruel décide alors de prendre du recul et de laisser du temps au temps pour protéger son image. Il prévient sa maison de disques et demande au nouveau directeur de tout faire pour réhabiliter son image auprès des médias. Pas question pour lui de sortir un nouvel album dans ce climat de défiance à son égard. Quand les journalistes auront laissé leurs a priori de côté, alors là, il pourra proposer de nouvelles chansons.

"La chanson 'Tic, Tic, Tac' devient le tube de l'été 1996 et se classe N° 1 au Top 50 pendant trois semaines en se vendant à un million d'exemplaires et devient ainsi disque de diamant."

En attendant, il prend le temps de vivre, de s'amuser. Il retrouve sa passion d'adolescent pour le poker. Au cours de l'été 1994, il va à Las Vegas pour les besoins d'un reportage photo pour un magazine de mode avec le grand photographe David Lachapelle. À cette occasion, entre deux séances de photos, Patrick fréquente les casinos, rencontre un champion du monde de poker qui l'encourage à participer à des tournois. Ce qu'il va faire avec plaisir et de plus en plus souvent.
Pendant cette période, Patrick Bruel se tourne aussi vers son autre passion, le cinéma.
Tout d'abord, il s'envole pour le Nord-Ouest brésilien, à Manaus, en Amazonie, pour le tournage du nouveau film de Francis Veber, *Le Jaguar*, aux côtés de Jean Reno. Dans ce film, Patrick joue le rôle de François Perrin, un joueur de poker criblé de dettes qui se voit confier une mission en Amazonie par un chef indien.
Lors de ce tournage, Patrick Bruel rencontre au *Havai*, l'un des plus grands clubs de Punta Negra, un groupe de sept musiciens dont le chanteur, Zezinho Corrêa, et quatre danseurs réunis sous le nom de Carrapicho. Patrick, qui s'y connaît en tubes, repère immédiatement leur chanson « Tic, Tic, Tac ». Il est convaincu qu'elle peut très bien

fonctionner en Europe. Il fait donc le nécessaire pour exporter et produire le titre sur son label 14 Productions et le fait distribuer par sa maison de disques BMG. Un véritable coup de maître pour Patrick, puisque la chanson devient le tube de l'été 1996 et se classe N° 1 au Top 50, dès le 13 juillet 1996, pendant trois semaines. Le disque se vend à un million d'exemplaires et devient disque de diamant. Un tube non seulement en France, mais aussi dans plusieurs pays d'Europe, en Israël et en Amérique du Sud.

En attendant la sortie du film *Le Jaguar*, le 9 octobre 1996, le 7 février, Patrick Bruel est à l'affiche de *Sabrina*, un film américano-germanique réalisé par Sydney Pollack. Il partage l'affiche du film avec Harrison Ford. Excusez du peu !

Le 28 août 1996, c'est la sortie du nouveau film de Claude Lelouch, *Hommes, femmes, mode d'emploi*, dans lequel Patrick Bruel joue son propre rôle.

Au cours des deux années suivantes, toujours discrètes sur le plan musical, Patrick Bruel est très présent en revanche dans les salles obscures.

À Berlin, il retrouve son réalisateur fétiche, Alexandre Arcady, pour le tournage du film *K*, adapté du roman *Pas de kaddish pour Sylberstein* de Guy Konopnicki. Dans ce film qui traite du nazisme, Patrick Bruel tient le rôle de Samuel Bellamy, un inspecteur qui est ami avec un brocanteur juif dont la famille a été massacrée par des officiers nazi pendant la Seconde Guerre mondiale. Un tournage éprouvant pour l'acteur, qui se détend en participant au Championnat d'Allemagne de Poker, où il gagne.

En 1998, Patrick Bruel joue également son propre rôle dans le film *Paparazzi* d'Alain Berberian et dans *Hors jeu* du jeune réalisateur franco-tunisien Karim Dridi. Cette même année, on peut le voir dans *Les Folies de Margaret*, une co-production franco-américano-britannique réalisée par Brian Skeet.

Cette même année, au mois de mai 1998, Patrick Bruel remporte un tournoi de poker de renommée internationale au championnat du monde World Series of Poker à Las Vegas. Plus qu'un simple passe-temps, le poker deviendra pour le chanteur et acteur une véritable activité sportive qu'il va populariser en France, en présentant des émissions sur ce thème sur Canal+ et en devenant actionnaire de Winamax, un site web de poker et de paris sportifs en ligne.

Retour en grâce juste avant l'an 2000

Même si, depuis son troisième album, Patrick Bruel a été beaucoup occupé entre le cinéma, le poker et les voyages, il n'a pas pour autant arrêté de créer des chansons. Bien au contraire. Depuis 1995, sur les tournages de films, et au fur et à mesure de ses déplacements et de ses séjours à

l'étranger, il a enregistré des possibilités de chansons sur un dictaphone. Il en a plus de soixante-dix, lorsqu'il démarre réellement le travail sur un nouvel album au cours de l'été 1997. Il sélectionne trente titres de ses enregistrements, mais finalement, il n'en gardera que douze !

Dans cette période de création, d'incertitude sur la direction musicale qu'il souhaite suivre mais aussi sur la réaction des médias et de son public à son retour, Patrick Bruel peut compter sur le soutien de son ami Johnny Hallyday, qui l'invite, contre l'avis général de son entourage, à chanter en duo avec lui lors de son premier méga concert au Stade de France. Ainsi, le 4 septembre 1998, Patrick Bruel se retrouve sur scène aux côtés de Johnny Hallyday et chante en duo avec lui « Et puis je sais » devant 80 000 spectateurs. Un moment très fort pour Patrick, qui ne l'oubliera jamais et qui lui redonne l'envie de faire son retour sur scène avec de nouvelles chansons.

Artiste humaniste, toujours prêt à s'investir dans des œuvres caritatives, Patrick Bruel accepte de participer à l'album *Ensemble*, un disque qui réunit quarante artistes

francophones au profit de l'association de lutte et de recherche contre le sida.
Pour cet album, Patrick participe à la chanson de groupe, « Sa raison d'être », et compose un titre inédit, « Demain », sur un texte d'une jeune auteure, Marie-Florence Gros, dont il apprécie beaucoup les mots.
L'album *Ensemble* paraît à la fin de l'année 1998 et se retrouve dans les premières places des Tops pendant 14 semaines.
Au mois de janvier 1999, Patrick Bruel fait son retour en studio d'enregistrement pour finaliser les chansons de son nouvel album. Sur ce disque, il travaille avec ses deux frères, David Moreau, qui compose trois titres et réalise et arrange le disque, et Fabrice Moreau, batteur, également arrangeur et réalisateur de l'album. Patrick s'entoure aussi de nombreux grands musiciens dont Basile Leroux pour des guitares, Thierry Eliez au piano, Roland Romanelli à l'accordéon, Dominique Bertram à la basse...
Patrick compose huit musiques de cet album et huit textes et collabore également avec Gérard Presgurvic, son ami depuis les débuts, qui signe le titre « Pour la vie ».
Patrick Bruel poursuit également son travail avec Marie-Florence Gros, rencontrée à l'occasion de l'album *Ensemble*. Elle écrit ou co-écrit avec lui six chansons.
Ce nouvel album, intitulé *Juste avant* parce qu'il sort juste avant l'an 2000, rassemble douze chansons aux sujets personnels, profonds, sincères dont Patrick a envie de parler à ce moment-là. L'artiste veut partager des émotions, des sonorités, des ambiances, des souvenirs heureux ou plus mélancoliques.
Parmi les douze titres de ce disque, il y a « Au café des délices », composé par son ami Félix Gray, une chanson qui va connaître un immense succès.
L'album aborde de multiples sujets : l'amour, la solitude, le désir toujours renouvelé, le temps qui passe, l'abandon, les illusions perdues, le va-et-vient passionnel qu'il y a entre les hommes et les femmes. Chaque chanson trouve sa justification dans un souci de vérité, de profondeur, de transparence.
Après un silence musical de presque six ans, Patrick Bruel fait donc paraître *Juste avant* le 19 octobre 1999.
Et c'est un retour gagnant. À tout juste quarante ans, l'artiste prouve qu'il sait se renouveler et qu'il fait partie du cercle très fermé des stars de la chanson. Le premier extrait de l'album, « J'te mentirais », amorce ce retour, dès le mois de septembre 1999, et reçoit un excellent accueil non seulement de la part des fans de l'artiste, mais aussi des critiques, qui soulignent que *Juste avant* est l'album de la maturité. Le quotidien *Le Parisien* écrit : « Avec ce disque, un nouveau Bruel s'est révélé, enfin débarrassé de son bandana et de son imperméable, frusques d'idole d'une génération en mal de romantisme. Ce Patrick Bruel-là, c'est du passé. Le chanteur a mûri... Dorénavant, ses chansons ne se contentent plus de surfer sur un spleen post-adolescent, mais abordent des rivages plus adultes, plus nostalgiques aussi. »
Ce nouveau succès musical offre au chanteur un passeport pour une grande tournée qui démarre à l'Elispace de Beauvais, le 27 avril 2000, pour se terminer par la Fête de l'Humanité, à La Courneuve, le 16 septembre 2001. Un moment très fort pour Patrick Bruel qui, ce jour-là, seulement cinq jours après les attentats du World Trade Center, chante main dans la main « Au café des délices » avec la star du raï, Cheb Mami, devant 80 000 personnes réunies à La Courneuve. Un superbe symbole de tolérance entre les religions.
Dans ses nouveaux spectacles, Patrick Bruel chante bien sûr ses grands succès, comme « Place des grands hommes », « J'te l'dis quand même », ou « Alors regarde ». Il interprète aussi ses nouvelles chansons : « Pour la vie », « Au café des délices » ou « Tout s'efface ». Il rend hommage à Serge

Gainsbourg en interprétant « La Javanaise » et reprend aussi un titre de Charles Aznavour, « Non, je n'ai rien oublié ».
Patrick inclut aussi dans ses tours de chant la chanson qu'il avait écrite pour Johnny Hallyday en 1991, « Et puis je sais », que le rocker vient d'ailleurs chanter en duo avec lui au Zénith de Paris.
Au cours de ces concerts, en plus de tous ses grands tubes, Patrick Bruel fait un medley rétro en reprenant de grandes chansons du XXe siècle comme « Mon amant de Saint-Jean », « La Romance de Paris », « Comme de bien entendu », « Le Petit Vin blanc », « La Java bleue » et « Avoir un bon copain ». Coiffé d'une casquette de titi parisien, Patrick Bruel se laisse aller, assis sur un tabouret et seul à la guitare, à reprendre ces rengaines du patrimoine musical français.
Ce moment est très apprécié par le public et donne lieu à de merveilleuses scènes de danse dans les salles.

Cette tournée 2000-2001 est un véritable triomphe. L'artiste confie alors : « Chaque soir, j'ai de plus en plus de mal à sortir de scène tellement je m'y sens bien. Honnêtement, je vis un rêve. D'autant que l'ambiance avec le public et sa qualité d'écoute sont telles que je ne les avais jamais connues. »

Après cette longue tournée, gravée sur un double album live sorti le 23 août 2001 et intitulé *Rien ne s'efface*, et à la suite du succès de son medley sur scène des grandes chansons de notre patrimoine musical, Patrick Bruel décide d'enregistrer tout un album de reprises de grandes chansons des années 30 à 50. Un pari audacieux et risqué que Patrick Bruel a envie de faire. On reconnaît bien là l'excellent joueur de poker qu'il est. Il confie alors : « C'est un voyage en pays de nostalgie, entre émotion et frissons. Entre deux guerres, les Français retrouvaient un semblant de légèreté et s'enivraient au son de l'accordéon... »

"'Chaque soir, j'ai de plus en plus de mal à sortir de scène tellement je m'y sens bien, honnêtement, je vis un rêve.'"

En attendant ce nouveau projet musical, côté cinéma, le 19 septembre 2001, sort le film *Le Lait de la tendresse humaine*, une comédie dramatique de Dominique Cabrera. Et le 14 novembre 2001, Patrick est à l'affiche du film *Les Jolies Choses*, de Gilles Paquet-Brenner. Il s'agit de l'adaptation du roman de Virginie Despentes. Patrick y joue le rôle d'un papa qui élève seul ses trois enfants. Dans ce film, il a pour partenaire une star montante du cinéma français : Marion Cotillard.

Le 3 juin 2002, l'album *Entre deux* arrive dans les magasins. Ce sera le succès colossal, stupéfiant de l'année. Patrick y reprend les grandes rengaines de l'entre-deux-guerres, période mythique de bonheur entre deux cataclysmes, d'où sont sorties ces immortelles chansons que sont « La Java bleue », « Mon amant de Saint-Jean », « Ménilmontant », « La Complainte de la butte », etc. Il les chante en duo avec Aznavour, Cabrel, Hallyday, Jean-Louis Aubert, Pascal Obispo, Jean-Jacques Goldman...

Combien en vend-il ? Près de 3 millions. L'album d'une envie devient ainsi l'album de l'année.

Cet album lui rapporte le plus gros revenu de la Sacem cette année-là : 5,2 millions d'euros !

Une grande tournée suit la sortie de cet album. Elle démarre le 4 juillet 2002 au Théâtre André-Malraux de Rueil-Malmaison et s'achève à Nyon, en Suisse, le 24 juillet de l'été suivant. Dans cette tournée, Patrick Bruel ne chante que les chansons de son album *Entre deux*.

Le concert est enregistré à l'Olympia les 12 et 13 septembre 2002 et fait l'objet d'un album live et d'un DVD.

Au cours de cette tournée, le 25 juillet 2002, Patrick Bruel se produit à Eauze, dans le Gers, et ce jour-là, son

père, Pierre Benguigui, dont il est sans nouvelles depuis l'année 1996, vient assister au concert. Dans les loges, c'est l'occasion pour le père et le fils de renouer le dialogue.
Le 47e grand Concours Eurovision de la chanson se déroule le samedi 25 mai 2002, à Tallinn, en Estonie. Cette année-là, c'est Sandrine François, une jeune artiste révélée par Mireille Dumas et Pascal Sevran, qui représente la France. Sa chanson a pour titre « Il faut du temps ». Patrick Bruel a co-écrit les paroles avec Marie-Florence Gros et a composé la musique avec Rick Allison. Le titre se classe à la 5e place, avec 104 points. Un score plus qu'honorable, et surtout le meilleur à ce concours depuis 1995.

Les bonheurs d'une vie nouvelle

Si, sur le plan professionnel, tout va très bien pour Patrick Bruel, c'est aussi le cas sur le plan sentimental.
Il a rencontré Amanda Sthers, le 2 août 2001, dans un célèbre club de Saint-Tropez, aux *Caves du Roy*, dans une ambiance très VIP. Amanda est la fille d'une avocate parisienne et d'un père psychanalyste. Elle n'a que vingt-trois ans et Patrick quarante-deux ans. C'est un véritable coup de foudre entre eux. Deux jours plus tard, Patrick doit se rendre dans un festival de cinéma dans le sud de la Suisse, à Locarno, et il propose à Amanda de l'accompagner. Elle accepte, et dans l'avion, le 4 août, Patrick lui demande si elle serait d'accord pour avoir deux enfants avec lui. Patrick sait qu'Amanda est la bonne personne pour fonder une famille.
À la rentrée 2002, Patrick Bruel fait son retour au théâtre aux côtés de Jacques Weber. Cela faisait dix-sept ans, depuis *On m'appelle Émilie*, que Patrick Bruel n'était pas monté sur les planches, et quatre ans qu'il cherchait une pièce. « Je me suis manifesté auprès des directeurs de théâtre, j'ai lu beaucoup de choses, mais rien d'intéressant, explique-t-il. Et puis, un jour, en attendant, chez moi, quelqu'un qui n'arrivait pas, j'ai pris un texte qui traînait sur mon bureau depuis trois semaines. J'ai commencé à lire, expédié mon rendez-vous enfin arrivé, terminé ma lecture. C'était *Le Limier*. J'avais trouvé... »
À partir du 26 février 2002, Patrick Bruel est donc à l'affiche du Théâtre de la Madeleine, dans *Le Limier*, une pièce d'Anthony Shaffer. Il y interprète l'amant de la femme de Jacques Weber qui apprend la vérité et décide de lui régler son compte... Le théâtre affiche presque complet pendant deux mois.
En 2003, Patrick Bruel et Amanda Sthers accueillent un premier enfant, Oscar, qui pèse 3,300 kg pour 49 cm. Il voit le jour le 19 août à la clinique parisienne de La Muette. Juste avant ce grand bouleversement dans sa vie personnelle, Patrick fait des démarches pour prendre officiellement le nom de Bruel, qui figurera désormais officiellement sur tous ses papiers d'identité. Patrick Bruel choisit aussi ce moment pour avoir une véritable discussion avec son père, Pierre Benguigui. Patrick expliquera : « *Un jour j'ai décidé, parce que j'allais avoir un enfant, de ne pas faire supporter à mon enfant le poids de ce passé, de mon histoire, de l'absence de mon père. Donc j'ai appelé mon père. Et on s'est vus. La discussion a été forte, elle était serrée, elle était violente. Il fallait que ce soit soutenu, pour mieux se dire les choses, parler vraiment. Et ça a été constructif.* »

"La compilation Puzzle, qui reprend ses plus grands tubes, atteste la place qu'occupe désormais Patrick Bruel dans le paysage musical français."

En 2004, histoire de fêter dignement ses vingt ans de succès dans la chanson et ses plus de 10 millions d'albums vendus, Patrick Bruel sort, pour la première fois depuis le début de sa carrière, une compilation intitulée *Puzzle* qui reprend ses plus grands tubes, dont la version espagnole de « J'te l'dis quand même », ainsi que quelques duos de légende comme « L'Italien » avec Serge Reggiani ou « Sorry Seems to be the Hardest Word » avec Joe Cocker. Ce bilan discographique atteste, s'il en était besoin, la place qu'occupe désormais Patrick Bruel dans le paysage musical français. Une place à part et au sommet qui lui permet d'être l'un des rares artistes de sa génération à avoir su fidéliser un public à travers les années et les modes si changeantes. C'est peut-être bien parce que lui-même ne change pas que Patrick réussit ce tour de force.
Le 11 février 2004, Amanda Sthers publie son premier roman aux éditions Grasset, *Ma place sur la photo*.
Le 10 mars, Patrick Bruel est à l'affiche du film de Thierry Klifa, *Une vie à t'attendre*, aux côtés de Nathalie Baye. La bande musicale de ce drame romantique est signée du frère de Patrick, David-François Moreau.
Cette même année, le 21 septembre 2004, Patrick Bruel et Amanda se marient à la Mairie du 4e arrondissement de Paris, puis à la Synagogue de la rue de la Victoire. Ce mariage se déroule en présence de Johnny Hallyday et de sa femme Læticia, d'Élie Chouraqui, d'Arthur et sa femme Estelle. Sûr de ses sentiments, sûr de lui-même, Patrick Bruel peut désormais dire sans retenue à celle qu'il aime un « oui » pour la vie.
L'année suivante, le 28 septembre 2005, ils ont un deuxième enfant, un autre garçon, prénommé Léon, qui pèse à la naissance 3,400 kg et mesure 51 cm.

En 1969, grâce à sa mère, Augusta, Patrick Bruel a une véritable révélation musicale pour Serge Reggiani, lors d'un concert à Bobino. En 1995, lors du concert des Enfoirés à l'Opéra-Comique, Patrick a le bonheur de chanter en duo, avec lui, *L'Italien*.

Grand amateur de poker et champion lui-même, Patrick Bruel accepte aussi, en 2005, de commenter les grandes parties pour Canal+, du « World Poker Tour ». De vraies parties de plaisir pour l'artiste, qui connaît toutes les ruses du poker pour l'avoir pratiqué très tôt.

Cette même année 2005, sous la houlette d'Élie Chouraqui, marque le grand retour de Patrick Bruel devant les caméras, aux côtés de Saïd Taghmaoui, dans une adaptation d'un best-seller de Dominique Lapierre et Larry Collins, *Ô Jérusalem*. Le tournage de ce film, qui relate la création de l'État d'Israël, le 27 novembre 1947, démarre au mois d'avril.

Quelques semaines après, au cours de l'été 2005, Patrick décide d'accélérer la création de nouvelles chansons. Une fois passée la difficulté de revenir derrière les œuvres des autres, l'envie de la création reprend le dessus. Patrick a déjà composé pas mal de mélodies mais il lui manque des textes. Il a vécu tant de choses, ces dernières années, que l'inspiration ne manque pas. Pourtant, il n'a pas encore le déclic. Et c'est sa femme, Amanda Sthers, qui va le lui donner et lui mettre le pied à l'étrier, en lui proposant le début de texte de « Je fais semblant ». Très touché par ces paroles si vraies qu'il n'aurait pas osé les formuler lui-même, Patrick va donc finir la chanson et surtout écrire presque une chanson par jour, alors que cela faisait deux ans qu'il traînait des textes qui n'avançaient pas.

Dans ce nouvel album qui sera intitulé *Des souvenirs devant…*, Patrick Bruel met en chanson ses émotions personnelles liées à sa nouvelle vie de père de famille dans laquelle bonheur et anxiété sont indissociables. Cet album qui raconte des tranches de vie, entre espoir et inquiétude, est enregistré au Studio Gang, dans un quartier que Patrick Bruel connaît bien, entre le Jardin des Plantes, le Quartier latin et la place d'Italie. L'album, arrangé et réalisé comme les deux précédents par David Moreau, paraît le 20 mars 2006 et va rapidement atteindre la première place des ventes et devenir triple disque de platine, avec plus de 700 000 albums vendus.

Un mois plus tôt, le 22 février 2006, Patrick Bruel était à l'affiche du film de Claude Chabrol, *L'Ivresse du pouvoir*, aux côtés d'Isabelle Huppert et de François Berléand.

Avant de reprendre la scène, au mois d'octobre 2007, pour une tournée de près de 150 dates qui le conduira jusqu'aux États-Unis, Patrick Bruel tourne le film *Un secret*, de Claude Miller, d'après le roman autobiographique de Philippe Grimbert.

Dans ce long-métrage, Patrick Bruel tient le rôle de Maxime, un lutteur taciturne, juif, confronté aux lois de Vichy, que l'on voit à différents moments de sa vie, de sa jeunesse à sa vieillesse. Pour Patrick Bruel, ce tournage est une véritable épreuve. Il sort de certaines scènes terriblement ému. Et la seule lecture du scénario l'a dévasté. Mais heureusement, la jolie histoire d'amour avec Tania, interprétée par Cécile de France, illumine toute cette histoire.

Ce film fera un beau score au box-office, avec un peu plus de 1 600 000 entrées en neuf semaines d'exploitation, entre octobre et décembre 2007. Il aura 10 nominations à la 33e cérémonie des Césars, mais aucune pour Patrick Bruel, qui avait pourtant un rôle important dans lequel il s'est beaucoup investi. Une terrible injustice qui blesse beaucoup l'acteur. Il avouera : « Ça me rend triste... Pas le fait d'être privé de statue, mais de sentir que, pour les gens du métier, ceux qui arbitrent, je ne fais pas vraiment partie de la famille du cinéma... »

Après avoir participé, comme chaque année, à la tournée des Enfoirés, du 24 au 27 février 2006, à la Halle Tony-Garnier de Lyon, Patrick Bruel démarre sa tournée au Havre, le 6 octobre 2006. Il enchaîne ensuite avec Laval, Beauvais, Reims, Nancy, Dunkerque, Douai, puis du 17 au 22 octobre au Zénith de Paris. Chaque soir, pendant plus de deux heures, les milliers de spectateurs applaudissent, dansent et chantent en chœur ces nombreux tubes qui restituent les souvenirs de tous. Une vraie relation particulière s'est installée entre Patrick Bruel et son public au fil des années.

Pour ce retour sur scène, Patrick Bruel commence ses concerts avec « Alors regarde » avant de reprendre ses plus grands succès, parfois en les revisitant avec de nouveaux arrangements, comme « Décalé », en version malgache, « Marre de cette nana-là », en version jazz, ou « Mon amant de Saint-Jean », devenu un tango.

Parmi les surprises de ce tour 2006-2007, Patrick reprend « Help », des Beatles, en racontant l'anecdote de sa présence à New York, lorsque John Lennon a été assassiné, le 8 décembre 1980. Bien évidemment, dans cette nouvelle tournée, l'artiste présente aussi ses nouvelles chansons extraites de l'album *Des souvenirs devant...* comme « Adieu », « J'm'attendais pas à toi », « Lettre au père Noël », « Où sont les rêves », « Gosses en cavale », qui sont toutes très bien accueillies. Et chaque soir, Patrick Bruel termine ses concerts avec cette belle déclaration d'amour à son public avec la chanson « Vous ».

Cette première partie de tournée se poursuit jusqu'au 22 décembre 2006, à Toulon, avant de reprendre entre mars et juillet 2007. La seconde partie de la tournée conduit Patrick Bruel une nouvelle fois aux quatre coins de la France, avec un arrêt à Paris Bercy les 25 et 26 mai. Le mois de juin est consacré à l'international, avec des concerts à San Francisco, Los Angeles, New York, Washington, Ottawa, Québec, Montréal et Neuchâtel.

"Chaque soir, les milliers de spectateurs applaudissent, dansent et chantent en chœur ses nombreux tubes. Une relation particulière s'est installée entre Patrick et son public au fil des années."

Ce Tour 2006-2007 se termine en Vendée, au Festival de Poupet, le 29 juillet 2007.

Quelques mois après, le 26 novembre 2007, sort un DVD et CD LIVE de cette grande tournée, intitulé *Des souvenirs ensemble*.

Le 8 décembre, Patrick Bruel préside le jury de l'élection de Miss France 2008, qui est remportée par Miss Réunion, Valérie Bègue, en direct au Palais des Congrès Le Kursaal, à Dunkerque.

La valeur du temps

En 2007, après trois ans de mariage, Patrick Bruel et Amanda Sthers divorcent sans haine, sans rancœur. Une complicité différente s'installe entre eux. Ils ont chacun la garde partagée des enfants, et grâce à leur intelligence respective, tout se passe au mieux dans l'intérêt d'Oscar et de Léon. Patrick confiera : « On est formidables avec les enfants, on ne l'était plus ensemble. »

En bon père de famille, Patrick Bruel acquiert cette année-là une propriété dans le Lubéron, à L'Isle-sur-la-Sorgue, ce village du Vaucluse si cher au poète résistant René Char.

Quand Patrick découvre, sur le plateau de Margoye, une ancienne ferme du XIIe siècle, reconstruite au XVIIe et entourée d'oliviers centenaires, d'amandiers, de vignes, il a un véritable coup de cœur. Il baptise l'endroit *Le Domaine Leos*, contraction des prénoms de ses deux fils.

Patrick confiera : « C'est à eux que cette oliveraie sublime de 2 600 arbres et de 22 hectares est destinée. La transmission, c'est sacré pour moi. »

Patrick se lance alors dans la production d'huile d'olive et obtient plusieurs récompenses de qualité du produit, adopté par de nombreux grands chefs étoilés.

Du 23 au 28 janvier 2008, Patrick Bruel retrouve la troupe des Enfoirés au Zénith de Strasbourg pour le spectacle *Les Secrets des Enfoirés*.

Au mois de février, il s'envole pour Montréal en vue de participer à un concert privé pour la station Rythme FM.

Le mois suivant, il est à Monaco pour participer à un hommage à Serge Gainsbourg.

Le 26 mai, le chanteur donne un concert exceptionnel à Raanana, au nord-est de Tel Aviv, à l'occasion des soixante ans de l'État d'Israël. Très engagé dans la cause israélienne,

Patrick y était aussi venu quelques mois plus tôt pour y présenter le film *Un secret*.
Le 24 août 2008, Patrick Bruel est de retour au Québec pour participer à l'émission de Daniela Lumbroso, *Paris-Québec sous les étoiles*, pour célébrer les quatre cents ans de la fondation de la ville de Québec, par Samuel de Champlain. Dans ce programme, devant une immense foule réunie dans le parc, Patrick interprète « Les Plaines d'Abraham », « Place des grands hommes », mais aussi, en duo avec Diane Dufresne, « La Complainte du phoque en Alaska ».
Le 13 septembre suivant, de retour en France, devant 45 000 personnes réunies dans le parc de Saint-Cloud, Patrick Bruel participe à un concert hommage à Luciano Pavarotti, disparu un an plus tôt. Au cours de cette soirée présentée par Michel Drucker et Ève Ruggieri, Patrick Bruel reprend la célèbre chanson napolitaine « O sole mio ».
Dès le 3 octobre 2008, à Colombes, en banlieue parisienne, Patrick Bruel commence une nouvelle tournée intitulée *Patrick Bruel seul... ou presque*. À la différence des tournées précédentes, il opte pour une tournée acoustique, plus intimiste, dans des salles moins importantes. Cette tournée se poursuit sur plusieurs mois jusqu'au mois de décembre 2009. Du 6 au 11 avril, elle passe par le Casino de Paris, où le spectacle est enregistré pour un album live qui paraît deux mois après, en juin 2009.

"Entre pop-rock et hip-hop, Patrick Bruel prouve qu'il est à l'aise dans tous les styles et toujours dans l'air du temps, trente ans après ses débuts dans la chanson."

Dans cette tournée, le chanteur reprend seul au piano ou à la guitare, et parfois soutenu par un autre guitariste, ses grands succès, teste quelques nouveautés comme « Oui » « Lequel de nous » pour un futur album, reprend « You've Got a Friend » de la chanteuse américaine Carole King et rend un vibrant hommage à Barbara, une chanteuse qu'il adore, en reprenant « Vienne », l'un de ses grands succès.
En fin de concert, Patrick Bruel appelle les spectateurs à se lever tandis qu'il entonne « Mon amant de Saint-Jean ». Une chanson qu'il n'avait pas incluse à son répertoire au début de cette tournée mais qu'il a rajoutée à la suite de la déception d'une dame qui l'avait attendu à la sortie d'un concert pour lui exprimer toute sa tristesse de ne pas l'avoir entendue.
En 2009, Patrick Bruel s'illustre aussi au cinéma dans le film *Le code a changé*, réalisé par Danièle Thompson, dans lequel il interprète le rôle d'un cancérologue, Alain Carcassonne, aux côtés de Dany Boon et Karin Viard. Ce film, sorti le 18 février, atteint plus de 1 600 000 entrées au box-office.
Sur le plan sentimental, l'année 2009 est marquée par une nouvelle histoire d'amour dans la vie de Patrick Bruel. Il rencontre en effet une jeune journaliste de vingt-quatre ans, Céline Bosquet, qui présente Le journal décalé sur la chaîne CNews. Pour préserver leur bonheur, le chanteur et la journaliste se font le plus discrets possible et n'apparaissent que très rarement ensemble. Tous les deux passionnés par le tennis, on peut les voir régulièrement dans les tribunes du Tournoi de Roland-Garros.
La jeune femme est plutôt bien acceptée par les deux garçons de Patrick, avec lesquels elle instaure une certaine complicité. Licenciée en chinois, la jeune journaliste aide Oscar, qui étudie cette langue en CE2, et comme elle a étudié aussi pendant dix ans le saxophone au conservatoire de Nice, elle aide Oscar et Léon en musique.
L'année 2010 marque le retour de Patrick Bruel au théâtre. Huit ans après *Le Limier*, l'acteur revient à partir du 7 septembre 2010 sur les planches au Théâtre Édouard-VII avec *Le Prénom*, une comédie de deux jeunes auteurs, Matthieu Delaporte et Alexandre de La Patellière, dans une mise en scène de Bernard Murat.
Dans cette pièce drôle et caustique, Patrick Bruel incarne Vincent Larchet, un quarantenaire qui va être père pour la première fois. Invité à dîner chez sa sœur Élisabeth, interprétée par Valérie Benguigui, et son beau-frère Pierre, joué par Jean-Michel Dupuis, il retrouve Guillaume de Tonquédec dans le rôle de Claude, un ami d'enfance.
En attendant l'arrivée de son épouse Anna, dans une bonne humeur générale, les invités interrogent Vincent sur sa future paternité. Mais quand arrivent les questions sur le choix d'un prénom pour l'enfant à naître, les choses se corsent, plongent la famille dans le chaos et deviennent le théâtre de règlements de comptes.
Au sujet de cette pièce, Patrick Bruel confie alors : « C'est une belle étude sur les rapports humains, la famille, les amis... Les auteurs ont beaucoup de talent. C'est très agréable de travailler avec Bernard Murat. Je découvre un metteur en scène qui a une très bonne oreille "actorale", comme d'autres ont l'oreille musicale. Il entend la justesse de la situation, du ton. »
Le Prénom devient le succès de la rentrée théâtrale 2010. La pièce va se jouer plus de 243 fois.

Face à ce triomphe, les auteurs adaptent leur pièce au cinéma avec les mêmes acteurs. Le film sort dans les salles le 25 avril 2012 et rassemble plus de 3 347 000 entrées en vingt semaines à l'affiche. Le film est adapté aussi en plusieurs langues, et il est distribué aux États-Unis sous le titre *What's In a Name ?*

Malgré cet immense succès au théâtre et au cinéma, Patrick Bruel n'oublie pas pour autant la chanson. Six ans après *Des souvenirs devant*, le 26 novembre 2012, il publie un septième album studio intitulé *Lequel de nous*. Un disque subtil, éclectique et surprenant qui regroupe douze chansons comme « She's Gone », « Où es-tu ? » ou « Maux d'enfants ». Entre pop-rock et hip-hop, Patrick Bruel prouve qu'il est à l'aise dans tous les styles et toujours dans l'air du temps, trente ans après ses débuts dans la chanson.

Pour la sortie de ce nouvel album, Patrick Bruel participe à de nombreuses émissions de télévision comme *Danse avec les Stars* ou *Le Grand Show de Céline Dion*. L'occasion pour lui d'annoncer une nouvelle tournée qui débutera le 16 mai 2013 à l'Arène de l'Agora d'Évry et passera par le Zénith de Paris du 29 au 31 mai.

Entre Patrick Bruel et la scène, c'est une histoire d'amour qui ne finira jamais. Véritable show-man, il sait mieux que quiconque instaurer un lien entre lui et son public et l'entraîner dans un tourbillon de souvenirs et d'émotion en chansons pendant plus de deux heures trente.

Dans ce nouveau tour de chant, il reprend « Le Métèque », de Georges Moustaki, et dédie sa chanson « À mon ami Alfred T », adaptée d'un poème d'Alfred de Musset, à son ami Guy Carcassonne, disparu subitement, le 27 mai 2013.

Artiste généreux, toujours disponible pour de bonnes causes, les 6 et 7 décembre 2013, Patrick Bruel est le parrain de la 27e édition du Téléthon. Il explique alors : « Bien sûr, l'objectif premier est de collecter des fonds pour la recherche, mais aussi de montrer à ces gens éprouvés qu'on les soutient et que seule la maladie est orpheline, pas les malades ni leur famille. » Plus qu'un parrain, l'artiste entend être un « maillon fort de cette magnifique chaîne de solidarité » et espère battre un nouveau record.

Après une pause de trois mois en début d'année 2014, le temps de participer comme chaque année au concert des Enfoirés, du 14 au 20 janvier, au Zénith de Strasbourg, Patrick Bruel reprend sa tournée au Millesium d'Épernay, le 25 mars 2014, avant d'enchaîner avec le Zénith de Paris, du 27 au 30 mars, et de très nombreuses dates à travers toute la France.

Cette tournée triomphale se termine à la fin de l'année 2014 avec plusieurs dates à l'étranger. Le 18 septembre, Patrick Bruel chante à Dubaï, le 22 septembre, il se produit au Royal Albert Hall de Londres, le 30 octobre à Miami, le 1er novembre au Beacon Theater de New York, le 2 novembre à Boston, le 4 novembre à Houston, le 5 à Washington, le 6 à Montréal et le 8 à Los Angeles.

Si la chanson et la scène ont beaucoup occupé Patrick Bruel durant l'année 2014, le cinéma n'est pas en reste pour autant. Le 9 avril, il est à l'affiche, aux côtés d'Emmanuelle Béart et de Julie Depardieu, de l'adaptation cinématographique du roman de Katherine Pancol, *Les Yeux jaunes des crocodiles*. Le 1er octobre, on le retrouve dans le film de Tonie Marshall *Tu veux ou tu veux pas*, avec Sophie Marceau et Sylvie Vartan. Patrick tient le rôle de Lambert Levallois, un conseiller conjugal, ancien accro au sexe qui va bien avoir du mal à résister à sa nouvelle assistante, interprétée par Sophie Marceau.

Le 12 janvier 2015, au lendemain des marches républicaines organisées en réaction aux effroyables attentats djihadistes du début de l'année, Patrick Bruel chante à l'opéra Garnier, à Paris, à l'occasion des quarante ans de l'Institut Pasteur-Weizmann. Lors de ce concert symphonique, il interprète notamment « Vienne », une chanson de Barbara. Ce jour-là, après ce moment tellement émouvant, il a un déclic.

Il racontera : « Après avoir repris "Vienne" avec un orchestre symphonique, je ne pouvais pas en rester là. Je me suis donc lancé en douceur, pour voir si ses chansons voulaient bien de moi. »
Patrick Bruel comprend alors que le moment est venu d'enregistrer un album de reprises des grandes chansons de la dame en noir.
Le disque, intitulé *Très souvent, je pense à vous...*, est réalisé par David-François Moreau et enregistré au studio Orgeville, dans le 5e arrondissement de Paris. Sur les quinze titres, douze sont enregistrés en une seule prise. « Le mal de vivre » est la première chanson de l'album à être diffusée en radio dès la fin du mois d'octobre 2015 et va servir de single promotionnel à l'album, qui paraît le 27 novembre 2015.
Le chanteur explique alors : « J'ai essayé de faire miennes les chansons de Barbara, qui, au niveau de leur propos me correspondent. Je me sens bien avec ce que ça dit et la manière dont ça le dit. J'ai voulu le faire dans un immense respect mais pas dans un respect béat et tiède. J'ai apporté beaucoup de choses personnelles et j'ai fait un grand voyage avec ce disque. C'est ce que j'ai fait de plus intime jusqu'à présent. Je suis allé loin en moi. Je suis retourné dans mon enfance, mon adolescence, mon parcours, dans mon histoire avec mon public. »
La sortie de cet album hommage à Barbara est suivie d'une tournée qui démarre le 8 mars 2016 au théâtre de Yerres, en banlieue parisienne, et se poursuit dans toute la France et même au Québec, en Belgique, en Suisse, en Allemagne... jusqu'en septembre 2017.
Lors de ses concerts à Paris, Patrick Bruel chante dans des salles où avait chanté Barbara, comme le théâtre Mogador, où il l'avait d'ailleurs rencontrée, en 1990, et lui avait présenté sa mère, Augusta, le théâtre du Châtelet ou la salle Pleyel.
L'album live de cette tournée est enregistré au Châtelet le 6 juin 2016 et paraît le 2 décembre suivant.
Depuis la comédie romantique *Ange et Gabrielle*, sortie le 11 novembre 2015, dans laquelle il partageait l'affiche avec Isabelle Carré, Patrick Bruel n'avait pas tourné d'autres films.
En 2017, Patrick fait son grand retour dans les salles obscures avec pas moins de trois films et le doublage en français de Buster Moon le Koala, dans le dessin animé *Tous en scène* de Garth Jennings.
Tout au début de l'année 2017, c'est avec la sortie, le 15 janvier, du film *Un sac de billes*, adapté du roman de Joseph Joffo, que Patrick avait lu quand il avait douze ans, sur les recommandations de sa mère, qu'il démarre l'année. Dans ce long-métrage de Christian Duguay, Patrick incarne Roman Joffo, le frère de Joseph, deux frères juifs qui traversent une France occupée pour se rendre en zone libre. Un très bon film qui réunit 1 300 000 entrées.
Le 4 septembre suivant, c'est dans un film dramatique italien, *Una famiglia*, de Sebastiano Riso, que Patrick Bruel crève l'écran dans le rôle de Vincenzo. Ce film est présenté en sélection officielle à la Mostra de Venise 2017.
Enfin, le 8 septembre, c'est dans un film américain de Jim Houck, *The Writer*, que l'acteur Patrick Bruel s'illustre dans le rôle d'un chauffeur de taxi.

Comme depuis toujours, Patrick Bruel prend plaisir à cumuler cinéma et chanson avec gourmandise. En 2018, il finalise un nouvel album de quinze titres inédits dont le premier extrait, « Tout recommencer », est dévoilé au mois de septembre 2018. Ce titre, composé par Mickey 3D et réalisé par Vianney, permet à Patrick Bruel de se réinventer et d'explorer de nouvelles sonorités.

L'album *Ce soir on sort*... est publié le 2 novembre 2018 et devient en quelques semaines un grand succès populaire encensé par les critiques. Le disque est certifié platine au bout de deux mois seulement, avec plus de 100 000 exemplaires vendus.

Une grande tournée commence le 12 février 2019 au Millesium d'Épernay. Les billets se sont vendus avant même la sortie de l'album. Patrick avoue alors : « J'ai été extrêmement rassuré et surpris de voir à quel point les gens ont répondu présent, à l'ouverture de la billetterie pour les concerts de 2019. »

Cette nouvelle tournée de 120 dates, qui passe par le Palais des Sports de Paris, du 20 au 23 février 2019, est un véritable triomphe.

La tournée rassemble, jusqu'au mois de décembre 2019, plus de 600 000 spectateurs dans toute la France, avec deux concerts événements à la Défense Arena de Paris, les 6 et 7 décembre 2019. L'un d'eux est retransmis en direct sur TF1 devant 2,3 millions de téléspectateurs. En cette année 2019, Patrick Bruel est omniprésent non seulement sur scène, à la télévision, mais également au cinéma.

Dès le 16 janvier, il participe au film *Holy Lands*, réalisé par Amanda Sthers, d'après son roman paru en 2010.

Le 4 décembre, il est à l'affiche aux côtés de Fabrice Luchini de la comédie *Le meilleur reste à venir*, dans lequel il retrouve les réalisateurs du film *Le Prénom*, Matthieu Delaporte et Alexandre de La Patellière. Tourné entre la France et l'Inde au début de l'année 2019, ce film rassemble près d'un million d'entrées.

Après quelques jours de vacances au ski pour Noël et un début d'année 2020 à Los Angeles, où vivent ses enfants, depuis 2015, avec leur mère, Amanda Sthers, Patrick Bruel revient en France pour participer, le 15 janvier, au traditionnel concert annuel des Enfoirés. Pendant les répétitions de ce spectacle, le chanteur est victime d'une mauvaise chute de deux mètres qui lui provoque une rupture des ligaments croisés, ce qui ne l'empêche pas pour autant de participer au concert.

La seconde partie de la tournée *Ce soir on sort* doit reprendre en mai 2020, mais l'artiste est contraint de reporter toutes les dates à la rentrée à cause de la pandémie de Covid-19 qui suspend toute l'activité culturelle.

Pendant cette période de crise sanitaire inédite, pour ne pas perdre le lien avec son fidèle public, Patrick Bruel lui offre régulièrement des directs intitulés *Stand Up at Home*, sur Facebook et Instagram, depuis son appartement parisien, où il reste confiné à partir du 16 mars 2020. Dans cette période particulière, sa chanson « Héros » prend tout son sens et le chanteur décide de faire don, à compter du 23 mars, de l'ensemble des revenus générés par ce titre à la Fondation Hôpitaux de Paris-Hôpitaux de France, en soutien à la crise du Covid-19.

“Chanteur aux 15 millions d'albums vendus, acteur dans près de cinquante films, la force de Patrick Bruel, sa quintessence, même, c'est de n'avoir jamais cessé de croire en ses rêves.”

Un geste pas étonnant de la part de Patrick Bruel qui est un artiste citoyen, toujours impliqué, très attaché aux valeurs humanistes, et qui ne cesse de le prouver en participant depuis longtemps à de nombreux événements associatifs.

Chanteur aux 15 millions d'albums vendus, acteur dans près de cinquante films, la force de Patrick Bruel, sa quintessence, même, c'est de n'avoir jamais cessé de croire en ses rêves. Dans ses yeux malicieux et son sourire enjôleur, on retrouve toujours l'audace d'un ado de quinze ans pour qui le mot impossible n'existe pas. Travailleur acharné, tout ce qu'il a eu, il l'a mérité. Avec détermination, pugnacité et gourmandise, depuis plus de quarante ans, Patrick Bruel s'est fait une place dans le cœur des Français. Ses chansons sont les souvenirs de tous.

Sans jamais se renier, sans jamais sombrer dans le jeunisme imbécile, en se réinventant et en innovant sans cesse avec conviction, Patrick Bruel a su traverser le temps et rester toujours d'actualité ! Cette capacité à croire que le plus beau reste à venir est vraiment l'une des grandes qualités de cet artiste.

Fidèle à lui-même, fidèle à ses idéaux, devenu père de deux enfants, réconcilié avec son propre père, Patrick Bruel peut aujourd'hui regarder l'avenir sereinement et exister pleinement.

Son histoire comprenait des blessures et des failles, comme chacun d'entre nous. Avec détermination, il a su se forger un destin comme personne.

Vide

LE BLUES DU CHANTEUR

Tout premier 45 tours de Patrick Bruel, « Vide » est sorti en 1982, aux disques Barclay. Une première chanson assez triste et déprimante, à l'opposé de l'enthousiasme et de la jeunesse pleine d'espoir de l'artiste.

Révélé par le cinéma en avril 1979, avec le film d'Alexandre Arcady *Le Coup de sirocco*, puis au théâtre, en avril 1981, avec le spectacle *Le Charimari*, qui se joue pendant deux saisons à Paris, Patrick Bruel est un acteur qui a le vent en poupe en ce début des années 80. Même si le cinéma et le théâtre occupent beaucoup son temps, Patrick n'a pas oublié son rêve de devenir chanteur. Il est toujours en contact avec Gérard Presgurvic, qu'il avait rencontré à New York au début de l'année 1980. Ils se voient souvent et travaillent ensemble sur des chansons. Parmi ces titres, il y en a un que Presgurvic lui avait joué pour la première fois à New York et qui s'intitule « Vide ».

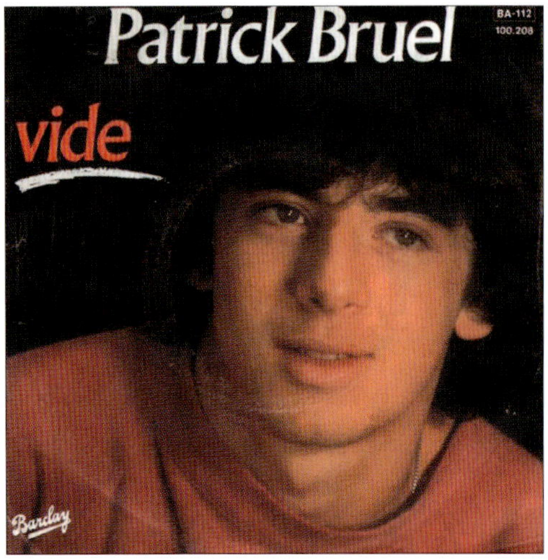

Entre deux tournages, Patrick Bruel travaille comme chanteur et animateur au Club Méditerranée. Et aussi surprenant que cela puisse paraître, c'est là que le destin de cette chanson va se sceller. En effet, au début de l'année 1980, le directeur artistique des disques Barclay passe ses vacances au Club Med et entend Patrick Bruel chanter « Vide ». À ce moment-là, comme la mode est au slow, avec Richard Cocciante qui est N° 1 avec « Le Coup de soleil », il a l'idée de faire signer un contrat de disque à Patrick pour enregistrer « Vide », qui est un peu dans le même esprit musical, aux disques Barclay.

La chanson est enregistrée au Studio Family Sound Aquarium sous la direction artistique de Jean-Claude Feitussi, plus connu sous le nom de Philippe Monet. Sur la seconde face du disque, il y a une autre chanson, « Jusqu'au bout », composée par Mario Santangeli, sur des paroles de Patrick Bruel, bien sûr. La photo de cette première pochette de disque est réalisée par Jean Lebreton.

Ce tout premier 45 tours est publié en 1982 mais ne connaît pas le succès. Un échec que Patrick Bruel expliquera plus tard par le côté triste et déprimant de la chanson, qui contrastait avec sa pêche, son physique et son côté solaire. Bref, une chanson qui ne lui correspondait pas vraiment. ■

> ***“Même si le cinéma et le théâtre occupent beaucoup son temps, Patrick n'a pas oublié son rêve de devenir chanteur.”***

Marre de cette nana-là

L'ALCHIMIE DE LA CHANCE

Sortie tout au début de l'année 1984, « Marre de cette nana-là », interprétée par Patrick Bruel, devient un beau succès seulement huit mois plus tard et permet de révéler au grand public ce chanteur plein de charme et de talent. Flash-back sur un premier succès né d'une belle histoire d'amitié.

Pour bien comprendre la naissance de ce premier succès discographique de Patrick Bruel, il faut remonter à la fin de l'année 1979. Patrick Bruel a alors tout juste vingt ans. Après quelques petits rôles au cinéma, notamment dans *Le Coup de sirocco*, d'Alexandre Arcady, il décide de traverser l'Atlantique et s'envole pour New York, le temps d'un séjour prévu pour quinze jours mais qui durera finalement neuf mois ! Là-bas, avec sa petite amie de l'époque, Patrick se fait plein de copains, qu'il voit régulièrement. Et c'est d'ailleurs chez l'un d'eux qu'il rencontre un certain Gérard Presgurvic. Comme lui, Gérard est passionné de cinéma et de musique. Ce fils de médecin a fait le Conservatoire libre du cinéma français et a déjà à son actif plusieurs courts-métrages et plusieurs musiques de film. Entre Patrick Bruel et Gérard Presgurvic, de six ans son aîné, le courant passe immédiatement. Gérard fait écouter à Patrick les chansons qu'il écrit et Patrick lui fait découvrir les siennes. Une vraie alchimie s'installe entre les deux garçons et donne naissance à une solide amitié qui va véritablement leur porter chance.

De retour en France, grâce à Gérard Presgurvic qui l'invite chez ses parents, dans le Sud, et insiste pour qu'il se rende au Festival de Cannes, Patrick Bruel fait de bonnes rencontres qui lui permettent de reprendre son métier d'acteur. Pendant ce temps, Gérard crée avec un autre ami, Philippe Bourgoin, le premier rap français pour le groupe Chagrin d'amour, qui sort en novembre 1981 et se vend à près de 2 millions d'exemplaires. En 1983, Gérard Presgurvic décide de passer de l'ombre à la lumière et sort un premier album chez Polydor, intitulé *Détective*. C'est un joli succès d'estime mais pas franchement un grand succès populaire. Toujours très proche de Patrick Bruel, Gérard Presgurvic va alors proposer au jeune acteur désireux de chanter une mélodie qu'il a composée, et sur laquelle ils vont co-écrire un texte plein d'humour, inspiré par leurs désespoirs amoureux respectifs. Cette chanson de 4 minutes 50, intitulée « Marre de cette nana-là », est enregistrée en décembre 1983. Le disque sort quelques semaines plus tard sur le label Barclay. Patrick fait sa première émission de télévision en tant que chanteur, le 16 janvier 1984, à l'invitation de Pascal Sevran, dans *La Chance aux chansons*. Le 10 mars, Patrick est invité par Michel Drucker dans *Champs-Élysées*. En dépit d'une importante promotion à la télévision et sur les radios, la chanson a bien du mal à décoller. Et c'est finalement après un passage dans l'émission *Passeport pour la forme*, sur TF1, en plein mois d'août 1984, que « Marre de cette nana-là » va enfin entrer dans les hit-parades. Le 45 tours va s'écouler à 200 000 exemplaires et permettre à Patrick Bruel de faire ses vrais débuts dans la chanson. ■

“Patrick fait sa première émission de télévision en tant que chanteur, le 16 janvier 198 à l'invitation de Pascal Sevran dans La Chance aux Chanson

En 1984, parmi les choristes et les danseuses qui accompagnent Patrick Bruel lors des émissions de télévision pour la promotion de « Marre de cette nana-là », se trouve l'actrice Sophie Duez.

Comment ça va pour vous ?

EXPÉRIENCES DE SOIRÉES !

Succès de l'été 1985, « Comment ça va pour vous ? » permet à Patrick Bruel de conforter son début de carrière de chanteur. Avec ce titre léger et enjoué, le jeune artiste fait son entrée pour la première fois au Top 50.

Après un deuxième 45 tours, « Marre de cette nana-là », qui s'est vendu à 200 000 exemplaires, Patrick Bruel et son complice Gérard Presgurvic créent une nouvelle chanson intitulée « Comment ça va pour vous ? ».

C'est en s'inspirant de soirées qu'ils ont souvent fréquentées que l'idée de cette chanson leur est venue. Les soirées où tout le monde fait semblant de se connaître et d'aller super bien, Patrick et Gérard en ont souvent fait l'expérience. Et quand en plus la fille qu'ils attendent n'arrive jamais à cette soirée, ils préfèrent en rire et en faire une chanson. Et c'est ce qu'ils font au début de l'année 1985. Au même moment, Patrick est choisi par le réalisateur Patrick Schulmann pour tenir un rôle important dans sa prochaine comédie : *P.R.O.F.S.*

Aussi, quand Patrick ne tourne pas les scènes de ce film dans lequel il campe le rôle de Frédéric Game, un prof de lettres modernes, aux côtés de Fabrice Luchini, il rejoint le studio d'enregistrement pour finaliser la création de la chanson « Comment ça va pour vous ? ».

En studio, il est accompagné de Jean-Yves D'Angelo aux claviers, de Kamil Rustam aux guitares, de Thierry Durbet aux synthés, et du grand Manu Katché à la batterie.

Ce troisième 45 tours sort aux disques Barclay au mois de mai 1985. Beaucoup diffusé sur les radios, il connaît un beau succès commercial et va devenir l'un des tubes de l'été 1985. Entre le 8 juillet et le 24 août, Patrick Bruel part en tournée avec Patrick Sébastien, dont il assure la première partie avec les trois chansons qu'il a à son répertoire, dont « Comment ça va pour vous ? » qui chaque soir est acclamée par les foules de vacanciers. Dès le 29 juillet, le disque fait son entrée au Top 50, à la 48e place, et va rester dans ce classement pendant 19 semaines, atteignant la 27e place le 16 septembre 1985. Deux jours plus tard, le 18 septembre, le film *P.R.O.F.S.* arrive dans les cinémas, et là encore le succès va être grand, puisqu'il rassemble 3 millions de spectateurs. Patrick Bruel devient la nouvelle coqueluche de la presse jeune. Les magazines *Girls* et *OK!* lui consacrent des articles. Entre cinéma et chanson, Patrick Bruel devient alors incontournable. ■

"Entre cinéma et chanson, Patrick Bruel devient incontournable."

PATRICK
BRUE

1986

Tout l'monde peut s'tromper

AU GÉNÉRIQUE DU FILM DE CLAUDE LELOUCH

Troisième extrait du tout premier album de Patrick Bruel, « Tout l'monde peut s'tromper », paru en 1986, figure également au générique du film de Claude Lelouch, *Attention bandits !*, dans lequel Patrick joue l'un des rôles principaux.

Après le succès de « Comment ça va pour vous ? », qui s'est imposé comme l'un des tubes de l'été 1985, la perspective d'un premier album se dessine. Patrick Bruel passe du label Barclay à Philips et publie son premier album au début de l'année 1986. Cet album comprend dix chansons inédites, dont « Tout l'monde peut s'tromper », une nouvelle collaboration entre Patrick et son ami Gérard Presgurvic. Cette chanson pleine d'humour, qui part du constat que l'erreur est humaine, est portée par une mélodie au piano très efficace qui n'est pas sans rappeler l'univers des compositions de Michel Berger.

Le titre est produit par Philippe Abitbol et enregistré au Studio du Palais des Congrès à Paris. Manu Katché est à la batterie et Carole Fredericks dans les chœurs.
Lorsque la chanson sort en troisième single de l'album *De face (2 faces)*, elle ne remporte pas plus de succès que les deux précédents extraits « Non j'veux pas » et « J'roule vers toi ».
Au moment où Patrick Bruel enregistre ce premier album, il tourne un film réalisé par Claude Lelouch et intitulé *Attention bandits !*
Dans ce film, Patrick Bruel, aux côtés de Jean Yanne, joue le rôle d'un jeune bandit surnommé Mozart.
Claude Lelouch choisit la chanson de Patrick « Tout l'monde peut s'tromper » comme générique d'*Attention bandits !* Et pour illustrer également une scène de son film.

Aussi, lors de la sortie au cinéma d'*Attention bandits !*, le 5 août 1987, le public redécouvre la chanson. ■

*"Claude Lelouch choisit la chanson de Patrick comme générique d'*Attention bandits *et pour illustrer également une scène de son film."*

Casser la voix

LA CHANSON DE L'AUBE…

Titre phare de la carrière de Patrick Bruel, « Casser la voix » a été écrit une nuit, à La Rochelle, après un concert de Jacques Higelin. Zoom arrière sur la petite histoire de cette grande chanson de l'année 1989…

Après des premiers succès comme « Marre de cette nana-là », « Comment ça va pour vous ? » ou « J'roule vers toi », Patrick Bruel se fait une place de choix dans la chanson française, tout en commençant en parallèle une carrière cinématographique prometteuse. Mais la véritable consécration musicale arrive en octobre 1989, avec la sortie de l'album *Alors regarde*, produit et réalisé par Mick Lanaro, sur lequel figurent plusieurs tubes en puissance, dont ce fameux « Casser la voix » qui va faire de Patrick une véritable idole, donnant même naissance à un phénomène que l'on appellera « la Bruelmania ».

Pour la petite histoire, « Casser la voix » est une chanson qui est née au cours d'une nuit de réflexion sur le métier de chanteur, à La Rochelle. Patrick est venu assister aux Francofolies, ce célèbre festival de la chanson française créé par Jean-Louis Foulquier. Sur la grande scène installée place Saint-Jean-d'Acre, c'est Jacques Higelin qui se produit ce soir-là. Patrick ne rate rien de la très longue prestation de ce merveilleux show-man qui se donne à fond, allant même jusqu'à se casser la voix pour plaire aux nombreux jeunes en liesse. En rentrant à l'hôtel, au petit matin, Patrick, qui n'a pas sommeil, s'installe sur le petit bureau de sa chambre qui donne face à la mer et se met à écrire et à composer le début de « Casser la voix ». Son fidèle alter ego, Gérard Presgurvic, l'achèvera plus tard, et ainsi naîtra un immense tube. L'enregistrement de la chanson se déroule le 14 juillet 1989, à New York, au studio Hit & Sounds. Ce jour-là, la communauté française de New York fête Bastille Day. Patrick est attendu pour assister à une soirée organisée pour l'occasion au Palladium. Avant de s'y rendre, Patrick enregistre « Casser la voix » en une prise, pensant qu'il s'agit d'un test pour une voix témoin et qu'il recommencera une prochaine fois. Pourtant, après l'enregistrement, Mick Lanaro, les yeux embués, lui dit : « On ne fait rien d'autre, c'est fini pour moi ! » Ce soir-là, Patrick est parti à la fête le cœur léger. « Casser la voix » est le premier extrait de l'album *Alors regarde*. Il sort le 2 octobre 1989. Dès le 25 novembre, il entre à la 27e place du Top 50 et va y rester 19 semaines. ■

"'Casser la voix' est une chanson qui est née au cours d'une nuit de réflexion sur le métier de chanteur, à La Rochelle, aux Francofolies, ce célèbre festival de la chanson française."

Avec son deuxième album studio vendu à plus de 2 millions d'exemplaires, Patrick Bruel devient un véritable phénomène de société au début des années 90 et incarne la voix de toute une jeunesse.

J'te l'dis quand même

ÉCRIRE JE T'AIME EN CHANSON

Chanson culte du répertoire de Patrick Bruel, « J'te l'dis quand même » est le deuxième extrait du deuxième album de l'artiste. Une ballade d'amour qui prend toute sa dimension sur scène quand des milliers de voix féminines la reprennent en chœur avec le chanteur.

L'histoire de la chanson « J'te l'dis quand même » s'inscrit dans la collaboration de Patrick Bruel avec Mick Lanaro, en 1989. À cette époque, la maison de disques BMG vient de signer un contrat avec Patrick Bruel. Bien décidé à mettre tous les atouts de son côté, Bernard Carbonez, qui dirige BMG, fait appel à Mick Lanaro pour produire le disque. Mick a une très bonne réputation dans la chanson et son palmarès parle pour lui. En 1987, c'est à lui que l'on doit le retour gagnant de Claude Nougaro avec la chanson « Nougayork ». Il a aussi travaillé avec Bernard Lavilliers, William Sheller et beaucoup d'autres. Mick Lanaro connaît un peu le jeune artiste Patrick Bruel pour l'avoir croisé quelques fois en studio ou dans les coulisses de certains concerts. L'idée de travailler avec un artiste de la nouvelle génération lui plaît bien et Mick accepte donc la proposition de BMG.

Après plusieurs semaines de travail préparatoire sur des maquettes à Paris, Patrick Bruel et Mick Lanaro s'installent pendant quinze jours au Studio Polygone, à Blagnac, dans la banlieue de Toulouse. Ils commencent alors les premiers enregistrements avec six musiciens : Gérard Bikialo aux claviers, Éric Berdeaux à la console, Christian Padovan à la basse, Pierre Teodori aux guitares acoustiques, John Woolloff aux guitares électriques, Marcello Surace à la batterie, et Alain Lepas pour les arrangements. Après avoir enregistré trois premières chansons, Patrick Bruel est sur le point de commencer à travailler sur un quatrième titre mais il y a un problème, il n'arrive pas à trouver de refrain. Lorsqu'il en fait part à Mick Lanaro, ce dernier lui suggère tout simplement de l'écrire et c'est ainsi que Patrick trouve les paroles : « Et je trouve pas de refrain », et plutôt que de dire « à ma chanson », il rajoute « à notre histoire ». Ainsi naît le refrain de « J'te l'dis quand même ». Mick Lanaro conseille ensuite à Patrick Bruel de parler d'amour dans sa chanson et de dire « je t'aime ». Une idée qui au départ n'enthousiasme pas du tout le chanteur, qui n'a encore jamais dit « je t'aime » dans une de ses chansons et n'a pas l'intention de le faire. Pourtant, Mick Lanaro insiste, et Patrick va finir par céder. L'album est ensuite finalisé à New York pendant cinq semaines.

Après «Alors regarde», le premier extrait de l'album qui paraît en novembre 1989 et devient un immense tube, «J'te l'dis quand même» sort en single le 2 mars 1990. Il fait son entrée au Top 50 le 21 avril 1990 et y reste 14 semaines, atteignant la 12e place au mois de mai.
Cette chanson sur une séparation amoureuse connaît un immense succès lorsque Patrick Bruel l'interprète sur scène pour la première fois à Liège, en Belgique, lors de sa grande tournée de 1990-1991. Dès lors, chaque soir, au moment où il joue les premières notes de la chanson au piano, des centaines de milliers de voix de jeunes filles chantent ce morceau avec lui et hurlent «je t'aime». Chaque fois naît un grand moment d'émotion pour le chanteur, qui leur répond : «moi aussi».

Pour la petite histoire, en 2011, le chanteur Amir, qui n'a pas encore été révélé par l'émission *The Voice* ni par sa participation au Concours Eurovision de la chanson, enregistre un album sur lequel il reprend «J'te l'dis quand même» en hébreu. Très touché par cette reprise, Patrick Bruel invite Amir sur scène avec lui lors d'un de ses concerts à Tel Aviv, devant 11 000 personnes. ■

Alors regarde

DERNIERS MOTS DANS L'ASCENSEUR

Sorti en single le 3 septembre 1990, « Alors regarde » est l'un des nombreux tubes du deuxième album de Patrick Bruel. Découvrons la genèse d'un titre ébauché à Paris et terminé dans un ascenseur, à New York.

En 1989, Patrick Bruel a trente ans. Depuis son premier rôle au cinéma, dix ans plus tôt, dans *Le Coup de sirocco*, sa carrière s'est littéralement envolée. Les rôles se sont multipliés et il a aussi fait des débuts remarqués dans la chanson avec des hits comme « Marre de cette nana-là », en 1984, ou « Comment ça va pour vous ? », en 1985, sortis aux disques Barclay. Après un premier album au succès modeste et un passage triomphal à l'Olympia, en 1987, Patrick Bruel trace sa route. Tout en enchaînant les films, il se met à travailler sur son deuxième album. C'est d'ailleurs sur le tournage de *L'Union sacrée* qu'il commence à ébaucher des textes, et notamment celui de la chanson « Alors regarde ». L'idée de ce titre lui est venue en réaction aux réflexions de ses conquêtes féminines de l'époque qui lui disaient souvent qu'elles ne s'intéressaient pas à l'actualité ni à la politique. Très agacé par ce manque d'intérêt pour l'état de notre monde, Patrick écrit donc les premières paroles de cette supplique à l'éveil des consciences.
Patrick signe un contrat avec la maison de disques BMG et travaille sur la réalisation de son nouvel album avec le producteur Mick Lanaro. L'enregistrement des chansons se fait en deux temps. D'abord au Studio Polygone, à Toulouse, au début du mois de mars 1989, puis dans un studio de New York. C'est d'ailleurs juste avant de se rendre dans ce studio, alors qu'il se trouve dans l'ascenseur de son hôtel, que Patrick Bruel trouve les derniers mots manquants de la chanson « Alors regarde ».

L'album *Alors regarde* arrive chez les disquaires, le 9 novembre 1989, et va connaître un succès phénoménal, atteignant les 2 millions d'exemplaires vendus. Les extraits se succèdent et se classent tous au Top 50. « Alors regarde », qui a donné son titre à l'album, est la troisième chanson qui en est extraite. Elle sort en single, le 3 septembre 1990, et se retrouve vite à la première place des meilleures ventes. Toute la jeunesse du début des années 90 se retrouve dans ce titre qui dénonce les dérives de notre monde. Dès lors, Patrick Bruel apparaît comme un chanteur engagé, désireux d'exprimer ses idées et de défendre ses convictions. À ceux qui le lui reprochent, le chanteur répond alors : « Je n'ai pas le tempérament et pas l'envie de fermer les yeux. »
Lors de ses concerts au Zénith de Paris, du 9 au 17 octobre 1990, puis du 20 au 23 décembre, les salles reprennent en chœur « Alors regarde », son tube du moment.

Pour la petite histoire, en 1992, Patrick Bruel a enregistré une version espagnole de son titre « Alors regarde » qui a connu un beau succès dans les pays hispanophones. ■

"C'est sur le tournage de* L'Unio *Sacrée* qu'il commence à ébauch *le texte de 'Alors regarde'."

Place des grands hommes

LES ANNÉES LYCÉE

En octobre 1989, à tout juste trente ans, Patrick Bruel se retourne sur son passé en chanson, avec « Place des grands hommes », dans laquelle il évoque avec nostalgie les amis de ses vingt ans. Gros plan sur ce titre aux allures de flash-back auquel pourtant Patrick ne croyait pas du tout.

Dans les carrières d'artiste, il y a toujours des titres plus emblématiques que d'autres. C'est le cas de « Place des grands hommes » pour Patrick Bruel. L'histoire de cette chanson commence le 8 mai 1988. À ce moment-là, Patrick Bruel prépare un deuxième album. Il demande alors à un de ses amis doué pour l'écriture et qui a toujours cru en lui, Bruno Garcin, rencontré en juillet 1977 au Club Méditerranée de Tignes, de lui écrire un texte de chanson faisant référence à un rendez-vous entre anciens camarades de classe. Une fois de retour chez lui, très inspiré par ce thème, Bruno écrit le texte de « Place des grands hommes » en une heure. Quelque temps après, lorsqu'il montre son texte à Patrick Bruel, Bruno a beaucoup de mal à le convaincre de composer une musique. Il lui suggère même de s'inspirer de celle de James Taylor, dont il lui rappelle trois accords. Finalement, Patrick compose une mélodie sur le texte de Bruno Garcin auquel il change quelques mots afin de personnaliser la chanson. Ainsi, dans l'énumération des prénoms, il choisit évidemment des personnes qui lui sont proches, comme François, Marco, Laurence, Évelyne, Gégé… Une fois la chanson terminée, Patrick Bruel hésite jusqu'au bout à l'inclure à son album. C'est au tout dernier moment qu'il décide à contrecœur de l'enregistrer. Signe qu'il n'aime pas beaucoup cette chanson, il la relègue à la septième position du disque, qui sort en octobre 1989.
Pour la promotion du nouveau film d'Alexandre Arcady, intitulé *L'Union sacrée*, dans lequel il joue le rôle de Simon Atlan et partage l'affiche avec Richard Berry, Patrick Bruel participe à de nombreuses émissions de télévision, dont *Avis de recherche*, sur TF1, le 24 février 1989. Le principe de ce programme présenté par Patrick Sabatier est de permettre aux invités de retrouver leurs camarades de classe à partir d'une photo. Pour cette occasion, Patrick Bruel interprète pour la première fois « Place des grands hommes », qui colle parfaitement avec la thématique de l'émission.
Après la sortie de *L'Union sacrée*, le 15 mars 1989, Patrick Bruel peut terminer l'enregistrement de son nouvel album. Sa maison de disques BMG lui permet de travailler avec le producteur Mick Lanaro. Celui-ci a notamment réalisé le fameux *Nougayork* qui a marqué le come-back de Claude Nougaro.
L'enregistrement des onze nouvelles chansons de Patrick Bruel, dont « Place des grands hommes », se fait en deux temps : d'abord au Studio Polygone, à Toulouse, puis dans un studio de New York, avec les meilleurs musiciens du moment.
« Place des grands hommes » sort en single en janvier 1991, en quatrième extrait de l'album, après les succès de « Casser

la voix», «J'te l'dis quand même» et «Alors regarde». Pour la pochette du CD deux titres, Patrick Bruel choisit une photo de classe de l'année 1973-1974.
À l'instar des trois premiers singles, «Place des grands hommes» connaît un immense succès et se classe en tête du Top 50. En quelques semaines, l'album, qui avait déjà atteint le score très honorable d'un million de ventes, atteint le record phénoménal de 2,4 millions d'exemplaires vendus en mai 1991. À partir de là, Patrick Bruel n'est plus seulement une vedette. Il est devenu une véritable star.

Pour l'anecdote, en 1999, Patrick Bruel compose «C'est la vie», une chanson qui fait écho à «Place des grands hommes» et aborde une nouvelle fois le thème de l'amitié face au temps qui passe. ■

Décalé

LA CHANSON POUR PATRICIA

Cinquième extrait de l'album de la consécration pour Patrick Bruel, « Décalé » est une chanson aux sonorités de bossa nova entraînante. Un titre qui lui a été inspiré par Patricia, une de ses premières amoureuses, d'origine brésilienne.

Pour bien comprendre l'histoire de la chanson « Décalé », il faut remonter quelques années en arrière, quand Patrick Bruel était encore étudiant en classe de 4e au lycée Henri-IV. C'est à cette époque qu'il rencontre sa première bande de copains et de copines, et surtout Patricia, sa première grande histoire d'amour. C'est lors d'un après-midi avec sa bande chez leur copine Marion Suffert que Patrick rencontre Patricia pour la première fois. Elle a quinze ans, il en a dix-sept. Elle est brésilienne et c'est la fille d'une diplomate. Comme lui, elle chante et joue de la guitare. Patrick est fasciné par ses yeux et sa jolie voix quand elle reprend les airs de bossa nova de Vinicius Cantuaria, de Chico Buarque ou d'Antonio Jobim. Dès lors, Patrick ne va cesser de passer des après-midi chez elle, où ils font de la musique et chantent ensemble leur chanson fétiche, « O que será ». Seulement, en 1979, la mère de Patricia est mutée à New York et la jeune fille doit quitter Paris. Avant son départ, elle organise une grande fête où elle chante toute la soirée avec Patrick, et avant qu'ils se quittent, sur le palier, ils tombent dans les bras l'un de l'autre. C'est donc en pensant quelques années après à cette belle histoire d'amour sur fond de bossa nova brésilienne que Patrick Bruel imagine sa chanson « Décalé ».

Le titre est enregistré à New York et figure sur l'album *Alors regarde*, qui paraît le 9 novembre 1989. Il est publié également en single le 4 juillet 1991 et reste dans le Top des ventes tout l'été. Dans le clip réalisé pour la promotion de la chanson, le rôle de la jeune Brésilienne est tenu par une comédienne de vingt-quatre ans, compagne de Francis Huster : Cristiana Reali.

Pour la petite histoire, le 24 février 1989, dans l'émission *Avis de recherche* spéciale Patrick Bruel, les téléspectateurs découvrent le visage de Patricia, qui est en duplex depuis le Brésil. Elle avoue alors : « C'était une superbe histoire d'amour qui passait par la musique, le Brésil. Je suis tombée complètement amoureuse de Patrick lors de notre première rencontre. Cela a duré pas mal de temps jusqu'à ce que l'on en vienne au fait de la chose. On a beaucoup joué de la guitare, beaucoup chanté et voyagé ! »

Très ému de revoir cette fille qui a tant compté dans son adolescence, Patrick interprète ce soir-là avec elle leur chanson fétiche, « O que será ».

En 2000 et 2001, lors de sa tournée *Rien ne s'efface*, Patrick Bruel interprète « Décalé », et à la fin de la chanson, avant d'enchaîner avec la reprise de « Non je n'ai rien oublié », de Charles Aznavour, Patrick rappelle qu'il a écrit « Décalé » pour son premier amour dont il a été obligé de se séparer à cause de l'opposition des parents de la jeune fille. ■

"C'est au lycée Henri-IV qu'il rencontre Patricia, sa première grande histoire d'amour."

Lors de sa tournée dans l'océan Indien, en 1991, Patrick en profite pour tourner, à l'île de la Réunion, le clip de sa chanson « Décalé », pendant trois jours, avec le réalisateur Élie Chouraqui.

Qui a le droit…

L'ABSENCE D'UN PÈRE

« Qui a le droit » est l'un des plus grands tubes de Patrick Bruel, sorti sur un album live, en 1991, vendu à plus de 500 000 exemplaires. Pourtant, cette chanson intimiste qui évoque l'absence d'un père a bien failli ne jamais voir le jour. C'est grâce à Augusta, la mère du chanteur, qu'elle va renaître sur scène.

En 1986, le premier album de Patrick Bruel, intitulé *De face (2 faces)*, ne rencontre pas le succès escompté. Il se vend à seulement 20 000 exemplaires, mais il permet à Patrick de se faire connaître du grand public, et surtout de faire son premier Olympia, du 5 au 8 mai 1987. C'est seulement deux ans après que le jeune chanteur de trente ans connaît la consécration, avec l'album *Alors regarde*, produit et réalisé par Mick Lanaro. Ce disque enregistré à New York comporte onze chansons mais il aurait dû en regrouper douze. En effet, Patrick Bruel avait prévu un 12e titre, intitulé « Qui a le droit ». L'histoire de cette chanson commence donc précisément à ce moment-là. Au départ, il s'agissait d'une chanson d'amour en anglais composée à Tahiti, en 1988, mais la traduction française ne donnait rien. En partant de l'expression que lui donne Patrick, « qui a le droit », sans changer la musique, Gérard Presgurvic écrit de nouvelles paroles plus intimistes qui abordent l'absence d'un père, sujet qui touche personnellement Patrick, élevé seul par sa mère. Patrick Bruel enregistre le titre durant le mois de juillet 1989 avec les 11 autres chansons de son deuxième album. Seulement, au moment de choisir les titres définitifs du disque *Alors regarde*, Patrick Bruel décide de ne pas y inclure « Qui a le droit ». La raison, c'est qu'il n'est pas satisfait de l'arrangement. La chanson est donc une nouvelle fois mise de côté.

L'histoire aurait pu s'arrêter là et « Qui a le droit » aurait pu être oubliée. Pourtant, après l'immense succès de l'album *Alors regarde*, sorti le 9 novembre 1989, Patrick Bruel entame une grande tournée de 130 dates qui passe par le Zénith de Paris. Ce soir-là, Augusta, la mère de Patrick, lui conseille d'inclure « Qui a le droit » à son tour de chant. Elle adore cette chanson et elle sait qu'elle est importante pour son fils. Patrick Bruel suit le conseil de sa mère et c'est un triomphe. Il est acclamé par le public, qui reprend les paroles avec émotion, en chœur avec lui. La séquence est enregistrée pour un double album live intitulé *Si ce soir* qui sort à la fin de l'année 1991. « Qui a le droit » est la chanson qui va soutenir cet album live, lequel se vendra à un million d'exemplaires. Elle entre au Top 50 le 2 novembre 1991 et va y rester jusqu'au 18 avril 1992, dont 7 semaines à la première place. « Qui a le droit » demeure, aujourd'hui encore, l'un des plus grands succès de Patrick Bruel. ■

" 'Qui a le droit' est la chanson qui va soutenir le double album live* Si ce soir, *qui se vendra à un million d'exemplaires."

Et puis je sais

UNE LONGUE COMPLICITÉ AVEC JOHNNY HALLYDAY

En 1991, Patrick Bruel écrit deux chansons pour Johnny Hallyday, dont « Et puis je sais », qui se classe au Top 50 durant l'été 1992 et qu'il interprétera en duo avec lui six ans après, au Stade de France.

Si Patrick Bruel a souvent interprété ses chansons, il lui est arrivé aussi d'en écrire pour d'autres. Et c'est le cas, en 1991, avec le titre « Et puis je sais », écrit et composé pour Johnny Hallyday.

Les deux artistes se connaissent bien. Leur première rencontre remonte à 1984, quand la programmatrice musicale de RTL, Monique le Marcis, lui avait présenté Johnny dans les coulisses du Zénith de Paris. Trois ans plus tard, en 1987, Patrick n'est encore qu'un débutant dans la chanson. Il a seulement un album à son actif et vient de faire son premier Olympia au mois de mai précédent. Le 4 octobre 1987, Johnny Hallyday l'invite à sa dernière à Bercy pour l'accompagner sur les chœurs de sa chanson « Gabrielle ». Un moment inoubliable pour le jeune Patrick Bruel. À l'issue du concert, dans les coulisses, le roi du rock l'encourage et lui promet une grande carrière. Ils se retrouvent quelques mois après, le 14 juillet 1988, à Saint-Tropez, où Johnny donne un concert. Ce jour-là, ils chantent ensemble « La musique que j'aime ». Après l'immense succès de son album *Alors regarde*, Patrick Bruel est nommé dans trois catégories aux Victoires de la musique, le 2 février 1991, mais il n'en obtient pas une seule. Johnny Hallyday, qui reçoit celle du meilleur spectacle musical, défend son ami Patrick Bruel qui, selon lui, méritait légitimement d'en avoir une. Une attention qui touche beaucoup Patrick Bruel. Quelques semaines plus tard, ils se retrouvent au cours de l'émission *Sacrée Soirée* sur TF1, le 7 mars 1991, où ils interprètent ensemble le titre de Patrick, « Casser la voix ». À ce moment-là, le rocker prépare un nouvel album pour la fin de l'année, produit par le même Mick Lanaro qui a produit le deuxième album de Patrick Bruel. Johnny demande des chansons à Patrick Bruel. Et c'est ainsi que ce dernier va composer et écrire deux titres pour l'idole : « Pour exister » et « Et puis je sais ».

L'album de Johnny Hallyday, intitulé *Ça ne change pas un homme*, sur lequel figurent les deux titres de Patrick, sort le 10 décembre 1991. « Et puis je sais » est le troisième extrait du disque à paraître en single, le 17 juin 1992. Il connaît un petit succès durant l'été 1992 et se classe à la 16e place du Top 50.

Six ans plus tard, en 1998, alors que Patrick traverse une période un peu plus compliquée sur le plan musical, avec pas mal de doutes quant à son avenir, son ami Johnny Hallyday l'invite, contre l'avis général de son entourage, à chanter en duo avec lui lors de son premier méga concert au Stade de France. Ainsi, le 4 septembre 1998, Patrick Bruel se retrouve sur scène aux côtés de Johnny Hallyday et chante en duo avec lui « Et puis je sais » devant 80 000 spectateurs. Un moment très fort pour Patrick, qui ne l'oubliera jamais.

Au moment de la disparition de Johnny Hallyday, le 5 décembre 2017, très ému, Patrick Bruel écrit un long message dans lequel il dit notamment : « Je n'ai jamais oublié et je n'oublierai jamais ce que tu as fait pour moi. Nos échanges, nos fous rires, tes conseils, nos duos… Tellement de duos, je n'arrive même pas à les compter, avec à chaque fois ce sourire bienveillant et fraternel… Je t'ai aimé comme un grand frère. » ■

Le 7 mars 1991, lors de l'émission *Sacrée Soirée*, sur TF1, Patrick Bruel interprète « Casser la voix », en duo avec Johnny Hallyday. Un grand moment dans la carrière de Patrick.

Combien de murs...

LA CHUTE DU MUR DE BERLIN

Inspiré d'un fait historique, la chute du mur de Berlin, la chanson « Combien de murs », publiée en avril 1994, écrite et composée par Patrick Bruel, interroge sur les lendemains qui chantent après la liberté retrouvée.

Après le succès retentissant de son deuxième album, *Alors regarde*, vendu à 3,5 millions d'exemplaires, que suivent une tournée triomphale et une Victoire de la musique de l'artiste masculin de l'année, en 1992, Patrick Bruel retourne au cinéma. Il joue le rôle de l'inspecteur Christophe Vade dans *Toutes peines confondues*, de Michel Deville, qui sort le 8 avril 1992, puis l'inspecteur Julien Segal dans le film de Claude Zidi, *Profil bas*, dans les salles le 8 décembre 1993. Le même jour que la sortie de son album *Alors regarde*, le 9 novembre 1989, un événement avait beaucoup touché Patrick Bruel : la chute du mur de Berlin. En regardant la destruction de ce mur érigé en 1961 et qui coupait Berlin en deux, Patrick Bruel s'était mis à écrire une chanson. Devant la liesse populaire, Patrick s'interrogeait sur les jours d'après. Il s'était mis dans la peau d'un homme face au mur qui s'effondrait, dans une ambiance d'immense joie, mais lui gardait une certaine froideur, en se demandant combien de murs se cachaient devant ce mur qui tombait.

De cette interrogation sur la liberté retrouvée, Patrick Bruel fait donc une chanson, « Combien de murs », qu'il enregistre quelques années plus tard, en 1994, sur son troisième album. Ce disque de quatorze chansons, beaucoup plus rock que le précédent, est enregistré entre New York et Toulouse. Patrick s'est chargé lui-même de la réalisation avec Mick Lanaro et s'est entouré d'excellents musiciens, comme le guitariste Aldo Nova.

Intitulé au départ tout simplement Bruel, ce troisième album est mis en vente le 26 avril 1994. « Combien de murs » sort en deuxième extrait et reçoit un très bon accueil. Cette chanson prendra encore plus de dimension sur scène, et d'ailleurs Patrick Bruel l'inclura souvent à ses concerts.

Sur sa tournée *Ce soir on sort Tour 2019-2020*, Patrick Bruel est accompagné sur la chanson « Combien de murs » par une violoncelliste, un clin d'œil au violoncelliste Mstislav Rostropovitch qui avait joué une sonate de Bach, symboliquement, devant le mur effondré, le 11 novembre 1989, filmé par les caméras du monde entier. ■

"En regardant la destruction de ce mur érigé en 1961 et qui coupe Berlin en deux, Patrick Bruel se met à écrire la chanson 'Combien de murs'."

Patrick Bruel au théâtre d'Enghien-les-Bains, en 1995, pour le tournage du clip de la chanson « J'suis quand même là », réalisé par Jean Achache. Dans ce clip, Patrick tient le rôle d'un réalisateur de théâtre.

Gibson

Tic, Tic, Tac

DANS UN CLUB DE MANAUS

Même si Patrick Bruel n'a écrit ni les paroles, ni la musique de « Tic, Tic, Tac », tube de l'été 1996, il a été pour beaucoup dans son succès dans toute l'Europe, et même au-delà. Un titre qui reste une grande fierté pour le producteur qu'est aussi Patrick Bruel.

S'il est à la fois chanteur, acteur et producteur, il arrive parfois que ces trois activités se télescopent dans le parcours de Patrick Bruel. C'est le cas en 1996. Après un troisième album et une grande tournée en France et en Europe, Patrick Bruel revient au cinéma.

En novembre 1995, il tourne dans le Nord-Ouest brésilien, à Manaus, l'ancienne capitale brésilienne du caoutchouc, en Amazonie, un nouveau film, *Le Jaguar*, réalisé par Francis Veber, dans lequel il tient le rôle principal, aux côtés de Jean Reno. Dans ce film, Patrick Bruel est dans la peau de François Perrin, un joueur de poker endetté qui se voit confier un chef indien malade de passage à Paris, une mission en Amazonie pour retrouver son âme.

Lors de ce tournage, Patrick Bruel rencontre au Havai, l'un des plus grands clubs de Punta Negra, un groupe de sept musiciens dont le chanteur, Zezinho Corrêa, et quatre danseurs réunis sous le nom de Carrapicho. Patrick, qui s'y connaît en tubes, repère immédiatement leur chanson « Tic, Tic, Tac » *(prononcez tchic, tchic, ta)*. Cette chanson est un véritable appel à faire la fête et s'accompagne d'une danse appelée le boi-bumba (le bœuf et le tambour), qui est une sorte de samba mêlant des origines brésiliennes à d'autres de la cordillère des Andes. La danse se pratique en rang d'oignons, le plus compliqué étant de se baisser rapidement en basculant le bassin d'avant en arrière.

Patrick est convaincu que cette chanson et la danse qui l'accompagne peuvent très bien fonctionner en France et au-delà. Immédiatement, il décide de signer le groupe pour le produire et le faire connaître en Europe. Quelques jours plus tard, l'équipe de son label 14 Productions arrive à Manaus et signe un contrat avec Carrapicho. Le disque sera distribué ensuite par la maison de disques de Patrick Bruel, BMG, via son label RCA, en partenariat avec Europe 1, France 2 et la boisson Cap Tea. Dès le mois de mai 1996, France 2 et Europe 1 matraquent le titre sur leurs antennes et invitent le groupe dans toutes leurs émissions.

Un véritable coup de maître pour le producteur Patrick Bruel puisque la chanson devient le tube de l'été 1996 et se classe N° 1 au Top 50, dès le 13 juillet 1996, pendant trois semaines. Le disque se vend à un million d'exemplaires et devient disque de diamant. Un tube non seulement en France mais aussi dans plusieurs pays d'Europe, en Israël et en Amérique du Sud. ■

« C'est le tube de l'été 1996, il se classe N° 1 au Top 50 en se vendant à un million d'exemplaires. »

1999

J'te mentirais...

MEA CULPA D'ADULTÈRE

Sortie en 1999, sur le quatrième album studio de Patrick Bruel, « J'te mentirais » est une chanson audacieuse sur les rapports humains au sein du couple. Entrons dans le secret de cette chanson écrite et composée à New York, au petit matin d'une nuit blanche.

Après un rôle remarqué dans un film d'Alexandre Arcady, *K*, Patrick Bruel se lance dans la production théâtrale avec une pièce intitulée *La Grande Magie*, au théâtre Hébertot, à Paris. Même si cette nouvelle aventure le passionne, il n'oublie pas pour autant la chanson et continue d'écrire et de composer en vue d'un nouvel album. Au cours de l'été 1997, alors qu'il se trouve à New York, en repensant à une histoire personnelle, il a l'idée d'écrire une chanson qui aborde le douloureux problème d'un homme qui a trompé sa femme et qui, en le lui avouant, lui demande de l'aider à sauver leur couple. En quatre minutes, Patrick se livre à une sorte de mea culpa un peu pervers et original pour sauver une histoire d'amour en danger. Sur ce texte autobiographique, il compose une mélodie sur un piano dans la grande boutique Steinway, sur la 57e rue, à New York, au petit matin, après une nuit où il n'avait pas réussi à trouver le sommeil.

La chanson est enregistrée et mixée avec Didier Lozahic quelques semaines après, avec le producteur Mick Lanaro, au Studio du Palais des Congrès de Paris.
« J'te mentirais » sort chez RCA/BMG, en octobre 1999, sur l'album *Juste avant* et devient rapidement l'une des chansons phares de ce nouveau disque qui marque les quarante ans du chanteur et sa véritable maturité artistique.

Pour la petite histoire, presque quatorze ans après sa sortie, le samedi 16 février 2013, Patrick Bruel a interprété « J'te mentirais » en duo avec la chanteuse Shy'm, sur le plateau de *Champs-Élysées*, présenté par Michel Drucker. ■

"La chanson aborde le douloureux problème d'un homme qui a trompé sa femme, qui lui avoue et lui demande de l'aider à sauver leur couple."

Pour la vie

UNE HISTOIRE D'AMITIÉ

Deuxième extrait du quatrième album de Patrick Bruel paru en octobre 1999, « Pour la vie » est une chanson qui célèbre l'amitié à travers le temps qui passe. Véritable chanson bilan d'un homme de quarante ans, à l'aube de l'an 2000, « Pour la vie » marque un nouveau départ dans la carrière du chanteur.

Même si son troisième album, paru en 1994, ne s'est pas aussi bien vendu que le précédent, Patrick Bruel a fidélisé un très large public et fait désormais partie du paysage musical et médiatique français. Sa tournée *On s'était dit Tour 95*, qui a duré un an, a rassemblé énormément de spectateurs, et la « Bruelmania » est loin d'être terminée. Pourtant, l'artiste ressent le besoin de s'éclipser, de prendre du recul afin de recréer chez lui l'urgence d'écrire de nouvelles chansons. Après sept ans d'effervescence et de folie médiatique, Patrick Bruel comprend qu'il lui est nécessaire de se ressourcer. Il va alors voyager, profiter de ses amis et tourner quelques films pour le cinéma comme *Le Jaguar* de Francis Veber ou *K* d'Alexandre Arcady, qui ne connaît pas un grand succès.

En partant à la recherche de nouvelles émotions, de nouvelles rencontres, Patrick retrouve l'inspiration pour composer de nouvelles mélodies et de nouveaux textes.

Pour ce nouveau disque, même si Patrick Bruel écrit beaucoup de chansons lui-même ou en collaboration avec Marie-Florence Gros, il y en a une que son complice des débuts, Gérard Presgurvic, a écrite et composée tout seul : « Pour la vie ».

Qui, mieux qu'un ami de longue date, comme Gérard, pour faire une chanson sur l'amitié... Patrick retient cette chanson car pour lui c'est en quelque sorte la suite de « Place des grands hommes ». Dix ans après, un homme fait le bilan de ses amitiés de jeunesse et de l'évolution des uns et des autres. Le titre parle du temps qui passe et qui fait et défait certains liens. Émouvantes, réalistes, un brin mélancoliques, ces paroles sont universelles et tout le monde peut s'y retrouver. Patrick enregistre la chanson, qui est subtilement arrangée par ses demi-frères, David-François et Fabrice Moreau.

Elle est publiée le 19 octobre 1999 sur l'album *Juste avant*. Elle est le deuxième extrait à paraître en single, le 28 février 2000, et se retrouve dès le 4 mars à la 13e place du Top 50. Le 31 mars 2000, une émission spéciale présentée par Jean-Pierre Foucault est consacrée à Patrick Bruel, sur TF1, et elle est intitulée *Pour la vie*. ■

"La chanson parle d'un homm qui, dix ans après, fait le bilan de ses amitiés de jeunesse, de l'évolution des uns et des autre. du temps qui passe et qui fait et défait certains liens."

Au café des délices

UNE AMITIÉ ENSOLEILLÉE

Extrait du quatrième album studio de Patrick Bruel, sorti en 1999, « Au café des délices » a connu un immense succès. Devenue un titre incontournable du répertoire de l'artiste, cette chanson pleine d'émotion évoque le déracinement et la nostalgie d'un paradis perdu. Gros plan sur la jolie histoire de cette chanson de l'amitié.

L'histoire de la chanson « Au café des délices » est avant tout une belle histoire d'amitié entre Patrick Bruel et Félix Gray, qui s'est fait connaître en 1987 avec son succès « La Gitane », puis grâce à ses duos avec Didier Barbelivien, au début des années 90. Patrick et Félix se connaissent depuis très longtemps et ils s'apprécient beaucoup. En 1998, un vendredi soir, jour du shabbat, les deux artistes se retrouvent avec des amis de même confession pour dîner. Avant de passer à table, Félix Gray prend sa guitare et joue deux couplets d'une chanson qu'il vient de composer et qui parle de sa Tunisie natale. Patrick Bruel est très touché par cette chanson pleine d'émotion. Bien qu'il ne soit pas né en Tunisie, comme Félix, Patrick connaît bien ce pays qu'il apprécie beaucoup. En plus, il a vécu lui aussi cette sensation de déracinement quand il a dû quitter l'Algérie, où il était né. Cette chanson émeut donc beaucoup Patrick, qui demande à son ami Félix Gray de l'interpréter. Félix accepte et Patrick va apporter quelques modifications au texte original. Il va en effet changer quelques mots, notamment pour ne pas enlever l'identité de la chanson à Félix. Ainsi, au lieu de chanter « Mes souvenirs se voilent... », Patrick chante « Tes souvenirs se voilent ». Après avoir testé la chanson sur scène, Patrick se rend vite compte de son efficacité. Chaque fois qu'il l'interprète, une grande émotion envahit la salle. Il décide donc de l'enregistrer pour l'intégrer à son quatrième album studio, qui s'intitule *Juste avant* et qui sort à la fin de l'année 1999.

Après les succès des deux premiers extraits, « J'te mentirais » et « Pour la vie », Patrick sort en troisième extrait « Au café des délices », qui confirme le succès de l'album, vendu à plus de 900 000 exemplaires. Sur scène, quand Patrick Bruel interprète « Au café des délices » et que Félix Gray se trouve dans la salle, il lui demande souvent de venir l'interpréter avec lui. Ce fut le cas notamment le 14 mai 2000, au Zénith de Paris, pour les quarante et un ans de Patrick. Ce soir-là, ils ont même été rejoints par Khaled pour une magnifique version de leur chanson.

Pour l'anecdote, depuis le succès de la chanson, le célèbre café *Sidi Chaâbane*, à Sidi Bou Saïd, dont la terrasse offre une vue imprenable sur le golf de Tunis, a été rebaptisé *Le Café des Délices* et fait le bonheur de nombreux touristes qui adorent se faire prendre en photo devant la pancarte de l'établissement. ■

Élie

D'UNE GÉNÉRATION À L'AUTRE

En 1999, sur son quatrième album, Patrick Bruel rend un vibrant hommage à son grand-père maternel, Élie, disparu quelque temps plus tôt. Sur une musique de son demi-frère David, Patrick écrit un texte émouvant sur le sens de la vie et de la transmission entre générations.

Tandis qu'il prépare un nouvel album, à la fin des années 90, Patrick Bruel perd son grand-père maternel, Élie Kammoun, à l'âge de quatre-vingt-seize ans. Quelque temps auparavant, David-François Moreau, son demi-frère, est devenu papa d'un petit Yohann, né de sa relation avec la comédienne Emmanuelle Béart. Et c'est la rencontre de ces deux générations, l'une qui arrive et l'autre qui s'en va, à près d'un siècle d'écart, qui inspire Patrick pour écrire une très émouvante chanson. Son grand-père, qui était en fin de vie, n'avait pas parlé depuis longtemps. Un jour, David lui amène le petit Yohann à l'hôpital, et là, comme par magie, Élie s'est mis à parler, il a souri, et c'est toute l'intensité de ce moment que Patrick a voulu restituer en chanson. Après un démarrage un peu laborieux, dès qu'il a trouvé ce qu'il voulait dire dans sa chanson, Patrick l'a écrite en une heure.
La musique est signée de son demi-frère David-François Moreau. Comme l'expliquera plus tard Patrick Bruel : « David a composé une merveille, un jour, quelque chose qui venait de loin, de très loin... L'impression que cet air lui était dicté par des anges... »

C'est ainsi que naît cette touchante chanson sur ce grand-père, au seuil de la mort, qui laisse en héritage à son arrière-petit-fils son dernier regard sur le monde.

« Élie » figure en 8e position sur l'album *Juste avant* et Patrick l'interprétera sur scène au cours de sa tournée en 2000 et 2001, juste avant un medley de chansons rétro qu'appréciait beaucoup son grand-père. ■

Patrick Bruel avec son demi-frère David-François Moreau, né le 14 février 1972. Une véritable complicité musicale unit Patrick et David, qui travaillent régulièrement ensemble sur des albums.

"C'est la rencontre de deux générations, l'une qui arrive et l'autre qui s'en va, à près d'un siè d'écart, qui inspire Patrick pou cette très émouvante chanson.

Nunca mas

PLUS JAMAIS ÇA

Artiste engagé et toujours sensible face à l'intolérable barbarie humaine, Patrick Bruel enregistre, en 1999, dans son album *Juste avant*, une chanson dédiée aux mères argentines qui ont perdu des enfants au moment de la dictature militaire. Intitulée « Nunca mas », cette chanson est enregistrée en duo avec le chanteur espagnol Nilda Fernandez.

Patrick Bruel n'avait que quatorze ans lorsqu'au Chili le général Augusto Pinochet a pris la tête du pays par un coup d'État militaire, le 11 septembre 1973, en renversant le président socialiste alors en place, Salvador Allende. Un événement qui avait beaucoup marqué le jeune Patrick, d'autant que sa famille, très engagée à gauche, trouvait intolérable ce coup d'État contre un président élu démocratiquement. Face à cette situation au Chili, la mère de Patrick et son beau-père avaient accueilli des réfugiés politiques et, de fait, Patrick avait été mis face au drame de ce peuple. Il confiera plus tard au journal *l'Humanité* : « J'étais dans un milieu très à gauche, où on s'indignait. Je me rappelle que des Chiliens sont venus à la maison, que des groupes comme les Quilapayun traversaient la France, nous avions tous leurs disques. On vivait tout cela de manière forte. »

Aussi, lorsque Patrick Bruel apprend au journal télévisé de 20 heures, le 10 octobre 1998, l'arrestation à Londres d'Augusto Pinochet pour génocide, terrorisme et tortures, il ressent une véritable satisfaction et écrit un début de chanson intitulé « Les diables sont jugés ».

Comme le Chili n'a pas été le seul pays d'Amérique latine à connaître la dictature dans les années 70, Patrick décide finalement de faire une chanson sur les femmes argentines dont les enfants ont disparu au moment de la dictature militaire et qui, depuis le 30 avril 1977, font des rondes chaque semaine, sur la place de Mai, devant le siège du gouvernement à Buenos Aires. Surnommées avec mépris par la dictature militaire *les folles de Mai*, ces mères résistantes deviennent au contraire à travers le monde les symboles d'un héroïsme revendicatif. C'est donc pour leur rendre hommage que Patrick Bruel écrit, avec Marie-Florence Gros, « Nunca mas », qui signifie « jamais plus », en espagnol. Pour accompagner ce texte plein de poésie sur les souffrances provoquées par les régimes totalitaires, Patrick choisit une très jolie mélodie composée quelque temps plus tôt par son frère David Moreau.

Comme la chanson est un duo, Patrick voudrait la chanter avec Peter Gabriel, qu'il apprécie beaucoup. Il lui fait donc une demande, mais l'ex-chanteur du groupe rock Genesis refuse la proposition car cette chanson aborde le même thème que « They Dance Alone » (« Cueca solo »), enregistré avec Sting, en 1987.

Patrick Bruel songe alors à Nilda Fernandez, le célèbre interprète de « Nos fiançailles », sorti en 1991. En écoutant le titre, Nilda le trouve très beau et très pertinent. Il accepte donc de chanter le refrain en espagnol et apporte l'idée d'inclure un enregistrement des voix de ces mères combatives sur l'introduction musicale. Le résultat donne donc un très beau duo franco-espagnol que les deux artistes ont interprété plusieurs fois à la radio et dans des émissions de télévision.

Après la disparition de Nilda Fernandez, à seulement soixante et un ans, le 19 mai 2019, Patrick Bruel, très ému, écrit : « Nous avions fait un si joli duo ensemble 'Nunca mas'... Nilda s'en va, salut l'artiste. » ■

Mon amant de Saint-Jean

PROMESSE D'AMOUR

En 2002, Patrick Bruel triomphe avec « Mon amant de Saint-Jean », une chanson à laquelle il donne une nouvelle jeunesse, soixante ans après sa création. Une valse d'amour créée en pleine Seconde Guerre mondiale par Émile Carrara, que l'on surnommait alors « le Poète de l'accordéon ».

Pour les jeunes générations, « Mon amant de Saint-Jean » est tout simplement un tube de Patrick Bruel. Pour les cinéphiles, c'est le titre emblématique du film aux 10 césars de François Truffaut, *Le Dernier Métro*, en 1980. Et pour d'autres, plus anciens, c'est l'air de leurs vingt ans, quand, pour oublier les affres de la guerre, ils allaient guincher sur cette valse, certains que l'amour finirait par avoir raison de la barbarie humaine. Car en effet, c'est en pleine Seconde Guerre mondiale qu'un célèbre accordéoniste de l'époque, Émile Carrara, qui n'a pas été mobilisé, à cause d'un lourd handicap, imagine cette valse pour faire danser dans les cinémas et les cabarets parisiens, puisque les bals sont alors interdits. Sur cette musique de Carrara, le parolier et éditeur Léon Agel écrit un premier texte intitulé « Les Barbots de Saint-Jean ». Mais cette référence à la prostitution et aux souteneurs, appelés populairement des « barbots », ne plaît pas beaucoup à Émile Carrara, qui préférerait quelque chose de plus romantique. C'est alors que Léon Agel lui propose « Mon costaud de Saint-Jean », et c'est sous ce titre qu'une première version de la chanson est créée par une certaine Jane Chacun, qui est alors la reine du musette. Mais voilà, le titre ne devient pas un succès.

Émile Carrara et Léon Agel sont pourtant persuadés qu'ils ont un tube. Aussi, ils ne baissent pas les bras et décident une troisième fois de changer le texte. En repensant à la promesse d'amour qu'il a faite à sa fiancée, dans une auberge de Saint-Jean-aux-Bois, dans la forêt de Compiègne, Léon Agel écrit « Mon amant de Saint-Jean ». Avec son complice, il propose alors la chanson à une chanteuse dont on parle beaucoup depuis qu'elle a remporté un radio-crochet, en 1939 : Lucienne Delyle. Compagne du musicien Aimé Barelli, Lucienne Delyle accepte d'enregistrer « Mon amant de Saint-Jean », en 1942, et c'est elle qui va en faire un immense succès. Le titre est diffusé sur Radio Paris et dans plusieurs stations de province, et comme le texte n'a rien de subversif, il échappe à la censure allemande. Pour l'anecdote, en 1943, Lucienne Delyle se produit à Bobino accompagnée par l'orchestre de son amoureux, Aimé Barelli. Chaque soir, en quittant la salle, comme il n'y a pas de taxis, ils prennent le métro, et tandis qu'ils se blottissent l'un contre l'autre, plusieurs passagers les reconnaissent et leur chantent en chœur la chanson.

En 2002, Patrick Bruel, avec son album *Entre deux*, remet au goût du jour « Mon amant de Saint-Jean », qui redevient un tube, soixante ans après sa création. Quelques années plus tard, en 2009, au début de sa tournée acoustique *Seul ou presque*, Patrick Bruel n'avait pas remis la chanson à son tour de chant. Mais, ému par une vieille dame qui, à la fin du spectacle, l'avait attendu pour lui dire en pleurs : « Mais pourquoi n'avez-vous pas chanté "Mon amant de Saint Jean" ? », Patrick Bruel a réintégré dès le lendemain la chanson à ses concerts ! ■

Harcourt
PARIS

La Complainte de la Butte

AMOUR ÉPHÉMÈRE

En 2002, Patrick Bruel remet au goût du jour une merveilleuse chanson écrite au milieu des années 50, pour la bande originale du film de Jean Renoir, *French Cancan*. Deuxième extrait de l'album *Entre deux*, ce titre retrouve une nouvelle jeunesse grâce à Patrick Bruel en duo avec Francis Cabrel.

En 2002, lorsque Patrick Bruel décide d'enregistrer un double album concept intitulé *Entre deux*, il reprend 24 grands succès des années 30 aux années 50. Parmi ces chansons, il choisit notamment « La Complainte de la Butte », qu'il interprète en duo avec Francis Cabrel. C'est le deuxième extrait de l'album à paraître en single au mois de novembre 2002.

Ce titre est à l'origine une chanson de film. En effet, en 1954, le célèbre réalisateur Jean Renoir tourne un long métrage intitulé *French Cancan* dont l'action se déroule dans le Montmartre du début du XXe siècle. De nombreux artistes de l'époque, comme André Claveau, Patachou, Giani Esposito, Philippe Clay, Jean-Roger Caussimon, et même la grande Édith Piaf, participent à ce film qui relate l'histoire d'un music-hall parisien tenu par un certain Henri Danglard, interprété par Jean Gabin. Pour les besoins de l'histoire, Jean Renoir écrit sur une musique de Georges van Parys une chanson d'amour qu'il intitule « La Complainte de la Butte ». Dans le film, c'est l'actrice italienne Anna Amendola qui tient le rôle d'Esther Georges, qui est censée interpréter cette chanson. Mais comme elle est avant tout comédienne et pas chanteuse, il faut trouver celle qui la doublera. Soufflé par Édith Piaf, le nom de Cora Vaucaire est avancé. Il faut dire que son interprétation pour un autre film, quelques années plus tôt, du titre « Les Feuilles mortes » n'était pas passée inaperçue.

Tout le monde semble donc être emballé par l'idée de faire interpréter la chanson par Cora Vaucaire, sauf le producteur du film. Il préférerait une chanteuse à accent ou Édith Piaf. Georges van Parys et Jean Renoir savent très bien qu'Édith n'acceptera jamais de doubler une comédienne, aussi ils vont tout faire pour convaincre le producteur de choisir Cora Vaucaire. Après avoir retravaillé la chanson en y rajoutant beaucoup de violons, ils finissent par obtenir gain de cause et c'est bien Cora Vaucaire qui enregistre « La Complainte de la Butte ». Cette chanson pleine de poésie sur fond d'amour éphémère va devenir avec le temps un grand classique de la chanson française. Avant Patrick Bruel, de nombreux chanteurs comme André Claveau, Patachou, Marcel Mouloudji, Francis Lemarque ont enregistré cette célèbre complainte. ■

"Ce titre est à l'origine extrait d'un film de Jean Renoir pour lequel il écrit une chanson d'amour, 'La Complainte de la Butte'."

Quand on s'promène au bord de l'eau

EN SOUVENIR D'ÉLIE

Parce que son grand-père maternel, Élie, adorait la valse musette, et plus particulièrement la chanson « Quand on s'promène au bord de l'eau », interprétée par Jean Gabin dans le film *La Belle Équipe*, de 1936, Patrick Bruel choisit de reprendre ce célèbre refrain en duo avec Jean-Louis Aubert, pour son album *Entre deux*, publié en juin 2002. Ce succès des guinguettes à l'époque devient l'hymne des fins de semaine des ouvriers qui fêtent le Front populaire et les premiers congés payés.

Pour la petite histoire, c'est au printemps de l'année 1936 que démarre véritablement l'histoire de la chanson « Quand on s'promène au bord de l'eau », au moment où se tourne dans les Studios de Joinville et à Chennevières, sur une île de la Marne, le film *La Belle Équipe*, avec Charles Vanel, Raymond Aimos, Viviane Romance, Charles Dorat... et Jean Gabin. Pour ce long-métrage, le producteur Arys Nissotti, grand amateur de valse musette, demande au réalisateur et scénariste, Julien Duvivier, de prévoir une ou plusieurs chansons pour illustrer l'esprit des guinguettes, que réclame toute une jeunesse française en cette période de Front populaire. C'est ainsi que Maurice Yvain, chargé de la bande musicale du film et compositeur de nombreux succès pour Mistinguett, Maurice Chevalier, Georges Milton et Dréan, crée un soir sur le piano d'un hall d'hôtel, à Joinville, la musique de la future chanson « Quand on s'promène au bord de l'eau ». Dans la précipitation des tournages, c'est Julien Duvivier qui, sur un week-end, écrit les paroles du titre. Le lendemain, le réalisateur impose en fin de tournage une répétition avec Jean Gabin et les accordéonistes du film, Marceau Verschueren, Médard Ferrero et Adolphe Deprince. Le résultat est fantastique, Gabin adore cette chanson qui, selon lui, symbolise parfaitement l'esprit des guinguettes à Nogent-sur-Marne, le bonheur et l'ivresse du monde ouvrier fêtant les congés payés. À l'issue des tournages du film, afin d'accompagner la sortie en salles de *La Belle Équipe*, le 15 septembre 1936, un disque 78 tours est enregistré par Jean Gabin, accompagné par Pierrot et son orchestre musette. Hélas, le film ne remporte qu'un succès d'estime. En revanche, la chanson sur laquelle il danse, drague et s'amuse en fin de semaine devient l'hymne des travailleurs.

En 1960, les cinéphiles redécouvrent l'œuvre de Julien Duvivier à travers *Les Cahiers du cinéma*. Le film est alors reprogrammé dans plusieurs salles et la chanson « Quand on s'promène au bord de l'eau » est à nouveau chantée par les séniors, nostalgiques d'une époque.

En 1973, Georgette Plana enregistre la chanson chez Vogue, elle en vend plus de 500 000 exemplaires et

obtient alors un disque d'or. Depuis, de très nombreux artistes ont repris « Quand on s'promène au bord de l'eau », de Francis Lemarque à Jean-Marc Thibault, mais aussi Lambert Wilson... Et soixante-quatre ans après sa création, à la suite de la disparition de son grand-père Élie, à l'âge de quatre-vingt-seize ans, c'est au tour de Patrick Bruel de reprendre ce célèbre refrain des guinguettes. Il enregistre alors cette valse musette en duo avec Jean-Louis Aubert, pour son album *Entre deux*, publié le 3 juin 2002. ■

La Romance de Paris

LA BATAILLE DES CHARLES POUR UN SUCCÈS MONDIAL

Parmi les vingt-quatre chansons de l'album *Entre deux*, publié en 2002, Patrick Bruel a repris « La Romance de Paris », un grand classique de Charles Trenet. Une chanson enregistrée pour la première fois en 1941 et qui depuis a fait le tour du monde.

Dans le film musical *Romance de Paris*, réalisé par Jean Boyer, en 1941, Charles Trenet joue le rôle principal aux côtés de Jean Tissier, de Jacqueline Porel, de Robert Le Vigan et de Raymond Bussières. Trenet se retrouve alors dans la peau d'un jeune électricien qui devient chanteur, sous le pseudonyme de Jean Papillon. Pour ce rôle, il interprète quatre chansons, « Un rien me fait chanter », « Bonsoir jolie Madame », « Tout ça, c'est pour nous » et, bien sûr, « La Romance de Paris », un titre qui fera faire le tour du monde au fou chantant.
C'est avec son pianiste, Léo Chauliac, que Charles Trenet compose un soir la musique de « La Romance de Paris », sur le vieux piano d'un ami qui habite rue de la Convention, dans le 15e arrondissement de la capitale. Lorsque le film musical sort, le 3 octobre 1941, « La Romance de Paris » est reprise dans toutes les salles de cinéma par les spectateurs. Un disque 78 tours est gravé en urgence et vendu à tous les patrons de brasseries, de guinguettes et de dancings à la mode. Toutes les jeunes filles réclament cette romance, elles veulent danser avec un amoureux sur cette valse musette dont la partition se vend à plus d'un million d'exemplaires dans toute la France. En 1945, et pour honorer des contrats que Charles Trenet avait signés avant le début de la guerre, il se produit aux États-Unis et au Canada. Et c'est durant cette période qu'il se lie d'amitié avec Charlie Chaplin, l'idole de son enfance. Charles Trenet a vu tous les films de Charlot et rachète même des bobines originales des films en noir et blanc de Charlie Chaplin dans des vieux cinémas new-yorkais. Ce dernier connaît toute l'œuvre de Charles Trenet, il lui arrive quelquefois de fredonner les refrains du fou chantant. Trenet et Chaplin s'écrivent, se téléphonent et s'invitent parfois à déjeuner. Pour les quarante ans de Charles Trenet, le 13 mai 1953, son éditrice, madame Breton, invite quarante personnalités au *Grand Véfour*, à Paris. Autour de Trenet, il y a Jean Cocteau, Joseph Kessel, Mireille, Emmanuel Bern, Colette... et Charlie Chaplin, de passage à Paris. Ce soir-là, tous les invités chantèrent les grands succès du fou chantant dont « La Romance de Paris », que Charlie Chaplin connaissait par cœur.
Mais au moment où le film *La Comtesse de Hong Kong*, produit par Charlie Chaplin Productions, sort sur les écrans, le 5 janvier 1967, Charles Trenet trouve que la musique de la chanson « This Is My Song », signée Charlie Chaplin et interprétée par Petula Clark, ressemble étrangement à « La Romance de Paris ». Trenet intente alors un procès à Chaplin. Le procès des deux Charles se plaide le mercredi 27 juin 1968, à la troisième chambre du tribunal de Paris. Trenet réclame un million de francs à Charlot, en se proclamant victime d'une étrange inspiration, d'un plagiat, d'un pillage de « La Romance de Paris » composée vingt-sept ans plus tôt. Dans la salle d'audience, les magistrats écoutent des enregistrements des deux œuvres en versions chantées et instrumentales. Un premier débat s'institue sur le nombre de notes combinées qui se retrouvent dans les deux chansons. Après avoir beaucoup tendu l'oreille, le président de la cour, monsieur Mouzon, et les avocats des parties, maîtres Floriot, Badinter et Chaperon, s'accordent sur quatre notes. Le débat s'ouvre alors entre les parties, sur les premières notes de la valse du refrain et les premières notes d'une barcarolle des couplets... Pour la défense de

Charlie Chaplin, son avocat annonce : « Si vous donnez raison à monsieur Trenet, il sera impossible désormais aux compositeurs d'échapper à la contrefaçon ! »
Avant que le tribunal donne sa décision, une table ronde est organisée entre les avocats et un protocole d'accord est signé entre Charles Trenet et Charlie Chaplin. Tous deux renoncent alors à toute procédure judiciaire. Chaplin reconnaît avoir entendu cette merveilleuse chanson lorsqu'il venait applaudir Trenet dans les grandes salles nord-américaines. Inconsciemment, il pense sincèrement avoir été inspiré… Dans ce cas précis, la coïncidence des notes frôle alors le plagiat. Et Trenet regrette amèrement son geste et ses poursuites à l'égard du grand Charlot, avouant alors avoir été mal conseillé.

Le succès planétaire de « La Romance de Paris » oblige Charles Trenet à se produire sur toutes les scènes du monde entier. Beaucoup d'artistes obtiennent alors l'autorisation des Éditions Raoul Breton pour reprendre la chanson. Colette Renard, en 1957, Lina Margy, en 1965, Francis Lemarque, en 1988, et bien évidemment Patrick Bruel, sur son album *Entre deux*, paru le 3 juin 2002. ■

Je fais semblant

LES VÉRITÉS D'UNE AUTEURE

En 2006, Patrick Bruel connaît un beau succès avec son sixième album, sur lequel figurent plusieurs chansons écrites par sa femme, l'auteure Amanda Sthers, ou en collaboration avec elle. C'est le cas pour « Je fais semblant », une chanson bilan qui résume bien le parcours de l'homme et de l'artiste.

Après avoir touché un large public avec des airs évocateurs de libération et de légèreté réunis sur l'album *Entre deux* et la longue tournée qui a suivi, Patrick Bruel songe, à partir de l'année 2005, à revenir sur le devant de la scène avec un album de chansons inédites. Concernant les musiques, il en a plusieurs de prêtes, mais il hésite à propos des textes et n'arrive pas à avancer. Il a du mal à trouver l'inspiration, jusqu'au jour où un événement va lui donner le déclic. C'est sa femme, l'auteure et romancière Amanda Sthers, qui va lui donner la clef de son nouvel album.

Un jour de l'été 2005, elle commence à écrire un premier texte, « Je fais semblant », et demande à Patrick de le terminer. Très touché par ces paroles si vraies qu'il n'aurait pas osé les dire tout seul, Patrick va donc finir la chanson et surtout écrire presque une chanson par jour, alors que cela faisait deux ans qu'il traînait des textes qui n'avançaient pas. Dans les premiers mots d'Amanda, Patrick retrouve une part de sa personnalité, faire semblant que tout allait bien, par pudeur et pour rassurer son entourage, même si parfois il a eu des périodes de doute.

Patrick avouera : « J'ai été très ému que quelqu'un qui est si proche de moi, tout en me connaissant depuis, au fond, assez peu de temps, puisse être si juste. »
Sur un texte d'Amanda Sthers, Patrick avait déjà composé une chanson pour Isabelle Boulay, parue en 2004 et intitulée « En t'attendant », sur la naissance d'un enfant. Patrick avoue : « Quand on a quelqu'un de talent à ses côtés, on aurait tort de s'en priver. »

Le titre est réalisé et arrangé par David Moreau, le petit frère de Patrick, au Studio Gang, sur des consoles « vintage » où ont été enregistrées de grands albums pop. Tout naturellement, comme « Je fais semblant » est la chanson qui a déclenché l'inspiration de Patrick Bruel pour l'écriture de son nouveau disque, cette chanson tellement autobiographique ouvre l'album. ■

"C'est sa femme, l'auteure et romancière Amanda Sthers, qui va lui donner la clef de son nouvel album."

DAMS
Holland

J'm'attendais pas à toi

POUR L'AMOUR D'AMANDA STHERS

En 2006, dans son sixième album studio, avec la chanson « J'm'attendais pas à toi », Patrick Bruel fait une belle déclaration d'amour à sa femme, Amanda Sthers, qu'il a épousée le 21 septembre 2004 et qui lui a donné deux enfants : Oscar et Léon.

Après l'immense succès du double album studio *Entre deux*, paru le 3 juin 2002 et vendu à 2,8 millions d'exemplaires, dans lequel Patrick Bruel reprenait quelques grands succès des années 30, 40 et 50, comme « Mon amant de Saint-Jean », il revient avec des chansons inédites au début de l'année 2006. Des chansons plus personnelles, plus intimes, presque autobiographiques. C'est le cas notamment avec « J'm'attendais pas à toi », une chanson dans laquelle il évoque la nouvelle femme de sa vie, l'écrivaine Amanda Sthers. Patrick et Amanda se sont rencontrés le 2 août 2001, dans un célèbre club de Saint-Tropez, aux *Caves du Roy*, dans une ambiance très VIP. Amanda est la fille d'une avocate parisienne et d'un père psychanalyste. Elle n'a que vingt-trois ans et Patrick quarante-deux ans. C'est un véritable coup de foudre entre eux. Deux jours plus tard, Patrick doit se rendre dans un festival de cinéma dans le sud de la Suisse, à Locarno, et il propose à Amanda de l'accompagner. Elle accepte et, dans l'avion, le 4 août, Patrick lui demande si elle serait d'accord pour avoir deux enfants avec lui. Patrick sait qu'Amanda est la bonne personne pour fonder une famille.

En 2003, ils accueillent un premier enfant, Oscar, qui voit le jour le 19 août à la clinique parisienne de La Muette. L'année suivante, le 21 septembre 2004, Patrick Bruel et Amanda se marient à la Mairie du 4e arrondissement de Paris, puis à la Synagogue de la rue de la Victoire. L'année suivante, le 28 septembre 2005, ils ont un deuxième garçon, prénommé Léon. Tous ces bouleversements dans la vie de Patrick Bruel lui donnent envie d'écrire de nouvelles chansons. Et c'est ainsi qu'il écrit « J'm'attendais pas à toi », une merveilleuse déclaration d'amour à la femme de sa vie et à la mère de ses enfants.

Produit et réalisé par David Moreau, le demi-frère de Patrick, « J'm'attendais pas à toi » est enregistré au studio Davout, à Paris. C'est ce titre qui est choisi comme premier extrait du nouvel album de Patrick Bruel, intitulé *Des souvenirs devant*.

Quelques mois avant la sortie de ce disque, Patrick réserve la primeur de sa nouvelle chanson à l'émission de TF1, les NRJ Music Awards, le 21 janvier 2006. L'accueil de cette chanson autobiographique est excellent et sert de locomotive à l'album, qui est l'un des albums le plus vendus de l'année 2006. ■

> ***"Les bouleversements dans la vie de Patrick lui donnent envi d'écrire de nouvelles chansons comme 'J'm'attendais pas à toi', une merveilleuse déclaration d'amour à la mère de ses enfant***

Raconte-moi

D'UN FILS À SA MÈRE

Parue en 2006, « Raconte-moi » est une belle chanson écrite, composée et interprétée par Patrick Bruel qui s'adresse à une personne importante de sa vie : sa mère, Augusta.

Entre Patrick Bruel et sa mère, Augusta Kammoun, il existe une grande complicité du fait même de leur histoire. Patrick n'avait qu'un an quand son père, Pierre Benguigui, a quitté le foyer familial, et c'est Augusta seule qui a élevé son fils. Ensemble, ils ont quitté l'Algérie et se sont installés à Argenteuil, en banlieue parisienne. Véritable mère courage, Augusta, tout en exerçant son métier de professeur de français, a été une mère parfaite. Elle a emmené le jeune Patrick partout avec elle, que ce soit en voyage, au théâtre, où il a vu *L'Idiot* de Dostoïevski alors qu'il n'avait que six ans, à Rome, où ils ont assisté à une représentation de *La Tosca*, où à des concerts de Serge Reggiani et de Barbara. De cet amour fusionnel entre une mère et son fils, Patrick Bruel garde éternellement un respect et une admiration sans bornes pour cette femme qui lui a donné la vie. Quelquefois, dans ses chansons, Patrick Bruel a évoqué sa mère, mais la première fois où il écrit vraiment une chanson sur elle et sur sa vie, c'est en 2006, dans le titre « Raconte-moi ».

Connaissant bien sa mère, très pudique et si discrète, Patrick a longtemps cherché sous quel angle aborder en chanson cette femme qu'il admire tant. Et finalement, il a l'idée de le faire sous la forme d'un questionnement d'un fils pour sa mère. Dans « Raconte-moi », Patrick Bruel évoque beaucoup de choses de la vie sentimentale d'Augusta, des hommes qu'elle a laissés passer pour ne pas délaisser son petit garçon, des sacrifices de cette femme pour offrir la meilleure éducation à son fils. Devenu lui-même père, Patrick Bruel se sent prêt pour cet échange avec sa mère.

Le titre est enregistré au Studio Gang, au cours de l'été 2005. Il est réalisé et arrangé par David Moreau, un des deux demi-frères de Patrick, qu'Augusta a eu avec son second mari, Philippe Moreau, un architecte épousé en 1969.

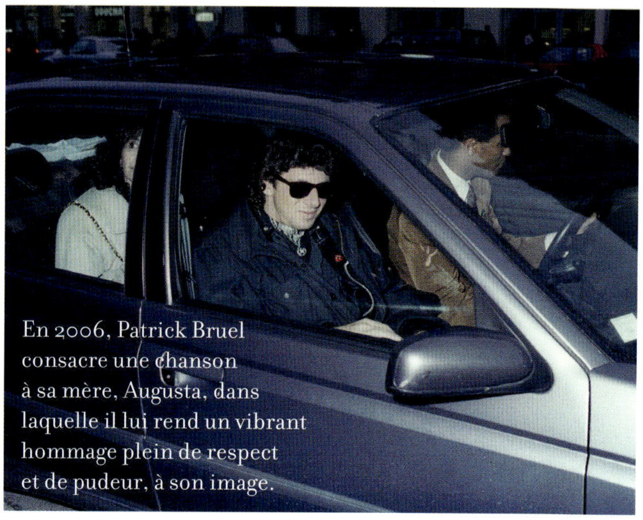

En 2006, Patrick Bruel consacre une chanson à sa mère, Augusta, dans laquelle il lui rend un vibrant hommage plein de respect et de pudeur, à son image.

Cette chanson pleine d'émotion paraît le 20 mars 2006 sur l'album *Des souvenirs devant* et connaît un grand succès parmi les fans du chanteur, qui l'interprète sur scène lors de sa tournée 2006-2007 intitulée *Des souvenirs ensemble*. ■

"Dans 'Raconte-moi', Patrick Bruel évoque beaucoup de choses sur sa mère, des hommes qu'elle a laissés passer pour ne pas délaisser son petit garçon, de ses sacrifices pour offrir la meilleure éducation à son fils."

Où sont les rêves

SOUVENIRS D'ADO

Extraite de son sixième album, paru en 2006, « Où sont les rêves » est une chanson autobiographique composée par le fidèle Gérard Presgurvic dans laquelle Patrick Bruel évoque les souvenirs nostalgiques de ses quinze ans.

Il y a des chansons qui mettent plusieurs années à exister. « Où sont les rêves » en fait partie. Au départ, Gérard Presgurvic l'avait composée à la fin des années 90 et elle aurait dû figurer sur l'album *Juste avant*, paru en 1999, mais comme il y avait déjà assez de titres, elle avait été mise de côté. Et puis, six ans après, en 2005, Patrick décide de la reprendre, d'autant que le texte qu'il a co-écrit avec Marie-Florence Gros et Gérard Presgurvic fait référence aux artistes et aux musiques qui lui ont donné envie d'en faire. D'ailleurs, au début du travail en studio, Patrick Bruel a demandé à son frère David, qui est chargé de la réalisation et des arrangements du disque, de le faire dans un esprit pop 70. Patrick veut un son chaud et un peu vintage pour accompagner ses chansons intimes et faire ressortir l'intensité émotionnelle.

Et dans « Où sont les rêves », avec les subtils arrangements de David Moreau, l'émotion est bien présente quand Patrick évoque ses souvenirs d'ado et ses premiers textes. Dans la chanson, il rappelle aussi plusieurs noms d'artistes, et au moment d'écrire ce vers, il a beaucoup hésité entre citer Maxime Le Forestier, Bernard Lavilliers ou Jacques Higelin... Pour finalement n'en garder que trois dans le texte final : George Harrison, Michel Polnareff et Georges Brassens. Et encore, Michel Polnareff ne devait pas être dans la chanson, mais lorsque Gérard Presgurvic est venu au Studio Gang pour écouter la chanson, en entendant l'intro, il s'est exclamé : « Tiens, ça fait très Polnareff ! » Et c'est donc pour cela que Patrick Bruel a rajouté Polnareff dans sa liste. ■

Patrick Bruel et Gérard Presgurvic, une indéfectible et solide amitié qui a donné naissance à d'immenses tubes.

"Patrick veut, pour ce nouvel album, un son chaud et un peu vintage pour accompagner ses chansons intimes et en faire ressortir l'intensité émotionnelle."

Gosses en cavale

UNE AMITIÉ FIDÈLE

Fidèle en amitié, Patrick Bruel consacre, en 2006, une chanson à son ami le peintre Philippe Benichou, rencontré en 1979, à New York. Une chanson pleine d'émotion qui évoque les vingt ans du chanteur.

C'est au cours de l'été 2005 que Patrick Bruel commence à songer sérieusement à son sixième album. Il a déjà plusieurs musiques composées mais a du mal à trouver les mots pour les accompagner. C'est un texte écrit et proposé par sa femme, l'auteure et romancière Amanda Sthers, qui lui donne le déclic et l'encourage à finaliser l'essentiel des textes. Dans l'un d'eux, intitulé « Gosses en cavale », il évoque sa longue amitié avec un garçon rencontré à New York, en 1980, Philippe Benichou, un élève comédien dans une école d'art dramatique new-yorkaise vers qui l'avait orienté un ami parisien.

Patrick et Philippe sympathisent. Ils sont tous les deux originaires de la même ville algérienne de Tlemcen, ils ont à peu près le même âge et tous les deux rêvent d'une carrière artistique. Pendant plusieurs mois, Patrick s'installe dans l'appartement que Philippe partage avec son frère Pascal, un jeune danseur qui rêve lui aussi de gloire. Pour gagner un peu d'argent, ils s'improvisent photographes et réalisent des books pour de jeunes acteurs comme eux. Malgré la distance qui les sépare, Patrick n'oubliera jamais son ami Philippe et leurs premiers pas dans cette fascinante ville américaine.

Vingt-cinq ans après, Patrick est devenu un chanteur et acteur à succès, tandis que Philippe Benichou s'est imposé dans la peinture et est devenu acteur et fondateur d'une importante école de théâtre. Leur solide amitié fait dire à Patrick : « Philippe est mon double, mon alter ego. Nous avons vécu ensemble des choses très fortes, comme la mort de John Lennon. Si pendant toutes ces années il m'est arrivé de le perdre de vue, je ne l'ai jamais perdu de cœur. »

Et donc, en hommage à leur indéfectible et longue amitié, Patrick Bruel écrit et compose, au cours de l'été 2015, la chanson « Gosses en cavale », dans laquelle il écrit : « On s'est trouvé en cherchant la même étoile ».

Le titre est enregistré en analogique au Studio Gang. Il est arrangé et réalisé par David Moreau et paraît sur l'album *Des souvenirs devant*, le 20 mars 2006.

Pour la petite histoire, du 2 au 31 mai 2006, Philippe Benichou a fait une exposition de peintures au Luxembourg, intitulée « L'Art de l'amitié », une exposition évidemment dédiée à son ami Patrick Bruel. ■

Notre plus beau visage

LA JOIE DE DEVENIR PÈRE

Parue en 2006, sur son sixième album studio, « Notre plus beau visage » évoque le jour où Patrick Bruel apprend avec joie qu'il va devenir père pour la première fois. Une belle chanson sur le bonheur de la vie qui naît.

Dans la vie d'un homme comme dans celui d'une femme, apprendre l'arrivée prochaine d'un enfant reste un instant inoubliable. L'histoire de la chanson « Notre plus beau visage » commence le 10 décembre 2002. Ce jour-là, Patrick Bruel est à Paris. Le matin, il reçoit un appel téléphonique de sa compagne, Amanda Sthers, alors en vacances à Eilat, en Israël. Comme elle aime le faire depuis son enfance, elle est allée au delphinarium pour nager ce jour-là avec les dauphins, mais elle a remarqué que, curieusement, ils ne l'ont pas approchée comme d'habitude. Elle évoque cette bizarrerie au téléphone avec Patrick en lui précisant qu'en revanche les dauphins se sont mis en cercle autour d'elle. À l'autre bout du fil, le visage du chanteur s'illumine. Comme il avait lu que les dauphins possèdent des sonars qui leur permettent de reconnaître une femme enceinte, et par protection ne l'approchent pas, Patrick suggère à Amanda de faire un test de grossesse. Et effectivement, le test sera positif, et c'est donc grâce à l'attitude des dauphins que Patrick et Amanda ont découvert la bonne nouvelle.

Quatre ans plus tard, c'est en se remémorant cette anecdote que Patrick Bruel décide d'en faire les paroles d'une chanson sur une musique qu'il a composée avec Jérôme Bardon-Lewy. Enregistrée au Studio Gang, à Paris, à la fin de l'année 2005, la chanson fait partie des douze titres de l'album *Des souvenirs devant*, paru le 20 mars 2006. ■

Patrick Bruel et l'écrivaine Amanda Sthers, qu'il rencontre le 2 août 2001, à Saint-Tropez, et qu'il épouse le 21 septembre 2004.

Lequel de nous

CHANSON DE RUPTURE

Premier extrait du sixième album de Patrick Bruel paru le 26 novembre 2012, cette chanson aborde la séparation d'un couple et ses conséquences. Enregistrée d'abord en 2001 par le chanteur Félix Gray, son ami Patrick Bruel la reprend onze ans après, quand le thème devient de circonstance pour lui, après sa séparation avec sa femme, Amanda Sthers.

Après avoir triomphé au théâtre dans la pièce *Le Prénom*, de Matthieu Delaporte et Alexandre de La Patellière, puis au cinéma, avec l'adaptation de cette même pièce qui réunit plus de 3 millions de spectateurs dans les salles obscures au mois d'avril 2012, Patrick Bruel revient à la musique à la fin de cette même année. C'est sur sa page Facebook officielle qu'il présente, en octobre 2012, une nouvelle chanson intitulée « Lequel de nous », qui va d'ailleurs donner son titre à l'album.

Ce titre est en fait la reprise d'une chanson de 2001 enregistrée par Félix Gray, un ami proche de Patrick Bruel avec lequel il a notamment travaillé en 1999, sur « Au café des délices », l'un des succès de son quatrième album.
Dans la chanson originale, telle que l'avait écrite Félix Gray, il était question d'un couple qui se sépare. Un thème qui avait immédiatement interpellé Patrick Bruel puisque, sur le plan personnel, il était lui-même en plein divorce avec sa femme, Amanda Sthers. C'est d'ailleurs pour cette raison qu'au départ Patrick a eu envie de reprendre cette chanson qui, dans ses paroles, dit qu'au-delà de la séparation les enfants restent un lien éternel entre deux êtres.
En revanche, pour s'éloigner de l'intime et de l'aspect personnel, Patrick Bruel a voulu élargir le propos de la chanson à la différence, à la tolérance et au respect de l'autre, et ainsi lui donner une lecture supplémentaire dans différentes situations comme les relations humaines, l'amitié, la politique, les différentes communautés…
Pour la musique, Patrick Bruel s'accompagne à la guitare sur un air de musique klezmer, une musique juive ashkénaze d'Europe de l'Est. Pour promouvoir sa nouvelle chanson, Patrick Bruel tourne un clip réalisé par Jean Sacuto, dans les entrepôts de la Plaine Saint-Denis. Le titre est largement diffusé à la radio à la fin de l'année 2012 et Patrick Bruel participe à de nombreuses émissions de télévision, dont le JT de 20 heures sur France 2, dans lequel il répond aux questions de Marie Drucker.
À cinquante-trois ans, l'artiste prouve une nouvelle fois que, en musique comme au cinéma, il reste très apprécié du public français. ■

"C'est sur sa page Facebook qu'il présente, en octobre 2012, une nouvelle chanson, 'Lequel de nous', qui va donner son titre à l'album."

Lorsqu'il interprète « She's Gone » sur scène, Patrick Bruel utilise le drapeau anglais comme accessoire et son fidèle public se met aussi au diapason !

She's Gone

SOUVENIR D'UN CONCERT DES STONES

Sortie le 26 novembre 2012, sur le septième album studio de Patrick Bruel, « She's Gone » est une chanson en partie autobiographique. Découvrons l'histoire de ce titre made in London.

Après avoir triomphé au théâtre, dans la pièce *Le Prénom*, Patrick Bruel reprend avec succès son rôle de Vincent Larchet au cinéma, dans l'adaptation cinématographique de ce film, sorti le 25 avril 2012. Après cette longue parenthèse d'acteur, Patrick Bruel prépare un nouvel album. En cherchant l'inspiration pour de nouvelles chansons, le chanteur se souvient d'une scène qu'il a vécue alors qu'il était adolescent. Venu assister à un concert des Rolling Stones, à Brighton, en Angleterre, il se rappelle d'une jeune fille du même âge que lui, qui portait un T-shirt sur lequel était inscrit *Come on.* Durant le concert, Patrick s'était rapproché de cette jeune Anglaise et avait flirté avec elle avant qu'elle ne s'éclipse avec les amis qui l'accompagnaient. Ce souvenir autobiographique inspire donc Patrick pour le début de « She's Gone ».

La suite est purement fictive. Durant le mois d'août 2012, alors qu'il se trouve à Londres pour assister aux Jeux olympiques d'été, Patrick Bruel prend un jour le métro pour se rendre au Stade olympique et, à la station South Kensington, il voit des banderoles sur lesquelles est écrit *Come on.* Cette expression lui rappelle le T-shirt de cette jeune fille qu'il avait connue à seize ans au concert des Stones. Il a alors l'idée, pour terminer sa chanson, d'imaginer des retrouvailles furtives avec elle, et c'est ainsi que naît la fin virtuelle de la chanson « She's Gone ».

Par la suite, Patrick Bruel enregistrera le titre sur une musique de son guitariste, Roman Chelminski, avec l'arrangeur et réalisateur Benjamin Constant, au Studio Guillaume Tell. Il en fera deux versions, dont une acoustique et totalement en anglais. « She's Gone » sortira dans les deux versions sur l'album *Lequel de nous*, au mois de novembre 2012, et sera le deuxième extrait, dans la version française, à être diffusé sur les radios à partir du mois de janvier 2013. ■

« Venu assister à un concert des Rolling Stones à Brighton, il se rappelle d'une jeune fille avec un T-shirt sur lequel était inscrit Come on. »

Maux d'enfants

DUO ENGAGÉ SUR LES DÉRIVES D'INTERNET

Patrick Bruel et le rappeur La Fouine ont uni leurs voix, en 2012, pour la bonne cause… Ensemble, les deux artistes se sont lancés dans un combat contre le cyber-harcèlement des adolescents, avec la chanson « Maux d'enfants ».

L'histoire de la chanson « Maux d'enfants » commence en 2011, à la suite d'un incident dont a été victime Oscar, le fils aîné de Patrick Bruel. Élève dans une école bilingue franco-américaine, le jeune garçon est victime d'antisémitisme de la part d'un de ses meilleurs copains qui ne veut plus lui parler quand il apprend qu'Oscar est juif. Quand Oscar raconte cette altercation à ses parents, le soir même, Amanda Sthers et Patrick Bruel sont choqués. Dans la nuit qui suit, Patrick Bruel commence à écrire une chanson intitulée « Maux d'enfants ».

Quelques semaines plus tard, alors qu'il travaille sur son septième album studio, Patrick Bruel décide de reprendre son idée de chanson mais d'élargir la thématique au cyber-harcèlement sur Internet. Il complète ainsi son texte initial avec Marie-Florence Gros et le rappeur Laouni Mouhid, plus connu sous le pseudonyme de La Fouine. Ainsi, sur une musique de Roman Chelminski, le titre « Maux d'enfants », en duo avec La Fouine, est créé et vient compléter les onze autres chansons de l'album *Lequel de nous*, qui paraît le 26 novembre 2012. « Maux d'enfants » est le troisième extrait à paraître en single, le 19 juin 2013. Pour la promotion de la chanson, un clip interactif est tourné dans lequel Patrick Bruel tient le rôle d'un professeur de lycée dont les élèves sont victimes des dérives d'Internet et des réseaux sociaux. Ce clip est réalisé en partenariat avec l'association e-Enfance, il est disponible sur le site mauxdenfants.fr et permet aux jeunes qui se sentent concernés par ces harcèlements d'entrer directement en contact avec l'association. Une belle initiative saluée par les uns mais critiquée par d'autres, notamment *les Inrocks*, qui reproche à Patrick Bruel de stigmatiser une technologie qui va trop vite. L'artiste s'en défend alors en expliquant qu'il ne dénonce pas Internet, qui est un outil extraordinaire, mais simplement l'utilisation qu'en font certains, expliquant que les disputes de cour de récré se prolongeaient sur le Net, prenant parfois une ampleur excessive et dangereuse et faisant des cybervictimes. ■

> ***“Pour la promotion de la chanson, un clip est tourné dans lequel Patrick Bruel tient le rôle d'un professeur de lycée dont les élèves sont victimes des dérives d'Internet et des réseaux sociaux.”***

Avec les nouvelles chansons de son album *Lequel de nous*, Patrick Bruel entame une grande tournée entre le 16 mai 2013 et le 8 novembre 2014. Quelques fois, La Fouine le rejoint sur scène pour interpréter leur duo « Maux d'enfants », notammentpour l'enregistrement de l'album live de la tournée.

Où es-tu ?

HOMMAGE AUX REPORTERS DE GUERRE

Paru en 2012, sur le septième album studio de Patrick Bruel, « Où es-tu ? » est le quatrième extrait de ce disque à sortir en single. Dans cette chanson, Patrick Bruel se met dans la peau du mari d'une journaliste, reporter de guerre appelée à couvrir des conflits dans le monde entier. Un vibrant hommage à un métier de courage et de passion, imaginé à la suite d'une rencontre émouvante.

Fin observateur de son temps, conteur de son époque et toujours sensible à ce qui l'entoure, Patrick Bruel puise souvent son inspiration dans des événements et des rencontres. C'est le cas avec la chanson « Où es-tu ? ». L'idée de ce titre lui est venue, le 14 février 2005, après un concert à l'Olympia de soutien à la journaliste Florence Aubenas, disparue en Irak, avec son guide, le 5 janvier. Après le concert, Patrick Bruel a rencontré les proches de la journaliste et, en les écoutant lui raconter avec émotion comment ils vivaient la situation, il a le déclic d'en faire un thème de chanson. Avec sa complice, l'auteure Marie-Florence Gros, Patrick va donc écrire les paroles de « Où es-tu ? », texte d'une grande intensité émotionnelle, au réalisme très cinématographique.
Pour la musique, Patrick ne veut pas d'une ballade mélancolique mais au contraire un son pop-rock, dans l'esprit des chansons du groupe anglais Coldplay. Et c'est donc une mélodie dans ce style qu'il compose avec le pianiste franco-allemand Nicolas Neidhardt et Orlando Marais.
La chanson est enregistrée au Studio Gang, au cours de l'été 2012, sous la direction artistique de David Moreau, et mixée par Renaud Letang, au Studio Ferber, à Paris. Elle paraît le 26 novembre 2012, sur l'album *Lequel de nous*, et elle est choisie comme le 4e single de ce disque. Patrick Bruel l'interprète notamment aux Folies Bergère, le mercredi 6 novembre 2013, lors d'une soirée diffusée sur Europe 1, présentée par Wendy Bouchard et Nikos Aliagas, en soutien aux journalistes Didier François et Édouard Élias, retenus en Syrie depuis le 6 juin.

Pour la promotion du titre « Où es-tu ? », un clip émouvant est tourné. Patrick Bruel y tient le rôle du mari d'une reporter de guerre, interprétée par l'actrice Vahina Giocante, qui se fait enlever au Moyen-Orient. ■

“Patrick Bruel interprète la chanson aux Folies Bergère en novembre 2013, lors d'une soirée en soutien aux journalistes Didier François et Édouard Élias retenus en Syrie depuis le 6 juin.”

Véritable homme de scène, Patrick Bruel a tissé un lien authentique avec son public au fil du temps et de ses nombreux concerts. Il lui a d'ailleurs dédié une très belle chanson, intitulée « Vous », dans laquelle il lui déclare son amour. Un amour largement partagé.

PATRICK
ON
T'AIME

Le mal de vivre

SOUVENIR D'ENFANCE

En 2015, Patrick Bruel reprend quinze titres de Barbara dans un album sur lequel figure notamment « Le mal de vivre ». Un bel hommage à l'idole de son enfance et à ses grandes chansons.

C'est en 1967, alors que Patrick Bruel n'a que huit ans, que sa mère, Augusta, lui fait découvrir le répertoire de la grande auteure, compositrice et interprète Barbara. Le jeune Patrick est hypnotisé par les chansons de la grande Dame en noir. Il ressent une vraie émotion musicale en écoutant « Madame » ou « Mourir pour mourir ». Absorbé par ses mélodies, le jeune garçon est aussi touché par ses textes, dans lesquels il trouve parfois des réponses à ses questions existentielles. Les chansons de Barbara accompagnent, dès lors, chaque étape de la vie de Patrick Bruel. En 1974, il va la voir pour la première fois en concert au théâtre des Variétés, puis presque tous les soirs à l'Olympia, en 1978, grâce à une de ses amies qui est la petite-nièce de Charley Marouani, l'imprésario de Barbara.

Quand elle se produit à Pantin, en 1981, Patrick Bruel assiste encore presque tous les soirs au concert. Du fait qu'il commence à avoir une petite notoriété grâce au cinéma, il peut avoir accès aux loges, mais il ne préfère pas la rencontrer. Même chose en 1987, au théâtre du Châtelet. Charley Marouani lui propose de l'emmener dans les loges pour rencontrer son idole, mais une nouvelle fois Patrick refuse. Il a trop peur d'être déçu.

Ce n'est qu'en 1990, alors que Barbara se produit à Mogador, du 6 février au 14 avril, que Patrick Bruel la rencontre pour la première fois. Ce jour-là, Patrick était encore réticent à rencontrer la grande Dame mais Charley Marouani a insisté en lui disant que Barbara savait qu'il était dans la salle et que s'il n'allait pas la voir, elle se vexerait. Patrick se laisse donc convaincre, et lorsqu'il entre dans la loge, Barbara lui dit : « Enfin, vous ne pouviez pas me fuir indéfiniment ! »

Quelques jours après, Patrick Bruel revient à Mogador avec sa mère Augusta, qu'il présente à Barbara. Un moment très émouvant pour Patrick de voir sa mère rencontrer celle qui avait été si importante pour elle. Et ce soir-là, à la fin de son tour de chant, Barbara a chanté rien que pour Patrick et sa mère leur chanson préférée : « Madame ».

Quelques mois plus tard, Patrick Bruel est en concert au Zénith de Paris. Le soir de la première, le 9 octobre 1990, Barbara lui envoie un fax disant : « Je pense souvent à vous avec force et tendresse. » Et c'est en repensant à cette phrase que, en 2015, Patrick Bruel intitule son album de reprises de chansons de Barbara, *Très souvent, je pense à vous...*

Le disque réalisé par David-François Moreau est enregistré au studio Orgeville, dans le 5e arrondissement de Paris. Sur les quinze titres, douze ont été enregistrés en une seule prise. « Le mal de vivre » est la première chanson de l'album à être diffusée en radio, dès la fin du mois d'octobre 2015, et va servir de single promotionnel à l'album, qui paraît le 27 novembre 2015.

Patrick explique alors les raisons de son choix : « Cette chanson, c'est rester debout malgré cette chape qui vient vous prendre, se glisse de manière insidieuse, vous écrase. Il y a cet instinct de survie qui oblige à regarder devant, à vous dire "c'est possible". Au bout de chaque tunnel, il y a une éclaircie, une manière de se relever, le goût de vivre. Cette chanson est pour moi la plus forte du disque. Elle résume Barbara qui a tellement souffert. » ■

"Au bout de chaque tunnel, il y a une éclaircie, une manièr de se relever, le goût de vivre. Elle résume Barbara qui a tellement souffert."

Dis, quand reviendras-tu ?

LA CHANSON DE L'ABSENCE

Sur son huitième album, consacré au répertoire de Barbara, Patrick Bruel reprend « Dis, quand reviendras-tu ? », un titre de 1962 qui reste aujourd'hui encore un standard de Barbara.

Comme souvent chez les auteurs-compositeurs et interprètes, leurs chansons sont le reflet d'une partie de leur vie. C'est précisément le cas ici, avec cette chanson sur l'absence de l'être aimé, créée par Barbara, en 1959. Cette année-là, avec d'autres artistes du cabaret L'Écluse, Barbara part en tournée en Afrique. À Abidjan, à l'issue de son spectacle, elle rencontre un séduisant homme d'affaires et diplomate qui ressemble selon elle à l'acteur américain John Wayne. Il s'appelle Hubert Ballay et ils éprouvent un coup de foudre réciproque. Leur aventure est intense. Mais hélas, bientôt, Barbara doit repartir à Paris. Hubert lui promet de la rejoindre rapidement. Mais les semaines et les mois passent et Barbara s'impatiente. Hubert lui manque terriblement. Pour combler cette absence et adoucir sa tristesse, Barbara compose et écrit « Dis, quand reviendras-tu ? », véritable supplique digne et sans victimisation. Finalement, après plusieurs mois, Hubert abandonne ses affaires en Côte d'Ivoire et revient s'installer en France. Mais il est trop tard. Barbara l'a oublié dans d'autres bras.

Entre-temps, et sans oser avouer qu'elle en est l'auteur, Barbara a testé « Dis, quand reviendras-tu ? » sur le public de L'Écluse, et l'accueil a toujours été très chaleureux. C'est pour cela qu'elle se décide, en 1962, à graver la chanson sur disque.

Le premier enregistrement 45 tours de « Dis, quand reviendras-tu ? » se fait le 8 mai 1962, pour les disques Odéon. Barbara confie les arrangements à l'orchestrateur attitré de Jacques Brel, François Rauber. Ce 45 tours arrive dans le commerce le 15 mai.

En novembre 1963, après avoir signé avec une nouvelle maison de disques, CBS, Barbara réenregistre le titre avec le contrebassiste François Rabbath. Il sort alors sur le même 45 tours que la chanson « Nantes » et donne aussi son titre à un album. Soutenue par l'animatrice Denise Glaser, qui l'invite régulièrement dans son émission *Discorama*, Barbara va peu à peu se faire connaître bien au-delà des cabarets.

Pour l'anecdote, en 2004, lors de ses concerts au Grand Rex, à Paris, Bénabar a chanté « Dis, quand reviendras-tu ? ». Une autre chanteuse de la nouvelle scène, La Grande Sophie, a aussi repris cette chanson de Barbara, en 2008.

Pour la petite histoire, lors de ses récitals, juste avant d'interpréter « Dis, quand reviendras-tu ? », Barbara avait pris pour habitude de dire : « À cette époque, je chantais seulement les autres, quand un monsieur qui partit pour les croisades me donna l'occasion d'écrire ma première chanson... » Ce monsieur, c'était Hubert Ballay, et cette chanson, c'était « Dis, quand reviendras-tu ? ». ■

"Les chansons des auteurs-compositeurs sont souvent le refl[...] d'une partie de leur vie, comm[...] ce titre sur l'absence de l'être aim[...] créé par Barbara en 1959."

Cavagnolo

Tout recommencer

EN PENSANT À BARBARA

Premier extrait du neuvième album studio de Patrick Bruel, « Tout recommencer » arrive sur les ondes en septembre 2018. Sans aucune nostalgie et sans renier son passé, Patrick Bruel dévoile dans cette chanson son désir de renouvellement.

Dix ans après un septième album original intitulé *Lequel de nous* et trois ans après un album hommage à Barbara, Patrick Bruel fait son grand retour discographique, en 2018, avec quinze nouveaux titres. Trois mois avant la sortie de l'album intitulé *Ce soir on sort*, Patrick Bruel dévoile le premier extrait, « Tout recommencer », une chanson dont il a co-écrit les paroles avec Mickaël Furnon, le célèbre guitariste stéphanois, leader du groupe Mickey 3D, qui a aussi composé la musique. Ce titre est réalisé par Vianney et permet à Patrick Bruel de se réinventer et d'explorer de nouvelles sonorités. L'artiste confie alors que cette chanson lui plaît énormément grâce à son rythme et à sa production.

Concernant les paroles, Patrick Bruel précise que « Tout recommencer » ne veut pas dire tout renier et balayer le passé. Bien au contraire, pour lui, cette chanson est synonyme de nouveau départ pour aller de l'avant. C'est en pensant à Barbara, qui disait toujours « On ne continue pas sa vie, on la recommence », que Patrick a eu l'idée d'une chanson sur ce thème. À cinquante-neuf ans, le chanteur est bien décidé à avancer tout en restant à l'écoute des nouvelles tendances musicales. Et c'est pour cela qu'il a eu envie de travailler avec Mickaël Furnon. Les deux hommes ne se connaissaient pas. Un jour, Patrick Bruel l'a appelé en lui disant tout simplement qu'il écoutait ses chansons, qu'il le trouvait formidable et qu'il adorerait travailler avec lui. Trois jours plus tard, Mickaël lui envoyait deux chansons, dont la musique de « Tout recommencer ». Quant à la réalisation de cette chanson, Patrick a eu envie de la confier à Vianney, qu'il avait

rencontré sur un plateau de télévision, et avec qui il avait sympathisé avant de lui demander de travailler avec lui. Pour la promotion de la chanson, Patrick Bruel tourne un clip assez drôle dans une ambiance de fête, avec en filigrane une histoire d'amour avec une certaine Alice.
Le clip est énormément diffusé à la télévision et le titre passe beaucoup à la radio, au point de devenir l'un des succès de la rentrée 2018. ■

" 'Tout recommencer' ne veut pas dire tout renier et balayer le passé, au contraire, cette chanson est synonyme de nouveau départ."

Pas eu le temps

LE TEMPS QUI PASSE

Deuxième titre extrait du neuvième album studio de Patrick Bruel, « Pas eu le temps » est à la fois mélancolique et festif. Cette chanson marque une nouvelle collaboration réussie avec l'ami Félix Gray.

Depuis le succès du titre « Au café des délices », en 1999, Patrick Bruel, qui apprécie beaucoup Félix Gray en tant qu'ami de longue date, mais aussi comme auteur-compositeur, n'hésite jamais à interpréter ses chansons. Et c'est une nouvelle fois le cas, en 2018, avec « Pas eu le temps ». En fait, pour bien comprendre l'histoire de cette chanson, il faut revenir cinq ans en arrière. En effet, en 2013, Félix Gray publie un album au Québec, intitulé *Chanter*, sur lequel figurent onze chansons. Il y a des reprises mais aussi des nouveautés, comme une première version de « Pas eu le temps ». Quelques années après, lorsque Patrick Bruel prépare son nouvel album, *Ce soir on sort*, il cherche de nouvelles chansons et c'est alors qu'il décide de reprendre ce titre sur le temps qui passe, de son ami Félix Gray, dont il a été le témoin de mariage à Ramatuelle, le 18 août 2016.

Pour Patrick Bruel, qui est alors à l'aube de ses soixante ans, le temps qui passe n'est pas une fatalité. Selon lui, il ne faut pas le subir, il faut l'éclairer et l'aimer. Patrick Bruel décide donc d'enregistrer cette chanson de son ami Félix Gray, mais pour contrebalancer le côté mélancolique des paroles, il décide de faire appel à un producteur de hip-hop, Skalpovich, qui va y mettre un arrangement surprenant et très dynamique avec des trompettes, pour en faire une véritable chanson de scène. Et le résultat est à la hauteur des attentes du chanteur, qui le choisit comme deuxième extrait de son nouvel album.

Pour la promotion de cette chanson, un clip en noir et blanc est tourné avec des anonymes de tous les âges et de tous les horizons qui tiennent entre leurs mains des pancartes sur lesquelles ils font part de

leurs regrets et des opportunités manquées, avant qu'un esprit de fête ne s'impose au fur et à mesure du clip. Sur la dernière image, sur la pancarte tenue par Patrick Bruel, il est écrit : De vous dire Merci encore. Un beau message à son fidèle public qui va faire de cette chanson un nouveau succès. ■

"Pour Patrick, qui est alors à l'aube de ses soixante ans, le temps qui passe n'est pas une fatalité, il ne faut pas le subir, il faut l'éclairer et l'aimer."

Stand Up

UNE CÉLÉBRATION DE LA VIE

Avec cette chanson optimiste et volontariste sortie en troisième extrait de l'album *Ce soir on sort*, Patrick Bruel distille sa philosophie de vie et transmet un message positif à la jeunesse.

Le plus difficile, pour un artiste, c'est de savoir rester dans l'air du temps. Patrick Bruel l'a très bien compris, et c'est pour cela que, pour son 9e album, en 2018, il n'a pas hésité à s'entourer d'auteurs, de compositeurs et d'arrangeurs de la nouvelle génération. Parmi eux, un producteur plutôt habitué au R'n'B : Pascal Koeu, plus connu sous le pseudonyme de Skalpovich. Patrick et ce DJ producteur né en 1979, à Épinay-sur-Seine, se connaissent depuis 2012 et le 7e album de Patrick, pour lequel il avait remixé la chanson « She's Gone ». Étant plus habitué à travailler avec Youssoupha, Soprano, Vitaa, Magic System, Corneille où sa muse Indila, l'univers de Skalpovich peut sembler diamétralement opposé à celui de Patrick Bruel, et pourtant, leur association va donner naissance à plusieurs tubes, dont « Stand Up ».

Le texte de cette chanson, Patrick Bruel l'a co-écrit avec Paul École, un brillant auteur qui a travaillé avec Calogero ou Christophe Maé. L'idée était de transmettre un message d'espoir et d'optimisme à la jeunesse. Selon Patrick Bruel, il ne faut jamais se morfondre, jamais se plaindre, et prendre son courage à deux mains pour aller au bout de ses rêves. Même si la vie est difficile, il y a toujours, selon lui, une lueur d'espoir, et c'est le message qu'il a voulu transmettre dans cette chanson. Pour illustrer ces paroles, dans le clip, Patrick choisit de mettre en avant des extraits de sa tournée triomphale, qui rassemble alors des centaines de milliers de spectateurs. Les images de son public déchaîné se mêlent à celles des vidéos de ses fans qui dansent sur ce morceau très fédérateur. Des images qui rappellent les grandes heures de la « Bruelmania » du début de sa carrière et qui prouvent que, à soixante ans, Patrick Bruel est toujours au sommet de la gloire. ■

"Même si la vie est difficile, il y a toujours, selon Patrick, une lueur d'espoir, et c'est le message qu'il a voulu transmettre dans cette chanson."

Héros

TOUCHANT HOMMAGE

Avec « Héros », cette chanson parue en 2018, dont il a composé la musique, sur des paroles de Paul École, Patrick Bruel rend hommage à tous les héros du quotidien qui donnent beaucoup d'eux-mêmes pour sauver les autres. Un titre qui a pris tout son sens au moment de la pandémie de Covid-19 qui a touché la planète, au printemps 2020.

L'histoire de cette chanson commence tout au début de la création du neuvième album de Patrick Bruel, *Ce soir on sort*. Patrick a composé une mélodie et il cherche un texte dans lequel il voudrait rendre hommage à tous les humbles, tous les héros invisibles qui se démènent au quotidien pour rendre service à leur prochain. Comme il a du mal à trouver les mots justes pour cet hommage, il fait appel au parolier Paul École, auteur de nombreux succès pour Calogero, Christophe Maé, Claudio Capéo. Paul École, qui a été brancardier et a travaillé aussi à Pôle Emploi avant de devenir auteur professionnel, connaît bien tous ces héros du quotidien auxquels Patrick Bruel veut rendre hommage. Ainsi, chez lui, à Pleurtuit, en Ille-et-Vilaine, il écrit les paroles de « Héros ».

Même si Patrick Bruel reconnaît qu'un chanteur peut apporter du soutien aux gens grâce à ses chansons, il a bien conscience que c'est si peu, comparé aux médecins, aux pompiers, aux sages-femmes, aux hommes de sécurité, aux chercheurs, et à tous les héros invisibles sans qui la vie ne serait pas possible. Aussi, lorsqu'il découvre les paroles de Paul École, Patrick Bruel est emballé et il enregistre la chanson.

Réalisé par Skalpovich, le titre est inclus au neuvième album de Patrick Bruel, qui paraît le 2 novembre 2018. Lors de sa grande tournée triomphale Ce soir on sort, démarrée en février 2019 au Millesium d'Épernay, Patrick Bruel interprète chaque soir « Héros » et mesure combien ce titre touche le public. Pour illustrer cette chanson qui est le quatrième extrait de l'album à paraître en single, un clip est d'ailleurs tourné lors du concert de Patrick Bruel à Paris La Défense Arena, le 7 décembre 2019. Devant des milliers de petites lumières jaunes illuminant la salle, le chanteur, très ému, interprète la chanson pendant que des photos de héros anonymes apparaissent derrière lui sur des écrans. Envoyée aux radios et aux chaînes musicales en mars 2020, « Héros » devient une véritable chanson d'actualité et prend un sens gigantesque au moment où la France salue le dévouement admirable du personnel soignant face à la pandémie de coronavirus. Patrick Bruel a d'ailleurs l'occasion d'interpréter sa chanson en direct de chez lui lors de Facebook live qu'il organise régulièrement sur sa page officielle, mais aussi au cours d'une émission spéciale présentée par Samuel Étienne, Daphné Burki et Faustine Bollaert, diffusée sur France 2, le mardi 24 mars 2020, intitulée « Ensemble avec nos soignants ».

Pour la petite histoire, la chanson « Héros » a été reprise dans une vidéo par des anonymes montrant des pancartes à destination du personnel soignant, des caissières, des livreurs, des routiers, des auxiliaires de vie... sur lesquelles était écrits des mots d'encouragement. Une belle initiative et un bel élan de solidarité pour ces héros du quotidien. ■

“Le chanteur, très ému, interprète la chanson pendant que des photos de héros anonymes apparaissent derrière lui sur des écrans.”

On partira

LE DÉRACINEMENT

Dernier titre du neuvième album de Patrick Bruel paru le 2 novembre 2018, « On partira » raconte une touchante histoire d'émigration. À travers l'histoire d'un fils et de sa mère contraints de partir vers la liberté, Patrick Bruel aborde un thème d'actualité : la douloureuse crise des migrants.

L'histoire de la chanson « On partira » est avant tout le résultat d'une belle complicité artistique entre Patrick Bruel et Vianney.

Leur première rencontre remonte au 27 novembre 2015, lorsqu'ils interprètent en duo, sur le plateau de l'émission *Taratata*, la chanson « Get Down », de Gilbert O'Sullivan. Quelques mois après, le 10 mai 2016, Patrick Bruel assiste au premier Olympia du jeune artiste de vingt-sept ans qui célèbre en même temps le succès de son premier album, *Idées blanches*. À cette occasion, après le concert, dans les coulisses, les deux artistes discutent. Patrick Bruel aime la simplicité, le talent et la maturité de Vianney. Il confie : « Je suis bluffé. Que ce soit humainement, artistiquement, intellectuellement, culturellement, le garçon a quelque chose de rare. Il est étonnant par ses attentions et sa simplicité. Il a un regard circulaire. C'est une merveilleuse rencontre. »

Par la suite, Patrick Bruel et Vianney se retrouvent encore sur des plateaux de télévision et deviennent de plus en plus copains. Le 8 juin 2018, Patrick Bruel le rejoint même sur la scène de l'AccorHotels Arena pour chanter en duo avec lui « Je t'le dis quand même ».

Tout logiquement, Patrick, qui prépare alors son neuvième album, demande à Vianney s'il veut écrire un texte sur une musique uptempo qu'il a composée.

En effet, au départ, sur la musique de « On partira », Patrick Bruel avait imaginé une chanson qui racontait la traversée des États-Unis par deux copains. Après l'avoir fait écouter à Vianney, ce dernier a accepté de la retravailler. Quelque temps après, il revient voir Patrick avec une version beaucoup plus lente dont il a changé les trois quarts du premier couplet et qui raconte une histoire

de migrants qui quittent un pays sans savoir où ils vont aller. Très sensible à ce sujet, Patrick Bruel adore cette nouvelle version et décide de l'enregistrer. Dans ce titre, il est question d'un enfant qui dit à sa mère « on partira pour trouver mieux ». Patrick a bien conscience que ces personnes qui partent pour éviter de mourir, d'être massacrés, n'ont pas d'autre choix. Sans aborder le sujet d'un point de vue politique, la chanson traite le problème sur le plan humain, ce qui en fait toute sa force. ■

"Vianney a changé le premier couplet, qui raconte maintenant une histoire de migrants qui quittent leur pays sans savoir où ils vont aller."

Le 8 septembre 2013, Patrick Bruel se produit en concert, dans le cadre de la Foire de Châlons-en-Champagne, devant plusieurs centaines de milliers de spectateurs.

Qu'est-ce qu'on fait

LENDEMAIN DE LIESSE POPULAIRE

Parue en 2018, sur le neuvième album de Patrick Bruel, « Qu'est-ce qu'on fait » interroge sur les lendemains des grandes fêtes populaires. Une chanson dont les paroles sont nées après la victoire de la France à la Coupe du Monde du 15 juillet 2018.

Ce n'est un secret pour personne, Patrick Bruel a toujours été passionné par le football. Enfant, Patrick était un grand fan du joueur néerlandais Johan Cruijff, qui portait le numéro 14 et jouait à l'Ajax d'Amsterdam. Patrick a même failli devenir footballeur professionnel à quinze ans. Aujourd'hui fervent supporter du PSG, il assiste régulièrement à des matchs au Parc des Princes pour soutenir son équipe favorite. Bien évidemment, quand l'équipe de France a remporté la Coupe du Monde, en 1998, puis une seconde fois, en 2018, Patrick Bruel était très heureux. Et c'est justement cette joie de la victoire qui va l'inspirer pour écrire les paroles de la chanson « Qu'est-ce qu'on fait », en 2018.

L'histoire de cette chanson commence quelques mois plus tôt. Dans l'optique de son prochain album, Patrick Bruel compose de nouvelles mélodies avec le guitariste Roman Chelminski. L'une des premières qu'il aime bien sera celle de « Qu'est-ce qu'on fait ». À ce moment-là, il a la musique mais a du mal à trouver un texte. Il demande à une vingtaine d'auteurs de trouver des paroles pour habiller cette musique, mais rien de ce qu'on lui propose ne lui convient. Même Vianney s'y colle, pourtant aucune de ses quatre propositions ne plaît à Patrick Bruel. Patrick est sur le point de renoncer à cette mélodie. Et puis arrive la victoire de la France à la Coupe du monde de football en Russie, le 15 juillet 2018, et l'immense fête qui a suivi. Le 17 juillet, confortablement installé sur sa terrasse, Patrick, en repensant à toute cette merveilleuse liesse populaire, trouve les mots de sa chanson qui lui viennent tout seuls. Il conservera simplement une phrase de Vianney, qu'il trouve très belle et qui dit : « Est-ce qu'on peut s'aimer, tu crois, deux mille ans après ça ? »

Dans cette chanson, Patrick Bruel s'interroge sur les lendemains de ces fêtes populaires qui rassemblent dans la joie et le bonheur mais qui, hélas, ne durent pas longtemps et s'évaporent bien vite.

Un très bon titre inclus à l'album *Ce soir on sort*, double disque de platine, avec plus de 200 000 exemplaires vendus. ■

> ***"Patrick Bruel s'interroge sur les lendemains de ces fêtes populaires qui rassemblent dar la joie et le bonheur mais qui, hélas, ne durent pas longtemps et s'évaporent bien vite."***

Discographie
Patrick Bruel

Albums studio :

DE FACE – 1986
ALORS REGARDE –1989
BRUEL (3) – 1994
PLAZA DE LOS HEROES – 1995
JUSTE AVANT – 1989
ENTRE DEUX – 2002
DES SOUVENIRS DEVANT – 2006
LEQUEL DE NOUS – 2012
TRÈS SOUVENT, JE PENSE À VOUS… – 2015
CE SOIR ON SORT… – 2018

Albums de scène :

À TOUT À L'HEURE – 1987
SI CE SOIR… – 1991
ON S'ÉTAIT DIT… – 1995
RIEN NE S'EFFACE… – 2001
ENTRE DEUX À L'OLYMPIA – 2003
DES SOUVENIRS… ENSEMBLE – 2007
SEUL… OU PRESQUE – 2009
LIVE 2014 – 2014
BRUEL BARBARA – LE CHÂTELET – 2016

Casser la voix
Si ce soir, j'ai pas envie d'rentrer tout seul
Si ce soir, j'ai pas envie d'rentrer chez moi
Si ce soir, j'ai pas envie d'fermer ma gueule
Si ce soir, j'ai envie d'me casser la voix
casser la voix (bis
peux plus cacher tout c'qui est marqué sur le mur
peux plus voir la vie des autres, même en peinture
suis pas là, pour le savoir d'aujourd'hui
veux pas, si ce soir j'ai envie
d'me casser la voix (bis
ami qui s'en vont
les autres qui restent
prendre pour un con
qu'on déteste
temps qui se perd
jeunes morts
vieux qui espèrent
flashs qui aveuglent
télé chaque jour
salauds qui beuglent
de l'amour
qui trainent
je trahis mon ennemi
qui est le même
j'me réveille la nuit
fille de la nuit
voit jamais le jour
qu'on couche dans son lit
appelant ça d'l'amour
sourires honteux
d'vant sa glace
disant, j'suis dégueu
j'suis pas dégoûtant
les rires qui coulent
l'regard des parents
larmes qui roulent
des enfants
qui viennent
dans la gorge
d'crier sa haine
chat, qu'on égorge
casser la voix (bis
soir...
P. Bruel

Remerciements :

Patrick Bruel pour l'hommage qu'il mérite et sans qui nous n'aurions pu réaliser cet ouvrage.
Tous les auteurs-compositeurs qui travaillent aux côtés de l'artiste depuis si longtemps, et sans oublier : Ludovic Boulnois – Jacques Benaroch – Benjamin Constant – Jef Cortes – Serge Darmon – Hervé Desinge – Jean-Luc Drion – Damien Ferdel – Laurie-Anne Ferret – La Fouine – Félix Gray – Marie-Florence Gros – Augusta Kammoun – Mireille Launy – Rose Léandri – Françoise Levaillant – David Moreau – Fabrice Moreau – Bernard Mouillon – Fabien Perault – Gérard Presgurvic – Amanda Sthers – Emanuele Scorcelletti – Pierre Terrasson.

Crédits photos :

Emanuele Scorcelletti : Couverture
Alain Marouani : 4e de couverture (bas).
Gilbert Moreau/ FLO : pages 6-35.
Bernard Mouillon : pages 15-37 – 38/ 39-45 – 47-51 – 57-86.
Pierre Terrasson : pages 19-20 – 43-49 – 53 – 54 – 55 – 59-60/ 61 – 67-88.
Ludovic Boulnois : pages 27-28 – 64-65 – 68-70 – 73 – 77-79 – 81 – 82 – 83 – 85-87 – 89 – 90 – 91 – 93 – 95 – 96/ 97 – 98 – 99 – 100 – 101 – 102 – 103 – 104/105 – 107 – 109 – 110 – 111 – 118 – 120/121 – 122 – 124/ 125.
Laurie-Anne Ferret : pages 113 – 114 – 115 – 117 – 123.
Jacques Benaroch/ FLO : page 71.
Jean-Luc Drion/ FLO : page 69.
Jean Lebreton/ Barclay : page 34.
Jean-Pierre Bouquet/ Barclay : page 40.
Frédérique Veysset/ RCA Ariola/ BMG : pages 44 – 46 – 48 – 52.
Erick Ifergan : page 58.
Diane Sagnier : page 94.
Klaus Guingand/ FLO : page 127.
AFP : pages 22 (Jean-Marie Leroy/ Photo12) - 75 (Studio Harcourt Paris).
Collection Sunset Boulevard : pages 12 (Étienne George – Gaumont) - 25 (Cinegram – Films18).
Collection Christophel : pages 14 (Films 13/ Jean-Pierre Fizet) - 63 (Gaumont International/ EFVE)
EScoop : pages 8-11 (Patrick Soubiran/ Archives Filipacchi) - 13 (Bernard Leloup/ Archives Filipacchi) - 41 (Jean-Patrick Gamet/ Archives Filipacchi) – 4e de couverture (Jean-Claude Deutsch/ Paris-Match).
Gamma-Rapho : pages 16 (Eric Catarina) - 23 (Alain Benainous).
Getty Images : pages 21 (David Koskas/ Sygma) - 31 (Bertrand Rindoff Petroff/ Agence Angeli) – 32-126 (Rindoff Petroff/ Viteur) – 92 (Stephane Cardinale/ Corbis).
SIPA : pages 24 (Benaroch) - 112 (Edmond Sadaka) - 119 (Romuald Meigneux).

Achevé d'imprimer
en octobre 2020
en République tchèque (Finidr)

BEST OF
PATRICK BRUEL
Bruel
Les Secrets des Enfoirés
2006
Solidays
Qui sait ?
ANGGUN PATRICK BRUEL
STEPHAN EICHER FAUDEL PETER GABRIEL
LOKUA KANZA LÂÂM YOUSSOU N'DOUR
NOURITH AXELLE RED ZUCCHERO
Solidaires contre le Sida, solidaires pour l'Afrique
patrick bruel
Au café des délices
REMIX
BRUEL
QUI A LE DROIT...
Les Enfoirés
À L'OPÉRA COMIQUE
PATRICK BRUEL
PatrickBruelive
Rien ne s'efface...
Le Zénith des Enfoirés
BRUEL
Alors Regarde
patrick bruel
tout s'efface
PATRICK BRUEL
La boîte à musique des enfoirés
PATRICK BRUEL
J'TE L'DIS QUAND MÊME...
PATRICK BRUEL
Best of
Voulez vous...
Marre de cette nana-là!
PATRICK BRUEL
Barclay
isabelle boulay
UN JOUR OU L'AUTRE
BRUEL
Non, j'veux pas!
2007
LA CARAVANE DES ENFOIRÉS
PATRICK BRUEL
MON AMANT DE SAINT-JEAN
PATRICK BRUEL
GREATEST HITS
BRUEL
Si ce soir...
VOL 2
patrick bruel pour la vie
Patrick Bruel
Juste avant...
Et 31 jours d'essai gratuit à Infonie & Internet
PATRICK BRUEL
PLACE DES GRANDS HOMMES
Bruel
2CD
2005
LE TRAIN
PATRICK BRUEL
PATRICK BRUEL
SHE'S GONE
2 CD
2004
LES ENFOIRÉS
DANS L'ESPACE
PATRICK BRUEL
Entre-deux...
CE SOIR ON SORT...